A History of the Seven Holy Founders of the Order of the Servants of Mary

A HISTORY OF THE SEVEN HOLY FOUNDERS

Nihil obstat.

GULIELMUS B MORRIS, Cong. Orat.,
Censor Deputatus.

Imprimatur.

HENRICUS EDUARDUS,
Card. Archiep. Westmonast.

Die 15 Aug., 1889.

A HISTORY

OF THE

SEVEN HOLY FOUNDERS

OF THE ORDER OF THE

SERVANTS OF MARY

BY

FATHER SOSTENE M. LEDOUX

Of the same Order

TRANSLATED FROM THE FRENCH

LONDON: BURNS & OATES, Ld.

NEW YORK: CATHOLIC PUBLICATION SOCIETY CO.

Approbation

OF THE

MOST REVEREND FATHER-GENERAL OF THE SERVANTS OF MARY.

———

WE have had the work, *History of the Seven Holy Founders of the Order of the Servants of Mary*, by the Rev. Father Sostene M. Ledoux, of the same Order, examined by theologians of our Order; we vouch for its containing nothing contrary to faith and morals, and willingly grant leave for its publication, at the same time earnestly recommending it to the faithful, persuaded that from the study of it they will draw much spiritual good.

Rome, at our Convent of San Marcello, 7 August, 1889.

FR. ANDREA Mª CORRADO, *Prior-General.*

PREFACE.

My object in undertaking this work was to portray, as vividly as I could, the Seven Saints upon whom I look as my Spiritual Fathers, and the Order of which they were the originators and first members. As every household prides itself on possessing life-like portraits of its parents, so have I wished to obtain, both for myself and for others, an accurate sketch of these Holy Patriarchs, and an authentic account of their work.

The task was not an easy one; for, circumstances seem to have combined to cast the events of their lives into obscurity. They themselves were especially desirous of being unknown to all. With one solitary exception, they left no writings behind them. They were almost equally sparing of speech, and only a few words of theirs have been preserved and transmitted to posterity. So absolute was their love of humility, of being unnamed and forgotten, that they shrouded all particulars concerning themselves in a thick veil of reserve. Besides, unhappily, the brief narrative drawn up by St. Alexis, at the request of his younger Brethren, has perished. St. Philip Benizi, their most favoured disciple, endeavoured to record the first beginnings of the Order which they had founded, and the virtues which he had so much loved and venerated in them; but no trace of his work remains. In short, of all that was written of them by their contemporaries, we only possess a chronicle, in but a portion of which do we find well authenticated facts concerning them.

Nevertheless, as far as the materials at disposal permitted, I trust that I have faithfully depicted our Seven Founders. In painting a portrait, the chief aim of the artist is to seize a characteristic expression of the sitter, failing which the work is comparatively valueless. Those who read this book will, I hope, recognize their leading features in the characters of the Seven Holy Founders, the mould in which their lives were cast, the inner beauty of their souls, the true scope of their work. Although the task has proved to be beyond my powers, I have endeavoured to give some idea of their unearthly type of sanctity, which made them find this world as truly a place of exile as though they had been already disembodied spirits. I have also been careful to give due prominence to that devoted love of Our Lady, which so deeply coloured every phase of their existence that their identity would be lost without it.

The following list comprises the names of the chief authors whom I have consulted whilst engaged in this work :

Pietro da Todi, General of the Servants of Mary, the third successor of St. Philip. He entered the Order at fifteen years of age, about the year 1295. His *Chronicle of the First Beginnings of the Order* is the only document written by a contemporary of the Founders, and was compiled in 1317, seven years after the death of St. Alexis. It contains many interesting details, intermingled with considerations partly laudatory and partly mystical.

Niccolo Mati, O.S.M. *Diary of Reminiscences.* This Father wrote in the year 1384, being then of an advanced age. His mind and heart were well stored with recollections of the first Saints of the Order, and especially of the

Seven Blessed Founders. He gives, in particular, a somewhat detailed account of their deaths. This author's gracious simplicity and liveliness of style reflect most correctly the character of the Seven Holy Founders. The perfect naturalness and charm of his descriptions and reflections cannot be equalled.

Paolo Attavanti, O S.M. (*circa* 1456). In his *Dialogue with Cosmo di Medici*, written in Latin, the style of which is extremely elegant, this author has preserved many traits of the lives of the Seven Holy Founders.

Michele Poccianti, O.S.M. *Relation of all that has happened in the Order of the Servants of the Blessed Virgin Mary*, 1567. This book may be called a diamond edition of the Annals. It is written in Latin · it ably epitomizes, in a terse and manly style, the chief events affecting the Order : it does not contain an exaggerated or a superfluous sentence. The author is plainly heart and soul in his theme, and he possesses the power of placing before his readers in a striking manner the people of whom he writes and the events in which they shared He also wrote in Italian a short and charming *Memoir of the Seven Blessed Founders*.

Arcangelo Giani and Luigi-Maria Garbi, both members of the Servite Order, were the authors of the *Annals of the Order of the Servants of Mary*. The first edition, published by Father Giani in 1618, was revised and completed by Father Garbi in 1719. It is a great work, and a perfect mine of historical wealth : it is in three volumes, folio, and is written in Latin. The style is old-fashioned, stately, and dignified. In these latter respects, it is out of harmony with the characteristics of the Seven Founders. But, apart from this, the Annals furnish a complete, trustworthy, and valuable history of the Order.

Francesco M. Pecoroni, O.S.M., 1746. *History of the*

Origin and Foundation of the Holy Order of the Servants of Mary. This author was thoroughly acquainted with all that had been done to obtain the beatification of the Seven Founders, and with the efforts that had been made to procure their canonization. It is a well-written volume, and at the same time learned, and overflowing with sweetness and interest.

Augustine Morini, O.S.M., who published in 1882 a complete edition, with notes, of the *Diary of Reminiscences* of Niccolo Mati, and in 1888 his *Historical and Critical Studies on the Seven Holy Founders and their Times.* Both these works are treasures of learning.

Peregrine Soulier, O.S M. 1886, *Life of St. Philip Benizi.* 1888, *A History of the Seven Holy Founders.* The author of these two works has shown himself at one and the same time a hagiographer, an historian, and a man of learning. Both of his works are remarkable in every respect, and notably for their critical erudition.

Amongst the authorities not belonging to the Order, I have likewise resorted to the famous Bollandist Collection; to Darras, Rohrbacher, the learned Cardinal Hergenrother, the brilliantly-stored pages of M. Brugère, my revered professor at St Sulpice, and the *Regesta* of the mediæval Popes, published by Potthast, Berger, and others; the *Chronicles* of Villani and of Malaperti, and the *History of Florence* by M. Perrens, although unable to help regretting that sectarian prejudice so frequently guides the pen of the latter writer.

I cannot conclude without an expression of fraternal gratitude to the Rev. Father Soulier for the stores of valuable information, the fruit of his long and toilsome researches in the great libraries of Italy, with which he has generously supplied me.

These numerous helps will, I trust, have enabled me to produce a work which may in some degree promote the glory of those whose lives are here recorded, and which may tend to the edification of souls seeking for models from whom to learn how best to serve Our Lord and to love His Most Blessed Mother. In writing it I have found a solace in bearing the bitterness of exile; and I have learned, in tracing the chequered story of my Fathers and Masters in the spiritual life, the great lesson never to despair of seeing, even in this world, the triumph of Right, of Truth, and of Justice.

ST. MARY'S PRIORY,
264, FULHAM ROAD, LONDON, S.W.

CONTENTS.

BOOK I.

BOOK II.

BOOK III

EXTENSION—CONSOLIDATION—TRIALS—TRIUMPH
(1243-1310—1717-1888).

BOOK I.

PREPARATION (1196—1234,

CHAPTER I.

𝕿𝖍𝖊 𝕸𝖎𝖉𝖉𝖑𝖊 𝕬𝖌𝖊𝖘 𝖆𝖓𝖉 𝖙𝖍𝖊 𝕾𝖊𝖛𝖊𝖓 𝕳𝖔𝖑𝖞 𝕱𝖔𝖚𝖓𝖉𝖊𝖗𝖘.

(THIRTEENTH CENTURY.)

THE Seven Saints, of whose lives we are about to give an outline, were, like the Order which they founded, essentially mediæval in character. They were the outgrowth of that period which, beginning with the reign of one great Pontiff, St. Gregory the Seventh, closed with that of the scarcely less illustrious Pope, Boniface the Eighth. This space of time, comprising more than two hundred years, from 1073 to 1303, offers undoubtedly the fairest page in the history of the Christian Commonwealth. The theory of life was then wholly Christian, and the practical results, in spite of some few dark shades in the picture, were truly wonderful.

Faith ruled supreme during those two centuries ; and the world, under her maternal sway, enjoyed all the true benefits of the highest civilization. The Catholic Church was her interpreter, and, revered by all, was the greatest moral power, and exercised the widest influence, throughout the world. The Holy See, speaking in the name of the Universal Church, was the arbitrator in all questions concerning the rights and interests of humanity ; and the Papal verdicts were accepted alike by all, from the monarch to his lowliest vassal. In one word, Faith, with her divine teaching and her unchanging promises, was the great motive power of the age.

The union of the temporal and spiritual powers for one common object—the welfare of the people—was throughout this period held to be a sacred and inviolable principle ; and, maintaining this principle, the two powers respected each other's rights, gave and received mutual support, and by their concerted action were the

1

better able to insure success in the accomplishment of their task. Their close union is the ideal of governmental wisdom, whether we regard it with the eyes of reason or with those of faith : since thereby the strength of both is utilized for the same end, and both are enabled to work smoothly and harmoniously together for the good of all.

This happy state of things was much promoted by the spirit of the age, which subordinated temporal interests to those of the spiritual order, in conformity with the maxims of the Gospel. Thus, in all things the Church took precedence of the world ; or rather, precedence was freely granted to the Church by the world, towards which she faithfully fulfilled her duty, by instructing, correcting, and, when necessary, punishing those for whose souls she was responsible. By a spontaneous and strictly logical extension of her prerogatives, the Church was even invested with the right of trying and deposing temporal sovereigns, and of releasing their subjects from their allegiance. Nothing could more strikingly illustrate the supremacy of spirit over matter, of the Church over the civil power, of things of eternity over things of time.

To sum up, the guiding principles of the men of the Middle Ages may be said to have been as follows : that Faith ruled all men ; that the spiritual and temporal powers acted in concert ; and that the Church, whilst respecting all civil institutions, moulded them in a way which made them consonant with the good of souls. This system, founded on truth, was fruitful in good, as history has proved. In fact, at no period has the Church of God expanded more vigorously, or in more varied directions, than she did under the influence of these principles.

At the dawn of the Middle Ages, the Church found herself face to face with many obstacles which hindered the fulfilment of her mission. A venal spirit had crept into the sanctuary itself, and there was a simoniacal traffic in holy things. Many of the clergy led dissolute lives, and were thus powerless to exert influence for good over their flocks. The holders of the temporal power, particularly in Germany, had the presumption to claim a share of the spiritual order, and, by means of the abuse known as *lay investiture,* to pretend to confer powers which it was beyond their competence to bestow.

A Pontiff gifted with lofty intelligence and with an iron will, one who was at the same time a man of great personal holiness of life, undertook the formidable enterprise of abolishing these sacrilegious abuses. This Pontiff, St. Gregory VII., of glorious memory, died in exile ; but the results of his life's work were already beginning to be shown in the renewed purity and recovered independence of the Church. His successors carried on the work, and restored to the Spouse of Christ her pristine beauty and freedom.

The same Pontiff energetically opposed the encroachments of the German Empire, which, inheriting the pagan traditions of Rome, aspired to universal sovereignty both spiritual and temporal. One emperor after another mounted the throne, and all were more or less imbued with this extravagant ambition. But their contemporaries in the Chair of Peter stood firm as an impregnable rampart for the defence of the Church; and, by protecting her, they preserved all her rights. Nor did the crimes perpetrated by the emperors against the Church escape visible punishment.

Meanwhile, the Church pursued her task among the nations which had been first converted to Christianity, and year by year her institutions became more and more deeply rooted in their midst. The first objects of her zeal were the Græco-Latin populations, her legacy from the Cæsars; next she turned her attention to the Slavonic and German nations, the tribes of Central Asia, and many others, sending her missionaries to instruct them in the faith and to wean them from their rude lives and savage customs. In spite of enormous difficulties the Church provided for the needs of all these her children with unceasing watchfulness and with unwearying activity.

Nor did she rest satisfied with simply maintaining her hold over the nations which already owned her sway. She continually strove to make fresh conquests, and her envoys kept steadily advancing, braving danger, and ready to shed their blood for the cause hallowed by her sanction. Upon the establishment of the Mendicant Orders, whole troops of apostles set forth by land and by sea to carry to all people the glad tidings of salvation.

Moreover, the Church, armed with the truth which she had received from the Incarnate Word, civilized those whom she Christianized. Wheresoever she trod, barbarism was beaten back, and the relations of the different classes of society towards each other became marvellously changed. She softened the callousness of the rich; she scattered the darkness of prejudice and superstition; she checked the passion for gain; she lessened the hardships of slavery; she made her voice heard in opposition to unjust wars, and in furtherance of all useful progress. She lifted from the legal code of nations all pagan and barbaric elements, impressing in their place the seal of Christianity alike on the State, on marriage, on municipal life, and on family relations. She gave her sanction to all lawful authority, especially to the power exercised by sovereigns. In fine, she called civilization into existence where it was not, and, when she had conferred this boon, she unweariedly continued to foster and to advance it.

No sooner had she freed herself from interior trammels than she set herself to infuse vitality and harmony into every department of her sway, in order to discharge more fittingly her appointed work on earth. Hence arose ecclesiastical discipline, parochial organization, and all other regulations concerning the government of the flock. She also settled and classified the enactments of the civil law. The Cardinals composing the Privy Council of the Pope were now placed in a higher position than before. A greater uniformity in the ceremonies of divine worship was secured. Devotions to the Cross and Passion of Our Lord, to the Most Blessed Sacrament, and to Our Lady, were encouraged and popularized. Thus the Daughter of the King adorned herself with variety, and enabled herself to win more souls to Christ.

For it was to this end that all her efforts tended. She spared no pains to train up a learned, virtuous, and high-minded priesthood ; and knowing how much the secular clergy stood in need of auxiliaries to share their arduous duties, she eagerly sought the aid of the older established Orders, which she carefully reformed, and more especially that of the newer Orders which had been providentially raised for this purpose, and to which she gladly gave her approval. She did not shrink from strong measures when heresy reared its head among either clergy or laity, corrupting the faith and leading the simple astray. In defence of the souls of her little ones, she armed herself with her thunders ; and finally she established the tribunal of the Holy Inquisition, the main duty of which was to seek out and to condemn errors in doctrine.

More now than at any previous period of her history, was the Church the great centre of enlightenment, showing beyond all cavil how firm were her foundations, how admirable was her doctrine, how lofty was her moral code, how consoling were her divine precepts. She offered to all a perfect solution of the enigma of human existence, and she was in herself the one element which fused all others into a harmonious whole. To the assaults of unbelief and worldliness her answer was given by the voice of six Œcumenical Councils ; by the teachings of the Universities founded under her auspices in Bologna, Padua, and Salerno, in Paris, Toulouse, and Montpellier, in Oxford and Cambridge, in Salamanca and in Coimbra , and by the works of the great doctors whom she had herself trained—Lanfranc, St. Anselm, St. Bernard, Peter Lombard, Albertus Magnus, St. Thomas Aquinas, St. Bonaventure, and others.

The Church was likewise the great fount of inspiration for art, which thus became the handmaid of religion, and was carried to such a height of perfection that, in spite of the material progress of these latter times, the masterpieces of the Middle Ages, especially those in architecture, painting, sculpture, and music, may occasionally have been equalled, but have never been surpassed. Both the Byzantine and the Gothic styles then attained their full glory ; the latter type, more particularly, displaying a marvellous variety which added to its beauty. To this period we owe the vast fanes of

Canterbury, of St. Sernin at Toulouse, St. Stephen at Caen, and St. Remi of Rheims, the Cathedrals of Amiens, Salisbury, and Chartres, Westminster Abbey, and the Sainte Chapelle. These mighty fabrics, with their "storied windows richly dight," their exquisite carvings and frescoes, soared heavenwards like embodied hymns to the glory of the Lord and Maker of all; and the poorest and most ignorant who gazed upon them and therein worshipped, saw the greatness of God and of His Church as in a visible form. Thus faith became the principal factor in the lives of those whom we now call the masses.

In this spirit of faith all Christian nations armed themselves, and, burning with zeal, hastened to Palestine to wrest from infidel hands the sepulchre of Christ and the sacred spot which He had consecrated by His presence whilst on earth. Eight times, within the space of two centuries, the fleets of the crusaders set sail, amidst shouts of *" Dieu le veult ! "* for the shores where the fierce Mussulman had raised the standard of the Crescent, and whence he continually defied not only Christianity, but also civilization. Although these expeditions ended in failure, yet the results on the whole were of untold benefit to Europe. They served to delay the advance of the infidel on Constantinople. They bound the different kingdoms of the Christian commonwealth together by the strongest ties, and put an end to the international wars hitherto waged almost unceasingly. They increased the influence of the Church, of the Holy See, and of the priesthood. They roused and quickened the spirit of faith. They were the occasion of many acts of heroic virtue, and they even subserved the temporal interests of the countries which engaged in them, by promoting commercial relations with the far distant East.

In more peaceful spheres of action, the Church crowned her work by producing souls of the highest degree of sanctity. In countries which had been her own from the first, and in those which had but recently fallen under her sway, were seen alike—and alike, too, in every rank and in every state of life—wondrous examples of holiness. At no former period, perhaps, had so many spiritual flowers bloomed at once in the garden of the Church, nor had so many lives been lived, modelled on the life of Him Who was in all things perfect. These were the times of St. John Gualbert, the founder of Vallombrosa; of St. Margaret, Queen of Scotland; of St. Gregory VII., himself the promoter of this great movement; of St. Bruno, the father of the Carthusian Order; of St. Alberic, the founder of Citeaux; of the great St. Anselm; of St. Norbert; of St. Malachy, Bishop of Connor, in Ireland; of the honey-tongued St. Bernard; of St. Mechtildis; of St. Isidore, the husbandman; of the unyielding St. Thomas of Canterbury; of SS. Felix of Valois and John of Matha, both founders of Orders; of the illustrious SS.

Dominic and Francis ; the wonder-working St. Antony of Padua ; the gentle St. Elisabeth of Hungary ; of the undaunted St. Peter, Martyr ; of St. Clare, the pupil of St. Francis ; of St. Simon Stock ; of the good St. Louis, King of France ; of the Angel of the Schools, St. Thomas Aquinas, and the Seraphic Doctor, St. Bonaventure , of St. Philip Benizi, the glory of the Servants of Mary , of his disciple, St. Juliana Falconieri ; and lastly, of the Seven great Saints whose lives we are about to retrace, not to name countless other holy men and women whom we have not space to enumerate.

Such, hastily outlined, was the epoch to which our Seven Holy Founders belonged. Amidst all its brightness and all its glory, some dark shades were to be discerned ; yet these seemed only to place in higher relief the splendour of those times, when the Church of Christ reigned in the world triumphant and supreme.

The Seven Holy Founders formed, in common with their work, an integral portion of this, the culminating point of the mediæval age. They appeared on the scene when the pontifical throne was occupied by Innocent III., whose memory remains with us as the embodiment of the lofty thoughts and mighty deeds of those days. The first of the Founders was born two years before Pope Innocent's election, and the birth of the youngest took place when that great ruler of the Church had already sketched the outline of the vast undertakings which were to be accomplished during his pontificate. Their lives were passed during his reign, and under his successors who were inspired by his spirit, and who strove to carry on the work which he had begun and perfected.

We see, then, that the Seven Saints of whom we are about to speak were born in a time of grace which endowed them richly with most of its best gifts. In the wonderful uprising of the Church, which gave strength to her within her borders whilst she was expanding herself without, they were caught by the advancing wave and carried forward irresistibly. To them the Church was the visible embodiment of the Divinity, and to her they devoted all their faculties, rejoicing in being permitted to serve under her sacred banner. They placed themselves unreservedly in her hands, to be moulded like clay at the will of the potter. They showed on all occasions the deepest reverence for her ministers, in whom they beheld the rays of light reflected from the face of God Himself. They felt themselves powerfully drawn towards the Religious Orders, more especially those of recent foundation. Often and often had they eagerly listened in their childhood to the narrative of the marvels wrought by the founders and first members of these Orders. In the days of their youth the names of the two great patriarchs, St. Francis and St. Dominic, were on every tongue : there is even much reason to believe that some, at least, among the Seven had actually beheld these illustrious Saints. They were attracted by the magnificence of the Divine Office, by the bright rays of knowledge with which the doctors enlightened the world, and by the masterpieces of art which had been produced in each. Their imaginations were fired by the story of the Crusades, which were entered upon with the aim dearest to their own hearts—the liberation of the Holy Land. They grew to manhood thus surrounded by recollections of the glorious Saints whose warfare had so lately ended, and edified from day to day by the heroic virtues of those who were still living.

These external influences enabled them to profit to a yet greater degree by the interior graces which were at work within their souls. Their childhood was remarkable for innocence and their youth for self-restraint and the subjugation of all evil inclinations; and in their riper age they attained the loftiest degrees of holiness. The life which they led was the highest known on earth, the life of the crucified; that life which, by the threefold vow, renounces wholly the gifts of riches, pleasure, and freedom. Thus being perfect Religious, they were already fitted to serve as models to the members of the spiritual household which they were about to establish, and in which their virtues were to be perpetuated in the ages to come.

But, if the Seven Founders owed a large debt to the times in which they lived, they repaid it with usury. Doubtless, the spirit of the age had helped in no small measure to make them what they were, and they, in their degree, contributed to the beneficial influences of the era and shared in its glories.

In fact, nothing precisely similar had yet been seen: a constellation of Saints appearing together, winning the admiration and exciting the emulation of their fellow-Christians by the beauty of their holiness and by their zeal for the sole object worthy of human aspirations: to love and serve God here, and to be happy with Him for ever hereafter. All men were charmed and edified by seeing these seven holy youths united in the closest bonds of friendship, and linking themselves more closely thereby to the sole object of their love. They made their sacrifice with one heart and with one mind: together they renounced the world, wealth, comfort, rank, all ties of relationship, wedded love and parental joys, all which might lawfully have been theirs, and embraced instead a life of strict austerity. And not only did they edify all around them by their modest and humble demeanour, by their rigorous penances, their utter self-abandonment to the Providence of God, their perfect detachment from all earthly things, but, most of all, they checked the intestinal divisions and wars in the midst of which they lived, by the brotherly union and holy friendship which reigned among them, and which wedded the souls and the hearts of the Seven together as one. Their love of solitude and silence, foreign though it was to the joyous social temper of the age, yet served to remind all who witnessed their self-immolation that they had chosen the better part, by seeking God and living for Him alone.

Nor did they only give to their contemporaries the benefit of their personal example. They conferred a more lasting gift by founding a Religious Order having a distinctive aim of its own, which was well suited to the needs of the age, and formed a characteristic and beautiful adornment to its rougher features.

The spotless Virgin, who, without detriment to her perfect purity, became the Mother of God made Man, held a foremost place in the love and reverence of the mediæval mind. By a continual development, fresh tokens of veneration accumulated around her, and gradually formed her recognised cultus The different Religious Orders rivalled each other in striving to honour her. Each of these Orders possessed some special characteristic, which bound them more closely to Our Blessed Lady. The devotion of the Middle Ages to the Virgin Mother was marked by a beautiful and childlike simplicity of filial love. Still, something seemed yet wanting to fill up the measure of her praises : something which should bear the stamp of her perfections, and thus be capable of defying the assaults of time. To do this was reserved for the later portion of the mediæval period, and the Seven Holy Founders were the persons chosen by God to carry out the design.

That which was needed, and was by them called into existence, was an Order wholly dependent, so to speak, on the Blessed Mother, who, in return, would give to its members a foremost place in her affections. Far from withholding what was due to Our Lord, this Order was to lay at His Sacred Feet a lavish tribute of devotion, whilst yet consecrating itself wholly to the service of the Queen of Heaven, and seeking in all ways to promote her glory, both interiorly, by the saintliness of their lives and their constantly renewed homage, and externally, by kindling among the faithful a childlike love for so tender a mother.

The aim of this Order was to realize in practice, by following a lofty ideal of religious perfection, the sublime theories of which the Blessed Virgin formed the central point in the noble outlines traced by the earliest Fathers, both of the Eastern and of the Western Churches : theories which were subsequently developed in their fulness by St. Anselm ; by St. Bernard, who is looked upon as the Marian Doctor *par excellence ,* by Richard of St. Victor, and others ; which were finally cast into strict theological form by the great Schoolmen : theories, too, which the mediæval poets, headed by Dante, sang in immortal strains. This Order, in short, was to embody the theology, the poetry, and the art of that epoch, devoted to the service of the Immaculate Mother of God, seeming, indeed, to fill, in the Supernatural Order, the place of that poet whom, on his journey through the heavenly regions, St. Bernard thus addresses :

> "Now raise thy view
> Unto the visage most resembling Christ;
> For, in her splendour only, shalt thou win
> The power to look on Him". (*Paradiso*, xxxii.)

The post of the Servite was to be at the feet of that Blessed Mother, there to contemplate the marvellous gifts of the most perfect of the great Creator's works. To him was appointed the duty of gazing continually on the perfections of her whose wondrous beauty fills the Saints with joy in their heavenly dwelling, of supplicating her in fervent prayer, and of sounding unweariedly in her honour the praises due to her:

> "O Virgin Mother, daughter of thy Son,
> Created beings all in lowliness
> Surpassing, as in height above them all;
> Term, by the eternal counsel pre-ordained;
> Ennobler of thy nature, so advanced
> In thee, that its great Maker did not scorn
> To make Himself His own creation:
> For in thy womb rekindling shone the love
> Revealed, whose genial influence makes now
> This flower to germin in eternal peace:
> Here thou to us of charity and love
> Art as the noonday torch, and art, beneath,
> To mortal men, of hope a living spring.
> So mighty are thou, Lady, and so great,
> That he who grace desireth, and comes not
> To thee for aidance, fain would have desire
> Fly without wings.   Not only him who asks,
> Thy bounty succours: but doth freely oft
> Forerun the asking   Whatsoe'er may be
> Of excellence in creature, pity mild,
> Relenting mercy, large munificence,
> Are all combined in thee." (*Paradiso*, xxx.)

This hymn of gratitude to the beneficent Queen of Heaven, which is placed by the great Florentine poet in the mouth of St. Bernard, may well be taken as typical of the constant attitude of mind of those who claimed especially the title of her Servants: and the concluding lines of that most beautiful address, in which he beseeches her—

> "To drive
> Each cloud of our mortality away
> Through her own prayers, that on the sovereign joy
> Unveiled we gaze" (*Paradiso*, xxxiii, Cary)—

and goes on to entreat her, the "Queen who can do what she wills," that she should preserve all pure affections and quell all evil passions within us—these words, inspired by the poet's genius, do but represent the Servite's unceasing prayer for himself, his brethren, and all mankind.

Yes; the central point of attraction in the Order of the Servants of Mary, the pivot on which its very existence turned, was the love and veneration of each mystery in the life of Mary. All that had crowned her with glory, all that had flooded her with bliss, from the first moment of her Immaculate Conception to the endless morn of light when she was assumed into Heaven, was to her servant the choicest theme for meditation, the contemplation dearest to his heart. But, by the express command of the Blessed Mother herself, his thoughts and aspirations were to be employed, above all, on the great Mystery of Sorrow, with which her heart was filled to overflowing, when she stood beneath the Cross of Calvary, and shared in spirit the sufferings of her Divine Son.

This was to be the appointed task of the Servants of Mary, since it was one which mankind at large, careless and fond of ease, would be but too likely to neglect. It was for them to carry on the devotion to the sorrows of Mary and the sufferings of Jesus, since the faithful are usually more prone to contemplate the joys which were the fruit of those sufferings and those sorrows. Their post was to be on Calvary, at the foot of the Cross, beside the sorrowful Mother, because her children in the world dwell more frequently on her life as the spotless Maiden of Nazareth, as the Mother of the King in Bethlehem, as the enthroned Queen of Heaven, whose prayer is, with her Son, all-powerful.

In short, the Order sprang into existence when it was needed for God's work. It took its place in the thirteenth century, so rich in beauty and genius, in which great men had been raised up to battle for every great cause. St. Dominic and St. Francis each occupied a large space in this era: the work of the former was to exhibit the dogmatic truths of the Christian faith in all their radiant clearness : whilst the latter showed forth in his life all the moral beauty of Christ's teaching—the sweet honey of charity flowing from the strong rock of penitential austerity. The Seven Holy Founders were to follow with childlike love in the train of her who, without detriment to her virginal purity, bore Him Who is the source of all purity, of all good : of her who, by her Transfixion, co-operated with Our Lord in His sufferings for our redemption. who was the Mother of the Word made Flesh, full of grace and truth, and of the Saviour Who out of His infinite love offered Himself for the salvation of all men.

And thus, whilst St. Dominic and St. Francis set forth the Lord Jesus to the nations, yearning to know and to love Him, the Seven Florentine Saints pointed out to their fellow-citizens the gentle and holy Mother who, from Bethlehem to Golgotha, shed the halo of her maternal love round the great Master, the Glory of God revealed to us, the Conqueror of Death, and the Captain of our Salvation.

CHAPTER II.

𝕭irt𝕳 an𝖉 𝕺rigin.

(1196—1206.)

THE Seven Saints, who were elected to become the founders of the Servite Order, weie born when the mediæval period was about to attain its apogee, that is to say, at the close of the twelfth and the beginning of the thirteenth centuries. It was the will of God that they should be scions of seven Florentine families, conspicuous by their descent and their social position, but destined to far greater honour by being chosen severally to furnish a member to the ranks of these heroic Servants of Mary.

At that time Innocent III, in the full vigour of age and mental power, filled the Pontifical Chair, and with a firm and skilful hand directed the affairs of the Christian commonwealth. Germany was laid waste by ceaseless struggles ; France was under the brilliant rule of Philip Augustus ; England was governed by John, surnamed Lackland, whose reign was proverbial for every species of crime ; and the Catholic kingdom of Spain was preparing to inflict upon the followers of Mahomet, in 1202, the defeat of Las Navas, which dated their gradual decline in the Peninsula.

The East still continued to be the scene of disastrous events. The Greek schism had entangled in its snares a great multitude of souls, and Jerusalem had once more fallen, in 1187, into the hands of the infidel. The third crusade had been almost barren of results. Innocent III. then organized a fourth expedition ; but, this time, it was the empire of Constantinople that fell before the warriors of the Cross, and the holy places weie not yet set free.

In Italy, with the exception of the States of the Church governed by the Pope, and of the kingdom of Sicily, where a Queen Regent presided, nearly all the chief cities formed so many independent communities, or small republics. They were, as a rule, severally eager for ascendency, and lived on bad terms with their neighbours : hence a constant succession of petty wars was carried on between them. Florence was one of the most turbulent of these cities ; yet exceptionally peace reigned within and without her walls, and remained unbroken from 1187 till 1215.

It was at this period that our Seven Saints in succession came into the world.

The first, in the order of time, was Bonfilius Monaldi, who was born in 1196, two years before the election of Pope Innocent III. He had French blood in his veins, for, according to some old pedigree, his family belonged to the royal house of Anjou. One of his ancestors, Roderic Monaldi, leaving France, settled in Orvieto, and, towards the year 802, Charlemagne appointed him governor of that town. Subsequently a violent quarrel having arisen between the families of Filippi and Monaldi, one of the latter faction, a direct ancestor of our Saint, resolved to emigrate to Florence, where he took root and flourished. From him sprang a vigorous offshoot, which from this time forward held high rank among the citizens.

The Monaldi belonged to the Grandi or the old nobility, and to the Ghibelline party, which supported the Emperor. They were a powerful clan, owning palace and towers, chiefly situated in a street which still recalls their name—the Via Monalda—a striking proof of their civic consequence. We find that, in 1201, Hugo Monaldi was nominated consul, thereby becoming one of the thirteen councillors of the chief magistrate of the Republic, the latter being styled Podesta and never being a Florentine by birth.

It would seem that the members of the Monaldi family were, during the first part of the thirteenth century, of placid dispositions, and willing to live on friendly terms with their neighbours ; for, in glancing through the Florentine annals of that time, we do not find any Monaldi putting themselves forward in the fierce struggles through which Florence had so often to pass.

They lived near the old gate of the city known as the Porta Rossa, not far from the Church of the Holy Trinity, one of the thirty-six parishes into which the city was divided, and to which they belonged. This church was served by the monks of Vallombrosa. It was a church of great antiquity, dating at least from the ninth century, and was recorded in old documents by the name of Our Lady of the Swoon. This name seems in itself to be conceived in the very spirit of the Servite Order. It expresses, in familiar phrase, the mystery of that intense sorrow which pervaded the soul of the Blessed Virgin in the climax of her sufferings, when, as the Mother of God made Man, she stood beside Him on Calvary, and when, according to several doctors of the Church, the agony which her spirit endured caused so terrible a shock in her physical being. It was the devotion to this overwhelming grief of the Blessed Virgin which was, later in their career, to be the great characteristic of the Servants of Mary.

The parents of Monaldi bestowed on him at his baptism the name of Buonfiglio or Bonfilius (Good Son), thus expressing in one word a hope and a prophecy, both of which were to be realized in their child, who was to be a model son to them, and to fulfil a higher destiny by becoming in religion the eldest son and the true father of the Blessed Virgin's adopted family.

Bonfilius Monaldi was in his fourth year, when, in A.D. 1200, the second of our Saints, Alexis Falconieri, was sent to gladden the household of Bernard Falconieri and his bride. Alexis was their firstborn, and he was followed by seven other sons, amongst whom was Clarissimo, the father of the future Saint Juliana Falconieri.

The Falconieri family belonged originally to Fiesole, a city which at one time was one of the rivals of Florence, whither they removed in the year 1012. Leaving the smiling hills of Fiesole, and crossing the richly cultivated plain lying between the two cities, they passed by the venerated oratory of Our Lady of Cafaggio, and took up their abode in the quarter of Florence nearest to the cradle of their race. Here they were close to the Porta di Balla, and within a few paces of Santa Reparata and St. John the Baptist, two churches which, at a later period, were thrown into one.

The Falconieri, from the first, took rank as the foremost of the Popolani or Florentine gentry. In the year 1225 their name is seen among the members of the chief Council of the Republic. This is an incontestable proof that they were of the first rank, since, at that time, the great offices of State were exclusively in the hands of the magnates, a monopoly which was not destined to last much longer.

Bernard Falconieri was also one of the merchant princes of his time; commercial pursuits not being considered, in those simple days, as derogatory to men of rank. Subsequently to 1285 we find the names of the Falconieri, on several occasions, in the lists of the councillors and chief magistrates of Florence, and one of their number was chosen for the high dignity of Gonfalonier.

The family of the future Saint followed the Papal and ecclesiastical party, and were opposed to the Imperial faction. They steadily adhered to their political principles; but, at the same time, they were always desirous of bringing about a reconciliation between the two sides; and, in the year 1279, they were among the earliest who came forward to sign the treaty drawn up by Cardinal Latino, which, for a short time, had the effect of restoring peace to Florence.

The firstborn of the merchant Falconieri was baptized by the name of Alexis, which he retained in religion. This name was in itself an augury of the humility, the spirit of poverty and detachment, the heroic mortification and the virginal purity, which the holy Founder was destined to exhibit in the utmost degree of perfection.

In 1203, when Bonfilius Monaldi had attained the age of reason, and Alexis Falconieri was beginning to utter his first articulate words, our third Saint was born in the family of Antella or Antellesi. To him was given at his baptism the name of Benedict—one, indeed, most fitting for this blessed child, who was to receive and to dispense to others so many choice blessings. But, later on, the Saint himself, on the day of his religious profession, made choice of the name of Manetto or Manettus.

Historians are not agreed as to the origin of the dell' Antella family. Some say that it is of Persian, others of Teutonic, descent.

All that is known for certain is, that, on its first arrival in Italy, the family settled in the village of Antella, of which, in course of time, it obtained the lordship. About the year 1200 the Antellesi left the village from which they derived, or on which they had bestowed, their name, and established themselves in Florence. Being rich, they bought from the powerful house of Uberti and Cerchi two palaces in the district of the Porta di San Piero, and there they took up their residence in the street which still preserves their name.

The Antellesi ranked among the Grandi or first nobility. They belonged to the Guelph party, and they also held a considerable place in the financial world as bankers. One of them was consul of the money-changers, and for many generations banking continued to be the chosen profession of the family. From these facts we may conclude that they were wealthy, a proof of which may be also found in the palaces, towers, and *loggie*, or arcades, built by them, all singularly beautiful specimens of architecture.

Once established in Florence, the Antellesi became valuable citizens of the Republic, and they were often called upon to fill important posts. Many of them figure in the list of the Gonfaloniers and of the chief councillors.

In the following year, 1204, was born the Saint who of all the Seven bears the most illustrious name in the history of his native city. This was Bartholomeo Amidei. His family were, so to speak, incorporated with Florence. However far back her annals could be traced, there were the Amidei to be found ; and learned writers aver that, among the houses which boast of a Roman origin, none have a clearer right to that distinction than theirs.

Besides their palace and towers in the city, the Amidei owned a fortified castle in Val di Greve. In Florence, their dwelling was on the west side of the street of Por San Maria, facing the narrow street leading to St. Stephen's, one of the priory churches founded by Charlemagne.

They were both rich and powerful, and they held an important position in the city, where they were much looked up to ; they had intermarried with the chief families, and they exercised great influence in public affairs. They were chivalric by nature, as well as noble by birth ; and several of their number had shared in the dangers of the Crusades, and won fame for deeds of valour.

At the time of our Saint's birth, they had counted more than one chief magistrate among them ; and, in 1182, Bonogianni degli Amidei had been elected one of the consuls.

They were always the first among the partisans of the Imperialist faction ; and, therefore, they placed themselves at the head of the Ghibellines, when a quarrel, beginning at a banquet, fanned the flames of civil discord to a greater height than usual.

The little Amidei was baptized almost as soon as he saw the light.

The name bestowed on him was that of a holy Apostle, whose love of his Lord had been proved even to the shedding of his blood—St. Bartholomew. But the Saint exchanged it upon his religious profession for his family name, which, etymologically, derived from *Amicus Dei*, expressed far better than his baptismal appellation the ruling passion of this soul, and the sole aim of his existence—namely, that absorbing love of God, which so filled his heart that it visibly appeared in his countenance.

In the same year that St. Amideus came into the world, whilst Bonfilius Monaldi and Alexis Falconeri were progressing in childhood, and Benedict dell' Antella was emerging from infancy, the fifth chosen Servant of Mary was born in the family of the Uguccioni, who dwelt near the Porta di Bella, not far from the Church of St. John the Baptist. The house which he rejoiced by his birth was one of the most ancient in Florence, and was known also by the name of Lippi and Scalandroni. They were one family with the Buondelmonti, who were lords of the whole Val di Pesa. They had removed to Florence before 1186, when we find Uguccione degli Uguccioni one of the three consuls, who were the magistrates appointed to govern the Republic.

The family of Uguccione was of an elevated rank, among the Guelph popolani, and was likewise engaged in commerce. In 1219, one Bonaguisa degli Uguccioni was elected the consul of the merchants. This was a post of considerable importance ; for, at this period, the consuls of the merchants exercised joint authority with the consuls of the city in the government of the Republic.

Our Saint's father bore a title which added to the splendour of his name. He was a knight—an honour which was coveted by all the Florentine patricians. Before receiving that dignity, he had complied with all the requisite conditions. On the appointed day he had gone, in solemn procession, to the Baptistery of St. John the Precursor, and there had been plunged in the bath, symbolizing the purity which should distinguish those vowed to defend the cause of God, of the Church, and of their country. His sponsors then clothed him with a rich mantle, buckled the gilded spurs of knighthood on his heels, placed the helmet on his head, and girded on his sword. This function over, he had been escorted in state to the Piazza dei Priori, where he had taken the solemn oath of his Order. The Gonfalonier of the Republic had then embraced him, and presented him, in the name of the city, with a banner, a lance, and a shield adorned with the civic arms, after which ceremony the new-made knight enjoyed, from that time forward, the privilege of wearing in his belt a dagger with a golden sheath.

Throughout the Florentine annals we find the name of the Uguccioni constantly recurring in association with all the varied fortunes of the State.

The baptismal name of our Saint was Ricovero, which appears to signify the recovering of divine grace by means of that Sacrament— a grace with which, in after life, he so fully corresponded On his religious profession he adopted the name of Uguccione or Hugh.

Not far from the Porta di Balla, in a westerly direction, another gate existed, called the Porta di Spadai. It is generally believed that the family of the Sostegni, known also as del Migliore, or dei Migliorelli, lived here. The sixth of our Saints, born in 1205, belonged to this family, which, according to the chroniclers of the Servite Order, was one of the most distinguished in Florence. It has, however, left but few "footprints in the sands of time". It seems that they were of the gentry and Guelphs. Three of its branches bore the name of del Migliore; and it is to. be believed that our Saint sprang from the branch which settled at la Lastra, a small place situated on the road to Bologna, beyond Pratolino. He was baptized by the name of Gherardino; but he did not retain it in religion, exchanging it for that of Sostegno or Sostene (support or prop), a name well suited to one whose life, consecrated to God and to His Blessed Mother, was to be a sustaining prop to his family, to his country, and to the Church.

Whilst Benedict dell' Antella, Bartholomew Amidei, Ricovero Uguccioni, and Gherardino Sostegni were yet infants, and when Alexis Falconieri had arrived at the age of reason, and Bonfilius Monaldi was passing from boyhood to youth, the birth of the youngest of our Seven Saints, in 1206, completed the chosen band. This was Giovanni or John Manetti, son of Buonagiunta.

Several Florentine families bore the name of Manetti; all were of high rank, at least in the gentry, and all had distinguished themselves in the public service. It is uncertain to which of these our Saint belonged. Some authors think that he belonged to the Manetti of the district attached to the Church of Santo Spirito, built in the thirteenth century. Others suppose him to have been one of the Manetti of the Santa Croce district. Both these families claimed to be lineal representatives of the noble house of Benettini. Without entering at greater length into these genealogical questions, we may briefly state that they held a high position in Florentine society, although they were not equal in rank to the powerful houses of the Amidei, the Monaldi, the Antellesi, and the Uguccioni, whose chiefs owned fortified castles in the country, as well as palaces and towers in the city. They were wealthy, and, like all their fellow-citizens of the same class, they were engaged in trade; in fact, they belonged to the corporation of the silk manufacturers. They followed the Guelph party.

To the youngest of our Seven Saints was given the name of John, which was borne by that faithful Servant of the Blessed Virgin, the beloved Apostle. It is true that, later, at the solemn moment of his religious profession, John Manetti renounced this cherished name; but, ceasing to bear the name of Mary's adopted son, he chose one most expressive of his joy in being allowed to consecrate himself to her service—that of Buonagiunta, which signifies "happily arrived or admitted".

Thus, within the space of nine or ten years, our Seven Saints had made their entrance into the world, and from their cradles had begun to walk in that path which was to lead them to the loftiest height of perfection.

It is much to be regretted that we possess no details of their early days, for surely the most minute circumstances, relating to these chosen souls, would have been full of edification. Unhappily, an impenetrable veil has fallen between us and them, and our curiosity, legitimate though it be, is completely baffled. But, since we know so little of their beginning, we must try, for our edification, to penetrate more deeply into the designs of the Master Who called them.

In the first place, we are struck by the number needed for the supernatural work—Seven. The number Seven signifies, in the mystical sense, perfection; and, therefore, it would seem that Almighty God desired that the work should be a very perfect one. Usually we find but a single intermediary chosen for the communication of His gifts, or, at the utmost, two or three, as in the case of the Benedictine Order, of the Friars Preachers, of the sons of St. Francis, the Order of the Holy Trinity, and of that of Our Lady of Mercy. But here He appointed Seven to carry out what He might, had it so pleased Him, have put into the hands of only one.

And we may say, too, that Almighty God chose these His instruments with especial care. It was His pleasure that all those gifts, which, in the natural order, make their possessors conspicuous—birth, wealth, education, high-toned moral training, and all that it implies—should be united in them. For, when the ground, in which the seed of grace is to be cast, has already been cultivated to the highest degree by natural means, there are fewer obstacles to the growing up of the plant. And, from another point of view, the more costly is the sacrifice to be made in the renouncement of all natural advantages, the more striking is the triumph of divine grace. God has often dealt thus with His chosen Saints, but seldom has He done so in a more eminent degree.

Besides, Almighty God has no respect of persons: He chooses whom He wills, and for His own purpose. The seven households which had each the glory of giving a child to God were ignorant of the future reserved to those children by Him. For the most part, these families were not united to each other by any bonds of kindred or friendship: between some of them an active political rivalry, if not hostility, existed. The time for the undertaking and the means for its execution were also to be determined in the same unlooked-for way.

And, at last, all was to be for the honour of the Mother of the King, so that, in the designs of God, the promotion of the glory of the Blessed Virgin was at once the first beginning, and the final object of His work. It was His divine will that a new development of the homage paid to His Blessed Mother should now take place, and, as she is honoured by Him above all his creatures, He was pleased to decide that His plan should be carried out by means hitherto untried.

CHAPTER III.

First Training and Youthful Aspirations.

(1204-1221.)

THESE seven children whom God had chosen to execute His own design advanced in years and intelligence, surrounded by all the caresses and comforts of home life. As we can easily suppose, theirs were the innocent joys and transient sorrows of infancy. And then came the period when reason first begins to unfold, and when the serious work of education is inaugurated.

In the education of a child there are manifold influences which combine to form his character. Among these, the most important are such as act upon him in the very cradle, and upon which his future disposition may be said in a great measure to depend. Our Saints received this training under the parental eye; and in order duly to appreciate the nature of their bringing up, we must try to picture them in the midst of their several home circles, and to give some idea of their domestic life.

First of all we shall say that the seven families to which they belonged, although differing widely in politics, were one and all Catholic to the core. The Catharist heresy had existed in Florence for more than a century, and had seduced many souls; but not one of these houses had been tainted with it, nor had shown the slightest tendency in that direction. Those who had belonged to the Ghibelline party were still dutiful children of the Church, and obeyed the Holy See in all spiritual matters. All held the faith, and practised their religious duties: all strove to lead good lives, and devoted themselves to works of piety and charity: and all, both by precept and example, endeavoured to inculcate in their children the fear of God, the love of religion, respect for the Church, and a steady fulfilment of all Christian duties.

Religion, undoubtedly, held the foremost place in these seven households ; but patriotism came next, and was sometimes, perhaps, carried to an excess. All Florentines were at that time led away by a passionate devotion for their beautiful city, which made them think that the whole of Italy ought to bow down before her. It is true that the Sacerdotal and Imperial factions held different views as to the means of aggrandizing Florence. As we have already said, the Falconieri, the Antellesi, the Uguccioni, the Sostegni, and the Manetti supported the Papal party, whilst the Monaldi and the Amidei were Imperialists. The political predilection of each house entered into its private life and made it difficult, if not impossible, for those who belonged to it to avoid being carried away by the feeling of partisanship for the cause which it espoused, and of rivalry with those who were of the opposite faction—a rivalry which often brought about fatal conflicts. Nevertheless, all agreed upon one point : all wished to see their well-loved Florence great and glorious. This public spirit ran high in the families of our Saints, and was instilled with zealous care into the tender minds of the rising generation.

As we have already said, those families ranked among the first of the city. All had not attained, it is true, to the same degree of historical celebrity ; but all were genuinely patrician. The title of those who were really Grandi or Nobles implied the absolute possessorship of land, whether in the city or in the country, the owner of the title having dependent upon him free-holders who paid him a certain rental. About these, and under their orders and those of their lord, gathered artisans engaged in various trades and manufactures, soldiers retained in readiness for any warlike outbreak, farmers, and labourers or serfs who belonged to the estate. The civic spirit which prevailed in Florence, and which continually increased in strength, modified to some extent the feudal customs, and indeed seriously weakened the whole system. This being taken into consideration, we may easily form a general idea of the position held by the Grandi at this period. As to the Popolani or rich citizens, they occupied a position nearly equal to the others for feudal possessions, and sometimes greater for influence. All of them, however, enjoyed the consideration conferred by a distinguished name, the power given by a numerous body of dependants, and that which arises from belonging to the governing class. Their style of living was in keeping with their rank, and gave employment to large numbers.

Wealth and rank in those days went hand in hand. The families of our Saints were all rich, though not all in an equal degree. To maintain their dignity, to keep up their palaces in Florence, and their castles in the country, large incomes were required. Their dress, furniture, and food were most comfortable. In this state of life a more than ordinary degree of virtue is required to conquer the natural inclination of mankind toward self-indulgence. The climate of

Tuscany, too, so mild and temperate during one half of the year, so warm and sunny during the other half, no doubt had something to do with the readiness with which the great families adopted an easy mode of existence. The chroniclers describe with enthusiasm the sobriety and the absence of luxury of the time which preceded the installation, in 1267, of Charles of Anjou and of his court in Florence; yet it is certain that during the youth of our Saints an atmosphere of great comfort and abundance pervaded their households, and they had to undergo its influence.

Besides the feudal dues and rents the chief source of all this material prosperity was commerce—*la Mercatura*—in which all the families of our seven Saints were engaged, great nobles though some of them were. At the beginning of the thirteenth century Florence was unquestionably the most industrious city in the world, and was possessed of the largest trading interests. Men of rank were then equally men of business, and the fathers of our Saints were occupied in various profitable undertakings. The Antellesi were bankers : nearly all the others were manufacturers, chiefly of wool, of fine cloth, and of silk. These occupations left little room for idleness ; but the love of gain could hardly fail to creep in, and to prove a stumbling-block in the path of spiritual progress.

Another feature of a mediæval household which is not unknown, indeed, at the present day in Italy was this, that all the members of the same family, married sons, of whatever age, with their wives and children, continued to dwell under the paternal roof, to lead the same kind of life as their parents, and to share in the business and occupations of the elders. This system of life was practically patriarchal. All looked up to the grandfather, or to the father who was the head of the house, and whom all obeyed. It was he who led the family prayers at night or morning, who took precedence at table, or in the social circle, and who walked to church followed by the long line of his descendants. His permission was necessary if any member of the family wished to remove into another house, or into a different part of the city. The real estate of the clan remained undivided in the hands of its chief: only the income and the trade profits were shared. Each house thus formed a community in itself, a *Consorteria* as it was called, in which the ties of kindred were closely knit, and in which there was yet a sufficient divergency of taste and tempers to form a useful training school for the younger members, where they served their apprenticeship before taking a part in the wider theatre of the world.

The families of those whose daily lives we have tried to sketch an accurate outline were high-minded and thoroughly religious in principle ; yet they did not seek to avoid civic honours and dignities. In Florence the passion for glory was the ruling spirit of every house at that period. And the citizens, consequently, eagerly sought and gladly accepted those public offices which conferred distinction on their family name—a distinction coveted by each generation in turn. The feeling of clanship which existed among the members prompted everyone to use his influence to the utmost to forward the views of his family candidates. It would have required a high degree of Christian self-abnegation to induce a Florentine of those days to withdraw from the race for civic honours ; and, in fact, the seven houses to which our Saints belonged were no exception to the rule.

To finish the sketch of these families, we must add that, although by no means frivolous, they were, like all their fellow-countrymen, far from being austere or gloomy in their deportment : the beauty of their city, the charm of the climate, the fertility of the soil, their intellectual gifts, and their wealth, all disposed them to enjoy life and to love pleasure. The households of our Saints' parents were well ordered, but amusement was welcomed ; and although moderate recreation is not incompatible with piety, yet it is so difficult to draw the boundary line between the use and abuse of amusements, that we can hardly expect to find heroic virtue amidst gay surroundings.

Such was the atmosphere in which our Saints passed the first fifteen years of their lives ; for they do not appear to have left home, as St. Philip Benizi and many scions of the great houses did, to pursue their studies at the famous Universities of Bologna, Paris, or Padua, or to receive a mercantile education in the commercial centres of other lands. So far as we know, they were wholly home-bred and home-trained : under home influences their characters were formed, and through these influences were sown the seeds of holiness, which, later on, were to blossom forth so brightly.

In spite, however, of all the care bestowed on them, they might yet have been drawn from the right path by the fascinations of the world and the seductions of vanity, which, even when powerless to lead astray, too often dazzle the young mind and prevent it from following the inspirations of divine grace. They might easily have fallen into a careless, easy-going mode of life, in which self-denial becomes difficult, and a taste for the coarser pleasures gradually springs up. Many were the obstacles in their way, both from persons and circumstances, any one of which might have caused them to falter and turn back from their course.

But our Saints, young though they were, managed so well that they profited by both the advantages and the dangers of their state of life. In fact they gradually developed tendencies which seemed much at variance with their surroundings, and which are seldom displayed by young and ardent minds, eager, as a rule, for pleasure and distinction. There was something striking in the unanimity with which they all devoted themselves to the same pious exercises, as though they were following a rule of life in common, under the same roof, directed by the same superior, and with the same end in view. And yet they were unknown to each other. It is possible, of course, that those who lived in the same district of the city, as dell' Antella and Amidei on the one hand, or Uguccioni and Sostegni on the other, may have met in public. But there was no acquaintanceship between them ; and each trod his path alone, and prepared himself unconsciously for his unknown vocation.

As the years of the Seven increased, so did their growth in virtue ; and whether in their own homes or in the world, they were models of all that Christian youths should be. Flowers of the Church's garden, they shed around the sweet fragrance of the indwelling grace which manifested itself in their ways and bearing to the edification of all. "Day by day," records their pious chronicler, "did the supernatural seed planted in their souls by Holy Baptism, and purified by Penance from all taint of corrupt nature, take root and flourish more and more. Strengthened by faith, which Holy Baptism had infused into their hearts, and which Penance had clarified and enriched, they were enabled to see, to understand, and to lead that life which is the perfect expression of Christianity reduced to practice. Closely united to their Divine Model by virtue of His Sacred Passion, they were wholly bound to Almighty God, their Supreme End, by the never-ceasing interior homage which their souls rendered to Him. Thus did they early begin to toil at their own sanctification, nor did they cease from the plough ; and so year by year the harvest of their virtues increased and multiplied."

These virtues were displayed first and foremost in their home life, all the duties which it imposed being faithfully performed. Their obedience to the parental will knew no limit save that of the Divine Will. Their own wishes were sacrificed, except when a question was involved of giving up piety.

No pains were spared to acquaint them thoroughly with literature, science, industry, and commerce, but they began to show more and more that the things of God and His service possessed for them stronger attractions than aught else which this world could offer.

They lived constantly in the presence of God ; the thought of Him absorbed them ; their hearts were filled with love of Him. To the pure in heart this exercises an influence beyond all others.

So ardently did their souls yearn after God, that they ceased not to seek Him everywhere, but chiefly in the churches, where, in His boundless love for man, He deigns to dwell. In Florence, churches and oratories abounded. Each of our Saints had several churches close to his father's dwelling, and thus all, without difficulty, could follow the bent of their devotion. They spent much time in prayer before the altar, and all who beheld them were edified to see them so recollected and absorbed in communion with God.

They speedily became proficient in mental prayer, so as to converse with God familiarly, as friend with friend. Their biographers tell us that they absolutely thirsted for this holy exercise, and that they were ever eager to quit the world and to fly from the society of their companions, in order to give themselves to prayer and meditation. They were accustomed to withdraw to some remote part of the house, and there, kneeling on the floor, with eyes humbly cast down or raised in supplication, they would spend many hours daily, joyfully and lovingly, as a writer expresses it, a the feet of Our Lord and His Blessed Mother.

To them all that worldlings call pleasure was wearisome and insipid. Far from seeking human society, they shunned it. Pomp and luxury were for them really a penance. The ordinary amusements of young people had no attraction for them. They often saw all around them full of mirth , but the seven holy youths well knew how quickly the bounds of lawful enjoyment are passed, and how soon innocent merriment degenerates into revelry ; and, therefore, they abstained from everything of the kind, and thus escaped from the great danger of falling into the hands of bad companions. Society, in those days, though still kept within certain limits in manners, was pervaded by many evil influences, such as party spirit, hatred, greed, and immorality ; and the young were led away by the bad example which they saw on all sides. But the future Saints kept resolutely aloof from all those of their age and rank whose conduct was not above suspicion, and thus avoided the snares spread for them.

They loved also to hear the Word of God, to which they listened with rapt attention, applying to themselves the counsels of the preacher. The ministry of the pulpit was then exercised with great freedom, and priests, in their sermons, spared not to rebuke the vices and follies of the time. Our pious Founders, in their child-like docility, profited by all that they heard, and found therein great safeguards against the dangers by which they were surrounded.

So soon as their dawning intelligence enabled them to comprehend sufficiently the importance of their action, they approached the two wondrous Sacraments of Penance and Holy Eucharist. As to their subsequent communions, they were as frequent as the discipline of that period allowed. The faithful then approached the confessional much oftener than the altar ; even monthly communions were comparatively rare. In the case of our young Saints their fervour made up for the infrequency of their participation in the Eucharistic feast, and day by day they were more and more drawn towards the things of God, and detached from this world and all its goods.

In concluding this sketch of their youthful days, we must not omit to observe how closely their love of God was intertwined with that of His Blessed Mother. Their love of Mary, through the pious care of their families, took root early in their hearts, and they cherished it and made it the guiding star of their lives. For them Mary was a benefactress, the almoner who distributed her Son's gifts to them, and by whom all their offerings were to be presented to His Majesty. The city of Florence had a great devotion to Our Blessed Lady ; and thus all the surroundings of our saintly youths tended to preserve and develop that filial love for the Queen of Heaven, which was as a sweet perfume pervading their every thought, word, and action, in the morning of their young lives.

All these characteristics were possessed in common by the Seven ; but there was an individuality in each of them which became more marked as they advanced in age, and which gave a type of its own to the sanctity of each one of the group. This will be related later on. Meanwhile, we have given an outline of their course of education and of their training to the age of fifteen or thereabouts. We have seen them steadily pursuing a virtuous course, holding aloof from the world, and striving after a closer union with God. The rudiments of sanctity have already appeared in them, and only await the finishing touch of the Great Artificer of souls, Who alone knows when and how to bring His handiwork to perfection.

These seven youths must have indeed presented a spectacle full of consolation to those who looked upon them. We may picture them to ourselves, with their unruffled brows showing the untroubled innocence of their hearts ; with the dignity and self-possession of mature years in their bearing ; with the purity of their souls mirrored in their eyes ; with their modest looks, their recollected demeanour, their discreet speech, their manners gentle and courteous to all They are hedged round, as it were, by prayer and meditation ; and they live and move in the presence of God. They are always occupied, but their activity is devoid of haste or of eagerness. Their obedience to those who have authority over them is prompt and cheerful, and they edify all with whom they are brought into contact. Unbelievers and libertines cannot refrain from respecting them, even whilst affecting to turn them into ridicule. Their pious biographers tell us that they were more like angels than human beings. It is easy to believe that so it must have been : it is what the whole course of their lives showed daily more and more, and which will be found strikingly displayed in the years which we are now about to chronicle.

CHAPTER IV.

ᶠflorence and ᵍer ᵖerils.

(1211—1225.)

At the age of fifteen the home training of our Seven Saints was to a great extent completed. Henceforth the moulding of their characters was to be chiefly their own work, and it depended, above all, on the line which they took upon entering the world of Florence. Whether for good or for evil, their native city would, of necessity, largely influence the current of their thoughts and their habits of life.

Undoubtedly Florence was a city beautiful and attractive in no common degree, with her exquisite climate and her position. Set in a landscape of surpassing loveliness, she seemed like an enchanted palace in the gardens of Armida Charlemagne had decided that she should bear the name which was hers by right, and thenceforth she was called Florence, the City of Flowers. She was at that time hemmed in by ramparts, and she covered far less ground than at the present day; and the bright gardens and smiling meadows surrounding her walls crowned her, as it were, and made her still more lovely.

Within the walls a large population was gathered, numbering, at the beginning of the thirteenth century, about eighty thousand people. This alone made Florence one of the most important cities in Italy. Her nobles, or magnates, were of Tuscan or other Italian descent, or else were sprung from some German house which had come southwards in the train of the emperors. Next to the nobles came the *popolani*, the *popolo grasso*, the wealthy burghers, many of whom possessed large private fortunes, besides carrying on extensive business transactions. These often came in competition with the nobles, and contended with them for the possession of civic offices, until, at last, they formed together only one class, the highest in the city. At the bottom of the social scale was the *popolo minuto*—that is to say, the masses.

The community composed of these three classes ranked high in intelligence, and had already shown great capacity both for invention and for execution. But the day of Florentine genius was as yet only in the dawn. It was during the course of this thirteenth century, upon which our history now enters, that the full radiance of this noteworthy city burst upon the world, dazzling alike in letters, arts, and sciences, and culminating in the appearance of two of the most illustrious men of that or of any age—Dante and Giotto.

The Florentines appreciated intellectual eminence. But they had also a great predilection for the practical and the useful; industry and commerce were, therefore, in high esteem among them. Professions and trades were organized into corporations, and all the enrolled members were actively engaged in the business of their respective guilds. The commercial relations of Florence extended to all parts of the world as then known, and a constant stream of wealth was thus continually flowing into the city. This influx of capital caused the inhabitants of Florence to turn their attention from manufactures to banking, of which system they are said to have been the inventors, and which they had, at all events, a great share in bringing to perfection.

Besides their qualities of industry and energy, the Florentines were distinguished by their intense civic haughtiness, which sprang partly from their pride of race, partly from exultation in the natural advantages and beauty of their city, and partly from remembrance of the victorious career which had hitherto been hers. A spirit of independence was then passing over the Italian cities. Italy, although willing to acknowledge her suzerains, hardly endured the idea of absolute masters. Florence, in particular, though placed under the suzerainty of the Pope, who held the fief in right of the Countess Matilda's bequest, aspired to self-government. she was at heart thoroughly republican. Her tendencies in this direction were checked by the nobility, whose strong castles made them practically independent, by the Emperor, and by some of the larger cities of Tuscany. The great object of the Florentines was to overcome these three obstacles. Siena, being the most formidable rival of Florence, a constant hostility was, after a period of peace, to be kept up between them, and no opportunity of dealing a blow at their opponent was lost by the Florentines, until, after a long and obstinate struggle, the victory was theirs.

To satisfy her ambition, Florence, in spite of her commercial instincts, became also a military state. She gradually gathered together a standing army, on the organization and maintenance of which she spent enormous sums. The nobles at first held the highest military rank, and were enrolled in the formidable squadron of knights in plate armour, the branch of the service to which alone they would condescend to enter. The middle and lower classes were placed in other divisions; but almost all the citizens were obliged to serve in the ranks.

Although Florence was much busied in worldly pursuits, she was, nevertheless, essentially a religious city. The Florentines believed with that simple, child-like faith which it was the privilege of the Middle Ages to possess. They were devoted with their noble hearts to the Church. They accepted her teaching and obeyed her decrees with docile submission, and her censures were dreaded by them as the greatest of evils. Of their piety they gave substantial proofs in the six-and-thirty parish churches of which the city boasted; in the numerous chapels and convents which abounded in every district ; in the well-filled ranks of the clergy, and of religious men and women. Religion formed an integral part of civic life. Public meetings were held in the churches, and the temporal interests of the State were discussed beneath the shadow of the consecrated roof. Weapons of war even were stamped with religious emblems. And shrines and oratories arose on all sides throughout the surrounding country, and fed the devotion of the faithful.

There was no tendency among the pious Florentines towards minimizing in religious matters. On the contrary, they were ever ready to receive all devotions sanctioned by the Church. After the supreme worship due to God alone ranks devotion to His Blessed Mother; and to Florence this devotion was always especially dear. One of the first churches ever built there, upon the Capitol where the Roman power took refuge under the protection of its false gods, was dedicated to Our Lady of the Capitol. Then, during the Crusades, especially at the time of the first, the cultus of the Sorrows of the Blessed Virgin was introduced into Florence, under the title of Our Lady of the Swoon. The abbey, with all its attendant buildings, was erected as a tribute to Mary, in which every rank, from the emperor to the peasant, took its share. Chapels dedicated to Our Lady were to be seen in all parts of the city and throughout the Florentine territory; her statues were placed in niches in front of private houses, and it became customary to keep lamps burning before them.

Besides, the great mass of Florentine people, in spite of their independent spirit, was deeply attached to the Holy See. But for those powerful nobles who adhered to the empire, it might have been said that Florence was devoted heart and soul to the Sovereign Pontiff, not only as the Spiritual Ruler of Christendom, but also as being invested by general consent with the right of redressing the temporal wrongs committed by the great ones of the world, and as the natural protector of the interests of Italy where his See was established.

But, although the instincts and the feelings of the Florentines were strongly religious, yet these good tendencies were not powerful enough to eradicate and stop the evil propensities of weak human nature. At an early date, during the thirteenth century, simplicity of manners was lost, and a general relaxation began to be felt in society. Thus devotional practices often went hand in hand with defective morality. The higher and middle classes were full of worldliness and always ready for idle gossip. Like the ancient Romans, they spent as much time in the streets as in their homes ; they delighted to meet in the public squares, the market-place, the arcades, and wherever noise and bustle were to be found ; they were somewhat addicted to the pleasures of the table, and they readily indulged their sensual tastes.

This relaxation of morals began to give rise to a debased style of literature. Manuscripts of immoral tendency were passed from hand to hand, and they were eagerly read by many whose hearts were depraved, and whose intellects were frittered away by the perusal of these dangerous works. In this way many, too, lost their faith, made the holy mysteries of religion the subject of profane jests, joined the followers of Epicurus, as the freethinkers of the day were called, and, lastly, apostatized altogether.

Heresy found the greater number of its recruits among these votaries of free life; for, sad to say, Florence, the city of the Madonna and of the Pontiff, was yet honeycombed by the most frightful of all heresies, namely, Catharism, which was nothing else but Manicheism, with some slight differences, and bearing a new name. The Cathari, like the Manichees, held that there were two creative principles, one good, the other evil; and hence, through various subtle deductions, they reached, on the one hand, the negation of the fundamental dogmas of the Catholic faith, whilst, on the other hand, they taught doctrines utterly immoral and opposed to the Gospel. The mysteries of the Trinity, of the Incarnation, of the Redemption, of the Divine Motherhood, and of the Communion of Saints—these great truths were so wholly perverted by the Cathari as to be unrecognizable. They rejected all the Sacraments, with the exception of Baptism: they would not practise Invocation of the Blessed Virgin, nor of the Saints, nor show any reverence to the Holy Cross: they disapproved of public worship in churches, of priests and bishops, and of marriage · they disputed the right of the Church to possess lands or money: they abolished all magnificence of ritual   They looked upon the Old Testament as being inspired by the evil spirit: they mutilated the New Testament, accepting some portions and rejecting others. They adopted a Sacrament of their own invention as an assured pledge of salvation, and those who had received it were styled the *Consoled.* They circulated horrible slanders against the Church. Whilst such were their theories, their practice was even more reprehensible. Under an austere outward demeanour they concealed dissipated lives. They preached fasting and mortification, whilst giving themselves up to every excess. They were greedy of gain and keen in all matters of business. They were zealous in spreading their doctrines, and would willingly move heaven and earth to make proselytes. To sum up in one word, Catharism was a work of the Evil One. It had one vital principle—hatred of the Catholic Church; and it tended to one direction alone—that of the most abject materialism.

The Manichees had been long established in Florence, and they had considerable influence there. They were supported by several rich and powerful families, particularly by the Baroni. When they were left in peace, they celebrated their religious rites openly in the palaces of some of the nobles. When popular opinion turned against them, they took refuge behind strong walls or in subterranean buildings.

Nothing seemed to check them, and the severities to which the Church was compelled to resort in order to destroy this source of corruption did not terrify the Cathari of Florence. On the contrary, their enthusiasm was stimulated by the recital of the punishments inflicted on their brethren in the south of France and the north of Italy. The blow dealt against the sect by the Lateran Council of 1215 appeared to make no impression upon them, or, at all events, did not produce any signs of amendment. Thus by degrees the infection spread on all sides, and threatened the very existence of the social fabric.

Many could foresee these sad consequences, but few had resolution enough to attempt to stem the tide of evil. The result was that, during the first forty years of the thirteenth century, so many men and women were seduced by the Catharist doctrines that, as a trustworthy historian assures us, they numbered one-third of the population of the city.

Such was Florence when the boyhood of our Seven Saints was about to close ; and to complete the picture, we must briefly relate some events which, occurring after twenty-seven years of peace and tranquillity, made the political situation highly critical. These events were as follows.

In the year 1197, the consuls of the Florentine Republic had laid siege to Montebuoni, a strong castle belonging to the Buondelmonti family, and had taken it by storm. This hostile act sowed the seed of discord between the owners of the castle and the Uberti, who were supposed to be at the bottom of the affair. From thenceforth their enmity continued smouldering, till, in 1214, one Mazzingho di Figrimo Usazzinghi was knighted. He invited all the youth of Florence to a banquet in celebration of the event, to be given in his castle of Campi on the day when he was to be invested with the insignia of his new dignity. During the repast the jester of the Mazzinghi snatched away a dish of meat from Uberto Infangati. A friend of the last-named, Buondelmonte dei Buondelmonti, took up the quarrel. Upon this, Odo di Arrigo Fifanti sided with the jester, and, in the heat of the dispute, threw the dish with its contents at the head of Uberto Infangati. The guests hastily rose from table, and Buondelmonte, carried away by anger, wounded Odo Fifanti with a knife. Odo Fifanti, returning to Florence, called together all his relatives, and begged them to avenge him.

Among his connections he numbered the Uberti, the Gualandi, the Lamberti, and the Amidei. But these last, instead of fomenting the quarrel, strove to appease it ; and, in order to reconcile the hostile parties, they proposed a marriage between Buondelmonte, who had given the wound, and a daughter of Lambertuccio Amidei, whose wife was sister to the wounded man, Odo Fifanti.

The marriage was about to take place, when the wife of Forese Donati offered her daughter, a maiden of surpassing beauty, as a fitting bride for Buondelmonte. She contrived to arrange a meeting between the young people, and seeing that Buondelmonte was much attracted by the fair girl, she stimulated his pride by saying that it would be shameful if he allowed the Uberti to frighten him into a marriage, when he was free to choose whom he would. Buondelmonte upon this, no longer heeding his plighted word, broke off his engagement with the Amidei.

The Amidei were indignant at this breach of faith, and they instantly summoned their kinsfolk to meet in St. Stephen's Church, there to confer upon some plan whereby to avenge so gross an insult. Schiatta Uberti proposed that they should strike the faithless knight on the face, thereby proclaiming him to all the world as a perjured recreant ; but to this suggestion Mosca Lamberti fiercely replied : " If you mean only to give him a blow, you had better at once order your own coffin. Pay him rather in sterling coin. Let what you do be done thoroughly." All understood what the speaker meant by these dark hints. From that moment Buondelmonte's death was decided on, and the morning of Easter Sunday in the year 1215 was chosen for the doing of the deed.

Early on that Easter morning, Buondelmonte, clad in a white suit and mounted on a white palfrey, was riding slowly from the Ponte Vecchio through the street of Por-San-Maria, when the conspirators rushed out of the Amidei palace, and fell upon him ; Schiatta Uberti pulled him off his horse, and Mosca Lamberti, Lambertuccio Amidei, and Oderigo Fifanti slew him upon the spot.

After the perpetration of this horrible murder, Buondelmonte's body was placed by his betrothed upon a litter, and was carried through the city, she following it distracted with grief, and calling piteously upon her relatives to avenge the crime.

The citizens took part in the strife, some siding with one family, some with the other, till at length two distinct factions were formed, the members of which met constantly in fierce encounters. Eventually seeking for support beyond the bounds of their city, they both allied themselves, partly according to their several political tendencies, but chiefly from a sheer love of opposition, with the two great parties into which Europe at large was then divided. The Uberti and their followers pronounced for the Emperor, and declared themselves Ghibellines, this name having been bestowed by Henry IV. on his party, from the castle of Wibeling, where his father was born ; whilst the Buondelmonti and their adherents placed themselves under the standard of the Church, and proclaimed themselves Guelfs, the name being derived from Guelf d'Este, Duke of Bavaria, the opponent of Henry.

The struggle lasted for four years, during which Florence with her six *sesti*, or districts, presented the astonishing spectacle of six intrenched camps, where the enemy not only had a large number of spies, but also dwelt in the midst of them. The strong towers in which they took up their abodes were huge square masses of building with walls of great thickness, and doorways opening at a considerable height above the ground. They were capable of sustaining a siege, and could only be taken by storm under a shower of arrows. The inhabitants of these fortress-homes were constantly on the alert behind their movable fortifications of barricades, palissades, and *chevaux de frise*, all of which were shut, like the shops, at the slightest threatening sound. Weapons were only laid aside at night, when advantage was taken of the brief truce for the removal of the dead and wounded.

We may easily picture to ourselves the misery of Florence during these years, the disturbed state of men's minds, the deadly hatreds kindled in the hearts of all, the wild thirst for revenge too often slaked, the spirit of faction dividing house against house, and even, at length, the members of the same family one against another.

Such was Florence, bright with all the splendour of intellect, but shadowed by sin, when our Founders, ranging in age from fifteen to twenty years and upwards, stood on the threshold of manhood. It was amidst these surroundings that they entered upon a period of life, fair indeed with hopes and possibilities of good, but in which there are also many risks, many hidden rocks where the strongest ship often founders. At this age, when mere physical existence itself is a delight, when all the faculties are in their fullest vigour, when pleasure is most seductive, and when ambition wears an heroic aspect, they found themselves in this beautiful city, where good and evil were mingled together, where lofty virtue and degrading vice dwelt side by side. Their daily lives were spent amid these stirring scenes, their families held a conspicuous position in the Republic, and several of their relatives filled high offices of State. They lived in frequent intercourse with their kinsmen and fellow-citizens, and consequently they were familiar with the state of Florentine society.

It is easy to conceive that their path must have been beset with pitfalls. They possessed the advantages of birth, fortune, and education : the future lay smiling before them : the world welcomed them with open arms, and offered them a brilliant career. Their relatives urged them to enter on the road to fame and honours, or at least did not seek to withdraw them from it. A life of pleasure and worldly splendour was open to them. They had all in abundance ; they were caressed and sought after by all , nor were there wanting emissaries of evil who would fain have turned them from the straight way. In short, everything concurred to endanger their virtue and innocence. Who could say what the result might be at a time of life which even the most prudent have cause to dread? Who could tell whether the good effects of early training, aided by divine grace, would enable them to triumph over these obstacles in the way of their salvation, or whether they would fall under the repeated assaults of the enemies of their souls?

It was between the years 1211 and 1225, or thereabouts, that the Seven passed in succession through these crucial trials. But they had no lack of supernatural aid to support them ; and again, Mary, their guiding Star, shone through the darkness of the tempest to guide them to the haven where—

> " The fiery fight is heard no more,
> And the storm has ceased to blow ". (*Campbell.*)

CHAPTER V.

Overcoming the World.

(1211—1225.)

THE characters and dispositions of the seven holy youths did not suffer any deterioration from the seductive atmosphere which they breathed in Florence, during the most dangerous period of existence. On the contrary, during the years just recorded, the promise of their childhood and of their boyhood was amply fulfilled. Although the Florentine Republic was, at that time, seething with political passions, the line of conduct which they adopted kept them aloof from the turmoil, and formed a most edifying contrast to the doings of their fellow citizens.

They took no part, save when compelled by duty, in these exciting scenes. They loved the country of their birth with a strong and steady affection ; but their chief aim was to reach their true country, which is eternal in the heavens. Thus, whilst the two factions sought each other's destruction, our future Founders joined neither the Guelfs nor the Ghibellines, and never mingled in the street affrays, which cost so many lives throughout the city.

They had equally little taste for the more peaceful employments and amusements of their countrymen. They were far from censuring the energy and activity which the Florentines displayed in commercial and industrial pursuits, so long as their love of gain did not overpower their sense of duty. But, for themselves, they sought no possession, save that of the Sovereign Good. Nevertheless, they took a share, according to their capacities, in the various kinds of business in which their families were engaged : for they were not the less dutiful, less obedient, or less loving sons for being fervent Christians.

Brief as had been their experience of the world and its ways, they were not dazzled by the honours and dignities which it offered them. They knew exactly what these were worth, although the position held by their families did not permit them wholly to reject such distinctions ; and when the path was smoothed for them by the exertions of their parents and kinsfolk, filial obedience almost obliged acceptance In spite, therefore, of their youth, they began to occupy posts, which ultimately would have led to the higher dignities of the State. In the year 1225, the eldest of our Seven Saints was not more than nine-and-twenty, whilst the youngest was barely nineteen years of age ; but they were already employed in the public service, belonging to one or other of the many boards, the members of which were called upon to vote and act on certain important occasions. Thus they gradually learnt the mode of conducting the business of the State, and of fitting themselves for the highest offices.

At that period the army offered a career to many. Large numbers of officers were needed for the service of the Republic. The warlike temper of Florence increased as her ambition took higher flights. The combative propensities of the nobles, especially, seemed inbred. In the midst of this perpetual strife, the seven youthful Saints yearned for peace. War, in their eyes, was a chastisement, often a great crime, always a terrible misfortune. Military service not being then obligatory, they were able to follow the dictates of conscience, and to hold themselves aloof from the expeditions which were undertaken during their sojourn in the world

Meantime, they pursued and finished their studies according both to the wishes of their parents, and also to the duties of their state of life. They sought to excel in them, but not from any vain curiosity, not from ambitious views, such as often lead astray those who would eat of the fruit of the tree of knowledge. In that time literature and science were termed the liberal arts. Under these heads were comprised Grammar, by which they learned to speak correctly : Rhetoric, which taught them to express themselves eloquently : Poetry, which gives to language the charm of metre : Dialectics, to which is deputed the noble task of setting forth the truth : Physics, which teach all things concerning the bodies · Mathematics, to which belong numbers and all calculations connected therewith : and, lastly, Music, which adds the fascination of melody and harmony to the productions of Poetry. Their application resulted in considerable acquirements in the liberal arts, in a thorough dogmatic and practical knowledge of the Christian faith, and in a colloquial acquaintance with Latin, which was the language then employed in public business. They were also familiar with the newly developed tongue, the Italian, which Dante's teachers spoke and loved. But beyond this they did not go. In those days the period devoted to study was short, for the curriculum was comparatively restricted. Philip Benizi obtained the degree of doctor of medicine at twenty years of age, and he was considered a man of profound learning. The art of government was thoroughly understood in Florence ; she was a military city, an important commercial centre, the banking house of Europe, the home of luxury and pleasure, but she was not the nursery of learning and science. She was in too disturbed a state to devote herself to those mental toils for which silence and tranquillity are essential, for study is difficult whilst one is standing on the edge of a volcano.

As to the immoral tales which, in those times, were so enticing for a great many, our seven godly youths knew how great was the danger incurred by those who fed on their honeyed poison, and therefore they would never look upon them, and it was with pain that they saw others reading and circulating works of this description. Their own delight consisted in reading devotional treatises, and the lives of the Saints, the recital of whose heroic actions fired their souls with the ambition of following the same path and practising the same virtues.

Although the thoughts of the holy youths were busied about far different things, yet they were well aware of the state of Florence as regards morality ; and howsoever it might be disguised by outward refinement, they saw vice in all its native hideousness. Many around them, it is true, were leading angelical lives ; but, on the other hand, many in every rank were given up to sin. The yawning gulf of self-indulgence daily swallowed countless souls ; but the Seven saw and shunned that terrible peril, and by never ceasing to keep a strict watch over themselves, from their boyhood onwards, they preserved the innocence of their childhood.

Thus, by all their conduct, their piety was strengthened and ripened, as they advanced in age, and the grand outline of their religious life became irrevocably fixed. To a contempt of the world and its allurements, and to a dread of all that could displease Almighty God, they joined a continually increasing perfection in prayer, an ever growing love for all that helps the soul to attain closer union with her Creator, such as frequenting the Sacraments of the Church and hearing the Divine Word. And meanwhile their inward spiritual beauty shone forth in their outward demeanour, so that they edified all who beheld them. Indeed, it could not be otherwise, since in them the love of Jesus, their Lord and Master, was indissolubly blended with the love of His Most Blessed Mother, whom they had chosen to be their Mother, their Protectress, and their Queen.

Whilst these characteristics were possessed by them in common, we are enabled to gather, in some degree, an idea of the distinctive individuality of each one of our Saints at this period of their lives. There is, no doubt, a general likeness ; but it is interesting to mark the more salient points of each character. So far as we are allowed to penetrate into the interior of these seven souls, we find them reflecting, like a pure crystal, the divine image, at a time of life when it has become, in so many instances, blurred and well-nigh effaced.

We will now reproduce, from the old biographies of the Seven Saints, their portraits from a spiritual point of view ; for on nearly all other points the chroniclers are silent.

Bonfilius Monaldi was one whose soul, deeply impressed with a conviction of the nothingness of earthly possessions, had early fixed its affections on God alone. He had bound himself by a most solemn promise to serve his Divine Master throughout his life. The better to carry out this aim, he had set before himself the example of Our Blessed Lady, and he continually strove to practise her favourite virtues. So pure was his heart, that he seemed like an angel in mortal form. In order to avoid the least shadow of evil, he maintained a prudent and reserved demeanour, which his love of retirement helped to develop. He had a great gift of prayer : he fasted much, and inflicted many bodily mortifications on himself, by which rigid discipline he preserved his baptismal innocence to the day of his death.

Alexis Falconieri's holy and innocent childhood was marked by a strong predilection for the splendour of divine worship. His favourite pastime in early boyhood was to deck miniature altars, and to organize processions with his young companions. To please his parents, he devoted himself later on to literary and scientific studies, in which he made remarkable progress, surpassing all his fellow-students, and winning the approval of his instructors. But the chief features of his character—a genuine humility, and an earnest desire to be of the number of those who follow the Lamb whithersoever He goeth—led him soon to bind himself by vow to the celibate life, and from that moment to take all possible precautions to keep himself unspotted from the world. He, at the same time, consecrated himself to Mary Immaculate, in whose footsteps he desired to tread. His love for Our Blessed Lady made him take especial delight in the recitation of the Hail Mary, which he was accustomed to repeat daily one hundred times, remaining faithful to this pious practice to the last day of his life. His love of spiritual reading and of meditation was likewise great. And he shunned, we are told, all dangerous companions with particular care.

Benedict dell' Antella was wholly devoted to the practice of his religious duties. The pursuit of pleasure had no charms for him, and he held aloof from the youths of his own age who gave themselves up to it. His sole delight was in reading the lives of the Saints, in visiting churches, and in frequenting the Sacraments, every spare moment being devoted to those works of piety in which devout lovers of Our Lord rejoice to co-operate. His talents were above the average, and his parents had, therefore, desired him to apply himself to the study of theology, in which he distinguished himself. Although his piety was ardent, it was regulated by sound common sense, and consequently it was steady and solid. He was endowed with great personal beauty, which might easily have become a snare, especially as the atmosphere which surrounded him was one of worldliness and forgetfulness of God ; but he triumphed over all such obstacles, and his virtues seemed ever to increase more and more.

Notwithstanding the stormy life in which his family was involved, Bartolomew Amidei had been brought up in the fear of God, and this good seed soon blossomed into love of Him. From an early age he gave himself up to devotional practices, in which his whole pleasure consisted. His bearing was so composed and recollected, that he seemed to be of another nature to the youths about him, and experienced eyes could already see in him the dawn of great holiness. In conformity with the wishes of his parents he entered upon the course of studies usually pursued by young men of his rank, and made some progress : but, whilst he advanced step by step in human learning, he made rapid strides in the path of perfection. He eagerly seized upon every opportunity which presented itself for prayer, spiritual reading, frequenting the Sacraments, visiting churches, and almsgiving. To accomplish these pious duties he would willingly deprive himself of recreation, even of sleep, and he fulfilled them with such recollection and fervour that it might plainly be seen that his whole soul was absorbed in them. Worldly conversation wearied him, and he cared but little for the society of youths of his own age. He preferred remaining, as it were, in the background, unnoticed by all. His bearing was unassuming, his manners were charming, and his countenance mirrored the purity of his soul. Although he was quoted and admired by all, he remained perfectly simple and unconscious. His parents felt a kind of awe in the presence of a soul so dear to God, and they made no attempt to induce him to enter into any of their social or political intrigues, leaving him at liberty to follow the promptings of his heart. Worldly themselves, they could respect a spirit so wholly detached from all worldly things, and they were clear-sighted enough to recognize the superiority of their son's aims to their own.

Ricovero Uguccioni was, in early manhood, what those who had known him in childhood had always predicted that he would become. Duty was his guiding star ; and the most salient trait of his sanctity was his spirit of unquestioning obedience. The least sign from his parents or preceptors was sufficient for him, and he submitted his will to theirs in the smallest matters. Another of his great characteristics was his love for the poor, on whom he lavishly bestowed alms. Nothing distressed him more than to hear that the servants had sent away any poor person from his door. He, too, loved retirement, and well understood how to dwell apart in his father's splendid palace, and there to devote himself to prayer and spiritual reading as though he had already been an inmate of the cloister He spent many hours in the Church, and was particularly fond of attending public devotions and hearing sermons. His education had not been neglected ; his natural talents were considerable, and he had a great gift of witty and ready repartee, which made him easily hold his own among his young companions, who entertained a high opinion of him.

Gherardino Sostegni's was an interior soul. All his thoughts seemed to be fixed on spiritual things. He spent hours in meditation, either in the Church or in some quiet nook of his own house. His modesty and humility made him ever ready to yield to others. His parents were deeply attached to him, and appreciated his many virtues. He cared little for human knowledge, but much for that which makes men wise unto salvation. Faithfully corresponding with grace, he was ever on his guard against the dangers of worldly company, which he carefully avoided. Whilst still in the flower of his youth, his mind had all the ripeness of mature age. Most prudent in conduct, and profiting largely by experience, he shunned dissipation and idle amusements. He sought for happiness in the love of Our Lord and of His Blessed Mother alone. The heavenly expression of his countenance proved that his thoughts were busied only with the things of God.

The youngest of our Seven Saints, John Manetti, was highly educated, and possessed of a brilliant intellect. He was both talented and amiable, and from his earliest years he had been an apt scholar in the school of the Saints. Great as were his gifts, there was no room in his heart for intellectual pride, for it was wholly filled with the love of God and contempt of self. As he advanced in age he became more and more detached from the things of this world, nor could the influence of his parents bend him in a contrary direction. His courage in self-conquest and his eagerness in the pursuit of spiritual goods knew no bounds, and the fervour of his soul was reflected in the expression of his face. Had he been permitted to spend his days and nights in the Church, he would gladly have done so ; once there, he scarcely ever seemed able to tear himself away. Whilst reading the Lives of the Saints, he was as though he saw them and heard them in the flesh ; he never wearied of their society as he did of that of the young men whom he met in the world. He found a still, retired place in a corner of his father's palace, and there he spent daily many hours on his knees, weeping for very gladness in the presence of God, and at the feet of Mary, whom he had chosen to be his mother and his model.

Would that we could give fuller details of every incident in the lives of these youthful Saints, at this period when their spotless souls were ever holding sublime colloquy with God.   But the greater part of these fourteen years has been hidden from us.   Thus we can only get an idea of the holiness of these young Florentines by the light of sanctity shed by their after lives, the fruits enabling us to judge of the trees on which they were grown.

Be this as it may, one fact stands out conspicuously, namely, that they passed triumphantly through this period of probation.   Their faith, their piety, their holiness, remained intact amidst all the dangers which assailed them.   They fought with the spirit of the world, and overcame it.   They traversed the path so full of peril, and when they reached the end, their innocence was unclouded, their courage was unshaken, their generosity towards God was ardent and disinterested, as at the outset.   They were ready to do and to dare all things to please their good Master, and their Queen, His Mother, to whom they desired to belong in this world and in the world to come.

CHAPTER VI.

𝕿𝖍𝖊 𝕮𝖔𝖓𝖋𝖗𝖆𝖙𝖊𝖗𝖓𝖎𝖙𝖞 𝖔𝖋 𝖙𝖍𝖊 𝕷𝖆𝖚𝖉𝖊𝖘𝖎—𝕾𝖕𝖎𝖗𝖎𝖙𝖚𝖆𝖑 𝕱𝖗𝖎𝖊𝖓𝖉𝖘𝖍𝖎𝖕.

(1211—1233.)

IN the city of Florence the people were faithful clients of the Blessed Virgin.   Thence they enthusiastically welcomed all aids to the preservation and development of her cultus.   They had already inherited from their forefathers a goodly number of devotional practices in honour of the Mother of God; and these, together with the more recent ones, were a constant source of consolation to all pious souls.

Shortly before that time a new institution had been added to the others.   It had gradually spread through Christendom, and largely increased the store of spiritual treasures.   It consisted in forming an association of the faithful, classified according to their age, sex, and social position.   In it the members gave to each other mutual edification and support, and devoted themselves especially to honouring the Queen of Heaven, who has such power to win all hearts and lead them to holiness of life.   It bore the title of the Confraternity of the Blessed Virgin—an attractive title, indeed, since it made plain that the institution was to unite all the members together in the bonds of fraternal charity.

The Bishops of Florence had gladly availed themselves of this means of grace, and had done all in their power to promote the establishment, in their See, of Confraternities of the Blessed Virgin. Several of these existed in Florence ; but one among them was especially distinguished by its seniority, by the high character borne by those who belonged to it, and, of late years, by its extraordinary development. Pietro da Todi calls it "The Great Society of the Blessed Virgin".

This Confraternity was founded in the year 1183. At that time, as we have seen, the Manicheans, under various names, had spread through many towns in Italy, and formed a constantly increasing and encroaching body. Full of insolent daring, they shrank from no method, however impious, of propagating their vicious doctrines. The faithful children of the Church were panic-stricken, and looked on all sides for help. Then it was that the Confraternities of the Blessed Virgin were inaugurated, and chief among them was that of which we are now speaking.

This Confraternity was widely known, being entirely composed of members of those families which were most distinguished by birth or by wealth. As both sexes and all ages were admitted to its ranks, parents entered their own names and those of their children on the lists, thus placing themselves and those most dear to them under the special protection of the Blessed Virgin. For a moment, at Mary's feet, the party spirit, which raged in Florence, was quelled, and all sides forgot their animosities, and met in brotherly love, to pay her, with one heart and one voice, their filial homage.

The rules obliged members to meet at certain hours on certain days. At these reunions they engaged in prayer, listened to the pious exhortations of the director, and sang the praises of Mary : hence their name of *Laudesi,* or Praisers. At that time four feasts of Our Blessed Lady were celebrated during the year : those of her Nativity, her Annunciation, her Purification, and her Assumption. All these were observed with the utmost solemnity. The Priest, who was appointed director of the Confraternity, devoted himself wholly to the spiritual progress and welfare of the members individually and collectively. The meetings were held at Santa Reparata. The spot is still shown where this chapel stood, bearing an inscription commemorative of the ancient Confraternity of the Laudesi. Upon this site now stands that wondrous embodiment of strength and grace, Giotto's famous Campanile of the Cathedral. Forty years after the establishment of the Confraternity, it numbered, among the men, two hundred members of the Florentine nobility and gentry — a large proportion of those two classes, which did not consist of more than fifteen hundred. Excluding infants, the indifferent, and those who neglected religion altogether, we see that the greater part of the patriciate belonged to its ranks.

There lived, at that date, in Florence, a learned, pious, and zealous young priest named James d' Alberto of Poggibonzi. Associated with the Florentine clergy in their ecclesiastical duties, and devoted to Our Blessed Lady as he was, he naturally became a member of the great Confraternity, which admitted both priests and religious. It is even asserted, by some writers, that he was soon nominated director.

Such was the Confraternity of the Laudesi when our seven youthful Saints began first to feel that heavenly home-sickness which causes such keen pain to exiled souls, who find that this world but poorly satisfies their longings. Eagerly seeking after God, and loving daily more and more His Blessed Mother, they earnestly desired to enter among the Laudesi. It seemed to them that to consecrate themselves to the service of the Queen of Heaven would be the sweetest of graces—a powerful support and consolation amidst all the trials of this world. We may be sure that they had only to ask admission to be at once welcomed into the brotherhood.

There is every reason to believe that they were entered among the Laudesi whilst still very young. At all events, we may hold for certain that they were all enrolled between the years 1225 and 1227. Gladly must they have sheltered themselves under the motherly protection of Mary, and great must have been the happiness of each one in succession on the day of his reception—a day which was to be henceforth a landmark in their lives—the day on which each one resolved, more firmly than ever, to quit the world and devote himself to God alone. Many partial victories had they already gained over their spiritual enemies ; but the crowning triumph was to be won under the eye of Mary, and by the help of her maternal intercession.

Whether they were previously acquainted with each other or not, is not known , it is beyond question, however, that from the time of their meeting at the altar of Our Lady of the Laudesi, they became friends. Their love of God and of His Holy Mother, and their earnest desire to sanctify their souls, undoubtedly acted as powerful magnets to attract them to each other. But Divine Wisdom, which disposes all things with strength and sweetness, was at the same time guiding their steps, and by an invisible yet all-compelling power leading them more directly towards the goal which they were unconsciously striving to reach.

In any case, the community of thought and feeling, which first drew the seven holy youths together, speedily welded their souls as one in the bonds of intimate friendship. Pietro da Todi, the first of their biographers who gives much information on this point, tells us that their great delight was to be together, and that even a temporary separation caused them pain. This appreciation of each other's society was most praiseworthy, being wholly founded on supernatural motives ; hence this chronicler expressly says that " their friendship was built on holy charity ". Being supernatural, it knew neither change nor diminution throughout their lives. And in after years the strength of the bond which united the Seven Saints was even surpassed by that which linked the souls of St. Hugh and St. Sostene, and which Almighty God was pleased to confirm by signs and wonders.

The most striking figure in this holy band was from the first that of Bonfilius Monaldi. He was the eldest of them ; and being endowed with remarkable sagacity and correctness of judgment, with a courteous and winning manner, and with a spirit deeply religious and wholly detached from the world, he possessed all the qualifications of a successful leader. He probably was the first of the Seven to enter the Laudesi, and it is natural to suppose that he introduced the six others into this Confraternity, and that they looked upon him from that time forward as their mentor. Later on, when it became necessary to choose a Superior, all eyes turned to Bonfilius Monaldi ; and the choice which then fell upon him was clearly the result of the position which he had already taken among them.

Another influence, besides that of Bonfilius Monaldi, was also successfully exerted—that of the young priest who had early become known to the Seven, and who was never to be parted from them—namely, James of Poggibonzi, of whom we have already spoken as being a member, and a director also, of the Confraternity of the Laudesi. This holy ecclesiastic possessed their confidence ; they opened their hearts to him, submitted themselves to his direction, asked his advice in all things, and, in short, looked upon him as their friend and guide, without whose approval they undertook nothing. He was much edified by these beautiful souls, and felt himself powerfully impelled to holiness by their example, whilst they were seeking guidance from him ; and he applied himself earnestly to enable them by his counsels to correspond more and more fully to the impulses of Divine Grace. Their docility made his task both easy and consoling.

He was especially in perfect agreement of thought with Bonfilius Monaldi, who was nearly of his own age, and who, equally with himself, felt the responsibility which jointly rested upon their shoulders. The united efforts of the two leaders were well seconded by their followers, who strove with touching emulation to excel in that generosity of self-sacrifice which we see in youthful souls, where purity of life and the habitual practice of virtue combine to make the path of perfection less rugged than it proves to world-worn spirits. Thus the little group became, as it were, a centre from which an attractive and edifying piety was diffused throughout the Confraternity, winning all hearts to Jesus and Mary, and drawing numerous recruits to the ranks.

Upon these two events, the entry of the seven holy youths into the Confraternity of the Laudesi, and the friendship which sprang up between them, the whole future of our Founders may be said to have been moulded. By their enrolment in her army, Mary took entire possession of them, and their friendship paved the way for that community of life and mission, in which they were to act as though animated by a single soul.

The Confraternity of the Laudesi was, in truth, the cradle of the Servite Order; and the Founders may be said to have served their novitiate there There Our Lady bent down more lovingly towards them, as they looked up to her with a more fixed resolve. Hence grew that motherly affection on her part towards her sons, and that filial love of theirs towards the Divine Mother, from which was ultimately to spring an Order wholly consecrated to her. The Chapel of the Laudesi was the blessed spot where the first idea of the new institution was conceived, whilst Monte Senario was to have the glory of seeing it carried out. But, before this could be done, the project had to pass through various phases, some of which seemed destined to bring it altogether to naught, but all of which went finally to prove that the Blessed Mother can overcome all obstacles whatsoever when it is her pleasure so to do.

CHAPTER VII.

Vocations Fixed—The Fruits of Holiness.

(1218—1233.)

WHILST thus pursuing their daily course of life, the seven holy youths had not lost sight of an object which was to them one of primary importance · they decided upon their vocations. Three of their number successfully resisted the pressure put upon them by their relatives, who wished them to marry; the four others consented to be bound by earthly ties

Alexis Falconieri, who from his earliest years had desired to give an undivided heart to God, continued to shun with scrupulous care whatever might tarnish the crystal purity of his soul. He had even wished to take the vow of celibacy at once, instead of waiting till he had reached manhood. Of him the chronicler Niccolo Mati says, in speaking of the close of his life : " Happy indeed was this venerable man ; for at his death his virginity remained intact ". So well had he guarded that fragile flower, that he carried it with him to the grave in the freshness of its beauty.

The young dell' Antella possessed all the advantages which would have enabled him to marry well. He had birth and wealth and good looks : his parents, therefore, sought for him the hand of an heiress. The family of the young lady gladly consented ; all were ready but the bridegroom, who was determined never to contract an earthly union, but to consecrate his youth, and all his gifts, to Him Who is beautiful above the sons of men.

The example of the two whom we have just named was followed by Uguccioni. We do not know the circumstances which led him to resolve thus. Had he wished to marry, he could have made what the world would call a good match ; but he chose rather to complete the little band of celibates in the company of our Saints.

The four who entered the married state were Monaldi, Amidei, Sostegni, and Manetti. In those unsettled times marriage was a great safeguard against the twofold plague of immorality and heresy, both of which then raged in Florence. Many erroneous doctrines were then promulgated, especially about matrimony, which the heretics rejected as an evil in itself, in order the more readily to follow their own perverse inclinations. A Christian union, therefore, was at once a protest against these errors, and a protection from them.

The biographers of our Seven Saints maintain an absolute silence on the subject of the married life of these four. Beyond the bare fact nothing is known. We would gladly have had it in our power to describe their domestic life, which, we may be sure, would have presented to us a realization of that high ideal which so many married persons vainly strive to attain. We should there have seen that the only real happiness lies in the fulfilment of the divine behests : that true affection, which is the image of the love of Our God for His Church, is only to be found where husband and wife mutually respect His Law and reverence each other in Him.

We are told that several of these unions were blessed with off-spring ; but, here again, only the mere fact is known.

Of one thing we are, however, certain, namely, that their vocation being once decided, the seven saintly youths made no change in their train of thought, nor in their rule of life. The married, not less than the celibate, continued to aim at perfection. Their hearts were too much set on heavenly things for any outward circumstances to turn them aside. To sanctify themselves was now, as ever, their chief object in life. Those who remained unfettered by domestic ties, rejoiced in being free to give their time wholly to God. Those who were united to the souls placed by the Almighty in their charge sought and found, in the society of their youthful spouses, new ways of serving and loving Him daily more and more. Although in ordinary life we find that the husband's heart is of necessity divided, yet, in the case of these our Saints, it was not so : there was no antagonism in their souls between the earthly love and the heavenly. Their conjugal affection was pure and holy ; and although it was bestowed on a creature, it raised their minds to the Creator.

So far were they from losing anything of their first fervour, that we find them even adopting new methods for the attainment of perfection. The friendship already existing between the Seven was in no wise diminished by their different vocations; and their hearts and minds being ever as one, they resolved to establish among themselves a private association with rules of its own, which they proceeded to draw up, and only two of which have come down to us. They called that list of regulations "The little Book of the Constitutions". In a modest introduction they explain their reasons for founding this association, as follows: "Several of our members being engaged in the state of matrimony, and being thereby debarred from following a severe rule of life, we hereby determine to adopt a milder and more ordinary rule, so that the married, as well as the single, may readily conform to it".

Moreover, since Our Blessed Lady had never ceased to be the object on whom their thoughts, their affections, and their hopes were chiefly fixed, they consecrated themselves in this association to be her Servants wholly and without reserve for ever. We give the text of the Constitutions· "Fearing our own instability, and following an impulse which we believe to proceed from the source of Wisdom, we cast ourselves, in fervour of spirit, at the feet of the most glorious Queen of Heaven, Mary, ever Virgin, beseeching her as our Advocate and Mediatrix to reconcile us to her Divine Son, to recommend us to His all-bountiful goodness, to supply by His abundant charity all our shortcomings, and in His clemency to aid us by His most efficacious merits. We, therefore, taking service for the glory of God in the household of His Blessed Mother, desire henceforth to be her Servants; and we adopt, at the same time, a rule of life in accordance with the counsels of men experienced in spiritual things."

These Constitutions are a valuable relic. They speak clearly to us amidst the silence of history. They show us the seven youthful Founders full of ardent, yet unobtrusive and childlike piety, closely united in the bonds of holy friendship, drawing their spiritual nutriment from a common source. We see them attracted gently, yet powerfully, towards Mary the most admirable Virgin ; and whilst they think they are but preparing themselves to follow the guidance of the Spirit Who bloweth where He listeth, the Order which was to be given later to the world was already founded. The consecration of the Seven was registered and accepted on high.

The rules of the little Association were drafted and sanctioned by the director, James of Poggibonzi, and the holy youths found in them a constant spur to their zeal. They read them frequently, thus reminding themselves of what they had undertaken ; and they renewed their pledges in order to carry them into practice as perfectly as possible.

Whilst our Saints were becoming daily more and more united in the bonds of holy friendship, and whilst they were being enrolled in the Confraternity of the Laudesi, entering upon wedded life or devoting themselves to celibacy, joining in the performance of pious and charitable works, and seeking in all things the sanctification of their souls, and the freedom of the children of God, Florence was pursuing a far different course ; for she was torn by factious struggles within her walls, and beyond them she only ended one campaign in order to begin another.

Holy Church, too, had her full share of troubles   A new Pontiff, Gregory IX., was elected to the Chair of Peter on 18th March, 1227. Although he had reached the advanced age of eighty-six years, he was still full of energy, which was shown by his eagerness in promoting the Crusade.   He, especially, did not hesitate to threaten the Emperor Frederic II. with spiritual penalties if he did not fulfil his engagement of August, 1221, to take the Cross, and embark for Palestine.

Unfortunately, Frederic, so soon as the imperial crown had been placed on his head by his former tutor, Honorius III, who had always treated him with a kindness of which he was wholly undeserving, began to follow an evil course, and to indulge all his vicious inclinations.   In a short space of time he had become the scourge of Italy and the implacable enemy of the Church.   A tyrannical ruler, a faithless husband, a hypocrite, and a profligate at one and the same time, he seemed to be an epitome of wickedness.   He respected no law, civil or religious.   He scorned the authority of the Church, and he violated treaties on the most slender pretexts. He favoured Cathari and Mussulmans, and ridiculed all that Christians hold in reverence.   He even presumed to utter blasphemies against the Divine Person of Our Lord   His private life was one continued scene of riot and excess ; which, being noised abroad, caused fearful scandal.   During the years 1227 and 1228 he was excommunicated no less than three times by Gregory IX.   This, however, produced no real change in him ; for, although he was in a manner forced by the menaces of the Pontiff to set out for the Holy Land, yet his presence there only compromised the success of the expedition. Whilst far from making any serious attack upon the Saracen forces, he entered into friendly relations with the leaders of the infidel host.

In the year 1227 the Church in Florence was much disturbed by frightful revelations then made as to the progress of Catharism in that city.   Inquiries were instantly set on foot by the Bishop, Giovanni of Velletri, and the Inquisitor, Giovanni of Salerno. Paternone, who presumptuously styled himself Bishop of the Cathari, was seized and brought before the holy tribunal.   But he obtained his release by means of a feigned abjuration, and quitted Florence only to continue his iniquitous proceedings elsewhere.   Besides, he left behind him his two well-known auxiliaries, Torsello Brunetto and Giacomo of Montefiascone, who succeeded in turn to his imaginary See.

On all sides, therefore, was now exhibited a universal scene of strife, tumult, and every evil passion let loose, either in civil discord or in antagonism to God and His Church.

This troubled atmosphere was not one in which our Seven Saints could freely breathe ; hence they felt more and more confirmed in their distaste for the world, and for the frivolous pursuits and petty aims of worldlings ; whilst the love of God and the desire to serve Him increased in their souls day by day. They gladly sought refuge from the turmoil around them at the feet of her who is the Comfortress of all anxious souls. The Confraternity of the Laudesi became dearer to them than ever, since there they found unfailing consolation by interchanging pious and loving thoughts of which Mary was the fruitful theme.

They continued, moreover, to do all the good that lay in their power. They formed a nucleus of virtue and high principle, from which radiated far and wide an influence for good. Their holiness was widely recognized, and gave them great power in dealing with others, so that they induced many to enter the Confraternity, and these new members strove earnestly to follow in the same path.

As years went on, and the growth of divine grace increased in their hearts, the friendship of the Seven became yet more firmly cemented. They met frequently and compared their impressions of the events occurring around them, as to which their opinions perfectly coincided. Often did they complain of the force of circumstances which obliged them to remain in the world ; and ardently did they long to break asunder the ties which yet bound them to it, and fleeing from all its evil and corruption, to devote themselves wholly to the sanctification of their souls and to prayer for others ; and finally, after a life thus spent, to die in the peace of the Lord. Having well considered the nature of the bonds which kept them from the life they so earnestly desired, they resolved to have recourse to the Blessed Virgin, in order that their perplexities might be finally set at rest, although they could not foresee in what manner this should be done.

Even those who were married felt keenly the insufficiency of earthly things. In spite of the happiness which they enjoyed in domestic life, they still felt an attraction towards religious retirement. In their case, the obstacles to the accomplishment of their wishes were apparently insurmountable, and, no doubt, they sometimes regretted that they had not followed the example of Falconieri, of dell' Antella, and of Uguccioni, by making choice at the outset of the celibate life, since there they would have found that true spiritual freedom which they had sacrificed. But ere long two of the four who had married were called upon to mourn over the grave of their young brides. The thought of being now free to consecrate themselves to God could alone soften the blow. Those whom the grace of God draws to Himself most strongly are the most alive to the influence of home affections, and especially in the conjugal state. The two bereaved husbands looked for consolation to Our Lord and His Blessed Mother, and accepted in this trial the all-wise and merciful decree of the divine will. They blessed the hand which had parted them from those who were dearer to them than life itself, and whom they trusted to meet again in the world where mourning and sorrow are no more. Undoubtedly, this bereavement must have augmented in the hearts of all our Saints their distaste for the world, and their desire to belong wholly to Jesus and to Mary.

In fact, their devotion to Our Blessed Lady seemed hourly to become sweeter and more spontaneous, and it showed how familiar and childlike were their communications with the Queen of Heaven. Her love was really the sun and centre of their existence, and gave to the life of each all its tranquillity and charm. They took delight in adopting any fresh pious practices established in her honour, without, however, neglecting such as had the sanction of antiquity. Two notable instances of this occurred at the beginning of the Pontificate of Gregory IX. That Pontiff was very zealous in promoting the fervour of Catholic devotion towards Our Blessed Lady, and to him we owe two invocations redolent with filial love—firstly, the *Angelus*, which he ordered the faithful to recite thrice daily at the sound of the bell, at daybreak, at noon, and at sunset, in order continually to recall the great mystery of the Incarnation of the God-Man, of which the Blessed Virgin was the willing instrument; and secondly, the *Salve Regina*, admitted by him among the liturgical prayers of the Church No prayer is sweeter than this last, made up as it is of aspirations to the Queen of Heaven, expressing the consolation which the devout soul experiences during this earthly exile in the contemplation of her who is so truly named "Our life, our sweetness, and our hope". The seven youths eagerly adopted this twofold devotion so fully in accordance with the bent of their souls; nor did they weary of it, for in after years the Servants of Mary ever made it their chief delight to hail their Mistress and Queen in the *Angelus* and the *Salve Regina*.

The year 1230 witnessed the death of Giovanni of Velletri, the Bishop of Florence, who for a quarter of a century had ruled his important See under circumstances of extreme difficulty, having been forced, in particular, to exert his strength to combat the Manichean heresy. Ardingo dei Foraboschi was at once appointed his successor. The new Bishop was a pious and learned ecclesiastic, a Florentine by birth, and a member of one of the greatest of the Guelf houses.

He succeeded to the toils and perils, as well as to the honours and dignities, of his predecessor. One of his first undertakings was to give full scope to the devotion towards Our Blessed Lady, for which purpose he encouraged all the Confraternities already in existence, and strove to increase their number He felt that there was no more potent engine for the pacification of states, the uprooting of vice, and the destruction of heresies. He esteemed above all the great Confraternity of the Laudesi, and all the members, particularly our Seven Saints ; for he knew how zealously they laboured to sanctify their own souls, and to promote the spiritual welfare of their neighbours.

Thus, amidst all variations of outward circumstances, our seven youths were led by different paths towards the same goal, and were prepared for the mission to which God's Providence had destined them. To fill their allotted posts worthily, it was needful for them to ascend high in the scale of perfection, and it was accordingly the divine will that every event of their lives should concur to advance them on that rugged road. The troubled state of their native land, the calm joys of domestic life, the infinite devices of grace, all tended in one direction. In beholding the evil around them, they learned to detest it. In tasting the happiness of home, they felt the insufficiency of earthly joys. In receiving the graces of God, they gave up themselves wholly to Him. Surely the loving hand of their Mother Mary thus directed each incident of their lives to the furtherance of their sanctification : that work was dear to her maternal heart, and she wrought at it as though impatient of delay. The time was now at hand when the secret hitherto known in heaven alone was to be revealed on earth

What more beautiful picture can we find than the scene presented by these seven young men, in the full vigour of life, yet simple-hearted and innocent as children, eager to make any sacrifice which may be required of them, united to each other by the tenderest ties of friendship, and to Our Lord and His Blessed Mother by bonds of generous love ; unconscious of self, and willing to be passed over and forgotten by the world ? Leading, whilst yet on earth, angelic lives, they were the chosen ones of the Queen of Angels, who was now about to give them a proof of her favour by visibly manifesting herself to them.

CHAPTER VIII.

𝕬pparition of t𝔥e 𝔅lesse𝔡 𝔙irgin—𝔉arewell to t𝔥e 𝔚orl𝔡.

(AUGUST 15—SEPTEMBER 8, 1233.)

WE have now arrived at the year 1233. The Emperor Frederic had quitted Tuscany for a time. Florence and her rival Siena were at peace. Bishop Ardingo was exerting his utmost energies against the Cathari, and had succeeded in banishing two of their leaders to Rome. At the same time, his chief delight was to foster all pious practices in honour of the Mother of God, and especially to encourage the Confraternities established under her invocation.

The Seven Saints became daily more and more devoted to their Mother and Queen. Differing from each other in disposition and in gifts, they were as one in attachment to her service. Time, and the succession of events which it brings about, united to their own untiring efforts, had produced in them that solid virtue which stamps the action of divine grace. The world and its goods no longer possessed any attraction for them. They looked for other things, and their whole ambition was to be found worthy of attaining heaven. Their one idea of happiness was to be permitted to give themselves wholly to the care of their souls. They strove with a generous emulation to be foremost in responding with manly resolution to the inspirations of grace. They had now passed the season of youth; most of them had reached the age when the chief struggles of the soul are at an end; when all the faculties are in their fullest vigour, and when a man makes the offering of himself to God at his best, knowing well the cost of the sacrifice and rejoicing in it Such is the case, at least, with heroic souls; and to this number our Saints unquestionably belonged. Monaldi was at this time thirty-seven years of age, Falcomeri was thirty-three, dell' Antella was thirty, Amidei and Uguccioni twenty-nine, Sostegni twenty-eight, and Manetti twenty-seven.

Thus they awaited the heavenly call which the Blessed Virgin herself was about to convey to them. The chosen day was one dear to Our Lady's heart, being that of her Assumption. This feast was always celebrated by the Confraternity of the Laudesi with a splendour and solemnity corresponding to the greatness of the mystery. Our Seven Saints did not fail on such an occasion to cleanse their consciences in the tribunal of Penance, and to strengthen their souls with the Bread of Heaven. Their minds were thus prepared to receive communications from on high. Their thoughts were chiefly occupied with their beloved Mother, and their hearts were raised to her as they knelt together in the

4

Sodality Chapel. Then it was that it pleased the Queen of Heaven to reveal herself to them.

Whilst they united themselves with the other members of the Confraternity in singing her praises, they pursued their own meditations in undisturbed tranquillity. Each fixed his inward eye on the contemplation of her glory, whilst he rejoiced in picturing to himself the beauty and perfection of the purest of God's creatures. Suddenly each of them appeared lost to all outward surroundings, and remained motionless, gazing with rapt look at some object present to himself, but invisible to the rest of the congregation.

In their ecstasy, the Seven Saints beheld an orb of supernatural light from which darted forth rays so pure and penetrating that they remained, as it were, spellbound. At the same time, their souls were flooded with sweetness, and they felt an ardent longing for the joys of heaven, all the things of earth seeming to them beyond measure wearisome. Yet at first they understood nothing definite : but they had not long to wait before their expectant hearts were more than satisfied.

In the centre of the radiant orb appeared a Lady, bright and beautiful, surrounded by angels, and bending with a loving smile towards the Seven Saints. They knew that they could not be mistaken. It was Mary, the Mother of God, who deigned thus to show herself to her Servants.

Soon she spoke, and her words seemed even sweeter than her smile, as, in a voice of motherly gentleness, she thus addressed them : "Leave the world, and withdraw yourselves together into a solitary place, that so you may learn to conquer yourselves, and to live for God alone. Thus will you receive heavenly consolations ; and my aid and protection shall never fail you."

Then the vision disappeared, leaving the Seven Laudesi filled with sentiments which were not of this earth. When they came out of their ecstasy, every detail was indelibly stamped on the memory of each one ; but each one, also, was unconscious that the grace he had received had been granted to any other than himself. Each then remained in his place, pondering over the marvellous apparition which he had just beheld

The Office was over, and the members of the Confraternity, with the exception of these favoured ones, quitted the chapel. But these Seven continued kneeling, motionless, and unconscious of the lapse of time, each longing to impart to the others the wondrous vision, yet not knowing how to break the charmed silence. Bonfilius Monaldi was the first to speak. As he was the eldest, it would seem to be expected of him ; and, accordingly, doing violence to his natural humility, he related what he had just seen. He told how the Blessed Virgin had appeared to him, how she had invited him to withdraw from the world, and how gladly he had responded to her invitation. The others then, with one voice, proclaimed that they had had the selfsame vision, and that they were equally ready to obey the summons of their Queen.

These first revelations were followed by further confidences, which confirmed them in their project. It was then agreed among themselves that the initiative, in all that regarded the carrying out of their scheme, should be taken by Bonfilius Monaldi. Having been first to speak, it was fitting that he should be first to act in the matter, more especially as he possessed, in a greater degree, the requisite qualifications for the task. Monaldi, though reluctant, was thus forced to accept the post of leader. He spoke at once a few feeling words on the necessity of stripping themselves of all that they possessed, in order to become more generous followers of their Divine Master ; and then he and his companions left the chapel, with feelings too deep to be uttered or described.

Such was the great event, which has been so carefully handed down from generation to generation to the present day. Tradition has preserved the general outlines of the vision, but the details are lost to us. The Seven favoured ones jealously treasured their secret, instead of being eager to divulge it. Pietro da Todi, the contemporary of St. Alexis, speaks of the occurrence in so guarded a manner that its extraordinary character is scarcely to be recognized. He says : "Our Seven Saints, being drawn towards each other by the virtue of holy charity, determined to have all things in common, so as to receive mutual support and edification from the good examples which each would give to each in life, work, and word. They did not take this resolution lightly, or by chance, but after mature deliberation ; and this was the work of Our Lady herself, who, by her supernatural intervention, inclined them thereto." The author fails to explain the nature of this supernatural intervention, but his omission is supplied by the chronicler Nicolo Mati, who, writing about seventy years later, expressly states that the historian was alluding "to that marvellous vision of which all have heard". Then history has related the chief particulars which we have given above, and which bear every mark of authenticity.

We know, then, that Our Blessed Lady appeared to the saintly Seven, and spoke to them words of heavenly power, stamping on their souls that divine superscription which nothing earthly can efface. But the Saints, however they may be elevated in grace, always think distrustfully of themselves. They fear to be misled by the Evil One, hidden under the appearance of an angel of light. Seeing clearly the vast disproportion between the graces they receive and their own feebleness and wretchedness, they are often unwilling lightly to believe the invisible workings of God upon their souls, until they are confirmed by His visible authority on earth. For these reasons Bonfilius Monaldi hastened at once to the Director of the Confraternity, the devout and revered priest, James of Poggi-bonzi.

The good Director, taking into consideration all the circum-stances, and especially the personal holiness of the Seven, gave it as his opinion that all the signs pointed to a genuine intervention of Our Blessed Lady. He commanded Bonfilius to intimate this to his companions ; and, in conclusion, told him that it was the duty of each and all to respond to the call from on high. Straightway the message was communicated to those whom it concerned, and all, without loss of time, made suitable preparations for quitting their worldly ties and possessions.

Humanly speaking, the task that awaited them presented almost insurmountable difficulties. They had to reconcile their families to a step most repugnant, from a natural point of view—to part from loving relatives, whose opposition was likely to be violent and prolonged, to give up cherished occupations, and to relinquish appointments that they had already filled with credit, or which they had sought for with every chance of success, to break the strongest of all ties, those which bound them to attached wives and beloved children. But Mary had manifested to them the will of God, and the seven heroic men felt, in their hearts, courage and strength to overcome all obstacles. Having formed their plan, they forthwith proceeded to execute it.

Without delay they informed their families of their resolution. The news fell like a thunderbolt upon the houses of Monaldi, Falconieri, Antellesi, Amidei, Uguccioni, Sostegni, and Manetti. Although religiously disposed, the families in question did not view all things with the eyes of faith . and the seven members, whose lives edified and consoled all their kindred, were especially loved in their own homes. Their fathers were startled by the sudden resolu-tion, and their mothers felt acutely the pain of parting from them. Various arguments were urged against their project, but all fell upon unheeding ears ; for the Seven Saints felt that it was no longer lawful for them to remain in the world, when the will of God had so solemnly and unmistakably been made known to them.

The effect of the first announcement having subsided, the next step was to free themselves from all earthly ties and encumbrances. This was comparatively easy for Falconieri, dell' Antella, and Uguccioni, who, being unmarried, were to a certain extent their own masters. For the four others, however, who had wives or children to provide for, the business was much more complicated.

The law of the Church provides that, in similar cases, husbands and wives can only separate by mutual consent, both being bound to embrace the religious life, and the wife, moreover, being bound to observe perpetual enclosure. In the present instance, although our Seven Saints were not about to enter a religious Order in the strict sense of the word, yet they proposed leading until death the eremitical life, which is a most perfect form of religious life. How the matter was settled in detail we are not told; but that all was arranged in conformity with the mind of the Church we cannot doubt. A tradition, indeed, exists, that the wives of the two Laudesi had taken upon themselves the religious vows whilst yet in the world, and that they were, subsequently, affiliated to the Servite Order as Tertiaries. These young women, deeply religious themselves, and having every prospect of earthly happiness from their union with men so thoroughly Christian and noble in character, thus resigned all that was in this world the most dear to them; and the sacrifice was painful in proportion to the strength of the affection which existed on both sides.

There were children, too, whose future must have been the subject of serious consideration. Of all obstacles in the path of our Saints, here was one which seemed insurmountable. How hard is it for a parent to give up a child! Nature herself revolts against it, and worldlings are shocked and scandalized at the idea. But the love of God can override the most powerful and the tenderest feelings of the human heart. Such heroic acts are the outcome of the counsels of Our Lord Himself. Has He not said in His Gospel : "If any man come to Me, and hate not his father, and mother, and wife, and children, and brethren, and sisters, yea, and his own life also, he cannot be My disciple"? (St. Luke xiv. 26).

This great victory over nature was gained by those among our Saints who were called upon to make the hardest renunciation of all. But, at whatever cost of suffering to themselves, they, like Abraham, hesitated not when called upon to sacrifice what was dearest to them. With bleeding hearts they left their children, or placed them in safe keeping, in order to give themselves wholly to God.

With regard to pecuniary matters, provision was made for the maintenance of the wives, and for the education and settlement in life of the children. Whatever remained over and above was, in accordance with the precept of Our Lord, given to the poor and to the Church

As to appointments held by our Seven Saints in the Florentine Government, they were, of course, at once resigned, the holders aspiring henceforth to serve only the King of kings, and the Queen of Heaven. In short, they left all ; and in little more than three weeks they had stripped themselves of everything that they possessed, and were ready to obey the Master's call.

Naturally, the steps taken by the seven friends soon became known throughout the city ; and the Florentines being much addicted to seasoning "their discourse with personal talk," the subject was discussed in all its bearings. Pious souls were struck by the heroism of the sacrifice. The lukewarm, the freethinking, the dissipated, spoke of it with either scorn or anger. But our Saints, not concerning themselves with what others said or thought of them, went on their way, and finally achieved the object they had at heart, namely, that of being entirely free by the day they had fixed upon, the Feast of Our Lady's Nativity, September the 8th, 1233.

Meanwhile, Bonfilius Monaldi was occupied with the arrangements necessary for the little community, as well as with his own private affairs. His advice and exhortations were at the service of all. It was he who planned their new rule of life, at all events, as far as the general outline was concerned. It was to be a life wholly opposed, both in theory and in practice, to the spirit of the world, and leading to the attainment of the utmost degree of evangelical perfection It was to be the religious life, wanting only a special denomination and object, and the particular constitutions essential to Religious Orders. The holy Seven were to be simply Associates, united by the love of God and by fraternal charity, and devoted to prayers and penance. In short, they were to live as hermits, without retiring to a desert. Abiding almost within sight of their former homes, the dwellers in the Babylon from which they had fled would be edified by their utter renunciation of self, whilst their daily prayer and penance would be offered for these poor worldlings.

Bonfilius Monaldi, in concurrence with his friends, fixed upon a habit to be worn by them all, as an outward and visible sign of the new state of life which they had embraced. It was a tunic of woollen stuff of a dark ashen grey colour, symbolical of penance, fastened round the waist, after the custom of the Baptist, by a leathern girdle.

It was necessary for them to have a dwelling to shelter them, in which they could lead in common a life of retirement, secured from molestation from without. Such an abode was found.

In all these transactions Bonfilius Monaldi did not fail to consult James of Poggibonzi ; and he thus had opportunities of speaking to him on an equally important subject—the choice of a chaplain and director. This was indeed absolutely essential for their spiritual organization. Monaldi was of opinion that their best course was to retain the services of that holy priest sent by God to assist and support them in the Confraternity of the Laudesi. As all his companions shared his view, he earnestly begged of James of Poggibonzi to continue to be to them in the future even more than he had been in the past, and to devote himself exclusively to their spiritual service. The request was gladly acceded to, and it was decided that their Director should take up his abode with them.

Besides, it was their duty to inform the Bishop of Florence of their intention, and to obtain his official sanction and blessing ; for although the Seven Laudesi did not propose to found an Order, yet their association being of a purely religious character, it could not be established without episcopal approbation. The Bishop's permission also was needed for a private chapel where Mass could be said, and where the Blessed Sacrament might be reserved, and likewise for the appointment of their chaplain.

One Sunday, accordingly, they presented themselves before the holy Bishop Ardingo, who received them with fatherly kindness, and who was even moved to tears when they explained to him their plan. He spoke words of encouragement to them, telling them how he was weighed down by the charge of souls, and how gratefully he welcomed the help which Almighty God was now pleased to send him ; for he felt convinced that the silent example of the Seven Solitaries would do more to lead others to the paths of righteousness than the persuasiveness of human eloquence. He granted all their petitions, and they left his presence more than ever resolved to persevere in their holy resolution. Nothing now remained but to await tranquilly the appointed day for action.

Thus in the space of three-and-twenty days our Seven Saints had broken all their earthly ties, and were free to respond to the summons of their Queen. The sacrifice was great, and their hearts were rent asunder in the struggle ; but amidst the dregs of the bitter cup it was given to them to taste of that sweetness promised by the Divine Master to those who leave all things for His sake. Soon they were to receive the hundredfold both promised and granted to the followers of their Crucified Lord. And Mary, who had consoled them by her words, and whom they had been permitted to behold, was never henceforth to be far from them. More than ever was she to be the guide of their lives, leading them towards the goal which her maternal love wished them to attain.

CHAPTER IX.

La Camarzia—Visit to the Bishop—Crowds flocking to the Solitaries.

(8TH SEPTEMBER, 1233—31ST MAY, 1234.)

OUTSIDE the walls of Florence, at a short distance from the Porta dei Buoi, stood a country house, called La Camarzia, from the Campus Martius, which lay close at hand. The sons of St. Francis, the Friars Minors, had settled there after leaving Ripoli in the year 1221. There they had established their convent and opened a church, which was as simple as, in after years, Santa Croce was grand. To the right of the church the good Friars, in virtue of a privilege granted to the Mendicant Orders, enclosed their cemetery, in the corner of which, close to the entrance, was a small rudely-built dwelling.

Hither came our Seven Saints to find a refuge from the world. The spot chosen by them presented at once favourable and un-favourable aspects. It certainly could not be said that their surroundings were too luxurious, for everything about their new abode bore the stamp of evangelical poverty. It was sufficiently removed from the noise and bustle of the city to secure an amount of seclusion. Close at hand there was established a community of Religious practising poverty in great perfection ; the dead slumbered peacefully hard by , and both the living and the departed were suggestive of holy thoughts. An old author states that this house belonged to one of the Seven. If this were the case, it was natural that the abode should be devoted to the service of all. It is hardly probable that it should have been bought with any sum reserved from the sale of their property . there would have been a certain incongruity in such a proceeding, since their great desire was to be stripped of everything that they possessed.

They all assembled in this house early on the morning of the Feast of Our Lady's Nativity, 8th September, 1233. They arrived quietly and unostentatiously, still shaken by the conflict of feelings which they had gone through in parting from their families. All was ready for the celebration of the Holy Sacrifice, which was offered by their spiritual father ; and their first action upon entering their new dwelling was to receive the Bread of Heaven. Only the holy angels were witnesses of what passed in those solemn moments, or could measure the tide of divine grace and love which flooded their souls in receiving Him Who was henceforth to be their All.

A statue of the Blessed Virgin was installed above the altar, in token of their having chosen her for their Protectress and Guide, without whose counsel and assistance they would not undertake anything.

Another circumstance which marked this first day of their new career was their outward transformation. Hitherto their dress, although simple, had been in colour, material, and make similar to that worn by others of their age and station. But now they clothed themselves in the coarse grey woollen tunics, symbolical of holy poverty, which they had chosen to be their habit. They put on these not unmoved ; for it was for life that they adopted this garb : living and dying they were to be clad in these garments, in token of having given themselves to God alone.

The first day of their consecrated lives was passed under the influence of that supernatural gladness which fills the souls of those who give themselves up without reserve to the influence of divine grace. The hours sped on in an uninterrupted succession of acts of love, of confidence, and of gratitude. It was their first experience of the life they had longed to lead. Our Lady, who had taken so prominent a part in the work of their vocation, did not fail to receive an ample share of their thanksgivings. Prostrate before her statue, the Seven Solitaries promised to continue unremittingly in their retreat the devotions which they had practised in the Confraternity of the Laudesi, and to have her praises ever in their hearts and on their lips.

They lost no time in organizing their little band. The first thing necessary was to have a rule clearly and exactly formulated. This they drew up in characteristically simple and plain terms, and in a few brief sentences their code of internal legislation was set forth. It was a summary of the loftiest perfection, founded on the sublime precepts of the Gospel. A charity which so moulded the hearts and lives of all as to make of them but one . a poverty which crushed all outward or inward attachment to earthly possessions : an austerity of life which limited the supply of all bodily needs to what was absolutely necessary : an almost uninterrupted silence, only broken at intervals by the exchange of a few words of fraternal charity : a constant lifting up of the heart in prayer and meditation : a frequent contemplation of those eternal truths most calculated to impress the soul : a tender and childlike love of Mary, their Queen and Protectress, expressed by oft repeated utterance of her praises—these were the principles which were to guide their daily lives ; herein were realized all their most ardent aspirations ; and thus did they respond to the call which the lips of their Mistress had addressed to them.

In this rule they possessed an exact description of the life which was henceforth to be theirs. It was to be composed of penance and meditation, with an utter renunciation of self, and was fitted to unite them more and more closely to God ; alternated with religious exercises performed in common, so as to keep them in a constant state of spiritual activity : whilst in their free moments each of the Seven had permission to employ the talent given him in the way best adapted to the promotion of God's glory and to the salvation of souls.

Finally, they completed the organization of their brotherhood by a solemn election, in which they chose Bonfilius Monaldi as their Superior, promising to obey him without reserve.

Thus we may look upon them henceforth as a true religious community. Such indeed they were, although their rule was an exceptional one ; but at that period it was not unusual to find groups of Solitaries who, under one title or another, had joined together and lived apart from the world in the practice of penance, sometimes in remote and desert places, sometimes in the neighbourhood of a town or village.

Nothing was now wanting but the sanction of their Bishop to enable them to proceed on their course, with the assurance that they were carrying out the divine will in their regard. They well knew that in spiritual matters nothing can prosper save through the blessing of Holy Church. In consequence, they begged for an audience in which they could submit the plan of life which they had drawn out for themselves to their good Bishop. That prelate wished to see them all ; and on the day appointed by him they left their solitude and repaired to his palace. They must have felt a real emotion on finding themselves once more in the gay city from which they had so lately withdrawn, and in reflecting on the great change which had taken place in themselves in that brief space of time. They would gladly have avoided such publicity, but they were bound to obey.

As soon as they entered the city the news of their arrival quickly spread, and they were instantly surrounded by crowds of all ages and ranks, exclaiming, wondering, and commenting. the devout praising them, and weeping for gladness : the careless shame-stricken, and taking to heart the example set by the holy Seven : the hardened mocking them : whilst some of the more demonstrative natures were moved to kneel before them, kissing their hands and garments, and begging their blessing.

Soon an incident of a miraculous character roused the enthusiasm of the crowd to the highest degree. Suddenly, amidst the hum of the multitude, infant voices were distinctly heard exclaiming: "See, here are the Servants of Mary !" All were struck with astonishment at hearing such articulate sounds from the lips of children in arms, and all declared that the like had never been known before : whilst many proclaimed aloud that the Seven must be Saints, and Saints, too, especially dear to Our Lady. Meanwhile, the Solitaries passed along with downcast eyes, abashed at finding themselves the centre of so much excitement, and imploring God to spare them these undeserved praises.

On reaching the palace of the Bishop, they were received by him with every mark of good-will and even of reverence. He conversed with them at length, desiring them to speak without reserve, that so he might be enabled the better to counsel and direct them. From what they now told him, he drew the same conclusions as at his first interview with them, namely, that their call had come straight from above, through the direct interposition of the Blessed Virgin, who is the Queen of Heaven. If any doubt had remained to him on the subject, it would have vanished at once when he saw these seven men kneeling humbly at his feet, clad in their poor habits, and awaiting his commands. Their very look and bearing produced a deeper impression than the most eloquent discourse could have done. No one, accustomed to read souls, could mistake the expression of candour, innocence, and holiness which shone in their countenances.

Bonfilius Monaldi having fully explained their plans, the Bishop

approved unreservedly of all that they had done. He added a few
heartfelt words of advice and encouragement, and dismissed them
with his blessing, after having listened benignantly to the outpouring
of their gratitude. The Seven returned to La Camarzia, their hearts
overflowing with that childlike and tranquil joy which is the special
privilege of those who seek in all things to accomplish the holy will
of God. In silence they pondered over the wonderful way in which
their vocation had been brought about, and they rejoiced inwardly
as they recalled the sanction given out of the mouths of babes and
sucklings to their desire of consecrating themselves wholly to the
service of Mary. Truly it was a consoling thought that the title of
Servants of Mary should have been conferred upon them by their
Mother herself, speaking by those innocent lips.

"It is a great marvel, in truth," exclaims Pietro da Todi, "and one
which must be known to all, most worthy to be celebrated for all
time, that in the beginning our first Fathers were called Servants of
Mary; yet none could say how it was that this name was given to
them, as it were, spontaneously by all. Hence, it is plain that it
must have been Our Blessed Lady herself who devised this title, and
who willed that our Fathers should be so styled. Therefore, it was
said that Brother Alexis used to say: 'Neither I nor any other could
ever find that the name by which we are known had occurred to any
man; and it has always been my belief that Our Lady conferred it
upon us; and so did my brethren believe likewise'."

Our Seven Saints desired to express with their lips the gratitude
which filled their hearts. They, therefore, resolved to adopt a pious
custom followed by many devout Christians, who desired to honour
the Mother of God—namely, that of reciting her Office daily. This
Office of Our Lady being divided, like the Divine Office, into seven
portions, offered a welcome means of repeating seven times in the
day the praises of their heavenly Queen. The Church had always
encouraged this pious practice already in vogue for more than four
centuries. Our Solitaries, who knew, loved, and used to say this
Office, thought that now was the time to impose it upon themselves
as an obligation, in thankfulness to their Mother and Mistress for
having chosen them to be her Servants. This token of homage to
her was not destined to cease with the lives of the Seven chosen ones.
Their sons still faithfully keep the promise made more than six
hundred and fifty years ago, by daily reciting the Little Office of
Our Lady.

Not only is the Little Office an appropriate thanksgiving for
graces received, but it is also well adapted to the needs of souls
desiring to express their love of Mary. It recalls, with a marvellous
vividness and charm, the great mysteries of the Christian faith, in
which Our Lady took so prominent a part. It draws out clearly the
theological position of the Mother of God. It is dogma enshrined in

the loftiest strains of poetry, such as must ever give delight to all devout souls.

We read in the old Chronicles of the Order that, from the first day of their abode at La Camarzia, our Solitaries resolved to devote every Saturday to the celebration of the Joys of Our Lady. Although this devotion was not as yet formally recognized, still it was generally practised. During the twelfth century St. Thomas of Canterbury was among those who had a particular attraction to it. Like most other popular devotions, it was the outcome of individual piety under the guidance of the Holy Spirit. Saturday, then, was the day dedicated to the contemplation of the joyful events of Our Lady's life; and probably they made use of the lovely hymn, attributed to the holy martyr of Canterbury himself, for this purpose.

But this devotion, confined to one particular day of the week, was only, as it were, the corollary of a deeper and more extended devotion to which all their days were dedicated. Although they themselves have been silent on this point, it cannot be doubted that the Solitaries of La Camarzia, from the outset of their new life, were given up heart and soul to the remembrance of Our Lady's Sorrows. These formed their favourite subjects of meditation; to these their thoughts had turned whilst they were still in the world; and at La Camarzia they became yet more absorbed in the inexhaustible theme. Bonfilius Monaldi, whose mind was tenacious of all early impressions, spoke frequently to his companions of the sea of sorrow which had overflowed the heart of Mary. He never forgot the Church of Our Lady of the Swoon, under the shadow of which his childhood had been spent. The image of the suffering Mother of God had been stamped into his soul, and he wished to print it in the hearts of his brethren. At this time, apparently, the Chaplet of the Seven Sorrows—a form of devotion which was something on the plan of St. Dominic's Rosary—was adopted by them.

The internal organization of the little Community having been settled in a spirit of brotherly concord, our Solitaries now set to work in good earnest. We would fain depict the daily course of their lives, filled as they were with fervour, fortified by the grace which attends on sacrifices cheerfully accomplished, and generously eager to do all and more than all which the Master required of them. Their ideal of life was this, that it should be spent in contemplation, in penance, and in the service of the Blessed Virgin. This ideal they carried out to the letter. Their days, and, often, their nights also, were passed in an uninterrupted succession of prayers, hymns, meditations, fasts, and bodily penances. Their biographers relate that they wore the roughest haircloth and spiked girdles—in short, that they treated their bodies with the rigour usual in those ages of faith. They lived in perfect unity, wholly obedient to the authority of Bonfilius Monaldi and of their spiritual director. There was a constant brotherly emulation among them to attain the aim which they had set before themselves when leaving the world. All the time they kept the image of their Queen and Mother in the foreground of their thoughts, living in her presence, and attributing to her intercession the happiness they enjoyed in the fulfilment of their dearest hopes.

They had cast away all care for their daily maintenance, depending entirely on the good Providence of God and the charity of the faithful. From time to time some of their number went forth to beg a few scraps of coarse food, or some was left at their door as alms. Having a roof to shelter them, garments to cover them, and their daily bread, they were content. No regrets for worldly comfort and luxury disturbed these souls consecrated to God and His Blessed Mother.

In the service of their Master and of Mary they were tasting all the sweetness which is the heritage of those who have given up the things of time for those of eternity, when a memorable event in the Servite annals occurred. It was the 13th of January, 1234, the Octave of the Epiphany, Uguccioni and Sostegni set forth to beg in Florence. They crossed the river and went towards the Oltrarno district, where Giacomo Benizi, a member of the guild of apothecaries, resided with his family. Whilst the two Solitaries were going from door to door in quest of food for the Community, infant voices were again permitted to speak distinctly and plead with their mothers and nurses the cause of the holy Religious. One of these little ones was Philip Benizi himself, who, being then barely five months old, stretched forward smiling from his mother's arms, saying : "Mother, here come the Servants of Mary : give them an alms".

This marvel excited no less wonder and edification in this, the second occurrence, than when it first took place ; and the Solitaries of La Camarzia recognized in it a fresh proof of the Divine Goodness in their behalf, and an express recognition of their privilege as true and devoted Servants of Mary.

The humble dwelling at La Camarzia was rapidly becoming an object of devout curiosity, and attracting many visitors, who came from more or less interested motives. The Seven had been well known in the world, and their withdrawal from public life had created considerable excitement, which was increased by the reports of their austere mode of life, and of the supernatural favours which they had received. Crowds flocked to see them and to consult them in spiritual difficulties, knowing that here their souls would be enlightened by the rays of heavenly wisdom, and their hearts would be softened by the balm of consoling charity. The chosen ones of God have ever possessed this healing influence which attracts the sinful and sorrowful, and lightens all their burdens.

Thus La Camarzia was continually besieged by the Florentines, eager to see and to speak with our Saints; and these, severe as they were to themselves, were too gentle-hearted to give pain to others by refusing admittance; till gradually they found that serious inroads were made upon the life of solitude and prayer which they had planned.

Besides, the spot which they had chosen because it was so peaceful had begun to lose its retired character. The Franciscan Fathers were extremely popular, and constantly increasing numbers came daily to their church to join in the Offices, or to seek their spiritual guidance. The large open space adjoining the convent was still used for military drills and reviews, Florence not having been cured of her warlike propensities. The Florentines came there also continually to take part in outdoor sports, and meetings of a political character began to be held there about this time. Thus La Camarzia was no longer a country retreat, but, rather, had become a noisy suburb.

The Seven Solitaries could not disguise from themselves that their great object in withdrawing from the world was frustrated by the constant stir and excitement which existed around them. All that they had fled from seemed to pursue them. They asked themselves whether Our Lady could approve of these perpetual inroads on their solitude, and whether by remaining at La Camarzia they were not acting in opposition to her wishes—it might be, even, that they were unfaithful to grace. The mere thought caused acute suffering to these holy souls, whose one desire was to do the will of their Heavenly Father.

It was a salutary fear which now possessed them—a fear from out of the clouds of which a light was to shine and guide them to a yet higher degree of self-renunciation. This light, like a beacon-fire through the darkness, was to lead them to the desert where Our Lady willed to communicate to them her designs in their behalf. They were now to take unconsciously another step towards the goal which they would reach without fail, because they responded to the slightest impulse of Divine Grace

CHAPTER X.

Withdrawal from Florence decided upon.

(1234.)

THE Seven Solitaries of La Camarzia could not shake off the fear which haunted them that they were not responding with sufficient generosity to the call of God and of His Blessed Mother. Their dread lest this might be the case grew daily stronger and stronger, leaving them peace neither by night nor by day, and following them like a shadow. More especially did it weigh upon Bonfilius Monaldi, who, as Superior of the little Community, bore the burden of all upon his shoulders.

If they had seen sufficient grounds for believing that time would produce any change in the circumstances which now gave them so much uneasiness, they would have been content to wait until the cloud dispersed. But, on the contrary, it seemed vain to hope that the crowds of visitors would diminish, still less that they would cease altogether. The busy world, with all its cares and troubles, was too near the peaceful haven where balm was to be found for every woe.

Souls accustomed to weigh all things in the balance of the sanctuary, under the eye of God, are never hasty in deciding upon the course they are to pursue. Our Saints followed their accustomed round of prayer and penance and of devotion to their Queen, awaiting in a spirit of faith the guiding light promised to all men of good-will. They patiently bore the anxiety that weighed upon them, humbly submitting it to the Divine Will; and they discussed it together thoughtfully, endeavouring to trace it to its source, and to discover whither it was leading them. Gradually the idea of a retreat into a more distant solitude took root among them, and seemed to spring up and ripen spontaneously. Their Director, to whom their inmost thoughts were confided, had at their entreaty united his prayers to theirs, in order that a wise decision might be made, for the greater glory of God.

At last, reason and feeling both concurred to bring them to a definite resolution of leaving La Camarzia without delay: they felt that their vocation was in danger, and that the slightest hesitation might be fatal. But some time was to elapse before their plan was put into execution. Meanwhile they encouraged each other by reflecting that their eyes would no longer be wearied, nor their ears stunned, by the perpetual sight and sound of the busy throngs who had sought their retreat. They were about to remove as far as possible from their birthplace. They would not cease to love it, but they would bid it farewell, and think only of the abiding city, eternal in the heavens. They felt, too, that in a remote solitude, under a wider sky, and breathing a purer air, it would be far easier to realize the continual presence of God.

They were all agreed as to the necessity of a speedy departure. Complete harmony of thought reigned among them. Pietro da Todi says of them: "By virtue of that fraternal charity which made of them one household, one in heart and soul, and in their resolve to lead the same life, by that same charity were they all prepared as by one accord to accept the sacrifices entailed by their voluntary exile".

Thus we read that they often said one to another : " Come, brothers, let us quit this abode where our lives are frittered away in vanity, and where our souls are in such peril, and let us seek some spot where by God's guidance we may find our satisfaction in doing His will ". Nothing delayed their departure but the necessity of finding a solitary place in which to hide themselves.

The watchful Providence of God was over them now as heretofore. He Who had called them to His service by the intervention of His Blessed Mother, and Who had found them obedient to His summons, did not leave them long in suspense. They had put themselves unreservedly into His hands, and now He was Himself preparing for them a way out of all their perplexities.

In the territory belonging to Florence without the city walls, and called the *Contado*, to the north of the city, and at a distance of about eleven miles as the crow flies, rises the mountain now known as Monte Senario. In former times it had several other appellations, as Sonaio or Sonario, on account of the hollow sounds produced by the violent storms of wind that howled through the natural or artificial caves on its slopes ; Asinaio, either a rustic corruption of the previous name, or else bestowed as signifying that it was necessary to ride there on asses ; lastly, it was called Sanario, on account of the purity of the air, and the good health enjoyed by those who dwelt there. But the name which has survived all others is the noblest of all, for it is that by which we venerate the abode of holy men who there lived saintly lives, and died the death of the righteous. The name, too, well expresses the venerable aspect of the mountain which, clothed with its ancient forest, rears its lofty head above the six neighbouring heights. This mountain formed a portion of a considerable estate situated in the parish of Santa Felicita di Bivigliano, a village, the centre of which was about fifteen hundred yards from the top of Monte Senario. This estate belonged to the family of Lotteringhi della Stufa, one of the noblest of Florence.

Monte Senario, the height of which is not far short of three thousand feet, is one of the loftiest points of a detached range which, at its northern extremity, is joined by Monte Morello to a branch of the Apennines. It is thus a portion of the natural rampart which closes round the northern, western, and southern sides of the fertile valley of Mugello, to the eastward of which flows the river Sieve.

Owing to the inaccessibility of its situation, and to the sparseness of population in the neighbourhood, it is difficult to imagine a more complete solitude than Monte Senario presents, even in our day. The pine forest which covers it seems to intensify the silence which reigns there. In whatever direction the eye turns, the landscape lies so far beneath that the beholder might almost imagine himself suspended in the air. All sounds of human life seem to be hushed before they reach the mountain crest, and a recluse might there find a tranquillity wholly untroubled by outward influences.

Nature there presents one of her fairest aspects. On all sides appear masses of rock, clumps of dark pine trees, a wealth of climbing plants. At every turn a fresh picture is disclosed. The scenery is wild, yet inexpressibly charming. All around disposes the mind to recollectedness and meditation. The soul looks from Nature up to Nature's God, beholding Him in the wondrous variety of His works, and bending in loving adoration before His Infinite Being.

Each season of the year decks Monte Senario with its own special beauty. In winter this beauty is stern and wild, a deathlike silence prevails, which is only broken by the howling winds, and a snowy veil is spread over the rugged head of the mountain. But with—

" The regular return of genial months,
And renovation of a faded world " (*The Task*)—

all is transfigured ; the wide vault of brilliant blue arches above ; the sweet pure air brings health in its breath ; the wilderness rejoices and is glad ; the air is filled with the wholesome scent of the pines and the fragrance of countless flowers ; the hum of insects, the song of birds, and the clear trickle of the mountain rills mingle with the distant murmur of the Sieve as it flows over its rocky bed in the valley. The mountain is then a vision of beauty ; nor is the distant landscape less attractive. From this lofty observatory the domes and towers of Florence stand out on the horizon, half hidden behind the hills of Fiesole. The writers who have painted Monte Senario in dark and gloomy tints are unjust to one of the most beautiful spots in that beautiful land. In the year of which we are now writing, 1234, Monte Senario presented even a wilder aspect than in our own day. Where now are rough paths and roads, there were then almost impenetrable woods, where wild animals found a safe refuge, seldom, however, attacking travellers, as imagined some naive authors of the past.

This was the spot chosen by Divine Providence for the abode of the Seven Solitaries, and hither were they guided at the appointed time.

In order to know the Divine Will concerning their future dwelling-place, our Saints poured themselves out in prayer to God before the picture of His Blessed Mother, multiplying their fasts and penances. Then lo ! one night, as they were praying with redoubled fervour, a dazzling veil of light overspread the sky ; their souls were flooded with that heavenly sweetness more than once already vouchsafed to them, and each one saw distinctly, figured upon the horizon, an exact representation of Monte Senario Soon a clear yet gentle voice, of no earthly tone, addressed them, saying that "the mountain they now beheld was Monte Senario ; that they were to go up thither, and dwell there, leading a life of great mortification ; and

5

that, in this important undertaking, they would be encouraged by the help and favour of the Mother of God ".

The voice of Mary—for it was she herself who had spoken to them—ceased, and the vision of light disappeared, but the impression left in the hearts of the beholders could not be effaced. By the motherly tenderness of their Queen, their resolution was now ratified, and the spot which they sought was pointed out to them. Their joy was unbounded, for at last they knew where was the beloved solitude to which they were to withdraw. Their feet seemed to have wings to bear them to the wished-for spot, whither their hearts had already taken flight, and where the dearest hopes of their vocation would be realized.

At length, then, the Seven Solitaries of La Camarzia were about to withdraw far from the tumult of the world, to dwell upon the heights amidst the majestic silence of Nature, to apply themselves to the holy exercises of the eremitical life, and to unite themselves more closely to God, in order to prove their gratitude to the Queen of Heaven for her maternal care.

CHAPTER XI.

Departure for Monte Senario.

(31st May, 1234.)

Our Seven Solitaries knew now that Monte Senario was destined to them by God. It therefore became their duty to inform Bishop Ardingo of the commands which they had received from heaven, and to await from him the means to carry them out. The recollections of the many kindnesses which they had already received at his hands, and of his approval—reluctantly given though it had been— of their withdrawal to a more remote spot, emboldened them to seek the Bishop's presence without delay. Once more, led by Bonfilius Monaldi, they knelt before him humbly, and touchingly recorded to him all that had happened.

The good Bishop heard them with attention, and, filled with an ever-growing admiration of the heroic virtues practised with the greatest simplicity by these holy men, he assured them that he would put no obstacle in the way of their removal, and that they had his full consent to establish themselves in any part of Monte Senario ; he added that he was ready to lend them his full co-operation in order that they should execute their design.

In fact, a short time afterwards, on the 23rd of March, 1234, all was settled according to the desire of the Solitaries. And the Lottaringhi, who had the property of Monte Senario, made a generous donation of the top of the mountain to the Bishop of Florence, in order to be occupied by our Saints. Ardingo then told them to go and inspect the ground, to take possession, and do with it what they desired, for their own spiritual benefit and the greater glory of God. At this announcement the Solitaries were filled with gratitude, which, with tears in their eyes, they strove to express to the prelate, both for himself and for the pious and charitable family who had bestowed the site upon them.

No trace of any formal contract remains to show that this grant was made to the Solitaries. This, however, is not to be wondered at, for at the first there existed only a verbal permission to make use of the ground. The Solitaries were vowed to the strictest poverty ; and when the Bishop accepted the property for himself as a representative of the Church, and allowed them to make use of it, he was acting completely in accordance with the spirit of the recently founded Mendicant Orders, which, by their Rule, could not possess any property of their own, either as individuals or as communities.

The much-wished-for solitude was theirs at last. Full of gladness, they hastened to follow the counsels of their Bishop, and without further delay, on the following day, which was the Vigil of the Annunciation of Our Blessed Lady, they made the best of their way to the chosen spot, which they were anxious to inspect before installing themselves there provisionally. Accordingly, having climbed the steep paths leading to the top of Monte Senario, their surprise was great when they found a level piece of ground perfectly suited to their purpose. It was of small extent, but extremely beautiful. A clear cold spring of water flowed on one side, and the whole was encircled by a shady grove of trees, shutting in the little oasis from the surrounding desert. All that met their gaze surpassed their utmost wishes, and they gave thanks aloud to Him Who had so bountifully provided for them a home in a place thus removed from all contact with the world, and admirably fitted for the penitential life which they proposed to lead. They returned from their inspection enraptured with what they had seen, and they began joyfully to address each other in words which have been transmitted to us by Pietro da Todi : " Henceforth we have no need to seek a place of refuge from the world, since God Himself has prepared one for us : come, and let us together behold the dwelling which He has appointed for us ; let us go up into the mountain, where He wills us to lead a life of penance ". And then, under the influence of the joy which they felt in hearing these words, all broke forth enthusiastically as follows : " Why do we tarry ? Come, let us go forth from this city wholly given over to worldliness ; we will no longer keep up any intercourse with her people, nor will we remain in this part of the country, but we will go at once to the retreat which the Lord in His fatherly care has reserved for us : thus shall

His will be accomplished by us, and the desire of our hearts shall be fulfilled."

By these, and the like, ejaculations, they nourished in their souls that ardent desire which possessed them to fly far from the haunts of men, and to be completely hidden from the eyes of all. Also they lost no time in preparing to remove there ; and they often went to the blessed spot, spending there even several days, in order to make all the necessary preparations for a provisory dwelling. At last they fixed their final departure on the last day of May, being the Vigil of the Ascension. The Bishop of Florence granted them another interview, in the course of which he confirmed all their plans. No further obstacle remained, and the exodus of which they had so long dreamed was now about to be accomplished. Nothing, indeed, could be easier to carry out, for poverty and detachment were their only treasures. They were, in truth, able to repeat, in a Christian sense, the words of the heathen philosopher : " We bear about with us all that we possess ".

The news of their departure from Florence spread quickly, and all the former frequenters of La Camarzia hastened thither to express their sorrow During the last few days of May all the relatives of the Seven Solitaries came to lament over this fresh separation, which renewed and increased the grief of the former parting. With their kindred came friends and acquaintances—all whose souls had been strengthened and consoled by the inexhaustible patience and gentleness of the Seven Solitaries. Tears flowed abundantly. The farewells were distressing to those who were being left, and not less so to those who were leaving them ; for holiness, far from hardening the human heart, does but increase its tenderness.

Our Saints spent the greater part of their last night at La Camarzia in prayer and thanksgiving. Great as had been the trials which they had there endured during nine months past, they felt that much grace had there been granted to them, the prelude of higher favours yet to come. By daybreak they were ready to hear Mass. The Holy Sacrifice was offered by their faithful chaplain, James of Poggibonzi. Then, in haste, each took what he had to carry, and together they all set forth.

The Seven Solitaries, with their Director, thought it well to impress a devotional character on their departure by going processionally : one of their number walked first, carrying the Cross ; another, bearing the picture of the Blessed Virgin, which had hung in their Oratory, came next ; and the rest followed in order. The greater part of Florence was still wrapt in slumber, but our wayfarers did not enter the city ; passing along the ramparts, they advanced towards Fiesole, and, climbing the hills, soon found themselves on the only road leading to their destination, namely, the highway from Florence to Bologna, which they were to follow till they reached

Pratolino, situated a few miles from the top of Monte Senario. Having once reached the quiet country, then in all the fresh beauty of early summer, they gave vent to the gladness of their hearts by chanting the Church's glorious hymns, with which the birds mingled their sweet songs. Thus they went on their way, recollected and absorbed in prayer, and heedless of the wondering glances of those whom they encountered, till, in about two hours' time, they reached Pratolino, where they diverged from the main road, and entered upon the wild and rough mountain path which led to the table-land on the summit of the mountain. Soon they came to a small cluster of houses, now called Aquirico, and, a little farther on, to a spring which never fails, and which waters the ever verdant meadows round Pratolino

They were now weary with their journey, for they had strictly kept the fast of the Vigil of the Ascension. Bonfilius Monaldi saw that they were exhausted ; and he, therefore, proposed that, before climbing the steepest part of the mountain, they should halt awhile to rest by the spring. Sitting there, their souls filled with grateful and devout thoughts, they gazed on the wide landscape stretched before them. Far in the distance they beheld the city of Florence, still dear to their hearts, and as they spoke of her, Bonfilius Monaldi, pointing to a narrow valley called Valle delle Croci, a few thousand paces from where they were seated, said to them : " On that spot, more than eight hundred years ago, Radagasius was defeated in that fearful battle which saved our Florence". And then he repeated to them the story which has been enshrined in some of the most stirring pages of history.

Having briefly narrated the event, Bonfilius Monaldi added : "See, there, the narrow space between the hills of Mugello and the plain of Florence : narrow is it, indeed, yet it is the grave of that great army of two hundred thousand men, which, led by Radagasius, swept over Italy, was everywhere victorious, and laden with spoil ; and which, after all its triumphs, perished miserably, overpowered by the skill and courage of Stilicho, supported by the magnates of Florence. In remembrance of that day, so glorious for our ancestors, but so terrible for the great Gothic warrior and his troops, this valley received the name of Valley of the Crosses." Whilst thus speaking, the gentle and tender-hearted Superior could hardly restrain his tears, as he recalled the fate of these unhappy men.

The wayfarers now felt sufficiently refreshed to begin the final ascent of the mountain, and they resumed their toilsome march, still singing psalms and hymns, which took a more triumphant tone as they drew nearer and nearer the favoured spot appointed to be their home. Filled with joyful emotion, they could hardly realize that the happy moment had now arrived when they were to take possession of the promised land.

The sun was by this time high in the heavens, and the heat began to be oppressive. But our Saints were too happy to feel heat or fatigue. All that they saw around them was food for pious reflections. As they passed through the grove of pines, and beheld those hardy trees rearing their lofty heads towards heaven, the restful silence, the deep shade, the beauty of all the surroundings, seemed to them a picture of paradise.

They spoke then of the various symbols which the pine tree presents to the devout mind, for—like all true contemplatives—they found "tongues in the trees, books in the running brooks, sermons in stones, and good in everything". The root, they said, is faith, the foundation of all spiritual life; the depth to which the root penetrates the earth shows us that faith must be founded in humility; the trunk, like labour, is the support of the whole tree; the branches, growing with great regularity, each in its own place, represent justice, which disposes all things orderly and in proportion; the evergreen leaves are emblematic of hope, and being sharply pointed, and growing in the form of a cross, they remind us also of the cross of Our Blessed Lord, and of the sufferings of the martyrs; the drops of aromatic gum which exude from the bark are like Charity, which cements us together in the bonds of brotherly love; in the unity of the tree we see the divine nature; the branches invariably growing in triplets show forth the Trinity of the Divine Persons; and lastly, the crest of the tree towering towards the clouds tells us that our conversation should be in heaven.

Thus, with holy simplicity, the Solitaries exchanged their devout reflections, and their gentle Superior closed the conversation with a few edifying words: "Learn hence, my dear sons," said he, "by what links of ardent charity you are knit to Our Master and to His Blessed Mother, Who have prepared for you, in this solitude, a space enclosed by these trees, whose leaves will be to you an ever-open book, where you may read great and heavenly mysteries. Think what awaits you in heaven, when every object of this visible world inspires such glorious thoughts. You see now how true are the words of Holy Scripture: 'He will make the desert as a place of pleasure, and the wilderness as the garden of the Lord. Joy and gladness shall be found therein, thanksgiving and the voice of praise'" (Isaias li. 3).

Their minds being filled with these thoughts, the Seven hastened upwards, and soon they stood upon the summit of Monte Senario. An exclamation of joy broke from the lips of all. They at once planted the Cross in the centre of the level space, and unfurled the banner of Our Lady; then, falling on their knees, they kissed the ground, weeping, in a transport of gratitude, and turning towards the picture of the Blessed Virgin, they exclaimed: "Behold, we have left all things for thee, O Mary, Our Mother!" They could hardly cease from pouring out prayers and ejaculations to her, repeating again and again that it was for love of her Divine Son and of herself that they had retired to this solitude, and entreating her to accept the consecration which they desired to make of themselves to her service, now and for ever.

With this taking possession of their new domain, one epoch of the lives of our Saints closed, and a new one opened before them.

During the first period, since they had once set their feet on the way of perfection, they had made rapid and constant progress; and thus, whilst dwelling in a lax and self-indulgent world, they had practised the loftiest virtues, and had been capable of the hardest sacrifices. They had conquered all their natural inclinations, and, having at their disposal ample means for gratifying the love of liberty, of pleasure, and of wealth, by which the young are so often led astray—they had of their own free will put on the triple yoke of obedience, mortification, and poverty. They had crushed under foot the tenderest and most attractive of lawful attachments, family ties, civic honours, the laudable ambition in which generous spirits indulge, all the joys and consolations of private or public life, had been powerless to turn them aside. Some of their number had even gone beyond this, and had risen to the very heights of heroism, by giving up wives and children to follow the Master. They had adopted the most humble mode of life; they had withdrawn from all intercourse with their fellow-citizens; they lived in solitude, and practised every kind of penance

This had they done during the first period of their lives, watched over and guided by their Blessed ' Mother, encouraged by her motherly love and strengthened by her queenly power. Since their birth, the eye of Mary had been fixed upon them, her hand had directed them, her maternal heart had attached itself to them with a love of predilection, not for one moment had she left them, but had kept her purpose ever before them, and swept all obstacles from their path, until at length she had brought them safely to their mountain solitude.

During the second period, on which we are now about to enter, we shall see them, under the same guidance, do no less; nay, rather in accordance with the laws of progress, they will mount higher and higher still in the spiritual life, as energetically as they climbed the steep path to their mountain home Besides, they will know their new calling, and set at work to fulfil it with no less heroism than they have listened, in the Confraternity of the Laudesi, to the voice of Our Blessed Lady manifesting to them the will of her Divine Son.

BOOK II.

FOUNDATION (1234—1243).

CHAPTER I.

𝔗𝔥𝔢 𝔥𝔢𝔯𝔪𝔦𝔱𝔞𝔤𝔢 𝔬𝔣 𝔐𝔬𝔫𝔱𝔢 𝔖𝔢𝔫𝔞𝔯𝔦𝔬.

(1234.)

OUR Seven Saints had now taken possession of Monte Senario. After a short interval devoted to recruiting their bodily strength, they prepared to instal themselves in their hermitage. The beauty of the season, the freshness of the air, the contrasting verdure of the level turf, and the encircling pines, all presented a scene of surpassing fairness. The Solitaries would fain have continued to pour out their souls in prayer in presence of this magnificent scenery; but the day was on its decline, and they had to spend their first night on the table-land which they had now reached. Their first task was to arrange their Oratory, which they did with loving care in the best manner that they were able; for that rustic tabernacle was to be the dwelling-place of the Most High, where He would deign to speak with them face to face. With regard to the accommodation for themselves, they were easily satisfied: the wooden hut just large enough to hold them, and already built, served well their purpose for the present.

Then their thoughts flew at once to the morrow's Feast. They looked forward to it with the more eagerness, as it presented some analogy with their own circumstances. For Jesus, on the day of His Ascension, leaving the world, was taken up into heaven: so had they on this day ascended from the plains where all their worldly ties remained, and had found on these heights, as it were, an antechamber of the heavenly city. Thus they made ready for the festival with redoubled fervour, earnestly begging Our Lady to accept the first fruits of their new solitude. Then they lay down, for a brief but welcome repose, on their rude beds, where they enjoyed the sweetest slumber that had ever visited them. They felt that, having left all things for their Divine Master, He would come and dwell with them more familiarly than before. They chanted the Night Office, listened to the pious exhortations of Bonfilius Monaldi, and, having offered their morning tribute to Mary, they were ready for Mass.

It was early : the sun had scarcely shown himself above the horizon ; all around was fragrant with the dewy sweetness of the dawn, and nature sang her glorious hymn of praise to her Maker. And, in the rural Oratory, seven souls united as one were over-flowing with divine love, as they assisted at the great Act by which earth appeases God's justice, and obtains His infinite mercy. James of Poggibonzi began the offering of the Most Holy Sacrifice immediately after Prime. The Seven followed the successive parts of the Mass with sentiments of ardent charity. Frequently did they express their desire of serving their Lord in labours, and in sufferings here, that so they might share in the glory of His Ascension hereafter. Then followed their Communion, when it was their happiness to possess their good Master, from Whom they had received such unnumbered benefits. The Adorable Sacrifice being ended, they prolonged their thanksgiving in loving converse with Him, the Giver of that unspeakable gift. That morning of June, 1234, remained ever after a memorable anniversary for the Order, and hardly less for the inhabitants of the villages around Monte Senario. Each year the recurring festival has never ceased to draw a number of pious pilgrims to visit the scene of this first inauguration, and there to offer up their prayers.

The remainder of the day was spent in much the same manner as the morning, in chanting psalms and hymns, in prayer, in meditation, and in contemplation ; and in frequent renewals of the great resolution of their lives, namely, that of belonging to Our Blessed Lady, and of devoting themselves to the promotion of her glory.

The Feast being over, a period began, during which they had to carry on simultaneously three different kinds of work. First came the occupations proper to the eremitical life, which consisted in a due admixture of prayer and penance. That was indeed their true vocation in which they made neither break nor pause. Then came the duty of providing what was necessary for the body : for this it was requisite both to till their ground, and to beg for alms in the neighbourhood ; for they were vowed to strict poverty, and therefore they had to depend, like the birds of the air, upon the good Providence of God, for the food and clothing of eight persons. Lastly, they had to build a hermitage which would shield them from the weather. Simple and unpretending as it was to be in its construction, it was needful to lay out a plan, to seek for building materials, and to set about the work. This they determined to do at once.

The site chosen was on the side of the mountain looking towards Florence ; for, although our Saints had left their native city in order to serve God more undividedly, yet they did not love it the less ; and thus it was a consolation to them to have the fair city always in view. They furthermore selected the highest point of the table-land, where the ground was hard and rocky, their desire for solitude making them take every precaution to isolate themselves as much as possible.

These preliminaries were speedily arranged, and the work began. The hermitage occupied a limited space, and comprised the Oratory, looking in a south-westerly direction towards Florence, and surrounded by the cells of the Hermits, to which were probably added two or three community rooms. But, before beginning their work, they sought the blessing of the Church, and, having conveyed their wishes to the Bishop of Florence, the holy prelate promised to come to Monte Senario without delay to bless the foundation-stone of their chapel. The ceremony took place a few days later, when Bishop Ardingo appeared in the midst of the Solitaries, whose joy was great, for he had ever been a true father to them all; nor was his happiness less than theirs, as he proceeded to bless the stone The Seven Saints, silent and recollected, stood around, a fervent prayer going up from their hearts to Jesus and His Blessed Mother, that the virtue of the Most High might be poured forth abundantly on that humble building. They knew not how fruitful a cradle it was to prove, but their care in preparing the ground was to merit an abundant harvest. The Bishop took the opportunity of saying a few cheering words, exhorting them not to look back now that their hands were laid to the plough, but to be ever ready to fulfil the behests of the glorious Mother of God, who had called them. Then he returned to Florence, refreshed by the sweet odour of sanctity which pervaded the spot which he had visited.

From this time forward the Solitaries were actively engaged in carrying out their plans. The work was a good deal retarded by the paucity of means and the difficulties of transport; but the holy Hermits gladly toiled as masons or labourers, feeling no fatigue as they hastened the completion of their beloved retreat.

In their explorations on the mountain they made the welcome discovery of several grottoes or caves on the slopes, looking towards Pratolino and Bivigliano. These were well suited to the manner of life that they had adopted, and they decided to make use of them for exercises of contemplation and penance.

The little chapel was quickly completed; and, as soon as it had received the consecration of Holy Church, the Seven Saints took possession of it with grateful gladness. Almost all their aspirations were now satisfied. They had in their midst the House of God, where Our Lord and His Blessed Mother would receive their homage and hold communion with them; and it seemed to them that no joy on earth could be compared to their own.

A little before the winter set in, the hermitage was completely finished and surrounded by its enclosure. Lowly and simple as it was, nestled upon the summit of the mountain, and encircled by pine woods, its very existence was hardly suspected by strangers until it was closely approached. It was thus all the more suited to the seven noble Florentines whose sole desire was to be forgotten, who were now, in every sense of the word, Hermits ; and whose place of abode was henceforth to be called the desert.

These souls, hungering and thirsting after righteousness, and eager for a life of penance, now entered upon their new mode of existence with the same ardour that they had shown in seeking and adopting it. The generosity of their efforts had won them the right to carry out their lofty aims ; and now they were going to spend their lives in an atmosphere of holiness, and to be gradually purified from all earthly alloy.

CHAPTER II.

Austerities of the Hermits—Crowds attracted towards them—Visit of the Legate.

(1234-1239.)

HAVING effected their removal to Monte Senario, the holy Solitaries were free to continue the mode of life which they had adopted at La Camarzia ; the only difference being in its increased austerity.

It was the true eremitical life which they now practised. That life was no novelty in the Church, for it had been honoured and in use from the beginning of the Christian era. St. John the Baptist had prepared himself for his high office as the Precursor of Our Lord, and had promoted his own sanctification by his life of prayer and penance in the desert. It was the state of life which the God-Man Himself deigned to follow. The Holy House at Nazareth, though silent and solitary, was only in part a hermitage ; but Our Lord, before entering upon His public life, withdrew into the desert for forty days, and, afterwards, frequently retired thither, thus pointing the way to souls yearning wholly to quit the world. No age nor country has been without its illustrious hermits. We need but recall the ascetics, St Paul the Theban, St. Anthony, their numerous disciples and followers, and, even in these latter times, St. Colette, Blessed Nicholas of Flue, and many others.

During the youth of our Seven Saints, there had dwelt in the outskirts of Villamagna, a small market-town about three miles from Florence, a holy man who carried out the eremitical life in its fullest rigour. Blessed Gerard, the hermit in question, was born at Villamagna about the year 1174 : his parents were good and pious peasants, who died when he was twelve years old. On becoming an orphan, the noble family on whose estate his parents had dwelt brought him to Florence, and trained him religiously. Later in life, he twice took the Cross and fought bravely in the Holy Land, where he was made prisoner by the Saracens. On being ransomed he returned to Italy, and, passing through Assisi on his way home, he there received the habit of the Third Order of St. Francis, which he wore till his death.

On reaching Villamagna, he retired to a spot known as the Grottoes, and there he began to lead the life which he had long desired. He prayed in the most solitary places, begged on the highway, distributed to the poor the alms he received, and visited and nursed the sick. He spent much time in manual labour, fasted often, passed many hours in the neighbouring churches, and frequently continued whole nights in prayer, before a statue of the Blessed Virgin placed in a niche near his retreat. During this period he wrought many marvels, and so continued to do until his death, which took place on the 13th of May, 1258.

Our Saints had thus had an admirable example of the eremitical state placed before them to study and profit by ; and, knowing it to be a high and holy calling approved by the Church, they had themselves embraced it. Their first attempt had been made at La Camarzia, where it was only possible to follow out that state of life partially ; but now, on Monte Senario, they proposed to practise it in greater perfection. From the first day, therefore, of their installation they grasped the fundamental principle of the eremitical life ; namely, that the anchorite should in his solitude retire wholly within himself, remaining *Solus cum Solo.* The one aim on which their minds were concentrated was to think of God only, to see Him alone in all things, and to act in all things with the sole view of pleasing Him. For six years they relaxed not their endeavours to attain their object. They were as though dead to the world, to their kindred, and to all temporal interests. Isolated from all contact with their fellow-men, they strove to isolate themselves, as far as was practicable, from each other. As one who has long been seeking a precious jewel, when he has found it, cannot bear to let it out of his sight, but spends his time in gazing upon it, and seems to prize it hourly more and more, so these holy souls for years sought God, and God alone, the sole end of all created things in heaven and on earth ; and now they could say with the Spouse in the Canticle : " I found Him Whom my soul loveth ; and I will not let Him go " (Cant. iii. 4). So great, indeed, was their attachment to their cherished solitude, that they could hardly bear to leave it for a moment. They no longer traversed the streets of Florence to seek for alms. They took great delight in their grottoes, where often they spent all their free time during the day, and occasionally the whole night. We may easily conceive how strongly the Seven Hermits felt the attraction of these caves, where they could conceal themselves from every eye, and lose themselves wholly in God. Such a seclusion, far from the busy world, amidst the wild beauty of nature, was after their own hearts ; and, there, in the tranquillity of the night, the soft lustre of the moon, and the flashing light of the stars, they were led more easily to the contemplation of heavenly things.

Among the various avocations which filled their days, prayer occupied the largest space, since they looked upon it as the very soul of their life. In one form or another they prolonged this holy exercise, until their existence seemed one continued chain of praise and supplication. They adopted the psalmody which for a long time had been used in the Church. Seven times in the day they raised their voices in the magnificent strains of the Royal Psalmist, in the words of Holy Scripture, and in passages from the writings of the Fathers which make up the Office. The praises of Mary naturally followed those addressed to the Most High, in fulfilment of the promise made by them at La Camarzia to recite daily her Little Office.

Winter and summer alike, they rose at midnight to recite Matins and Lauds in their humble oratory, lighted only by a few dim lamps. Whilst all around was wrapt in repose, they fulfilled the welcome task of praising God. The intense and mysterious silence of night, which reigned undisturbed on Monte Senario, enabled them the more readily to unite their hearts to Him. Years gave a character of greater strength to their piety, but it always retained that childlike familiarity so often found in simple-minded and loving souls.

Immediately after Matins and Lauds our Hermits were accustomed to hold what they called a Conference ; that is to say, one of their number, usually Bonfilius Monaldi, addressed a few plain words to his brethren on the things of God ; words that, coming from the heart of the speaker, fell like refreshing dew or burning fire on the hearts of the hearers From time to time a short pause was made, during which all conversed interiorly with Jesus and Mary, thus making the Conference a true exercise of mental prayer. This practice has been preserved in the Order in the usual form of meditation, one of the Community reading out the points upon which all are to meditate.

The Hermits did not restrict their mental prayer to the time of Conference. During the course of the day, whether at the hour prescribed by the Rule or during their free time, whether in common or privately, in their cells or in the grottoes, by daylight or in darkness, the Seven Solitaries gave themselves up to it again and again, finding rest and food for their souls in alternating meditation and contemplation.

In the eremitical life, whilst the soul is being lifted up in prayer, the body must be abased by penance, in order to conquer its repugnance to all that is against nature. Our Seven Saints, therefore, employed simultaneously these two engines of perfection to curb and crush the craving of the natural man for pleasure and ease. They had served their apprenticeship in this stern school at La Camarzia ; now, in their hermitage, they were proficients in the science by which self is subdued. They availed themselves of the freedom of action which Bonfilius Monaldi accorded to each in respect to austerities, and they made use of every weapon known in the penitential armoury to their forerunners in the path of sanctity. Bodily labour in frost and snow, or under a burning sun ; meals spare in quantity, few in number, composed only of a few herbs or vegetables, a small piece of bread, and a draught of spring water ; short and interrupted sleep upon the bare earth, or on boards and stones ; prolonged vigils ; days and nights spent in complete solitude in the caves ; hair shirts, chains, disciplines—in not one of these things did they spare themselves in order to conquer the flesh and reduce it to absolute subjection.

Some among them fasted daily. Others remained, for more than one hundred consecutive days, in the absolute solitude of the grottoes, which they only quitted to hear Mass, or to fulfil some other obligation. These prolonged retreats were spent by the holy Hermits in unbroken silence, and in the closest union with God by prayer and meditation. Alexis, Hugh, and Sostene were especially drawn to this solitary life, and there are still grottoes on Monte Senario which are known by their respective names. Others disciplined themselves daily even to blood. Briefly we might say that there was a keen competition among them to surpass each other in mortifications ; and Bonfilius Monaldi, the only one of their number who might have induced them to moderate their penances, could not well condemn in them what he carried out so rigorously on his own person. To all these inflictions may be added the expeditions which they were obliged sometimes to make over hills and valleys among the neighbouring villages, for the purpose of procuring the necessaries of life. Though rare, they were for them the source of serious fatigues. Thus we have a tolerably distinct picture of their daily lives—lives truly heroic and edifying, spent in the continual practice of the highest virtues.

Undoubtedly they now led eremitical lives, but, at the same time, they did not cease to dwell in community ; it was therefore a mixed life, combining the advantages of both its component parts. So far as it was eremitical, it made them aim at the loftiest perfection, and practise great austerities. Through the Community life the ties of brotherly interdependence were not broken, the dangers of a too complete isolation were obviated, and the innocent gladness of a monastic household still prevailed among them. Thus had Divine

Providence preserved the balance between their two vocations ; and, whilst calling them to the solitary life, it had gathered them together in a sacred Community, in order that they might the better and more securely carry out their holy aspirations.

For the space of six years, then, they led this double life, more resembling that of purified spirits than of mortal men. It was as a furnace in which Our Lord refined them, to make them more worthy of His Blessed Mother, to whom He desired to offer them.

One single thought absorbed the pious Hermits in their new life—the desire of sanctifying themselves by serving Our Lady. With unwearied energy and an iron will, they strove by every imaginable means to attain this end, regardless of all obstacles. Their complete isolation on the crest of Monte Senario facilitated the accomplishment of the aim on which they concentrated all their powers. They continued all the practices they had adopted at La Camarzia to honour Our Blessed Lady. They took especial care not to address each other before first saying *Ave Maria*, and receiving the answer, *Gratia plena;* thus showing that they carried all throughout their lives the loving remembrance of that Heavenly Queen.

But having once started in the race, they knew not how to moderate their course, and they ran great risks of being urged beyond the bounds of prudence and discretion. In point of fact, they forgot the existence of their bodies, or rather they acted as though those bodies did not exist. Carried away by their fervour, they totally neglected the tenements of clay, which it was their duty to subdue, but not to destroy. Daily they imposed upon themselves greater privations, refusing to yield to any physical weakness. Their allowance of food was gradually reduced to a minimum, but with that they learnt to be content. Their physical strength grew weaker, but they were consoled by the growth of their spiritual strength. "What matters it," they said, "whether our time here below be short or long? All that really concerns us is that we should so live as to be admitted hereafter to the Beatific Vision in the company of Our Blessed Lady."

Thus they pursued their holy course : practising strict poverty, possessing nothing, making no provision for the morrow, living entirely on the herbs and vegetables which they themselves cultivated, with the scraps which they collected from door to door, when at long intervals they visited the neighbourhood, and trusting wholly to the good Providence of God, Who feeds the young ravens and clothes the lilies of the field. The bodily necessities, which so heavily clog the wings of the soul, were thus almost wholly cast aside ; but their detachment was, if we may say so, carried beyond the limits of what is permissible

Undoubtedly these excessive austerities were not wholly blameless. They were threatening destruction to bodily health, endangering life, and, in a manner, tempting God. But our Saints would never have discovered that they had gone beyond the bounds of moderation, had it not been for the watchful care of Providence.

Meanwhile our Hermits wished that Monte Senario might continue to be an inaccessible fortress, where they might live and die unknown and forgotten by the world. When they had first taken up their abode in that wild solitude, the difficulty and length of the road protected them from curious and importunate visitors. Since they had left Florence, they had scarcely been seen, and, nothing having occurred to draw attention to their movements, they were left unmolested to follow their vocation.

This tranquil state was not destined to be of long duration. The hopes of the pious Hermits were quickly dispelled. When they sometimes went out of their Hermitage, their pale and wasted looks, their poor and coarse garb, their modest and recollected demeanour, the holiness visibly impressed on their outward aspect, the humble office of mendicants so cheerfully fulfilled, spoke for them to all those who saw them pass by.

Soon the imagination of the susceptible Tuscans was captivated by all the circumstances of their extraordinary life. Their histories spread from mouth to mouth throughout the country. Everywhere their names were coupled with expressions of loving reverence, and, at last, they were, it may be said, canonized by popular acclamation.

In those ages of faith, the name of a Saint sufficed to draw together large numbers, eager to behold one on whom a brighter ray of the glory of Christ Our Lord was reflected—one who mirrored on earth a clearer view of His infinite perfection. Thus it was that in the neighbourhood of Monte Senario, and far around, many would have flocked to the dwelling of a single Saint: what, then, must have been the effect produced by the vicinity of seven?

But knowledge of the bare fact that they had Saints for neighbours did not satisfy the childlike simplicity of pious souls. They wished to see them, to hear them personally, and to feel the contact of their holiness. Little by little, pilgrims began to make their way to Monte Senario, and crowds followed, besieging the entrance of the Hermitage. The wilderness was no longer a solitary place; and the paths, hitherto untrodden, were now traversed by earnest throngs.

Then, as ever, mankind suffered from private sorrows, even when unafflicted by public calamities. It is the law of existence that we should never remain without suffering. Many who were troubled or oppressed sought the presence of the holy Hermits to lay down their burdens. Hither came those who were weary of life; members of torn and divided households; delicate and scrupulous consciences in search of strength, enlightenment, and consolation; persons broken in health and suffering from various diseases, seeking a cure ; profligates yearning to shake off the heavy yoke of sin ; devout and pious souls eager for instruction and edification ; even idlers who wanted to fill up a vacant hour of life.

Besides these sufferings and needs, which are not peculiar to any one period or any single country, Florence was oppressed by many troubles, which were the outgrowth of that turbulent age. With these the whole of Italy was likewise afflicted, and there was, therefore, good cause for the constant increase in the stream of visitors to Monte Senario. The humble Solitaries tried in vain to check this influx, so adverse to all their cherished plans ; but the distressing nature of many of the cases brought before them and their own tenderness of heart made the task well-nigh impossible. Then they resolved to submit to the inevitable, and, whilst endeavouring to secure as much retirement and regularity of life as was practicable, they gave up themselves with good-will to the service of the petitioners. They dispensed comfort, encouragement, counsel, and enlightenment to all in spiritual difficulties; they alleviated physical suffering ; often, by God's permission, they worked miraculous cures ; in a word, they dismissed no one without having poured the balm of consolation into his heart.

Among the many pilgrims, a certain number came with the hope of being received into the little Community ; but they were invariably refused. Although it cost the holy Hermits much to repulse souls impelled by the motions of divine grace towards the solitary life, they thought, in their humility, that in gathering others around them they would have been departing from their appointed mission.

In contemplating this new and unexpected state of affairs, we may well recall the words of the wise king : "The heart of man disposeth his way ; but the Lord must direct his steps" (Prov. xvi. 9). And this, which is true as regards the universal Providence of the Maker of all, is true also of the particular guidance which Mary, acting in His name, bestows upon her chosen children. We may ask what were now her designs concerning her Seven Servants. She had commanded them to flee from the world and to lead a solitary life, and now she allows it to be wholly disturbed. Whither, then, did she desire to lead them ? This was Our Lady's secret, which she was shortly about to disclose.

Meanwhile, those who had flocked to Monte Senario returned home, gladdened and edified by all that they had seen. Truly it seemed to them that a glimpse of heaven had been vouchsafed to them, and that they had been permitted to converse with angels in mortal form. None left that favoured spot without having received some special grace. Either their sufferings were assuaged, or they obtained patience to endure them. The pilgrims on their homeward way ceased not to bless and laud our Saints, and this inspired all who had not yet made their way to the Hermitage with an ardent desire to hasten thither. Thus the tide of pious visitants continued to flow on without any signs of decrease.

The holy Solitaries were at once alarmed and consoled by this invasion, which, however, they did not allow to alter their kind of life. In some industrious way, only known to Saints, they contrived to reconcile all their interior duties with their external calls. The task was a heavy one, nor could they refrain from frequent sighs and regrets, as they thought of the happy days of unbroken solitude, absolute silence, and perfect freedom, when they were able to realize their one desire, and to give themselves wholly to God and to His Blessed Mother. But to them the will of God was revealed in the daily events of their lives, and to do it gave them a far higher joy than any following of their own inclinations. Still there was a constant struggle to be maintained, and, at times, their way did not seem clear before them. This in itself became a source of keen suffering.

During the progress of these events, four years, from 1234 to 1237, passed away, and now the Cardinal Legate, Goffredo di Castiglione, was summoned to Florence on ecclesiastical business On hearing the story of the Seven Hermits, the illustrious prelate expressed a wish to visit them in their seclusion, in company with the Bishop of Florence. We may well believe that the Solitaries were deeply moved when they saw the representative of Christ's Vicar on earth and their beloved Bishop Ardingo standing together on their threshold. Their humility made them feel deeply so great a condescension, and they received the two ecclesiastics with profound respect mingled with childlike affection.

Cardinal Castiglione, a man to be reverenced both for his piety and for his learning, was most favourably impressed, after a strict examination, both by the Hermits and their work. So well satisfied was he that the chronicler Mati tells us: "He conceived a lively affection for the Rule of our Thebaid on Monte Asinaio" One point alone did not meet his approval, and on this he spoke strongly and plainly to the Seven. "Your mode of life," said he, "is too much like that of the wild creatures of the woods, so far as the care of the body is concerned. You treat yourselves in a manner bordering on barbarity; and you seem more desirous of dying to time than of living for eternity. Take heed: the enemy of souls ofttimes hides himself under the appearance of an angel of light. You run the risk of falling into the opposite sins of presumption and despair. Avoid, then, this snare by observing humbly and discreetly, over and above the commandments of God and of the Church, the three great precepts of poverty, the giving up of your own will, and the renunciation of earthly pleasures. Hear the counsels of your Superiors, remembering that obedience is better, in the sight of God, than sacrifice."

Less than this would have sufficed to secure the prompt obedience of our Hermits. The holy Seven hastened to request from their Bishop full instructions for the mode of life that they should prefer. They begged him to give them a Rule, to which they promised to conform as implicitly as though God Himself had spoken to them. Ardingo did not absolutely refuse compliance, but he told them that the matter was too important to be undertaken without special light from the Holy Spirit. He desired them, therefore, to pray earnestly for that intention: and, speaking with the most fatherly kindness, he entreated them not to persist in their determination to close their ranks against all applicants for admission. "Do not," he said, "discourage those souls who are drawn to consecrate themselves to God and Our Blessed Lady, in order the better to work out their salvation. Be generous, like the Apostles, and give freely of what you have freely received. Your mystical number of seven indicates, so it seems to me, fulness, expansion, increase. Although, at first, you may have shrunk from the idea of founding an Order, it is not permitted to you to continue in this determination, unless Mary, who called you, should so will. This problem is a difficult one, and it must be solved by her, and not by yourselves. If the ever Blessed Mother of God should desire you to receive new Brethren, you cannot refuse her. Pray, then, fervently, in order that you may arrive at a good decision."

The Seven Hermits were much impressed by these words, which from this moment dwelt in their minds and hearts. They promised him who was at once their superior, their father, and their friend, that they would do all in their power to conform themselves to his wishes.

The visit of the two prelates now drew to a close. They assured the Solitaries of their continued interest and protection, and they quitted Monte Senario highly edified by all that they had seen at the Hermitage.

Day by day Almighty God unfolded His designs, slowly but continuously. In the silence and solitude of Monte Senario He now began to reveal to His chosen ones somewhat of His intentions on their behalf. Mary, too, co-operated with motherly loving-kindness in a work so dear to her. The time was at hand when, all being in readiness, the Queen of Heaven was to speak the word, the light was to shine forth, and the mists of uncertainty were wholly to vanish.

CHAPTER III.

𝔄 time of 𝔄nxiety and ℘rayer—𝔐iracle of the 𝔙ine —𝔒ur 𝔏ady again appears to the 𝔖even.

(1239—13TH APRIL, 1240.)

THE visit of the Cardinal Legate and of the Bishop of Florence was an important event in the lives of our Hermits, causing them both intense joy and much anxiety. By degrees the joy subsided, but the anxiety remained. The Seven seemed to have reached a fresh stage, where they would soon have to leave the mode of life which they loved with their whole heart, and embrace another which they dreaded.

They could no longer blind themselves to the fact that their golden dream was about to vanish, and that they must shortly bid farewell to the purely eremitical life. The hope of giving their days to God alone, which had hitherto sustained them under all sufferings and sacrifices, was theirs no more ; and they no longer knew what to think or what to expect. They were like men rowing hard to reach the harbour, who find themselves baffled both by wind and tide, and think that it would be better to make no further effort, but to furl their sails and to ship their oars, leaving themselves to drift whither they would fain not go.

Whilst they still in imagination heard the words of the Cardinal Legate, as he exhorted them to moderate the severity of their penances, and those of the holy Bishop Ardingo, desiring them to open the ranks of their Community to all who felt called of God to belong to it, they were moved to make a generous sacrifice of their most cherished hopes. But again, when they withdrew into themselves, the irresistible longing for solitude seized them once more ; then in their humility they exaggerated to themselves their own infirmity, and, reflecting upon the secure refuge afforded by the eremitical life, they would gladly have entreated the prelates to leave them to follow their original vocation.

There is no more painful state of mind than this kind of moral perplexity, which rends the soul of the sufferer to its very centre. The life of our Seven Solitaries was now one prolonged torture. They felt, however, that it was their duty to fight against sadness and discouragement, and that, to this end, they must do violence in prayer to heaven, in order to obtain more abundant light. The prudence of this course was shown by the sequel.

Between seventy and eighty yards below the crest of the mountain, a rocky platform projected towards the south, thinly covered with earth, which the Hermits thought suitable for cultivation, and where they had accordingly planted a vine. Having done so, they took no further thought about it, till, on the third Sunday of Lent, February 27, 1229, they chanced to pass their rocky garden ; then great was their wonder on perceiving the strange transformation wrought thereon. The vine had put forth long shoots covered with leaves, and was bearing bunches of ripe grapes ; whilst all around the earth was decked with fresh springing grass and masses of flowers.

This premature productiveness filled the Hermits with astonishment, which quickly gave way to the desire of knowing how they were to interpret it ; for living as they did in constant communion with the Unseen, they doubted not but that this miracle had some connection with their present circumstances. But they were too self-distrustful to attempt to solve the enigma by themselves. As usual, Bonfilius Monaldi was called upon to decide what was best to be done ; and he at once despatched one of the Brethren to the Bishop of Florence, to whom the messenger was deputed to give an exact account of all that had taken place, and whose comments and commands he was to bear back to the Community.

The good Bishop of Florence was a man of great personal holiness, and was endowed with an extremely rare and elevated gift of prayer, by which he lived in most intimate union with God, from Whom he often received supernatural communications. For instance, some years previously, about the year 1229, when he had only recently been nominated to the See of Florence, a priest, celebrating without due care in the Church of St. Ambrose in that city, left a few drops of the consecrated wine unconsumed : when lo ! the outward appearance of wine was, seen no more within the chalice, but in its stead the Precious Blood. The Sacred Vessel was committed to the care of the Abbess Teida, Superioress of the monastery to which the Church of St. Ambrose was attached. The following night, as the Bishop of Florence lay asleep, he seemed to hear an awe-inspiring voice address him thus : "In poverty, O my Bishop, thou didst receive Me, and in poverty thou hast sent Me from thee ". Ardingo was startled by these words, and he at once caused a reliquary of gold and ivory, lined with purple silk, to be constructed, and within this the priceless treasure was enclosed.

When the holy Bishop heard of the miraculous vine of Monte Senario, he at once exclaimed that here was indeed an answer from heaven to the Hermits' prayers, and that it showed plainly that Almighty God desired their Community to grow and spread, even as the vine had stretched forth her branches laden with blossom and fruit. Before pronouncing definitely on the matter, however, he thought it well to take time for examination. He had recourse to prayer ; and, during the ensuing night, he received a communication from on high, which no longer allowed of any doubt.

The Bishop set out immediately for Monte Senario, and hastened to the spot where the marvellous vine could be seen by all. His soul was overwhelmed with gladness on beholding so incontestable a proof of the divine beneficence, and, calling together the Solitaries, he thus addressed them: "My sons, whom I have once again begotten in the Lord, hear what I am about to relate. I saw, in a vision, a vine from which sprang seven shoots, and from each of these shoots grew branches covered with leaves, blossoms, and fruits. The Blessed Mother of God appeared in dazzling beauty, and pointing to the vine, she commanded that it should be diligently cultivated, saying, 'My vineyard is before me . . . the vines in flower yield a sweet smell . . . let us see if the flowers be ready to bring forth fruit' (Cant.). If, now, you consider this vine which I beheld in my vision, and will then look upon the vine which has blossomed and borne fruit in this your hermitage, you will understand that, without doubt, it is the will of God that you should admit all those who so desire to draw water with joy out of the Saviour's fountains, whereat you yourselves are refreshed. O my dear Fathers, Holy Scripture rarely speaks of the vine, except in this sense, expressing the propagation and spreading of the Church, and the increase in the number of God's servants. And Our Lady desires to put the same thought into your hearts. Do not then resist the Holy Spirit of God. There will be great joy among the angels in heaven over all those chosen souls, who, weary of the false joys of the world, are led to consecrate themselves in your holy Community to the service of God and of His Blessed Mother, and who are admitted to drink the wine of heavenly consolation, pressed from the grapes of your mystic vine. We read that St. Ephrem, in his childhood, beheld a vine spring forth from his own mouth, the branches whereof were laden with grapes, and that the birds came in flocks to feed upon them. This was an augury of the great work for souls which this holy monk was to accomplish, by the persuasiveness of his eloquence and by the holiness of his life. Do you act, dear Fathers, likewise? Receive all who come to you, led by the Spirit of God, and may your Community, established under the auspices of Mary, develop rapidly, fostered by her maternal care, and contribute largely to the promotion of her glory. Make foundations wherever it may be practicable to do so, whether in cities or in country places, and cause the name and the loving kindness of the great Queen of Heaven to be known throughout the world. I shall be one with you in all things, provided you throw yourselves heartily into this plan. May the Holy Spirit guide you, and may the Father, with the only begotten Son, bless you, now and always!"

The fervent spirit of the holy prelate pervaded his every word, and thrilled the hearts of his hearers. Never previously had their souls been so deeply stirred by the thought of their vocation. At once their understandings were enlightened, and their wills were moved ; and that so powerfully as to cause them to accept generously the great sacrifice which was demanded of them. With a touching unanimity, they offered up the cherished dream of their lives, and they assured the Bishop that they were ready to adopt his views, and to take upon themselves the task assigned to them. Satisfied with this promise, Ardingo spoke a few words of congratulation and encouragement, and took leave of them, saying that they would shortly see him again.

The brief space of time, during which the Bishop had spoken as the mouthpiece of God and of His Most Holy Mother, and the Hermits had listened to his words and vowed obedience to them in the sincerity of their hearts, was, in reality. the turning-point in the lives of our Seven Saints. Until then they had been vowed to solitude, and wholly taken up with the care of their own salvation, shunning the world, and, above all, leading a life of penance. Now, all was to be changed. They were destined henceforth to lead a life of publicity, to have the charge of souls, to go forth into the world as Apostles. Hitherto, they had been devoted Servants of Mary interiorly ; now, they were also to be her Servants outwardly.

Although all shared in the responsibility incurred by this new mode of life, yet it fell most heavily on Bonfilius Monaldi, since he was expected to take the lead in all things, to arrange the ways and means, and to ponder well every step to be taken, before entering into consultation with his Brethren. The task was, indeed, a laborious one, and full of difficulty ; and he sought earnestly for help where it was most surely to be found—at the feet of Our Lord and of His dear Mother. He also frequently asked the advice of James of Poggibonzi, who, throughout, rendered most valuable assistance. The situation was especially trying just then ; for most important questions relative to the vocation of the Seven Saints had to be examined into and decided upon.

The discreet Superior considered that, under these circumstances, it was well to confer with his Brethren ; and no sooner had the Bishop of Florence taken leave of them, than he summoned them together, and spoke to them as follows : " My beloved Brothers, there is not, I am certain, one among you who is not desirous of complying with every wish of Our Blessed Mother. You are well aware, also, that without the divine concurrence, the best laid plans must fail. For some years past our one desire has been to serve God and Our dear Lady in solitude, poverty, and penance. You know how we fled from the city, and sought refuge in these mountain wilds. All has proved in vain. Heaven has decided otherwise, and has discovered us to the world. It has, then, become our duty to renounce our own inclinations, and to devote ourselves to the service of our neighbour. Neither must we any longer persist in our resolution of admitting no one to our Community. We must obey the will of God, we must carry out the designs of Our Blessed Lady, we must follow the advice of our Bishop. We enter upon this new course free from all motives of ambition, of self-interest, or of self-love. It is sufficient for us that we are doing what the spirit of obedience and piety dictates to us. It would have been rash to enter unadvisedly upon such a course ; but how encouraging is it to do so now that this great marvel has been vouchsafed to us. God has given us many blessings : how many more may we not look for, when we are striving to enlarge our Community under the auspices of our Mother Mary."

All concurred in the sentiments expressed by their Superior ; and it was decided that, in future, all suitable subjects who presented themselves at Monte Senario were to be admitted. There were, however, some necessary preliminaries to be arranged as to the foundations of the new religious Community, as to the name, the habit, and the Rule to be adopted ; and, also, as to the work to be undertaken. Several different types of Orders, both ancient and modern, were known to our Saints : upon which of these should they now model themselves ? It was impossible to proceed further until these matters had been settled. Both from the natural and from the supernatural point of view, it was essential that all should be clearly defined, before the seed was sown, from which they·hoped a great spiritual harvest would spring.

With one accord they insisted on the necessity of seeking for the guidance of the Holy Spirit by earnest prayer, at the same time consulting together and employing their best faculties on the subject. Prayer was to be their chief resource, and they resolved to besiege Our Lord and His Blessed Mother with supplications, that all things might be so disposed as to promote Their glory.

More than a year passed away, during which the Seven continued to discharge all their duties with unrelaxed fervour, whilst praying continually for light. Thus they entered upon the Holy Week of the year 1240. Having a presentiment, that, at this time, their dear Mother would make known to them her wishes, they resolved that the Paschal Feast should be preceded by a triduum of uninterrupted prayer.

The triduum had begun, and they had already spent the whole of Maundy Thursday in contemplating the great Mysteries commemorated on that day. With hearts full of grateful love, they had implored the spotless Lamb, offered perpetually as a Victim upon our altars, to obtain for them all of which they then stood in need. Then, as Good Friday dawned, they turned to the sorrowful remembrance of the Death and Passion of the Redeemer of the world. According to their custom, and following the promptings of their devotion, they mingled with these contemplations the unspeakable

Sorrows of Mary, the most perfect example of maternal love. Their souls overflowed with generous and loving compassion, as they dwelt alternately upon the Sufferings of the Son, and upon the Sorrows of the Mother. Perhaps, they may have lingered longest over the mental picture which each one drew of her whom they had chosen to be, after her Divine Son, the chief object of their reverence and devotion. Her inward martyrdom, endured with such loving resignation and self-forgetfulness, moved them intensely. To her and to her Jesus, they gave themselves for time and for eternity, imploring the King and Queen of Martyrs to point out the path ordained for them to tread, that so they might in all things act in concert with the Divine Will.

In the course of this Good Friday, which fell in that year on the 13th of April, Mary was pleased to bestow upon them the greatest favour which they had yet received at her hands, a grace which eclipsed all those which had preceded it. Night had already closed in, and the good Fathers, following the course of the Passion, had, like faithful children, accompanied the Blessed Virgin in spirit, as she trod her Way of Sorrows. From the foot of the Cross to the Sepulchre, from the Sepulchre to the house where Jesus no longer dwelt, they followed her footsteps, offering to her all the tenderest affection of their hearts for her consolation. Time passed unheeded, as these contemplations filled their minds, when they were, of a sudden, all rapt in one of those ecstasies which, whilst suspending the bodily powers, leave the faculties of the soul in complete freedom. It was then that Mary appeared to them in a glorious vision.

The Mother of God shone brighter than the sun, and the reflection of her perfect beatitude appeared in her countenance. In her hands she held a black habit. Her eyes rested with loving complacency upon her Servants A multitude of angels surrounded her, some bearing the different instruments of the Passion, others carrying black habits, one holding an open book, whilst another offered with one hand a scroll, on which appeared the title of Servants of Mary, surrounded by golden rays, and with the other a palm branch. The radiant host descended gradually from on high, thrilling the beholders with joyful awe. The Queen of Heaven reassured them, speaking as follows: "Behold me, the Mother of your God; I have yielded to the prayer which you have so often offered up to me. I have chosen you to be my first servants, and under this name you are to till my Son's Vineyard. Here, too, is the habit which I wish you to wear: its dark colour will recall the pangs which I suffered on this day, when I stood by the Cross of my only Son. You have already cast aside the gay and costly garb of worldlings, and you will, therefore, rejoice to wear these garments, which will outwardly recall the Sorrows I inwardly endured. Take also this Rule of St. Augustine, and may you, bearing the title of my Servants, obtain the palm of everlasting life."

Having thus spoken, Mary disappeared, and the vision vanished away.

It would be impossible to give an adequate idea of the effect produced upon the Seven by this heavenly apparition, which remained graven as a seal upon their hearts. Human language is too poor and weak to picture what transcends all powers of the imagination.

We are told that Our Lady appeared at the same time to the saintly Bishop of Florence, and made a similar communication to him, so that—on his being informed of the vision of Monte Senario —no hesitation whatever remained in his mind. Our Lady's plan was clearly defined, and she had spoken both to those who were to carry it out, and to him who was to sanction it.

By this supreme act of maternal loving-kindness, Our Blessed Lady completed what she had long designed, the foundation of the religious Community which she had chosen to be her own. From this time forth she may truly be styled the Mother, the Patroness, the Foundress of the Servite Order, for such she is, in all truth. It was she who gave it to the world ; it was from her that it derives its strength ; it was to her that it owes the elementary principles of its existence.

The Seven Saints, sons of Tuscany and of fair Florence, had now become the First Seven Servants of Mary. To them belong the honour and happiness of having received this appellation from her own lips. They were the first, but we shall find many following them in the course of the years to come, making them the Fathers of a race which is not destined to die out.

And Monte Senario might well now rejoice and be glad, like the mountains in the royal Psalmist's song, for not only had Seven great Saints chosen it for their dwelling-place, but Mary herself, their Mother and their Mistress, had descended upon its crest, there to inaugurate the cradle of the family of her Servants.

CHAPTER IV.

Our Lady's Cherished Plan.

IF Mary, in her marvellous benignity, had appeared to her Seven Servants simply for their spiritual consolation, the vision of the 13th of April, 1240, would have ever remained for them a most memorable occurrence. What more touching proof of her maternal tenderness could she have given than her appearing upon Monte

Senario, and revealing herself in celestial brightness, surrounded by glorious cohorts of angels, not to one alone of her children, but to all the Seven in a single vision?

But there was more in this great favour than could be comprehended at the first glance. Mary had not merely appeared to them, but she had deigned to tell them what she desired, and had herself traced the outline of the work which they were to carry out, so that she might truly be styled its Foundress. In this wondrous vision she unfolded her cherished plan, which she had long kept in view, and which, as she made known to them, was especially dear to her. In order to show what was this plan, we must give a brief sketch of the place which Our Lady fills in the divine scheme of Redemption, and, consequently, the homage which is due to her, and which she practically received at the period when our Seven Saints flourished.

We must go back far beyond the six thousand years of our epoch, and behold Almighty God in the bosom of His Eternal Beatitude. He was then contemplating that great design, in which His power and his love were to be so signally displayed. It was the wonderful scheme by which His only begotten Son was appointed the Medium of His boundless mercy towards the guilty human race.

But, by the particular disposition of His sovereign goodness, this scheme could only be carried out through the co-operation of a woman, of the Maiden Mother, who was to bear the Incarnate God. Her consent had to be asked, and she had to give it freely. Then, when she had spoken her fiat, the Great Mystery of the Incarnation was to be wrought, and the work of Redemption was to begin. Mary was the woman, the Virgin Mother, to whom this great office was to be entrusted. Chosen by God Himself, she was to be the instrument through which all these mighty things were to be accomplished. She was to be the Mother of her Creator, and by her means He was to enter the world clothed in mortal flesh.

To no creature could a higher office have been assigned than that which was allotted to Mary. The most astonishing graces and favours were, accordingly, to be lavished upon her who was thus raised to a dignity above that of all created beings. She was to be immaculate in her Conception, and free from even the slightest shadow of sin during her whole life. Grace was to be bestowed upon her without measure, and she was to attain the summit of all perfection. She was to wear the twofold crown of Motherhood and of Virginity. By an unheard-of privilege, she was not to remain in the darkness of the grave, but was to be borne bodily by angels to heaven, there to reign as Queen of the whole Universe. Moreover, she was to be so intimately associated with her Divine Son in His work, and was so efficaciously to co-operate therewith, as to be styled the Co-Redemptrix of Mankind. Without trenching on the office of Him Who is the One Only Redeemer, she was to promote and obtain the salvation of souls by the promptness of her co-operation, by the fervour of her prayers, and by the merit of her good works.

Such was the place occupied by Mary in the eternal plan of Almighty God. His plan was, in due season, carried out to the smallest detail, and the result was the masterpiece of grace and virtue—Mary, Mother of God, and our Mother. From the beginning the Church has published and taught the true doctrine concerning her, Councils have defended her prerogatives, and Doctors and Fathers have sounded her praises with all their powers of eloquence. In these words did St. Cyril of Alexandria, at the Council of Ephesus, in the year 431, express himself concerning the Blessed Virgin, speaking in the name of all the assembled Bishops, whose president he was:

"All hail to thee! Mary, Mother of God, most precious treasure of the whole world; by whom the Holy Trinity is worshipped and glorified; by whom the precious Cross is adored and celebrated; by whom Heaven triumphs, the Angels rejoice, the demons are put to flight; by whom that tempter the devil is overcome; by whom fallen man is again raised to Paradise; by whom all creation sunk in idolatry is brought once more to the knowledge of the truth; by whom holy baptism is vouchsafed to all believers; by whom the nations are brought to do penance. What more shall I say? By whom the Holy Son of God giveth light to them that sit in darkness and in the shadow of death; by whom the Prophets have spoken; by whom the Apostles have preached salvation to the world; by whom the dead are raised to life again; by whom kings reign! Who can give utterance to the praises of which Mary is worthy?"

In accordance with the pre-eminent position given by the Almighty to Mary in his plan, special homage was at once paid to Our Blessed Lady. The cultus of the Blessed Virgin may be said to date from the moment of her becoming the Mother of God and the Spouse of St. Joseph. The Word Incarnate and the Head of the Holy Family were the first two to do her homage. The lowly House of Nazareth was the first Sanctuary of this devotion. The Apostles, the Disciples of Our Lord, and the first Christians, followed the example of their Master during the lifetime and after the death of His Blessed Mother. When cruel persecutions broke out, they failed to check the advance of Christianity, to abolish the bloodless Sacrifice of the Altar, or to diminish the veneration of the Primitive Church for the Mother of God. The progress of the religion founded by the Son of Mary was made in silence and obscurity, and the Christians of the first ages were soon forced to take refuge in the catacombs; but there we still find touching evidences of their cultus of Mary, mingled with those of their adoration of the Divine Redeemer. Later, when the Church rose triumphant from the ground watered with the blood of Martyrs, the cultus of Mary was brought forth jubilantly into the full light of day. In many cities churches were dedicated to the Mother of God, such as the Cathedral at Ephesus, St. Mary Major at Rome, and at Constantinople St. Mary of the Blachernii. The practice of invoking her spread and became general ; her pictures were to be found everywhere. Soon, days were appointed for the celebration of her principal Mysteries, particularly those of her Nativity, of her Annunciation, of her Purification, and of her Assumption. Since that time, the cultus of Mary has formed an integral part of the divine system established by Our Lord Jesus Christ for the salvation and the happiness of mankind. More and more, as the ages rolled on, did it increase in fervour, and more inseparably was it blended with the very existence of the Church. It may be said, indeed, to have become the most distinctive mark of those who truly believe in the Incarnation. In all lands the great body of the faithful, the clergy, and the religious of all Orders, emulated each other in zealously offering to Mary the homage due to her. That homage was so far surpassing all which was rendered to the Saints, as to bear a special title of its own—that of hyperdulia, expressive of that higher veneration which we owe to her, the Queen of Saints.

In the Middle Ages, this cultus attained its full development ; and the religious writers of that period give full vent to their enthusiasm for the devotion to Our Blessed Lady, whilst carefully and clearly showing its solid foundation.

Among these, the illustrious St. Bernard is especially to be noted. In the middle of the twelfth century, about fifty years before the birth of our Seven Saints, this great Doctor exalted Mary in terms of the most touching eloquence, and he thus magnificently pictured the interior devotion of pious souls towards her.

"The name of Mary," he says in one of his discourses, " signifies Star of the Sea. This interpretation suits admirably with the title of the Virgin Mother : for she is with just reason compared to a star. For, as the Star gives forth light without losing any of its lustre, so did the Blessed Virgin bring forth her Divine Son without loss of her peculiar privilege. As the ray shooting from the Star deprives it not of the smallest particle of its brightness, so the birth of the Son in no wise interfered with the perfect integrity of the Virgin. She is the glorious Star coming forth out of Jacob, which enlightens the whole universe, which shines brightly in the highest heavens, whilst its rays penetrate even to the depths of hell ; which pours abroad light and warmth into souls ; and thus promotes the growth of virtue and destroys sin. She is that wondrous Star which, by the divine command, arose from out that boundless ocean over which she sheds the brightness of her merits and the illumination of her example.

" O man, whosoever you may be, thrown into the torrent of the world, become the sport of angry waves on a stormy sea, instead of treading on the solid earth ; if you wish to escape shipwreck, turn your eyes towards Mary. If temptations, like so many fierce winds, should rise around you ; if you find yourself in danger of perishing, look up to that Star, call upon Mary. Should anger, or avarice, or passion place your bark in peril, look up to Mary. If the horror, occasioned by the enormity of your sins, should bring trouble to your soul ; if, terrified by the judgments of the Almighty, sorrow should take possession of your heart, and you should find yourself drifting into the gulf of despair, think on Mary. In all dangers, difficulties, and doubts, think on Mary, invoke Mary, let her name be ever on your lips ; and, while beseeching the help of her prayers, seek again edification from her example. Follow her, and you will never go astray. Pray to her, and you will not be disappointed. Upheld by her, you will never fall. As long as she protects you, you need have no fear. If she leads you, the road will become easy to your feet. If only she be with you, you will safely reach the port for which you are bound. Thus will you experience for yourself with how great reason are we expressly told that the Virgin was called Mary."

We thus see that the homage rendered to Mary in the Middle Ages corresponded, in a most beautiful manner, with the divine idea. But, among all those who earnestly strove to promulgate it, the Religious Orders held the foremost place. And it is truly edifying to note the pious ingenuity with which they endeavoured to express the filial affection which filled their hearts.

But, notwithstanding the zeal displayed both by devout Christians in the world, and by Religious Communities, Our Blessed Lady desired to have an Order more especially her own than any of those hitherto founded had been. This project was dear to her heart, and she willed that it should be carried into effect. Does it seem over-bold in us to ascribe this project to the Mother of God, when she had already so many faithful Servants, and received such great and perfect homage from all, and more particularly from the Religious Orders ? Not so. The idea is in itself most just and reasonable. The place allotted by Almighty God to Mary in His divine plan for the salvation of mankind called for the establishment of a new Order to be wholly and entirely hers : the homage rendered to the Mother of God by the Universal Church made it opportune that an Institute should be called into existence, in order to have her service for its exclusive mission.

CHAPTER V.

Our Lady's Order.

A DESIGN which harmonized so beautifully with the plan of Almighty God, and with the homage due to Mary, although it may have appeared at the first glance to be a work of supererogation, was not so in reality. On the contrary, it came into being at the most opportune moment, at a time of great spiritual expansiveness, and it came to supply a want. It seems that it was called forth to blend together all the various characteristics which made the other Religious Orders then existing belong to Mary and be her Servants. This fact stands out distinctly in the religious history of that period. In order to place it more vividly before our readers, we will briefly refer to the Orders previously established, and point out the particular links which united them to Our Blessed Lady.

First, in order of time, come the monks of St. Basil and those of St. Antony, differing, indeed, in their origin, but both living under the Rule compiled by the great Bishop of Cesarea. These were the first pioneers by whom the road was opened, which was to be trodden by so many in the practice of religious life and the observance of monastic rule. The fundamental principle upon which these Orders were built, in the third and fourth centuries, was the renunciation of the world, self-abnegation, obedience, and the unreserved offering by the individual of himself to God. These monks engaged themselves by vow to observe perfect purity of life, to be obedient to the least sign, and to renounce wholly their own will. They were employed solely in manual labour, in prayer, and in penance. Whether isolated in hermitages or gathered together in monasteries, all were bound to devote their entire energies to the attainment of that perfection which is realized alone in Our Lord Jesus Christ.

All the members of the religious family of St. Basil were animated by the spirit of their holy Patriarch, who bore to Our Blessed Lady a love and a veneration which he shared with his brother St. Gregory of Nyssa, and which he bequeathed as a legacy to the many Communities of men and women that sprang into existence throughout the East, during his lifetime and after his death.

Among his disciples St. Basil numbered both Popes and Bishops, whose writings are mines of theological science concerning the Blessed Virgin, Mother of God, and wherein are likewise to be found most glorious lyric outbursts in her praise. We need only name St. Cyril of Jerusalem, St. Gregory Nazianzen, St. Epiphanius, St. John Chrysostom, St. Cyril of Alexandria, St. Ephrem, in fact, an army of illustrious writers, in whose works the glories of Mary are celebrated with all the richness of Eastern eloquence. When we peruse these Fathers, we feel that the source of their inspiration was the love which filled their hearts for Mary ; we feel that to these exalted spirits, and to every subject of St. Basil's Rule, she was the centre of their being and the life of their life.

Later, a famous member of the Order, St. John Damascene, who, like so many of his Brethren, shed his blood in defence of the veneration of images, especially those of the Blessed Virgin, was favoured by having his devotion to her rewarded by a striking miracle. The iconoclast, John the Isaurian, had condemned him, as a punishment for his writings on this subject, to lose his right hand. The valiant Doctor had just undergone the cruel sentence, when, turning towards a picture of Our Blessed Lady, he recommended himself to his powerful Protectress for whose cause he had endured this suffering. Hardly was his prayer ended when his hand was restored, whole and uninjured, being reunited to the arm as before.

The followers of St. Augustine, whether belonging to the Canons Regular, the Premonstratensians, the Hermits of St. Augustine, or to any other branch of the Order, were ever worthy of their illustrious Father, who had so eloquently written of the Blessed Virgin ; and, in their diversity, they had one common point of resemblance, viz., their love for the Most Clement Mother of men.

To St. Norbert, the founder of one of the most flourishing branches of the Augustinian Order, was vouchsafed an apparition of Our Lady herself, who, at Prémontré, in the Chapel of St. John the Baptist, showed him the habit in which the Religious living under his direction were to be clothed. In Friesland, Blessed Frederick, another member of the Order, had so great a devotion to the Most Holy Virgin that he obtained, through her prayers, the restoration to life of a child that had died unbaptized.

The Hermits of St. Augustine loved to have the image of her who was blessed among women engraved on their official seals, the design of which, as we read in the memorials of the Order, represented an Augustinian Religious kneeling at the feet of Mary, whose benignant gaze was fixed upon him. It would occupy too much space to particularize all the proofs of devotion to Our Lady given by this Order ; all the labours which it has undertaken to promulgate that devotion among the nations ; and all the favours which it has, in consequence, obtained from its loved and loving Mother.

The great Benedictine Order, the numerous branches of which had spread throughout the civilized world, propagated in every region the cultus of Mary, the Mother of God. All the great works of architecture which we owe to the indefatigable industry of these monks bear traces of their devotion to her. But the devotion which found a visible outlet in these triumphs of their skill was rooted in their hearts, and sedulously tended by them, as one of their greatest aids to perfection and one of their chief consolations. Consequently, at an early period, they adopted the pious custom, practised by so many Orders, of reciting, in choir, the Little Office of Our Lady. Indeed, many authors of weight attribute to them the compilation of that Office.

The Cistercians had special cause to be devout to the Virgin Mother, since, at the time of their foundation, they had received extraordinary favours from her. St. Alberic having, in conjunction with the Blessed Robert and Stephen, founded the Order of Citeaux under the patronage and name of Mary, Our Lady rewarded him by bestowing on him the white habit which was to be worn by the Community. This fact, so glorious for the Order, made it incumbent on the brotherhood to show their gratitude towards their Blessed Patroness. Hence, from the very beginning, the Cistercians were especially devout to Our Lady, and they have remained ever faithful to her. The tradition of the Order, which has become a rule, had decreed that their monastic churches should be dedicated to her, and should bear one of her titles. Besides the regular recitation of the Little Office, they made a commemoration of her at the conclusion of the Hours of the Great Office. The Order rejoiced, too, to recognize in Our Lady its chief Patroness and its especial Protectress, and to proclaim that on her it depended, that to her it belonged, and that it existed but to carry out her commands. Filled with this spirit, Citeaux became the nursing mother of many Saints, all fervently devout to the Blessed Virgin, among whom shone with the highest lustre the great Abbot of Clairvaux, St. Bernard, who, amidst the Fathers of the Latin Church, is fittingly distinguished by the title of Our Lady's Doctor, so sublime and so comprehensive is all that he has written of her.

When St. Bruno and his comrades were, in the year 1084, drawn to the wild solitudes of the Chartreuse, by that rigorously penitential spirit which had formerly prompted St. John the Baptist, their hearts were already the home of that tender filial love of Mary which was to characterize their Order. Thus, from the beginning, the building of their first sanctuary was sanctified by an act of devotion towards her. They consecrated to her the spot where they were to offer their praises and prayers, in order that she, hearing them, might present them before the throne of the Most High. This devotional spirit did not diminish, but rather increased, as time went on, in an Order so vigorously constituted that it has never relaxed from its first fervour. It was their devotion to the Queen of Heaven which contributed in a great measure to maintain that high standard of perfection, which contrasted so favourably with other institutions, whose relaxation in fervour caused a slow decline, and

7

made a reformation necessary. We find that, in the thirteenth century, the Carthusian Order, in its maturity, as formerly in its cradle, was one of the Orders most closely devoted to the Queen of Saints.

Devotion to the Blessed Virgin also characterized the Military Orders which arose, in the Middle Ages, for the purpose of freeing the Holy Places from the dominion of the followers of Mahomet. To the stern vocation which called them to be shedders of blood, if needful, for the Faith, they united the pious practices inspired by the love of Mary *inter omnes mitis*. The Knights of St. John of Jerusalem, we are told, dedicated to her the first church that they built for themselves, and they made it a rule to recite her Office daily.

The Carmelites, or Brothers of Our Lady of Mount Carmel, were founded, as their traditions affirm, by the Prophet Elias himself, for the purpose of leading a life of solitude and penance. One day the great prophet, absorbed in prayer in the seclusion of Mount Carmel, is said to have been shown a vision of the Spotless Virgin, who was to be the Mother of the Redeemer. and, from that time forward, his disciples whom he gathered round him, and their successors, held in profound veneration the Maiden destined to this glorious office. When Our Lord came on earth, these pious Anchorites enrolled themselves among His followers, and after the descent of the Holy Spirit, when the Apostles began to preach the Gospel, they are believed to have held personal communication with Our Blessed Lady, to whom their fathers had rendered anticipatory honour in their solitude, nine centuries before her birth. In token of their reverence for the Mother of the Messiah, they built a chapel dedicated to her on Carmel itself And, from age to age, they there offered to her their homage, until, in the year 1209, they were consolidated into a distinct Religious Order. Some time afterwards, Mary gave a proof of her maternal affection for the Carmelites by appearing to one of their number, St. Simon Stock, on the well-known occasion when the Confraternity of the Brown Scapular was established.

In the army of St Dominic, devotion to Our Lady was a constant watchword, and a most potent weapon, which their leader himself wielded, and taught them to use In a memorable conjuncture, he had instituted the holy Rosary, armed with which, he had overcome the most formidable obstacles, and broken down the obstinacy of the Albigenses, who had wandered from the true faith into the errors of Manicheeism. The Rosary, transmitted by the great Saint to his spiritual children, has ever remained the characteristic mark of the devotion of the Order to the Mother of God.

The sons of St. Francis yielded to none in their attachment to Mary, the purest of creatures. Their holy Founder had been one of her favoured children. To him was permitted the privilege of conversing with her familiarly; and, through her as intermediary, he obtained from Our Lord the wonderful Indulgence of the Portiuncula. The Order founded by him held in constant remembrance the favours received from his powerful Patroness, who was honoured by them as their Mother; and they already showed that special devotion to her Immaculate Conception to which all the branches of the Franciscan family have ever remained constant.

The Order of Our Lady of Mercy owed its origin directly to the Mother of God: all the members, therefore, were especially devout to her. St. Peter Nolasco, who had been called by Mary to institute this Order for the redemption of captives, communicated to his Brethren the love with which his own heart was filled for the Comfortress of the Afflicted: and, in accordance with his desire, a special festival was celebrated yearly in commemoration of the thrice-repeated apparition of Mary, to command the foundation of the new Institute.

Thus we see how universal was the devotion to Our Lady among the principal Religious Orders at the beginning of the thirteenth century. An equal degree of loving zeal distinguished the Orders of secondary importance, and all united to form a vast court, in the midst of which the enthroned Queen of Heaven received the homage of the succeeding generations of holy men and women who peopled the monasteries and convents throughout the world. These institutions formed so many schools, where the nations were taught to appreciate the virtues of the sinless Virgin, and to love her whom God so loved as to choose her for His own Mother

But, although there existed so close a connection between Our Blessed Lady and the Religious Orders, yet the greater number of these either bore the name of the Saint, their Founder, or of the place where they had first been instituted, thus clearly indicating that the cultus of Mary was not the chief object of their foundation, nor their principal employment. Each of these Orders had a special and a general aim of a different nature; and, although this cultus of Our Lady mingled, and influenced, and crowned every undertaking, it was still subordinate to the mission peculiar to each respective Institute. The Monks of St. Basil, the Religious of St. Augustine, the children of St. Benedict, all severally aimed at uniting the practice of perfection with the ministry of souls. The Cistercians and the Carthusians led a life of penance. The Military Orders were constituted for the defence of the Holy Places and of the Catholic Faith. The Carmelites gave themselves to seclusion, to penance, and to prayer. The sons of St. Dominic and of St. Francis sought their own salvation and that of their neighbour by word and work. And the Order of Mercy was devoted to the redemption of captives.

Thus, when we survey the Orders already existing, when we study their characteristics and the various objects for which they had been established, we see that there was room for a new Institute, which should owe its being to Our Blessed Lady, which should be her own inspiration and her own foundation, which she herself should train, and which should in all things seek to promote her glory.

Now this design, which we can see to be just and reasonable, was already planned and resolved upon by the Blessed Mother of God. Her love for the existing Orders, which emulated each other in loyalty to her, was in no wise diminished; yet she wished to possess an Institute to which she should be more intimately related than she was to these, and which should be more closely devoted to her than were the others. This Institute was to be hers by its very name, by its special vocation, by the whole tenor of its extistence. It was to serve her with its whole heart and strength. Its members were to rejoice in knowing themselves to be her cherished children; but they were to prefer before all things to be called her Servants, since that title implied that they were bound to work, to suffer, to deny themselves, for this great Queen, and also to have this thought constantly before them in their life of prayer and struggle. Their Order was to give itself utterly to her service, that so it might the more efficaciously manifest its devotion to her Son, the King of kings, the Lord and Master of all things, the Redeemer and only Mediator of mankind.

This Order was to publish everywhere the glories, the greatness, the prerogatives of the incomparable Mother of God, such being its duty, its mission, and the reason for which it was called into existence. And this Order was that which was actually founded by the Blessed Virgin herself, when in her Apparition she gave to it its name, its habit, and its Rule; this Order was the Order of the Servants of Mary or Servites.

CHAPTER VI.

The Name, Object, Characteristic Devotion, and Habit of the Order.

FROM the date of the Apparition of 1240, the existence of the Order of the Servants of Mary was an accomplished fact. But, to avoid any misapprehension on that head, Our Lady had taken care, by a few brief and simple words and actions, to regulate all that was essential for the constitution of the Order she had in view. A Religious Order must bear a name by which it may be publicly known, have an object to which all its energies are devoted, a special devotion which marks its spiritual life, a habit by which it is outwardly recognized, a Rule which regulates its life, and, lastly, an assurance that it will produce fruits of sanctity. All these requisites were supplied, when Mary vouchsafed to appear on that memorable day, 13th of April, 1240.

By the name which she bestowed on the first members of her Order, and all the attendant circumstances of her Apparition, she sufficiently expressed the aim which she desired them to pursue. The special characteristics of the Order were told to them in the most explicit terms. She held the habit in her hands, and mystically clothed them in it: there could be no doubt, therefore, upon that point. The beholders saw the Rule placed by Mary's side, and heard her proclaim it the Rule of their Institute: and, to crown all, the Mother of God, by holding out to them the palm of victory, gave an unmistakable proof of the fruitful holiness of the Order. Nothing, then, was wanting in the demonstration: Our Lady's plan and intentions were by this revelation shown completely and with the fulness of evidence

Long since, our Seven Saints had professed themselves Mary's Servants, and had chosen the service of the Queen of Heaven for their portion. To this had they felt called from their earliest youth ; and they had gladly suffered themselves to be severally drawn onward by this sweet magnetism, before they had met with, or become known to, one another. Subsequently, when they were enrolled in the Confraternity of the Laudesi, and united by the closest bonds of friendship, this devotion grew and strengthened till it became the leading characteristic of their spiritual lives. The summons which they heard from Mary's lips, on the 15th of August, 1233, made the desire of serving their Queen and Mistress their unceasing aspiration. The early days of their sojourn in the mountain solitude permitted them fully to realize their dream of spending their existence at her feet. The acclamations with which they were hailed by innocent babes made their vocation most dear to them. Finally, all was consecrated by the voice of Our Lady herself, when she bestowed their very name upon them on the 13th of April, 1240. Henceforward, among themselves, and by the world at large, they were to be known as the *Servants of Mary.* None could alter the title chosen for them by the Mother of God, which, coming from her, was more treasured than any rank that earthly monarchs could confer.

The name of Servants of Mary was prized also, because it signified that our Seven Founders and their spiritual descendants were to form, as it were, part of the household of the Queen of Heaven, with whom they would thus be in constant communication. They were to be, in a manner, attached to her person, to follow her everywhere, to be ever ready to obey her commands. None could approach her more closely than they, none could more uninterruptedly bask in the sunshine of her presence.

Simple as was the name, it bore a lofty meaning, and it expressed with the utmost precision the vocation of those who bore it. It showed, also, that this vocation was an active and thoroughly practical one. In one sense, it was a humble and lowly vocation; but, in another, it was a great and glorious one; for their service was to be like that of those who surround sovereign princes, and are appointed to watch over their dearest interests.

Bearing, then, this name, and called upon, as they were called, to exercise the functions appertaining to it, they were bound to discharge all the duties of faithful Servants to their Mistress, to whom they owed honour, respect, and obedience. Their duty it was to recognize more fully than others the incomparable dignity of Mary, her high prerogatives, her wondrous graces. To them the slightest intimation of her wishes was to be a command instantly executed. Her interests were to be their own, to be promoted by their strenuous efforts · and Mary's interests include all which relate to her glory, such as knowledge of her greatness, attachment to her person, imitation of her virtues, and the propagation of her cultus. Like good servants, they were to apply themselves to these various works, as though prompted by self-interest alone. They were not to be satisfied with bearing so honourable a name, but they were to labour hard to be worthy of it. And, in return for all that they did and suffered in her service, they were to count themselves overpaid by being allowed to remain in it, and to draw from their toils on earth the sure hope of belonging to her in heaven.

The title of Servants was the more beautiful, as it crowned the two other appellations of Children and Friends, and added a charm to both. A child is bound to honour his parents, to make their interests his own, to sacrifice himself for them ; otherwise, his sonship is merely nominal—love without sacrifice being but a poor and barren love. A friend must be ready to suffer, if needful, for his friend. Friendship, which does not include service, is undeserving the name : to speak of it as friendship is a profanation of the word. Now Mary chose for her Servants those who were already her cherished Children and her trusted Friends Therefore, as we have said, in giving them the title of her Servants, she ratified their other claims to her regard, and, by mingling the duties belonging to each relationship, she added to the beauty and dignity of all. Our Seven Saints had, therefore, good reason to consider the name they had received as the most glorious that could be borne by themselves, or transmitted by them to their successors.

The object which the Order was to keep constantly in view was clearly defined in this name, which showed that the aim proposed was a particular, not a general, aim. Undoubtedly, the object common to all Orders was to be theirs also. They were to serve God, and seek their own perfection, by the practice of the Evangelical

Counsels, and the observance of the three vows. But the particular aim was to be one belonging to the Order of the Servants of Mary alone, and was to consist in realizing the ideal which that name implies.

The true Servant of Mary was, therefore, to spend his life in constant endeavouring to realize this ideal, and to meet death with her name on his lips and her love in his heart, leaving gladly this world, where he had laboured for her, and looking to dwell with her for all eternity in heaven.

Such was the name conferred by Mary on her Order ; such was the aim which she proposed to it ; and both were beautiful and attractive as herself. We cannot wonder that, when they became known, many souls were won by them, and were solicitous to be called by that name and to embrace that vocation.

But Our Lady desired to attach this Order, so absolutely her own, yet more closely to her service, by pointing out to them one department of that Service to which she willed them more especially to devote themselves. We must now explain what was this central point of Mary's design, a point most important, whether we regard it in itself, or, as it was, in the estimation of the Heavenly Foundress.

It is needless to enter upon a theological disquisition to prove that Our Lady was associated with her Divine Son, in all that He suffered, and that her life was one long martyrdom, ending only with her last sigh. This truth must strike all, as being a necessary consequence of the great scheme devised by Almighty God for the Redemption of mankind ; the Mother's destiny was inseparable from that of the Son ; and her sufferings and humiliations co-operated with those of Jesus in reparation for the sins of men. She was the Sorrowful Mother, as He was the Man of Sorrows.

The groundwork of this doctrine is to be found in the Holy Gospels : all the Mysteries therein recorded prove how indissolubly Jesus and Mary, His Mother, were united throughout the Great Act of Redemption. The Doctors of the Church clearly discerned this ; and we find the idea pervading all their commentaries on the Sacred Writings. As Mary had her share in the glory and greatness of her Divine Son, so had she likewise her portion of His sorrows and His reproaches. To her is due, after Him, our deepest homage, since, next to Him, she has the highest place in heaven. She was, indeed, full of grace, but not less was she full of grief, during her earthly career.

When Our Divine Redeemer ascended in triumph to heaven, bearing with Him the marks of His Five Sacred Wounds for a perpetual memorial of His bitter Passion, in the sight of His Father, of the Angels, and of the elect, these wounds pleaded, and continue still to plead, for mercy, to Him Who is Infinite Justice. Thus man is redeemed from age to age, and the inexhaustible streams of the

Saviour's pity flow endlessly over guilty souls. And so, when Mary, on the triumphal day of her Assumption, was enthroned as Queen of Heaven, her heart retained the deep and glowing impress of the pangs which had rent it, and of the griefs which had weighed it down ; and the Most Holy Trinity and the courts of heaven rejoice in contemplating this sorrow-pierced heart, from which wells forth so copious a fountain of graces for the whole human race.

The Church Militant, always acting in unison with the Church Triumphant, from the first, has had set before her the Passion and Death of Our Crucified Lord as the great object of her faith, the most solid grounds of her hope, and the chief end of her charity. This is the watchword which rings out through all St. Paul's preaching, and which all faithful ministers of the Church have echoed, as century after century has passed away, and the Cross of Christ, placed on high in our sanctuaries, shows that the divine worship, offered at its foot, is permeated by the thought of the dogma of which that Cross is the outward symbol. Neither has the Church forgotten that, next to Jesus, the chief place, in this fundamental mystery, belongs to Mary.

Accordingly, from a very early period, the Transfixion of Our Lady has been honoured ; and, on the very spot where the Passion and Death of Our Lord took place, at Jerusalem, on the Mount of Calvary, the cultus of Our Lady's Sorrows was inaugurated. When the Christian Faith finally triumphed over Paganism, this devotion received a fresh impulse from the piety of St. Helena, the Mother of Constantine, who built a church, dedicated to "Our Lady of Anguish". From thenceforward it spread and developed in the bosom of the Church, although the scantiness of historic records makes it difficult for us to trace all its steps. But, in the Middle Ages, when the eyes and hearts of the faithful were lovingly turned towards the Holy Places, the mysteries of the Passion of Christ, and, by a natural concomitance, those of Mary's Transfixion, were the favourite devotions of all Christian souls. The Crusades increased this feeling, especially the first of these expeditions, which placed Jerusalem in the power of the Crusaders for the space of eighty years. From this time we find everywhere Our Lady represented as the Mother standing at the foot of the Cross, or as the Mother receiving the dead Body of her Son in her arms, or weeping over Him as He is laid in the sepulchre. All Christian people, in short, were passionately devoted to the Pitiful Virgin, the Sorrowful Mother. At length Fra Jacopone da Todi gathered up all the sweetest blossoms of this touching devotion, and bound them in an immortal garland, in his *Stabat Mater dolorosa*, which the Church has incorporated into her Office, and which we never cease to hear, recite, or meditate upon.

From her throne in heaven Mary contemplated all these pious

souls, intent on honouring her Sorrows, and rejoiced as she beheld them. She could not but feel a personal satisfaction in a devotion to what had been so intimate a part of her existence, and the recollection of which was so indelibly impressed upon her heart. Her satisfaction was the more intense, because she saw how great a source of grace to men this devotion would prove. What could, in fact, more efficaciously inspire all those who practised it with patience, under the trials of their state of life, with confidence in their tender Mother, with a desire of imitating her virtues, and with a dread of all that could displease her? It was also eminently calculated to promote the glory of her Divine Son, because one most certain fruit of meditation on her Sorrows is to show forth His Mercies, and to make us love Him in the Mysteries of His Passion and Death, these overwhelming tokens of the love for man, with which His heart is filled.

We may even suppose that Our Lady desired to prevent the possibility of her trials and sufferings fading from the remembrance of men ; for, undoubtedly, there is a natural tendency in human nature towards joyful rather than towards sad recollections. When we fix our minds on the Blessed Mother of God, we prefer meditating on her Joys and Glories to recalling her Sorrows. A devotion which places before us thoughts of tears and afflictions would soon wither away, unless it had a strong supernatural basis. This would have evidently been the case for the devotion to the Passion of Our Lord, or to His Mother's Sorrows.

The Blessed Virgin, then, designed to give her appointed Servants who were already devoted to her interests the special duty of honouring her Sorrows, of constantly wearing the outward tokens of their charge, and of expounding it to the world at large. And, on the 13th of April, 1240, on which day, in that year, Good Friday fell, and consequently on the anniversary of the day on which she had sounded the depths of sorrow, she put into execution this part of her plan. She had only spoken briefly of the general vocation of her Servants, because they already understood well its obligations and its spirit, and, for some years past, they had practised them in great perfection. But, as regarded the special point of devotion to her Sorrows, she spoke with much minuteness of detail. Holding in her hands the black habit which she wished them to wear, she said : " Behold the habit with which I desire you to be clothed, the sombre colour being emblematic of the grief which I felt on this day, when my Beloved Son died upon the Cross. You have not cared for the gay and glittering garb of this world, and, therefore, you will gladly wear this habit, which will recall to you outwardly the Sorrow which I inwardly endured." Thus did Our Blessed Lady, at one and the same time, confer upon them their distinctive character, and invest them with the religious habit which typified it.

This special mission of the Servants of Mary imposed on them the obligation of exploring the little known region of the sufferings of their Mistress, that so it might become familiar to them from end to end. On these sufferings they were to feed in meditation, and the secret thereof they were to reveal to the faithful. The devotion to these sufferings was to be held in high honour among them, for to keep this alive was to be their function in the Church of God : it was to be their task to preserve it intact, free from the seeds of decay, which so quickly begin to spring up in all human enterprizes. They could never for a moment forget their calling, since their habit, which Our Blessed Lady had deigned to hold in her own hands, and to invest them with herself, brought it perpetually to their minds.

There was nothing absolutely new in the shape of the habit destined to be henceforward worn by the Servants of Mary. It was the primitive religious garb, so admirably combining all that is needed for health, convenience, and modesty. The principal garment was the ample and simply cut tunic, reaching from the throat to the feet, and girt with a leather belt round the waist. Over this was worn the scapular, composed of two long strips of stuff falling in front and behind. This scapular had the gift of protecting and inspiring purity of heart in the wearer of either sex ; and therefore, Mary, the Most Pure Virgin, chose it to be the distinctive mark of her Children and her Servants. Lastly, a large cloak, with a hood, completed the habit, which bore a character of religious dignity. It resembled the dress of several other Orders, either in colour or shape, but, as a whole, it had a type of its own, and it has ever remained exclusively the habit of the Servants of Mary.

By this habit, those whom Our Lady had called especially to serve her were to be known to the world, and so to be distinguished from other Orders. To its wearer it was to be an honour, a memorial, and a shield : an honour, because it was the livery of their Queen ; a memorial, because it recalled to them what she expected from them ; and a shield, because so long as it covered faithful hearts, it would keep their lives spotless.

This habit, therefore, and the office of which it is symbolical, were two inestimable gifts bestowed by Mary's bounty upon our Seven Saints, and added to the name which she had already bestowed on them, and the aim which she had placed before them, these favours displayed, in a yet more brilliant light, the benefits implied in her Apparition. They formed an additional stone in the building up of the Order, and they manifested distinctly a fresh aspect of Our Lady's design. The Rule appointed for the new Order will fully unfold that design, and will show with what wisdom all the constituent parts have been prepared and harmonized by the celestial Foundress.

CHAPTER VII.

Rule of the Order.—By whom originated.—Provisions of the Rule.

Our Blessed Lady in her Apparition gave also to her Order a Rule. At this period the essence of Religious Life was clearly defined Papal Bulls and theological writings alike showed a perfect comprehension of it, whilst the ancient and modern Orders continually demonstrated it in practice ; and it was soon to be formulated in Raymund of Pennafort's celebrated Collections of Canon Law, and in the stupendous works of the Scholastics   But, if the teaching as to the essentials of the Religious Life had been always one and the same, such were not its particular forms and developments, which were many and various , and it was the Rule which made the chief difference between one Order and another.

Several Rules flourished at the period of which we are now speaking. Some were of considerable antiquity, as the Rules of St. Basil, St Augustine, and St. Benedict   Others were more recent, and had been supernaturally inspired, like those of St Bruno and St. Francis, for their Religious families.   Other Orders, as the Cistercians, the Camaldolesi, the Religious of Vallombrosa, the Premonstratensians, the Carmelites, and the Dominicans, followed one of the old Rules, either that of St. Benedict or of St. Augustine, to which they added divers regulations concerning the discipline and organization of their body, called the Constitutions.   The first Rules had been chiefly compiled for the direction of monks living inclosed, and devoting themselves more to contemplation, study, and manual labour than to the ministry of souls.   The Rule of St. Bruno was exclusively concerned with the eremitical life.   That of St. Francis took an entirely new departure : it inaugurated a religious body, as much occupied about the salvation of others as about that of its own members, preaching penance, and teaching of the divine precepts, more by example than by words.   The new Orders which had adopted the old Rules had, by means of their Constitutions, considerably modified the ancient monastic life, by making it include the ministry of souls.   Among those who took this line were the Franciscans, the Dominicans, Carmelites, and Augustinians   But all these Rules, whatever was their origin, bore the impress of sanctity ; they were approved of by the Church, and, for the greater number, added to these qualities the guarantee of a long and fruitful experience.

Undoubtedly Our Lady, if it had been her pleasure so to do, could have framed an entirely new Rule for the Order which she was about to found.   But she preferred to take one already in existence.   Her choice fell upon that of St. Augustine ; and, though it is not for us to examine into the motives of the Mother of God, we may, to some extent, divine several of the reasons which made her determine to give it to her Servants.

St. Augustine is one of the most heroic figures that the history of the Church exhibits to our view. His return to God after so long an estrangement, the marvellous depth of his doctrine on the most perplexing dogmas of our Faith, the sanctity of his life, the vast labours with which it was filled, and the sweetness and gentleness of his disposition, place the whole man before us in so lofty yet so attractive an aspect, that his equal is hardly to be found. The Rule which he wrote was drawn from his inmost soul, the reflection of which we find in every line. This Rule was the fruit of much prayer and meditation ; it was also the outcome of the great Doctor's personal experience. We shall endeavour to give some idea of the circumstances under which St. Augustine first conceived and formulated it.

Augustine, having been converted and baptized, after wandering for twenty years in the wilderness of sin, was revisited by a dream of his youthful days, when, unwilling to give himself wholly to God, yet yearning after the beauty of His truth, he had formed a plan of gathering his friends about him, to live together in brotherly union, and in the peaceful prosecution of their studies. Many times was this scheme taken up, and as often laid aside, because some of his friends were married, and others wished to enter upon that state. But now all circumstances seemed favourable for carrying out the idea, and it was decided that, on returning to Africa, the experiment should be tried on the outskirts of Tagaste. Augustine was then thirty-three years of age.

He now studied unceasingly all subjects connected with the Religious Life. He examined and compared the Rules already in existence, especially that of St. Basil, as well as those in use among the Gauls. Before leaving Milan, he and his mother visited some Religious who were directed by St. Ambrose. On his way to Rome, with Monica and his friends, he halted at Pisa to make an excursion in the forest of the Apennines, and to see some Solitaries who dwelt there in high repute of sanctity. In Rome, where he only at first spent a few days, there were monasteries, both of men and women, existing in a flourishing condition ; and when, after the death of St. Monica at Ostia, he returned to the Eternal City, he spent a whole year there, visiting the churches, the catacombs, and especially these monasteries. The greater part of his time was passed in the society of the Religious, whose mode of life he examined assiduously, conforming himself to it as much as possible. Thus, in the space of a year, he acquired an extensive knowledge of monastic life and its requirements, and he had already drawn up, in thought, a project for carrying out, in his own country, that which he deemed the perfect life.

At length he set sail for Africa, and, on reaching his native land, he hastened to satisfy his thirst for solitude by founding, near Tagaste, the long dreamed of monastery where, with his chosen friends, he designed to pass his days in prayer and study, and in the practice of poverty, chastity, and obedience. He and his companions were all clad alike in black tunics with leathern girdles, and they adopted the monastic tonsure. The Rule which he had so long reflected upon in his own mind was now more fully drawn out, and, for the first time, reduced to the test of practice. Whether he committed it to writing on this occasion we know not ; the one which we are accustomed to call his Rule has been transmitted to us by other channels, as we shall see, and dates from a much more recent period.

St. Augustine was the Father and Superior of this new Thebaid. His biographer, Possidius, writes : " He dwelt there for the space of three years, a stranger to all worldly cares, living, with his companions, for God alone, and spending his time in fasting, prayer, and good works : meditating by night and by day on the great mysteries of the Christian Faith, and communicating freely to those both present and absent, in conversation and by letter, the wonderful light which he received from God in contemplation". His only desire was to become more and more hidden from the world in the obscurity of monastic life, when unexpectedly a journey made by him to Hippo occasioned his being promoted to the priesthood. Being, then, obliged to go thither, he left Tagaste, having completed what may be termed his novitiate ; but he only quitted his old monastery to enter another, which he established, in the neighbourhood of Hippo, with his old companions, who were now joined by some new recruits.

This monastery, under the direction of Augustine, priest and monk, speedily became a school of sanctity, and a nursery of bishops for Africa. Augustine, although he devoted himself assiduously to all the practices of Religious Life, especially to study, silence, and prayer, did not fail to preach regularly on Sundays in the church at Hippo. He also invited the surrounding heretics to public conferences ; he kept up an extensive correspondence, and wrote many works which were received with enthusiasm, and which produced a great harvest of souls. For about five years, from 391 to 395, he led this dual life, interiorly that of a perfect Religious, and outwardly that of an indefatigable Apostle, combining constant wrestling with the old man, the practice of submission to his own Rule, and perfect self-abnegation, with vigorous onslaughts on the foes of the Church and the enemies of souls. Thus it was given to him both to conceive a finished type of the religious man, and to embody it in his daily life.

This first stage of his abode in Hippo was followed by the unlooked for event of his episcopal consecration by his own Bishop, when he at once became the right hand of the prelate, whose successor he was destined to be. On being raised to this dignity, Augustine was constrained to quit his monastery, in order to become all things to all men : but he vigorously enforced Community life and the practice of a Rule in his episcopal residence. Thus did he enter upon a career which was to continue for thirty-five years : during which space of time, we are in doubt whether the chief share of our admiration is due to the Bishop, who with such wisdom and ability ruled his flock : to the Doctor, whose profound learning was the wonder of the whole Church : to the man so sweet-tempered, genial, and ready of access : or to the Saint, on fire with the love of God, who gave so great an example of all virtues.

It was towards the close of his episcopacy, so filled with action, during which he had never ceased to live as a Religious, though under a different form, that he committed to writing the Rule which bears his name. His experience had been vast : he knew thoroughly all the weaknesses of human nature, which religion prunes away and replaces by the fruits of grace. Some of these he had known in his stormy youth, with others he became acquainted during his long diocesan experience. Meanwhile, the work of grace in his own soul had gone on, with increasing strength, from the date of his conversion, causing him to strive continually after yet higher degrees of perfection, until he reached a level of sanctity approaching to that inculcated in the teaching of the Divine Master, that sanctity which, rooted and founded in humility, pierces the clouds through far-reaching charity. The character of St. Augustine's holiness became more and more marked, as years advanced, by kindliness, modesty, gentleness, sweetness of temper, benevolence, and compassion. In his dealings with others, however great might be their perversity, he always endeavoured, by prayer and the help of divine grace, to bend, rather than to bruise, or break, them. He still looked with longing to the Religious Life, and amidst all his countless occupations and duties, he continued to study it, and, as far as he could, to practise it. Who, then, could be better fitted than he was to formulate a Rule, bearing the impress of heavenly wisdom, and forming a safe guide for those desirous of entering Religion ? Certain it is, that he won universal approbation by his successful performance of this task, and his Rule was adopted by numerous Communities.

There was, then, everything in the personal character, the life, and the virtues of St. Augustine to cause Our Lady to look upon him with favour. He must, however, have been yet dearer to her on account of the many errors which he had retrieved, and of the preference which he showed for her own most cherished virtues : for humility, modesty, purity, meekness, patience, and charity. Mary could not fail to be drawn towards this great soul on fire with love of her Divine Son, and with zeal for the salvation of men. She remembered, too, the tears of Saint Monica her own trials had made her keenly alive to a mother's sorrow. And Mary, herself the Seat of Wisdom, delighted in observing the fostering effects of grace on the magnificent intellect of Augustine, who in all his works so nobly set forth the doctrine of the Incarnate Word, and so triumphantly maintained the prerogatives of the ever Spotless Virgin, Mother of God and men, and Queen of Heaven. Besides, the Rule which he had drawn up, not only presented the Religious Life in the mild and attractive form, so pleasing to Our Lady, but assorted perfectly with the vocation which she wished to give to her Order—that of being her Servants within the cloister and her Apostles beyond its boundaries. This Rule, in short, was compatible with every kind of good work, and allowed those who followed it to fulfil, without any exception, whatever mission was appointed to them.

The Rule of St. Augustine had, consequently, many claims to be preferred by the Blessed Virgin, and, therefore, she was pleased to choose it for her Servants, and to show it to the Seven Founders, written in letters of gold as a mark of honour, telling them, at the same time, that it was to be their Rule from thenceforth. The more we study the Rule, the more convincingly does it demonstrate the wisdom of Our Lady's choice, and the more grateful must her Servants feel to her for having followed up the bestowal of their name, mission, distinctive devotion, and habit, by giving them this Rule to regulate their lives.

The Rule which St. Augustine gave to his monasteries at Tagaste and Hippo, and which he himself practised, has not come down to us. Nor is it known whether he wrote it out, or whether he simply communicated it by word of mouth to those Communities. It is true that we possess two writings of his, each containing a summary of the Religious Life. There can be little doubt of the authenticity of these works, for the great Doctor's unmistakable style can be recognized in every line. The first is intended for monks properly so-called, and the second for clerics living in community within a Monastery, but without being engaged in the cure of souls It is well known that Augustine had established foundations of both kinds at Hippo, and that he had followed both vocations. These two Rules contain all that is essential for the lives to be led by monks and clerics. They are remarkable for their wise and noble spirit, and they display a marvellous insight into souls : but they have not the completeness and minuteness of detail which we expect in a work intended to outlive the author. They are but an outline of the perfected Rule, the substance of which they undoubtedly contain : and they form a collection of valuable counsels ; but they cannot be looked upon as a definitive code of religious legislation. Their conciseness, and a certain informality of tone, would seem to show that Augustine, supposing him to have left no other writings on the subject, whilst willing to give a few paternal precepts to his spiritual children, was by no means desirous of legislating for the Universal Church. But the unabridged Rule, fully unfolding St. Augustine's views on the Religious Life, and which his humility might have concealed from posterity, has been preserved for us through the abundance of his charity, as we will now relate.

At Hippo, there existed a convent of women, founded by the saintly Bishop himself. To use his own expression, he had planted it as a garden of the Lord, wherein to shelter the choicest and most fragrant flowers. His sister was the Superior, and, under her headship, this monastery fully responded to the designs of its founder, and was a source of great rejoicing to his soul. But, after a time, the tares of discontent and insubordination were sown by some rebellious members of the Community, who disliked the sister then filling the office of Superior, and who demanded her removal. Augustine was much distressed by these dissensions. Upon being requested to come himself to pacify the malcontents, he refused, saying that it was painful enough for him to hear of these scandals, without being compelled to witness them. He prayed for them with tears, and wrote a letter to the sisterhood, expressive of the sorrow with which his heroic soul was filled. He rebuked them with the compassionate tenderness of a father, and, at the same time, with the firmness of a Superior who is inflexibly opposed to all wrong-doing. In order to check all farther irregularities, he appended to his letter a complete and comprehensive Rule, wherein he carefully laid down all that must be done to restore piety, peace, and charity among themselves. This Rule was the masterpiece which has since borne the name of its author, St. Augustine.

It is this Rule which, by the addition of a fundamental principle at the opening, the alteration of a few words, and the omission of one or two sentences in the body of the work, has been transformed into the famous Rule which has directed, and still continues to direct, so many Communities both of men and women. Its plan is such that there has been no difficulty in making use of it for men ; yet, it is easy to trace, throughout the whole, that it was originally intended for women. The leading of Divine Providence with respect to this document has been truly most striking in all respects ; for it was issued in consequence of a private dispute, and it became a public charter. It was intended to remedy a temporary evil, and it proved a source of lasting good. It was addressed to women only, and it has been established as a favourite Rule for men. This marvellous adaptability is to be accounted for, no doubt, by the fact that Augustine, when composing his Rule, only repeated the precepts which he had already given, after long study and many trials, to his monasteries. Besides, writing, as he did, at the advanced age of sixty-nine, he infused into it all the extended knowledge which he had acquired during the twenty-eight years of his episcopacy. In fact, this Rule shows a consummate acquaintance with all the weaknesses of human nature, and an exact understanding of all the precautions and tact required in dealing with these, and a wonderful spirit of conciliation, such as can only spring from a long-continued intercourse with souls. It was only seven years previous to his death that Augustine produced this masterpiece, which may be looked upon as a kind of spiritual will.

The text of the Rule of St. Augustine was adopted in various monasteries soon after the death of its author. It was observed with great fervour in the Monastery of Tarnat, near Lyons, in the sixth century. St. Benedict of Aniano, famous for his monastic reforms, who flourished from the year 750 to 831, mentions it, with high approval, in his Concordance of Rules. After his time, we find it in every country where the Augustinians and the Orders following the same Rule existed. Chief among these were the Premonstratensians, whose numerous foundations were established in every part of Europe.

The Augustinian Rule, as it stands and has stood since the Middle Ages, starts from the fundamental principle with which the summary of counsels to the secular clergy opens. Augustine had not inserted it in the precepts addressed to the monks, nor in the Rule intended for the nuns of Hippo. That precept is as follows : "Above all things, most dear Brethren, let God be first loved by you, and, next to Him, your neighbour, for these are the two chief precepts that have been given to us". The slight difference in these cases is readily accounted for. It was essential to impress upon the secular clergy, who were to be devoted in a special manner to the service of their neighbour, the full importance of this part of their vocation ; whereas the monks and nuns being more exclusively devoted to their personal sanctification, there was no need to bring so prominently before them the twofold duty imposed by charity. In the endeavour to attain perfection, they were bound to practise all virtues without exception, and the love of their neighbour was, necessarily, included with the rest.

This great principle, the very soul and mainspring of Religious Life, having been enunciated, all the constituent elements of that life are enumerated, as maxims or as orders. Our Blessed Lord, His Apostles filled with the Holy Spirit, the first Christians in all the fervour of their zeal, are the models placed by Augustine before those who desire to enter upon the Religious Life. He follows, as he observes in his counsels to the secular clergy, the Apostolic tradition. Then he proceeds to the practical part of his work, showing the conclusions to which his premises lead, commenting on them with great acuteness, and proving that Faith and Reason unite in confirming the teaching of Authority.

8   .

He next puts forward the primitive idea, as he conceives it, of the Religious Life, namely, that of corporation, a bond of union, a link welding the members indissolubly together : whence naturally follows a dwelling in common, similarity of ideas and feelings, the same aspirations in the spiritual Order, so that all should have one heart and one mind, and that all should be fused together and centred in God Himself : in short, a true home of souls, where all should live in brotherly union, having the Father Who is in heaven for their Father, and the Order in which they have been born again to the Religious Life for their mother. Thus do all the members become inseparable, both materially and spiritually.

This idea of a kind of family coalition is pushed to its extreme conclusion ; insomuch that the civil rights of the individual, which are held to be inalienable in the eyes of the law, are transferred by exceptional privilege to the community, which holds property for the good of all. Thus is realized what, under the ordinary conditions of humanity, is looked upon as a mere utopian vision—the abolition of the distinctions of *meum* and *tuum.* Property, in itself a legitimate and necessary right, but the parent of so much that is evil, can, under these circumstances, afford to men all its inherent advantages, with none of the attendant drawbacks.

The members of a Religious Community, although they have renounced all personal possessions, have a right to share in the maintenance supplied by the common fund, which is expanded under the judicious and careful superintendence of the head of the household, the Superior who fills the place of their earthly Father. And this fund is dispensed, not in accordance with the cold rules of arithmetic, giving to each and all the same modicum, but in proportion to the needs of each one, thus obeying the dictates both of Reason and of Charity.

Here, the prudent legislator addresses some appropriate exhortations to those who were rich before entering Religion, and, likewise, to those who were poor. The former he counsels to be willing to have all their possessions in common ; and the latter he desires to be moderate in their requirements. Still, whilst he urges the poor to place their happiness in higher things than being simply placed beyond the reach of corporal privations, he forbids their being refused anything really needful. He commands all, both rich and poor, to be united in a spirit of intense humility, caring nothing for worldly distinctions ; for pride sows the seeds of death even in our good works. And he adds : " Honour one another as temples of the living God ".

Having spoken of the pivot on which the Religious Life may be said to turn, St. Augustine goes on to describe, in his masterly way, the chief exercises to be practised. First there is prayer, both in common and in private, for which he prescribes fervour, fixed hours, an Oratory always open and in which strict silence is to be observed, and other necessary conditions. Next comes mortification of the body, as to which everyone must go as far as his physical strength allows, by fasting, by abstinence, by taking neither food nor drink between meals, by keeping silence at table, and listening attentively to the spiritual reading. Those who are strong are not to cavil at the indulgences granted to the infirm, and those who are sick are to return to their ordinary mode of life as soon as they are recovered.

Having discussed the subject of mortification, he next treats of certain points of discipline and good order, touching upon all the chief acts of life so as to regulate them in a religious spirit. The habit is to be simple and modest, for it is not worn to please the eyes of the world. None are to go out or pay visits alone. In their walk and bearing, in all things and everywhere, they are to endeavour to give no cause for scandal. They are to be careful to keep the custody of the eyes. Augustine knew by experience to how many dangers the way is opened by carelessness in this respect, especially in the voluptuous African climate. He knew how small a spark kindles a great fire, and how easily the whiteness of the soul is sullied. He therefore sought to inspire a great dread of the first beginnings of that sin, and an intense horror of the sin itself.

In speaking of the obligation laid upon all the Brethren, to warn and correct any among them who do not keep the custody of the eyes, and even to inform against them, and punish them, as Holy Scripture commands, should they prove stubborn, St. Augustine takes occasion to observe that, in the fulfilment of this obligation, all must treat the offender with kindness and gentleness, and though there may be hatred of the sin, there must be none for the sinner.

Next, he strictly prohibits all clandestine correspondence, and the acceptance, without permission, of presents.

The question of clothing is by no means an easy one, since vanity finds so many unexpected loop-holes whereby to creep in. St. Augustine, therefore, orders that all the habits shall be kept in the vestiary, and given out indiscriminately; that all should take what falls to their share without remark or complaint, however old or ill-fitting the garments may be. He speaks much of the necessity, in all that concerns the clothing of the body, of forgetfulness of self, of unselfishness, and of letting others have the first choice. He considers this preference of the interests of others to our own as one of the surest signs of perfection.

The tropical heat of Africa made the frequent use of baths general, and there were many public establishments much patronized for this purpose by all classes. The kind-hearted Augustine, who was ever disposed to take a charitable view of poor human nature, does not forbid bathing, but he regulates the practice so as to prevent any excess, and takes every precaution to avoid any injury to the health of the soul from being caused by the care bestowed on that of the body.

His charity extends also to the sick. He desires that the physician should be called in to attend them, that this physician should be specially appointed for their service, and that, during their sickness and recovery, they should be supplied with everything that they required. Here, too, he exhorts the Procurator, the Vestiarian, and the Librarian, to be ever ready to place their services at the disposal of their Brethren.

He forbids lawsuits, if they can be avoided, and, if they are inevitable, he desires that they may be quickly ended, lest hatred and ill-will should arise. He also insists that, if disputes should occur, and uncharitable words should be spoken in the Community, reconciliation and reparation should immediately follow   To farther enforce this, he observes, that prayer cannot be efficacious and fruitful, if it be offered by unquiet and disunited hearts. But he does not wish Superiors to weaken their authority by apologizing to inferiors who imagine themselves affronted. Thus he shows that, with all his gentleness and large-heartedness, he is not weakly indulgent, but knows how to rule with wise firmness. And, whilst he dwells much on the necessity of brotherly love, he explains that it must be a wholly supernatural affection, free from all selfish and worldly motives.

Having thus gone through all matters concerning external discipline, he passes to the crowning point of all—obedience, which fills up every hiatus in the Rule, which solves all difficulties, and decides all questions. Ever leaning to the side of indulgence, he begins by saying that obedience should cause the Superior to be looked upon as a Father : then he describes, briefly, the obligations of those in authority, which are to keep up strict observance, to relax nothing, and to restore all that is capable of restoration. He then proceeds to enumerate, with a perfection hitherto unequalled, all the qualifications which a Superior should possess : "A Superior," he says, "should prize his Office, not because it confers on him authority, but because it enables him to exercise charity. Men honour him, but, in the sight of God, he must put himself under their feet. It is he who is bound to set an example in all good works ; it is he who must chastise the refractory, comfort the weak, watch over the sick ; it is he who must be patient with all, who must be ever ready to bend himself under the yoke of discipline, whilst he is cautious in laying it upon others ; it is he who must strive to make himself loved rather than feared by those under him, ever remembering the account which he is to render to God." Then, addressing himself to the Community generally, St. Augustine says : "Be, therefore, daily more and more obedient, out of compassion to yourselves, as well as to him who, as your Superior, is in greater peril than you all, inasmuch as he is more highly placed ".

Augustine had now finished his task, and he closes his Rule with a prayer to God, that He may give them all grace to keep it he then finally recommends that it should be read through weekly, so that each one, viewing his soul therein as in a mirror, should give thanks to the Lord for what has been faithfully observed, should repent himself of all that he has failed in, and should take means to avoid, for the future, whatever has been amiss.

Such is the epitome, though but a poor one, of St. Augustine's immortal work, which he has left almost unintentionally, to the Church. Such is the outline of that glorious picture of the perfect life, painted by the hand of one of the greatest masters in the science of sanctity. Such is the analysis of the Rule in which the genius of Augustine has condensed the whole spirit of the Religious Life, and has so skilfully and attractively pointed the way to the source of all perfection. Such is, briefly, his luminous commentary on the noblest maxims ever given to man for his guidance here below. It is of this Rule that another Saint, himself a bishop and doctor of the Church, St. Francis of Sales, has spoken in the following terms of praise : " The great authority of St. Augustine," he says, " the weight given to his words by the eminent holiness of his life, and by the marvellous writings with which he has adorned the Church, has caused his Rule to be of all spiritual codes the most generally followed. (For Our Lord, as St. Jerome says, dwelling within him, surely inspired this Rule, so much is it filled with the spirit of charity breathing nothing but sweetness, gentleness, and benignity, and it is thus adapted to persons of every disposition and constitution.) Therefore we find it adopted not only by several congregations of cloistered Religious, as those of the Canons and Clerks Regular, of the Hermits, of St. Dominic, St. Jerome, and St. Antony, the Premonstratensians, the Servants of Mary, and the Order of the Redemption of Captives ; but also by the Military Orders of Knights of St. John of Jerusalem, of SS. Maurice and Lazarus, the Teutonic Order, the Knights of St. James, and several others, have marshalled themselves under the banner of this great leader." And St. Francis of Sales himself adopted this Rule for the Order of the Visitation, founded by him.

The Doctor of these later days did but justice, in thus speaking and acting, to the Rule of the Doctor of the earlier ages of the Church. In point of fact, the Rule of St. Augustine is simply the pith and marrow of the Holy Gospels. It does but repeat, almost in the self-same words, the counsels of perfection which fell from the divine lips of the Son of Mary. For this reason it was that Mary chose it for her Servants, so that, by following it, they might more surely win the palm which she had held out to the Founders, the palm emblematic of the holiness which was to adorn their lives here, and of the infinite reward which was to be theirs hereafter.

CHAPTER VIII.

Character, Spirit, and Growth of Holiness in the Order.

THE Order on which Our Lady herself had been pleased to bestow the elementary constituents of name, mission, distinctive devotion, habit, and Rule had only just entered upon its existence ; yet, soon the sweet influence of the Mother of God so moulded it that it possessed a marked character of its own. In some points it resembled one or another of the contemporary Orders, but it had also an individuality which prevented its being mistaken for any other : it belonged to a type of its own, and at the same time, it readily fraternized with those to which it bore some affinity.

In the first place, there can be no doubt whatever that the Institution, which the Servants of Mary were about to form was to be a Religious Order in the strictest sense of the term. Our Blessed Lady had not said so explicitly, but her meaning was sufficiently clear. The part which she had taken in the work of the foundation proved this : for only a Religious Order would bear a distinctive name, or wear a habit like that which she had shown them, or observe the Rule of St. Augustine. It is true that this Rule, apparently, leaves the subject of the vows in the background : but to anyone who has studied the progressive phases of the Religious Life, this vagueness presents no difficulty.

The essentials of the Religious Life consist in the practice of the Evangelical Counsels, summed up in the renunciation of all worldly possessions, of all the pleasures of the senses, and of self-will ; or, in other words, in the observance of poverty, chastity, and obedience. This is the primary idea of such a life, but it is an incomplete one : for the Religious belongs absolutely and for ever to his vocation, being attached to it by a bond which cannot be severed; that is to say, that, in making the three vows, he makes them irrevocably.

In all ages the consecration of a life to God has been an understood fact. From the time of the Apostles there have always been souls desirous of walking in the paths of perfection, and who have engaged themselves to do so, by pledges binding on their consciences. The form under which this was accomplished varied considerably. In general, it was spoken of as a Consecration. In the case of virgins it was termed the Veiling. In the Rules of St. Basil and St. Augustine the vows are not mentioned; but they are implied in the fact of this Consecration, which was hedged round with strict obligations of a sharply-defined character. St. Benedict is the first who, in his Rule, expressly insists upon solemn and perpetual vows, and who prescribes the vow of stability, thus giving an exact definition of the Religious Life, and obviating all perplexity and confusion.

Now, in his Rule, St. Augustine speaks so expressly of the renunciation of all personal property, and of having all things in common, that it would be impossible to enlarge further on the subject of poverty. Obedience, too, is a point as to which he is equally clear. Chastity is not formally prescribed: but this virtue was considered as so essential a part of the Religious Life that the two were identical. The holy legislator only dwells on certain risks which might endanger this virtue: his care to guard it from all possible danger proves that he desired that it should be especially cherished.

The Consecration is not named; but it is to be inferred from the whole tone of the Rule, and from the counsels addressed to the monks by St. Augustine. In these counsels we find that a certain probation was required from those who wished to enter Religion, because the engagement was to be for life. History, tradition, and universal custom, abundantly prove that permanency was regarded as a necessary condition of the Religious State: it seemed so self-evident that it was unnecessary to speak about it.

Now that this new Religious Order had sprung into existence, the question was, what mode of life would it adopt in regard to its internal organization, and to its external mission? Would it prefer the tranquil and dignified retirement which broods over the old Abbeys, with their daily round of praise and prayer, the unceasing chant of the Divine Office, the remoteness from the tumult and hurry of city-life, the concentration of the energies of the inmates on study or manual labour? Not such were to be the lives of the Servites, in the first place, the spirit of St. Augustine's Rule differs from that of St. Benedict; and, in the next place, the young Order could not avoid being carried on by the current of ideas which was gradually replacing the old monastic traditions with institutions more suited to the actual needs of the age. About twenty years previously this new kind of Religious Life had been introduced under the initiative of two great Saints: Francis of Assisi and Dominic, and had attracted crowds of labourers to the Evangelical harvest-field, by whom great good had been effected; whilst other Religious Institutions were induced to walk in their steps. Under this hitherto untried system, monastic life, simplified in some of its details, was combined with works of external charity, and the ministry of souls, which became the secondary object of the Religious. The Convent replaced the Abbey, the Prior took the place of the Abbot, the solemn chant was succeeded by simple psalmody; instead of the old-world seclusion of the monks, the friars dwelt in the midst of the stir of towns; whilst in lieu of the mental and bodily labour pursued within the enclosure of the Monastery, the friars substituted prayer, study, and the duties of the Apostolate; besides which, the whole Order was mobilized under the command and inspection of the Superior in Chief, who was called the General, thus giving additional facilities for doing good.

It is this life which the Servite Order, by a leading which it sought not to resist, adopted for its own—the more readily, as it harmonized well with the mission which the Heavenly Foundress had imposed upon her Servants. For, surely, there could be no more certain way of procuring the glory of the Queen of Heaven than by propagating devotion to her among the multitudes, since nothing contributes more efficaciously than such devotion to the sanctifying and perfecting of souls. The Order of Mary accordingly entered upon this course, and has persevered in it even to our own day. At one period, indeed, certain members returned to the eremitical life; but this anomaly lasted but a short time, and finally disappeared.

Like other New Orders, the Servites at once cast off the trammels of worldly possessions. Instead of owning broad lands and vast wealth, as did some of the more ancient foundations, they had but the space absolutely necessary for a humble building to shelter them. Their wealth was to be but the alms which they gathered from door to door, whence their right to the name of Mendicants; and, thus living from day to day, and looking for the supply of all their needs to the Providence of Him for Whom they laboured, they wanted for nothing. Practising poverty so austerely, they had not to dread the creeping worm of prosperity, which devastates and destroys the most firmly established institutions.

In other external features, the Servants of Mary gradually assimilated themselves to the Orders which had preceded them by a few years. They could not have done better, for the two Orders in question—the Franciscans and Dominicans—bore all the marks of being dear to God; since they had received the Church's approval, their Founders had lived and died in the odour of sanctity, and had been already canonized. The ranks of both were filled with countless holy men, who were spread through the world doing good wheresoever they were found. It may with truth be said that these two Orders alone had regenerated the Church of God. They were, consequently, greatly beloved by the people, who put themselves under their direction, and thousands of whom entered the spiritual militia in which the laity can be enrolled, viz., the various Third Orders. The older Orders were inspired by the enthusiasm of the younger institutions, and, renewing their youth like the eagle, they strengthened their armour and prepared for fresh combats.

Notwithstanding the many important events which had caused these changes in the views of the Seven Founders, there lingered in their minds—and the Order, it may be said, inherited from them—a regretful memory of the eremitical life which they had relinquished: and traces of this regret were shown by their marked affection for the interior life. A dread of the tumult of the world, an aversion to all parade and ostentation, a strong preference for unambitious undertakings and humble works, an instinctive shrinking from public view, in order to live under the eyes of Jesus and Mary alone —such have always been the predominant characteristics of Our Lady's Order. And in its ranks were to be found souls so enamoured of the solitary life that only a hermitage could satisfy their craving. In this way several great Saints were given to the Order; whilst for a time a branch flourished which, without separating from the Order, led in it a different life from that prescribed to it. These were the Hermits, who, twice in the space of about three centuries, sprang into existence, and shed around them the perfume of holiness.

The Order in its earlier stages was also subject to slight external variations. The first Fathers were wholly taken by surprise when it was announced to them that they were to be Founders. They had already established themselves in a different vocation, and they had to grope their way in arranging for a new mode of life. Many circumstances combined to make their task a difficult one; moreover, they had to struggle against a formidable opposition, which was only overcome after sixty years of courageous efforts. Thus the Order, like a new-born child, had to pass through all the phases of life, and only attained to ripe age after a youth spent in many labours, and in overcoming tremendous obstacles: and these troubles left upon it deep traces of sorrow, as though to keep alive the remembrance of the mission assigned to it

But, if there were points in which some variation was to be found in the Order, there was one mark, so indelibly stamped upon it, that utter annihilation could alone efface it. This mark is that which is expressed in the name of Servants of Mary, which shows how absolute, how all-pervading, how ineradicable is the love of Mary, how tender and child-like is the remembrance of her sorrows, which her Servants cherish in their hearts, proclaim with their lips, display in their habit, and prove by the whole tenour of their lives. This is the mark which has been upon them from the beginning, and which they have borne with them from age to age.

Such was the general aspect of the Order of the Servants of Mary, in the early stages of its existence, when it had just been instituted by Our Lady. A little fragment of the thirteenth century has chanced to fall into our hands, the writer of which, doubtless himself one of the Religious, brings before us, in a dialogue of quaint simplicity, some of the salient features of his Order.

The conversation is held between a Servite named Benedict and a layman called Peter :

Peter. " Pray, Brother, tell me of yourself."

Benedict. " If you desire to know my name and country, I am called Benedict, and Florence is my birthplace."

P. " If you had told me that you were not a Florentine, I should have answered that you were saying that which is not, for your accent is easily to be recognized   But, I pray you, tell me to what Order do you belong, and what is this habit which you wear."

B. "Since you desire to be told of the Order to which I who wear this habit belong, know, then, that we are called the Servants of the most glorious Virgin, that we wear her mourning garb, and that her Sorrows are the food of our Meditations."

P. "Truly I like your habit much ; and, since you nurture your souls by meditation, I suppose that you must be hermits.   I, poor worldling that I am, cannot refrain from envying you your blest solitude."

B. "May Our Dear Lord and Our Blessed Lady be praised therefore, good Sir!   According as our Rule prescribes, and our leisure permits, we make to ourselves an interior solitude, for the purpose of meditation ; but it is not given to us to enjoy the holy and blessed peace which a hermitage offers ; for the life which we lead is like to that of the holy Apostles, as our blessed Father St. Philip said to the Dominican Fathers."

P. "Then, do you go about through the country, preaching the name of Christ Jesus our Lord ?"

B. "Certainly we do, good Sir, and some of our Brethren have even gone, with the blessing of His Holiness Pope Clement, into the land of the Tartars ; it was our holy Father St. Philip who sent them thither.   And tidings have come to us of their martyrdom ; they have given their blood for the love of Christ.   Another of our Brethren (Antonio of Viterbo) a man of great learning, and skilful in argument, dwells in Candia   he is in repute of sanctity, and has gained many inhabitants of that country to the Faith : he is even said to have wrought many well authenticated miracles "

P. "Then, do you mean to say that your mission is to preach the Faith to the Turks and Tartars ?"

B. "No, that is not what I meant.   Our mission is to be the Apostles of Our Lady's Sorrows : it was for this that our glorious Queen, the Sorrowful Mother of Our Sweet Lord Jesus, called us out of the world.   Consequently, it is her desire that the thought of her Son's Passion should be stamped deeply into our hearts, and that we should, moreover, steep our souls in the flood of grief which overwhelmed her, when, by that piercing sorrow of hers, she co-operated in the work of our redemption.   Then, also, she requires of us that we should preach everywhere, as much by holy and mortified lives, as by word of mouth or writing, the hatred of sin, since it was sin which caused the cruel martyrdom of her Divine Son.   This she willed us to do throughout the world.   Wonder not, therefore, if you find, that we, Servants of Blessed Mary, not only do penance in our own land by reciting office, by prayer, by acting as peacemakers in family disputes and party strifes, by preaching, and by teaching grammar and logic, but that we also when called upon, shed our blood in foreign missions."

This fragment gives a vivid idea of the external features of the Servite Order. But its inner life is also peculiar to itself, moulded by the spirit which directs it, and of which Mary herself is the source. In this spirit are comprehended several interior tendencies combining to form a whole of great sweetness and charm—a kind of after-glow of the life which Our Blessed Lady led whilst on earth. It comprises a marked love of tranquillity, of solitude, and of silence : extreme humility in thought, in aim, in enterprize ; a total exclusion of all worldly ambitions , perfect recollection, so that the soul readily withdraws from all outward surroundings to converse with God, and to unite herself more completely with Him ; in all dealing with others, kindness, patience, pitifulness ; and, lastly, an entire surrender of self into the hands of the Creator, accepting unreservedly all that He wills, and so utterly renouncing whatever is contrary to that Will, that not a particle of the creature's own thoughts or desires is opposed to the divine decrees.

Such being the distinctive features and spirit of the Order, we see that the vocation of the Servants of Mary is to remain within the charmed circle of thought where Our Lady reigns supreme. Their intellects and their hearts must alike be filled with the remembrance of her life on earth, and the contemplation of her life in heaven, with her prerogatives and her glories, as with her sufferings and sorrows. From these reflections they proceed to render her the homage which they owe to her, of praise and gratitude, of supplication and of compassion. Thus, they remain ever near her, like true and faithful vassals, and, in this life, they find ever new delights.

Is it, then, to be wondered at, if holiness becomes a second nature to those who faithfully observe this rule? Living in an atmosphere filled with the fragrance of Mary's virtues, they inhale the good odour, and are nourished by it almost unconsciously. Great, indeed, are the privileges accorded to those who consecrate themselves wholly to the Mother of God. It is theirs to win the palm which she held out to the Seven Founders, that palm of virtue which Our Lord crowns in heaven.

Devotion to Our Lady has long been looked upon in the Church of God as a sign of predestination. St. Alphonsus of Liguori has summed up the teaching of the Fathers and Doctors in the following proposition : " It is impossible that a client of Mary should be lost, so long as he serves her faithfully, and commends himself to her ". This sentence is but an echo of the words of St. Ephrem, who declared that "devotion to the Mother of God was a safe-conduct which would ensure us from falling into the abyss". But this teaching only exhibits one aspect of the supernatural influence of the cultus of Our Lady ; to set it forth fully, it should be said that this devotion is an overflowing well-spring of sanctity. Sanctity, in fact, flows hence by two different channels : on the one hand, by the efficacy of the prayers and good works which we offer through Mary, and, on the other, through the dominion which she exercises over those who honour her, by means of the example which she sets before them, and the encouragement that she gives them.

The Doctors of the Church perfectly understood how great was this efficacy, when they styled Mary the Highway of the King, because she leads us to Jesus, the sole source of all sanctity. Experience has confirmed the opinion of the Doctors, and we find all the Saints of God filled with a fervent devotion to Our Lady, knowing that she will be their most powerful Helper in their efforts to attain the steep heights of heroic sanctity.

But, in the cultus of Mary there is, as it were, an inner garden, a choicer flower, a more towering height It is the Devotion to her Sorrows, which includes every stage of her transfixion. And, as the love which is shown to a fellow-creature in a time of trial and suffering is of a higher kind than that which is displayed in a season of gladness and prosperity, so the commemoration of the Sorrows of Our Blessed Mother implies greater perfection than the celebration of her Glories and her Joys, and likewise abounds more in the fruits of sanctity. Our Lady, too, is more touched by this devotion, and shows herself more and more bountiful to those who practise it. It is easy to conceive that those who draw nigh to the Queen of Sorrows derive from her an influence which strengthens them for any sacrifice, and enables them to reach that degree of perfection which sacrifice alone allows them to attain.

A pious author, who has produced a celebrated work on the Sorrows of Mary, has well described this influence. He speaks thus :

" This devotion has also a remarkable connection with great interior holiness. For it is a devotion which makes us unworldly, because we live and breathe in an atmosphere of sorrow. It brings out the unreality of worldly joys. It sobers our thoughts. It keeps them close to Jesus Christ, and to Him Crucified. It communicates to our souls the spirit of the Cross : and the enviable gift of love of suffering full often begins in a prayerful familiarity with the sorrows of Our Blessed Mother. More than most devotions it tends to supernaturalize the mind, because its keeps us in a sphere of heavenly beauty, whose look and odour gradually pass upon ourselves. It is a sphere in which the most wonderful divine operations mingle with the common woes and sorrows of a suffering world, and so it expresses that union of self-abasement and self-oblivion in which all the greater graces of the spiritual life take root. Moreover the prevailing ideas to which it weds our minds, are just those which are the most solid and essential in any persevering endeavours after holiness.

For it unites us to an abiding sorrow for sin—sin which caused Mary's sorrow, sin which caused the sorrow over which Mary sorrowed, sin of our own which was actually present and influential in both these sorrows, wronging at once the Mother and the Son.   It equally unites us to the perpetual sense of needing grace, of absolute dependence upon grace, and of that ready abundance of grace on which our filial confidence reposes.   It is all stained with the Precious Blood ; and thus it puts us into the very depths of Our Saviour's Sacred Heart.   There is no soul which worldliness finds it harder to attack than one which is entrenched within the dolours of Our Blessed Lady.   There is nothing which the world can graft itself upon in that devotion.   There is nothing congenial to the spirit and way of the world, nothing even which the world can falsify for its own ends, or fraudulently divert for its own purposes.   Moreover it was in the dolours that the grandeurs of Mary's sanctity were fabricated, out of materials which in their degree are common to every one of us, her sons and daughters.   It is hard to live in the bosom of great examples, and be uninfluenced by them.   The lessons which the dolours teach us are wanted at almost every turn of life, and are most appropriate to the very seasons in which grace is wont to be most active in us ; and they are imparted with such loving tenderness, such pathetic simplicity, and in the midst of such countless similitudes between our sinless Mother and our sinful selves, that it is difficult to conceive of a school in which so much heavenly wisdom is taught so winningly as in the Compassion of Mary." (*The Foot of the Cross*, by Fr. F. W. Faber.)

It is thus that the Servants of Mary are bound to strive after sanctity, and to attain it.   They are bound to exemplify in themselves the truth of the words of a holy priest and devout client of Mary : " It is sufficient to stay at the feet of Mary to find great wealth " (M. Olier—*Vie Interieure de la Ste. Vierge.*)   They are bound to act thus in conformity with these earnest words which St. Alexis Falconieri continually addressed, in his touching and fatherly accents, to his spiritual sons : " My dear good children, remember that the spirit of our Order is yet higher and more wonderful than that of the Religious of St. Francis and of St. Dominic ; for it is that we should become holy ourselves, and make others holy, by meditating, and causing others to meditate with true compunction of heart, upon the Sorrows of the most afflicted Mother of God, and the Sufferings of her divine and most dear Son.   Nay, by whatsoever trials and temptations you may be assailed, never can you be lost so long as you are diligent to accomplish the will of Our Blessed Lady : but woe to you, if you should cross it !   My children, of this I have been assured by the mouth of Our Heavenly Patroness : believe it therefore and trust in it ! blessed will you be if you act upon it." (*Ricordi di Nicolo Mati.*)

The Servants of Mary, then, have but to sit at the feet of their Mistress, employing their thoughts and fixing their hearts upon her Sorrows, in order to gain the palm shown by her to our Seven Saints, and to be admitted at last to dwell near her throne in Paradise amidst endless joys.

We see that Mary, in her Apparition of 13th April, 1240, had planned the constitution of her well-beloved Order in all essential points : she had traced the general outlines of her Institution, and she had even permitted the Founders to behold the reward laid up for them. Theirs was now the task of setting the work on foot, and of completing by their own energy and perseverance that which their Heavenly Patroness had begun with such maternal loving kindness.

CHAPTER IX.

Ͳge Ørᴅer Begins fo Ɓaᴠe a Corporafe Ꞓrisfence.

(1240—1241.)

THE Blessed Mother of God had unfolded her plan to our Seven Saints in so unmistakable a manner as to leave no possibility of doubt as to her intention. From this time forth, accordingly, their one aspiration was to carry out her design. Therefore, when they assembled together, soon afterwards, in order to confer upon their affairs, they were unanimous in deciding that, at Easter, as a sign of the change which had taken place in their views, they would admit any suitable subjects, who might come to them to be received into the Community. The zealous Chaplain, who had followed them to Monte Senario, and had assisted them during their essay of the eremitical life, was taken at once into their confidence. He was deeply touched by all that they related to him, and he approved highly of all that the Saintly Seven had determined upon. He confided to them that he had resolved never to leave them, and to consecrate himself likewise to Our Lady in the Order which she had commissioned them to found. The Fathers of Senario rejoiced much in this decision, which gave them a new brother—indeed, the first addition to their family—in the person of their beloved Spiritual Father.

The Bishop of Florence, who had long been urging our Saints to embrace the Apostolic life, upon being made aware of their resolution, gave it his fullest approbation. As Our Lady herself had deigned to inform him of everything, he had well weighed and considered the subject before God, and he had come to the conclusion that the Fathers of Monte Senario were bound to go forward. He, therefore, desired to arrange with them all the points that still remained unsettled. In particular, it was his will that they should, without delay, assume the religious habit which was to be theirs for life, and which he wished to confer on them himself, in the little Chapel at Monte Senario. The question as to the Novitiate was examined and decided. A decree, issued by Gregory IX. more than twelve years previously, dated 12th July, 1227, expressly provided that no one should take the solemn vows until after a twelvemonth's probation. Our Seven Founders, already far advanced in perfection, were, nevertheless, prepared to begin cheerfully their Novitiate, as though they had everything to learn. St. Bonfilius was confirmed in his Office as Superior and Novice-Master, which functions he had filled, in reality, ever since he had begun to train his companions in virtue in the Confraternity of the Laudesi. On the day appointed for the clothing, Ardingo betook himself to Monte Senario. It was not long after Easter, and the zealous prelate rejoiced to find himself, after the toils of Lent, of Holy Week, and of the Paschal Feast, once more in this beloved solitude.

All was now in readiness for the ceremony. The habits had been made after the pattern shown by Our Lady to the Fathers of a plain coarse woollen material, such as was then woven in Florence. They consisted of a tunic reaching to the feet, and girded at the waist with a leathern belt, of a scapular, and of a cloak, to which a hood was attached. These various articles were all black in colour, and the woollen stuff of which they were composed was called Cisalpine cloth—Transalpine cloth being much finer in texture, and more expensive in cost. This last was only used for the white under-tunic worn next the skin. Linen was in those days an article of luxury ; and it was only occasionally permitted to be used by Religious in the form of a kind of stocking.

At this period, there was a custom which has since been disused. Those who were about to be clothed, first divested themselves almost wholly of their secular garb This part of the ceremony was a symbol of that casting away of all worldly possessions which is the essence of the Religious Life, and took place behind a curtain. We can picture to ourselves the feelings with which the hearts of the Seven Saints overflowed at this moment of outward humiliation. With what generosity must they have made the offering of their whole being to Jesus and Mary—an offering which was to be ratified by the subsequent course of their lives. They then received, with loving joy and gratitude, the habit of the Servants of Mary, each separate article of which was emblematic of high and holy things. Thirdly, their hair fell under the sacrificial shears, and the monastic tonsure was traced on their heads, in token of their spiritual royalty.

Lastly, according to a traditional custom, our Seven Saints took the names by which they were to be known in Religion, as a sign that all about them was now made new, including the appellation by which each man is distinguished among his fellows. The two oldest among them retained their baptismal names, relinquishing their surnames : these were Bonfilius Monaldi and Alexis Falconieri, who were henceforth known as Brother Bonfilius and Brother Alexis. No doubt, this abandonment implied their readiness to give up all those ties of blood which most strongly move the human heart. Three others, on the contrary, dropped the baptismal names which had sounded so sweet to them from kindred lips, and kept their surnames. We do not know their reason for so doing : it may have been—since the hearts of Saints are so full of tenderness—that they wished to prove to the dear ones whom they had left, that they would never cease to love them. Thus Bartholomew Amidei became Brother Amedeus, a name truly expressive of the character of that soul on fire with the love of God ; Ricovero Uguccioni was called Brother Hugh, and Gerardino Sostegni, Brother Sostene. The two last, Benedict dell' Antella and John Manetti were moved to sink their identity completely, and henceforth they were only known as Brother Manettus and Brother Buonagiunta, the latter name signifying " Welcome ". Perhaps the former thought himself unworthy of the name of Benedict, and the latter wished to please his father, who bore the same name, and also mark his gratitude for having been one of the earliest to be admitted into the Order of the Servants of the Queen of Heaven.

After the clothing and the conferring of the names in Religion, the Bishop of Florence addressed a few feeling words of counsel and encouragement to the Fathers, whom he truly looked upon as his spiritual children, and in whose foundation he had taken so prominent a share. He now told them that, from henceforward, the Rule of St. Augustine was binding upon them ; he reminded them that in it they would find the perfect type of the life which they wished to lead; and he promised them, that the more closely they approximated to this type, the more securely would they walk in the path of holiness. He exhorted them, in most fatherly words, to set forth boldly, assuring them of a happy ending to their journey. Lastly, the gentle prelate invited his children to the kiss of peace, which he gave to each in turn, receiving again from them this simple and touching sign of brotherly love, which the Church has so well appropriated for herself, giving to it a higher meaning, and expressing by it the welding together of souls. The Bishop then gave them from his heart his best blessing, saying, in a voice broken by strong feeling: " May the Blessed Mary, Queen of Angels, bless, increase, and preserve the Order of her Servants, in the Name of the Father, and of the Son, and of the Holy Ghost. Amen."

At the conclusion of the ceremony, the Fathers' hearts brimmed over with gladness. In the fulness of their joy, they embraced each other like loving brothers. They kissed their consecrated habits, which they were resolved to wear as a perpetual sign that their lives were now irrevocably devoted to the Service of Mary, and to the cultus of her sorrows. All agreed that no alteration should ever be made in this habit, since it had been given to them by their heavenly Foundress, and was typical of such great mysteries. They decided, too, that it should be exactly the same for members of the Order, whether priests or lay-brothers, since, as Servants of Mary, all were on the same level, far above the distinction conferred by monastic rank or office.

The holy Bishop hastened to bid farewell to his entertainers, who accompanied him for a part of his homeward journey. As they traversed with him the rough mountain paths, he edified them by speaking much of the habit which they wore. The dark colour, he said, would remind them of the unhappy fall of our first parents; and he exhorted them to meditate often on the reasons which had prompted Our Lady to bestow it upon them, and, meanwhile, to rest assured that the more earnestly they strove to make themselves worthy of so great a favour, the more abundantly would graces be showered upon them. Whilst they were still absorbed in this discourse, the time came for them to separate, and our Saints and Bishop Ardingo took leave of one another.

During his sojourn at Monte Senario, the Bishop of Florence had decided that the Seven Fathers were to prepare without delay for Ordination—this being essential to the work in hand. Our Saints experienced a thrill of awe and dread on hearing this, but they submitted to the obvious necessity of the case, one only among them entreating, as a favour, that an exception might be made in his case, so as to allow him to retain the lowly rank of lay-brother. It was St. Alexis who proffered this petition, and who for more than seventy years gladly filled the humble office of his choice.

The news was quickly spread that the Seven Hermits of Monte Senario were now to be the commanders of a religious troop, devoted to the service of Our Lady, whose destination was to go out into the world, fighting the good fight. Many were filled with consolation at the thought of so strong an additional bulwark being raised for the protection of Holy Church. Many vocations, hitherto offered to the Fathers and by them rejected, were now again laid at their feet, and this time were not repulsed. Among the happy souls who obeyed the call of grace were, besides Blessed James of Poggibonzi, Father Octavian, who was to be the first Procurator-General of the Order; Father Juncta, who was, later on, the socius of Father Octavian; Father Victor, St. Philip Benizi's future travelling companion; Father Marcellino, who became Prior of the Convent at Pistoja; Father Hildebrand, and others, whose names have not been recorded. Applications for admission were numerous, and, these being granted, were followed, in due course, by clothings, till at length the Novitiate was quite full: and, here, was to be seen an unwonted spectacle—that of the Superiors mingling in simple humility and cordial fellowship with their newly-arrived subjects.

This was the true beginning of the Order claimed by Our Lady. The heights of Monte Senario, although still tranquil and retired, presented a more busy scene than before. The life of regular observance now worked upon lines which harmonized the spiritual leadings of the past with present duties. The Seven Founders, having made those extensive alterations in the scope of their vocation which their Mother had sought from them, thought that it was still permissible for them to have a special preference for meditation, which is the very soul of the Religious and Apostolic life ; for bodily penance, that powerful lever for raising us to perfection ; and for a hidden and retired life, whence devout thoughts and holy desires spring. They treasured as much of their old spirit as was compatible with their new obligations, adding thereto all the ardent zeal with which their unconquerable humility and the conviction of their own unworthiness inspired them. Thus, whilst their mission was really changed, they seemed not to have forsaken their former paths. Silence, fasting, and retirement in their well-loved grottoes were still the delight of their lives.

All the duties of headship devolved upon St. Bonfilius, in whom the virtues of sweetness and gentleness, of wisdom and of prudence, so effectual in smoothing all difficulties, increased from day to day. In concert with his Brethren, he drew up a series of regulations, all stamped by extreme plainness and simplicity ; and, soon, under his paternal guidance, the little flock attained to a great degree of fervour.

It became evident that the original Hermitage of Monte Senario no longer sufficed for the increasing numbers of the devout Community . it was therefore necessary to set about erecting a new building eastward of the humble Oratory. To effect this the Lotharingi offered again their generous help, and it became possible to carry out the devised plan. This was the beginning of successive additions to the Mother-House of Monte Senario, which, however, have made it impossible for us, at this day, to trace out the exact site of the cells of the Seven Founders. Now the little Hermitage no longer exists : but there are some remains of the second structure, in which St. Sostene dwelt, for, by an unbroken tradition, his cell, now transformed into a chapel, is still preserved.

Meanwhile, there was no lack of activity among the inhabitants of Monte Senario. They were compelled by necessity to go, more than before, on their begging rounds to get the daily bread of their numerous family, and to continue to a certain extent their tasks of manual labour ; but the greater part of their time was now devoted to all the observances of the Religious Life, which were carried out with an ardour which the example of the Seven Founders did not allow to cool ; and the remaining portion was employed by those destined to the priesthood, in study. By the advice of the venerated Bishop Ardingo, the Founders themselves became students of theology, in preparation for their Ordination. With the exception of St. Manettus, who is said to have been versed in this science from his youth, they had been hitherto better acquainted with the lore of spirituality . but now, during their year of Novitiate, they set themselves to acquire all that was essential for them to know. Their chief source of instruction, very likely, was the Book of the Sentences, that well-known and admirable summary, which we owe to the genius of Peter Lombard, Bishop of Paris. The greatest Masters of the Schools had not yet made their mark. St. Thomas Aquinas was about fourteen years of age, and was beginning to feel the first yearnings for the Religious Life, upon which St. Bonaventure had entered a few years previously. Alexander of Hales was at the University of Paris, where he produced the first commentary on the Sentences of Peter Lombard.

The year of Novitiate, divided between study, prayer, and what may be termed the apprenticeship to the Rule of the Order, passed quickly away. It was a year most fruitful in grace, a year in which the foundations were sunk deep for the future building to rest upon. The Fathers rivalled one another in courage and good-will, striving first to perfect themselves, and then to train others to perfection. They knew that the harvest to come depended on the seeds now sown, and destined to spring up, year after year, through the course of ages. Their labours were indeed blessed, for among their Novices many became subsequently eminent both for holiness and learning.

At length, the Canonical term of their Novitiate being ended, they prepared for their Religious Profession. Long since, the irrevocable bond by which the soul gives itself wholly to God had been signed and sealed in their hearts. It had stood the test of time, and had triumphed over all obstacles. As regarded their interior dispositions, nothing more remained to be done ; but, in order to comply externally with the requirements of the Church, it was necessary to ratify by word of mouth the union which the heart entered upon by free will. Accordingly, during the spring of the year 1241, they went to Florence to make their profession in the hands of the Bishop. The ceremony was simple in the extreme. The good Bishop blessed with the customary prayers the habits, with which he clothed anew the Seven Founders, and then received their vows. St. Bonfilius, as Superior, made his profession to the Bishop ; and then he received the professions of his six companions. The form of the vows has been preserved, and is the same that was recorded in the first Constitutions of the Order. The words pronounced by St. Bonfilius were as follows :

" I, Brother Bonfilius, formerly Bonfilius dei Monaldi, profess and promise to Almighty God, to Blessed Mary, ever Virgin, and to the whole Court of Heaven, and you my Lord Bishop, as holding the place of the Superiors of this Order, who may come after me, to observe obedience and chastity, and to live without possessing aught of my own, as the Rule of St. Augustine prescribes, all my life long, in this Order".

The ceremony, though wholly without pomp or splendour, moved Bishop Ardingo deeply. The heart of the holy old man was touched, and he could not restrain his tears · he embraced the Founders tenderly, and gave vent to his inmost feelings in the words which he addressed to them. "My wishes are fulfilled," he said, "I now see that which mine eyes have desired to behold. You belong now wholly to the service of Our Lady . and your praises and homage will rise up to her unceasingly. Henceforth, she will be the Star of your lives Let us then jointly greet her in the words of our favourite hymn *Ave Maris Stella.*" Together they then recited antiphonally this hymn, which so well expressed all that they felt at so solemn a moment. The Bishop then again addressed them, saying "Hither-to you have been under my direction and wardship, like little children ; but, now that you are men grown, you are to be under the sweet yoke of Our Mother Mary, and you must obey your own Superior, according to the Rule of St. Augustine, who will hence-forth be your true Bishop." Having spoken thus, Ardingo desired them to choose their Superior, and they unanimously elected Brother Bonfilius to that office.

Finally, the Bishop, having sanctioned their choice, accorded to these first members of the Servite Order the most extended powers, both with respect to their outward development, and to their internal organization. By virtue of this grant they had the power of building oratories and houses in any part of the diocese, of ringing bells, of celebrating the Divine Office according to the Roman Rite, of admitting persons of all ranks and conditions to their Order, of gathering alms for whatever they required in the way of food and clothing, and for their general needs In short, Ardingo conferred upon them every privilege that he could bestow. One admonition alone remained for him which was to remind the newly professed that they must hold themselves in readiness to receive Ordination shortly, that so the work might be fittingly completed. In brief space, therefore, all, except St Alexis, who adhered to his original resolution, were admitted successively to minor Orders, the subdiaconate, diaconate, and priesthood. No record remains of these occurrences ; of their time of preparation, of their reception of Holy Orders, of their first Masses, of all circumstances of time and place, we know nothing. We can only feel assured that our Founders realized the tremendous importance of the event, and that they entered upon the priesthood adorned, even to superabounding, with the virtues essential to that state.

Thus was the Order of the Servants of Mary provided with living foundations well calculated to insure its success. But it likewise required an internal organization, depending on fixed rules, which should leave nothing to the hazard of caprice. This was the first task to be accomplished, since upon it hung the unity and regularity of the exercises of Religious Life. It was, therefore, the chief care of St. Bonfilius, and he set to work immediately to draw up certain Constitutions, which, appended to the Rule of St. Augustine, would bring it to completion for the greater general good.

CHAPTER X.

Ϯϐe First Constitutions of tϐe Order.

In the Rule of St. Augustine, the Community at Monte Senario possessed the guiding principles of Religious Life clearly defined. Nor was there wanting the means of interpreting its different clauses, so as to reduce them to practice. For the Orders which had followed that Rule, during a longer or shorter period, had thrown abundant light on the matter by their sagacious practice, and had sanctioned it by their use and authority. The Rule, however, was insufficient, since it only furnished general outlines, without entering into details. For example, in prescribing prayer and fasting, it did not mention at what time, nor to what extent, nor in what manner these exercises were to be kept. It enjoined that all were to obey the Superior, without explaining how his authority was conferred, or for what space of time he was to hold it. The Constitutions were to supply all that was omitted in the Rule. On this plan the greater number of the Religious Orders, especially the Dominicans and Premonstratensians, had hitherto acted.

Our holy Founders followed so good an example, and supplemented the Rule by a series of Statutes, or Constitutions, in which all that the said Rule left uncertain was stated with precision. As regards the drawing up of these Constitutions, two courses were open to the Founders of the Order. As other Founders had done before, they might conceive the first ideas after meditation and prayer, subsequently elaborate them after discussion, and finally consign them to writing for the guidance of the Religious. On the other hand, they might content themselves with legislating as occasions arose, whether of doubts to be solved, of abuses to be corrected, or of works to be undertaken. Of these two methods, our Saints preferred the second, as being more in accordance with their humility, which made them extremely mistrustful of them-selves. It was, therefore, during the course of years, as circum-stances presented themselves, that the body of the Constitutions was shaped, slowly and cautiously. The signs of this timidity are very legible throughout. But, whilst there might seem to be a want of vigour and promptitude in the proceedings, it was atoned for by greater solidity and security. There was an additional reason for this excessive circumspection and reserve. The Order was then in its infancy, feeble and powerless. It had come into existence at a critical moment No one knew nor was likely to know for some years to come, whether the designs of the Bishop of Florence would be approved of by the Holy See, and whether his cherished foun-dation would receive the Apostolic sanction. The law then in force respecting Religious Orders gave much reason to fear the contrary ; and the Servants of Mary were buoyed up wholly by hopes grounded on the promises of their heavenly Foundress—for, humanly speaking, all was uncertain.

It was, however, necessary, at the outset of their Religious Life, to frame a code of the most essential duties. This St. Bonfilius perfectly comprehended ; and, availing himself of all the counsels which he could obtain, he succeeded in reducing the chief points to a formula which has been traditionally preserved, and which was fully written out at a later period. This formula was the kernel of the complete Constitutions, the drawing up of which was reserved for St. Philip Benizi. Simple and brief though these earlier Con-stitutions were, they contained the marrow of the more extended code which was compiled thirty years later.

The first Constitutions are believed to have been taught by word of mouth, St Bonfilius and the other Fathers making them the theme of their spiritual Conferences , and, thus, all the Religious were trained in their school by precepts which, though unwritten, were none the less vigorously applied. Consequently all to a great extent were moulded after the pattern of the Seven Holy Founders, whose devotional leanings strongly influenced their teachings. Intense humility, love of meditation, a strong spirit of mortification, were inculcated unceasingly, and pervaded all their instructions. Whatsoever future might await the Order, our first Fathers thought their time well spent in endeavouring, by this method of direction, to train those under them to aim before all at sanctity.

The Constitutions by which the Religious Life of Monte Senario was organized were in the beginning, therefore, brief. But, although incomplete, they so clearly marked the character of the Order that it was impossible either for those who already belonged to it, or for those who desired to enter it, to be under any misapprehension We here give these Constitutions, taken from a text which was adopted some years later.

The Constitutions begin, as may be expected, with the Name of Mary, and proceed to treat of the duties owed to her. She who held so foremost a place in the spiritual history of our Seven Saints could not fail to stand at the head of their Rule. Accordingly, they decreed that all the observances in her honour, and for the promotion of her cultus, which had been practised by them in the Confraternity of the Laudesi, at La Camarzia, and at the Hermitage of Monte Senario, should be continued in their integrity, not the most insignificant omission being permitted. As they had reached by successive steps the fulness of their vocation, they made a point, now that they had arrived at the goal, of gathering together all the flowers which they had plucked on the road for Mary's shrine. Other observances might, they considered, be modified and relaxed in extreme cases; but such as concerned their Queen and Mother, they could only develop or preserve.

This first Constitution, therefore, decreed irrevocably for the Servite Order the observance of the following devotional practices: The recitation of the *Ave Maria* at the beginning of Mass, and of each hour of the Divine Office, and of the *Salve Regina* at the close of the same; the daily recitation of the little Office of the Blessed Virgin; the customary prayers in honour of Our Lady's Sorrows, on each day of the week except Saturday; and on Saturday the commemoration of her Joys.

This fundamental decree, inspired by that duty which all Servants of Mary must hold to be the most stringent, as well as the sweetest, ran as follows: "Before all things, the Statutes drawn up for the purpose of doing honour to the Most Blessed Virgin must be most strictly observed, particularly in the celebration of the Divine Office, and of Holy Mass, by reciting the *Ave Maria* at the beginning, and the *Salve Regina* at the conclusion. The Roman Breviary and Missal are alone to be used."

These various pious practices, although they did not in themselves amount to much, were important as regards their meaning. The intention of those who established them was to impress deeply on the hearts of all the conviction that, as their lives were devoted to Our Lady, to whom they consecrated the most solemn acts of their vocation, so to her all their most trivial actions should belong. The claims of their Mistress were to be ever present to their minds, and should they be tempted to a momentary forgetfulness, these constantly recurring devotions would quickly recall their wandering thoughts.

But there was little danger of such obliviousness, since, into the web of their daily lives was woven a thread of other habitual devotions to Our Lady, which made it well-nigh impossible. These pious observances were never formally recorded in the official Constitutions. Chief among them, we must class that cultus of the Sorrows of Mary, the offspring of which was St. Bonfilius' early piety, and which nurtured the riper years of his disciples. The retirement of the Hermitage fostered its growth in those loving hearts, and it was carefully watched over by the Blessed Virgin herself, who desired that it should be the distinctive badge of the Order of her Servants. It sprang up vigorously when the novices, for the first time, gathered round the Fathers; and, as years went on, it was to become so firmly rooted in the Order as to be perennial, and to flourish as luxuriantly after long years had passed as in its earliest days.

This devotion was a choice jewel, very precious to Our Lady; and, therefore, in the early days of the Order, she inspired her Seven Servants with the idea of placing it, as it were, in a casket where it might be more safely kept. This casket took the shape of that form of prayer which is called the Rosary. Instituted by St. Dominic between the years 1205 and 1213, during that war of the Albigenses which wasted the south of France with fire and sword, the Rosary quickly became known throughout Christendom. The Friars Preachers having settled in Florence in the year 1221, our Saints became acquainted with this devotion, and undoubtedly adopted it. But, as their thoughts dwelt chiefly on the mysteries which exclusively concerned Our Lady, and which recalled her Sorrows, they were moved to offer the homage of a new kind of Rosary, which they called a *Crown.* This Crown was composed of seven *Paternosters,* and seven times seven *Aves* in honour of the seven Sorrows of Our Blessed Mother, and concluded with three *Aves* in commemoration of her tears. This Crown must, undoubtedly, have proved most pleasing to Our Lady: and, though the flowers of which it was twined were of sombre hue, their perfume was none the less sweet to Mary, who would have her children ever remember the sword of grief wherewith her soul was pierced.

The Rosary of St. Dominic, as it was the first in order of time, kept the foremost rank, and became world-wide in its renown; whilst the humble Crown of the Servants of Mary flourished in the shade, so hidden from the general eye that its origin can scarcely now be traced. The same was the case with the entire Cultus, offered to the Queen of Sorrows by the Seven Founders and their first disciples. The Crown remained for many years a species of family devotion. It was transmitted by tradition from one generation to another, like an heirloom, which is handed on from father to son, without any legal document to attest the fact. We know, however, for certain, that St. Philip Benizi, the beloved son of the Seven Founders, always wore the beads of the Crown at his girdle, and that this was buried with him in his grave at Todi

The seven Sorrows, commemorated by the Crown, are all recorded in Holy Scripture—a warrant for the solidity of the devotion. We here give them in the very words of the Holy Gospels :—

The First Sorrow :—"A man named Simeon, just and devout, said to Mary : 'Thy own soul a sword shall pierce'" (St. Luke ii. 25, 34, 35).

The Second Sorrow :—"Arise, and take the Child and His Mother, and fly into Egypt : and be there until I shall tell thee" (St. Matt. ii. 13).

The Third Sorrow :—"Son, why hast Thou done so to us? Behold, Thy father and I have sought Thee sorrowing" (St. Luke ii. 48).

The Fourth Sorrow :—"And there followed Him a great multitude of women who bewailed and lamented. Daughters of Jerusalem, weep not for Me, but weep for yourselves and your children" (St. Luke xxiii. 27, 28).

The Fifth Sorrow :—"And when they were come to the place which is called Calvary, they crucified Him there" (St. Luke xxiii. 33). "Now there stood by the Cross of Jesus His Mother" (St. John xix 25).

The Sixth Sorrow :—"A certain rich man of Arimathea, named Joseph, asked the body of Jesus" (St. Matth. xxvii. 57, 58). "Our Blessed Lady received in her arms the Body of her Beloved Son." These last words were taken from the sacred Liturgy.

The Seventh Sorrow :—"And Joseph wrapped Him up in the fine linen, and laid Him in a sepulchre" (St. Mark xv. 46).

St. Luke narrates all these sorrowful events, except the second, which St. Matthew alone mentions in his Gospel : St. John joins with St. Luke to complete the history of the fifth : the last two have the privilege of being recorded by all the four Evangelists.

The Religious, as well as the faithful, learn, whilst telling the beads of this Crown, to draw from the purest source, and by the sweetest means, the true signification of the darkest and most perplexing of all mysteries—the mystery of pain and sorrow. As their lips repeat the *Aves*, they call to mind how this mystery pervaded the life of the most spotless Virgin ; and, hence, they are taught the most useful, the most strengthening, and the deepest lesson which is set before men. At each succeeding stage of the Way of Sorrows, there shining before them, in mild radiance, they read the watchwords of our holy Faith—self-immolation and charity : and, seeing these virtues so perfectly set forth by the purest of creatures, to whom so large a share of their love is given, they feel encouraged to overcome all obstacles, to make every sacrifice, and to practise the most heroic virtues.

Frequent repetition does but increase the fervour and efficacy of this prayer. As a great writer of recent times has said in speaking of the Rosary : "The free-thinker smiles as he watches long processions of people pass, repeating over and over again the same words ; but, those whom the Light has enlightened know well, that love's whole language consists of a single word, and, though it is spoken again and again, there is no sameness in it ".

Certainly, the Fathers of Monte Senario could have devised no better means than this Crown, whereby to impress on their own hearts, and on those of the faithful in general, the strange beauty of Our Lady's Sorrows.

In addition to the devotion to the Sorrows of Mary, the holy Founders also celebrated her Joys, consecrating to them the Saturday of each week. Thus, they lightened the somewhat sombre horizon of their contemplations, making them more acceptable to our infirm nature, and also more in accordance with the true history of Our Lady's life on earth. For, if the Mother of Jesus endured great sorrows, she also experienced immense joys. These joys were of brief duration, but they were deep as the sea, and continued to flow beneath the current of her grief. Our Saints showed herein their wisdom ; they well knew that poor human nature cannot thrive under an ever-clouded sky, and that light, hope, and gladness are as necessary to man, as space is to the birds that want to try their wings. On each recurring Saturday, therefore, they consoled themselves by meditating on the unspeakable joys by which Mary was visited amidst her many trials in this world, and those which have been hers in heaven since the close of her earthly exile.

The Little Office of the Blessed Virgin was another step of the ladder by which the spiritual household of Our Lady continually endeavoured to ascend to her, and to offer her the homage due from her Servants.

These observances were obligatory upon all the Religious ; but each one of them had, besides, full liberty, of which he frequently availed himself, to exercise his own ingenuity in various pious devices, whereby to keep himself, as it were, constantly in her presence, serving her, and expressing freely all his sentiments of reverential love and fidelity. Under the influence of this fervid spirit, the Seven Founders established the touching ceremony of crowning the statue of Our Blessed Lady on Holy Saturday, in remembrance of the joy with which her maternal heart overflowed on beholding her Divine Son risen from the sepulchre. On this occasion, they even celebrated Mass in the afternoon, a most unusual exception to the Church's rule ; and this was continued until the pontificate of St. Pius V.

We may hence perceive how perfectly our Founders fulfilled their vocation, and how ardently they carried out the wishes of the Most Blessed Virgin, whose heart must have rejoiced thereat.

In the second of the original Constitutions, the Fathers treated of fasting and abstinence. This was to them a fundamental point. They did not consider it possible that the Religious Life could be carried out without bodily mortification, and the renunciation of a great portion of the ordinary comforts of existence, particularly with regard to food.

This Constitution is as follows: "In the matter of fasting and abstinence, besides what the Church prescribes, the Brethren shall fast on Fridays, in remembrance of the habit which they have received, and of the mystery of the Redemption of mankind Likewise, in honour of the Virgin Mother, a fast shall begin in November and conclude on the Feast of the Nativity of Our Lord. As regards private mortifications, each one must defer to the decision of the Superior." Thus, with the observance of Lent as well, there were abundant opportunities provided for chastising the body by that most efficacious means of fasting: and in those days, fasts were kept with extreme strictness, only one meal a-day being allowed, and the evening collation being merely a slight refreshment taken before Compline.

The Third Constitution regulated the apparel of the Religious, in the following terms: "Under this head, all that was set forth, at the beginning, by the Seven Fathers and by the Bishop Ardingo, after the pattern given by Our Lady and adopted at the first Clothing, must be observed unalterably". Consequently, as we have already remarked, poverty and simplicity were to be the chief characteristics of the Servite garb.

The Fourth Constitution concerned the sleeping arrangements. "With respect to the beds," it says, "and to the regulations about sleeping, let beds of straw be used, with woollen sheets, and common coverlets, or skins of animals, according to the season—unless, it is added, any should desire a harder bed. In all these matters, the original custom shall be observed and, in particular, all shall sleep in their habits, only laying aside the cloak "

The Fifth Constitution completed all that was needful to say regarding bodily requirements, prescribing "that all should, like the Holy Apostles, take whatever was set before them, in the way of food or drink, by the charity of the faithful; and it enjoined that all should eat together, in the same place, at the same table, all sharing the same provisions ". This was wholly in accordance with the spirit of the Gospel, and also of the Rule of St. Augustine, which lays upon Religious the obligation of living like Brethren in unity and of having all things in common.

This principle, in itself most lofty and beautiful, gave rise to an unfortunate amount of difficulty and uncertainty as to what kind of food might allowably be eaten under these circumstances. In the Middle Ages great importance was rightly attached to this question of the different kinds of food. Four species were distinguished . the purely vegetable, especially fruits and herbs; fish and shell-fish, the products of birds and animals, as eggs and milk; and the birds and animals themselves. The free use of these various alimentary substances appeared incompatible with the Religious Life; therefore, in all the Orders, stringent restrictions were made, and the precepts of the Church for Lent and Advent were extended over the entire year. The Cistercians used vegetables only; the Benedictines employed fish in addition to these; and the Carthusians partook of eggs. Beyond these limits, none ventured; and thus they observed perpetual abstinence. The Apostolic life embraced by the Mendicant Orders, and the circumstance of their possessing no landed property, placed them in a difficult position. In their daily rounds, they could not always procure the abstinence fare prescribed by their Rule, and as they received alms in kind, they were often offered gifts of articles of food which the Rule prohibited. It was a question whether they should accept indiscriminately whatever was given to them, or whether they should take some things and refuse others. In some Orders, the Apostolic precept " Eat of anything that is set before you" (St. Luke x. 8 ; 1 Cor. x. 27) prevailed. In others, abstinence fare, in accordance with the Rule, was alone accepted. In the Servite Order, sometimes the former practice was observed, sometimes the latter; and, at length, when the custom of receiving alms in kind was finally given up, the mixed diet, as used by the Franciscans, of flesh meat and abstinence food was continued.

The last Constitution treated of the government of the Order. At first, there had been little need of legislation on this point, as the small group of Religious Associates were already provided with a Superior, and thus everything was perfectly well regulated. Besides, the Rule of St. Augustine fully instructed those in authority as to the proper method of discharging their Office. Nevertheless, a special Constitution was now drawn up, in order that nothing might be left in uncertainty, especially in view of possible eventualities such as the illness or absence of the Superior   "In each house," so runs this Constitution, " there shall be one who shall be the head, and who shall guide the rest and reprove them in perfect charity, and who shall furthermore provide for all their needs at a fitting time. He shall rightly be styled Prior, both because of his headship and of his usual office. All shall obey him, and he may choose to himself a Coadjutor, whose chief duty, among others, shall be to deal out to the Brethren all that they require in the shape of food. As the latter is to supply the place of the Prior, he shall of right be called Sub-Prior." This was a necessary ordinance : for, in all bodies of persons living in Community, it is necessary that there should be a living Authority, readily accessible, and taking the lead in everything. This is essential to the peace and well-being of all. By this Constitution, the Seven Founders completed their governmental code, the brevity of which was only surpassed by its opportuneness, moderation, and solidity.

Our Saints were now in a position to train their spiritual household, being aided by the traditions of the past, by the customs which had been adopted during those years spent in silence and retirement, and by the divine Oracles communicated to them by their Queen and Mother. The Rule and the Constitutions furnished them with the means of establishing that unity of purpose and feeling which enables a body of men to act as one, and thus of inspiring all the Servants of Mary with the true spirit of their vocation, that so they might glorify her by their daily lives within the Convent, and in the world without, by the apostolate of souls.

CHAPTER XI.

Course of Events in the Church—A Time of Suspense.

(1240—1243)

In the meantime, Gregory IX. had expired on the 21st August, 1241, amidst great trials, and at an advanced age. Some weeks later, Cardinal Goffredo de Castiglione, Bishop of Sabina, was elected in his place. This was the Cardinal who, when sent as legate to the North of Italy, a few years previously, had visited the Solitaries of Monte Senario, and had conceived a great admiration and regard for them. He took the name of Celestine IV. It is probable that he would have used the power given him by his supreme position in the Church, to promote the work undertaken by the Seven Founders; but he died after a pontificate of only fifteen days, just as he was about to enter upon negotiations with the Emperor of Germany. Thus ended all the hopes which were founded by the Religious of Monte Senario upon this Pontiff.

These events occurred whilst the Religious household of the Servants of Mary was establishing itself, arranging its internal organization, enlarging its ranks, and planning new foundations. The Fathers would willingly have settled in Florence, where they had always met with so much good-will from the devout Catholics; but the outlook was not, just then, particularly encouraging. The city was at the mercy of Frederick, whose headquarters were at Pisa, and whose partizans ruled absolutely in Florence. Hence, there was a complete separation between the Church party and that of the Imperialists, the Guelphs and the Ghibellines. The fire of civil discord was smouldering, and would have already burst forth, but for the presence of Frederick and his representatives, who enforced peace. The Fathers of Monte Senario were, besides, wholly destitute of funds : having resolved to possess nothing, they depended upon the generosity of pious souls who might be moved to offer them the necessary means of subsistence. Now, as they had not yet been formally recognized by the Pope, the faithful were somewhat reluctant to make sacrifices on their behalf. Moreover, though they were as yet but a young Community, they had already opponents who would not have been well pleased to see them settled in Florence. They, therefore, resolved to await some providential opportunity of making the wished-for foundation.

The Church was now passing through a time of much trouble. Having lost her Chief Pastor, she could not elect another because the Emperor of Germany refused to release the Cardinals whose persons he had seized. This widowhood lasted for a year and eight months, during which time Frederick continued to harass the faithful, to cause innumerable scandals, and to imperil an infinite number of souls. The wicked gave way to unrestrained excesses, and the good could only lament in silence. In this extremity, prayer was the only refuge; by prayer alone could Heaven be moved to grant the much-needed succour. The Bishops, therefore, ordained penitential exercises, to obtain the remission of these sufferings. Ardingo was not less fervent than his Brethren, and he summoned his flock to public expiatory ceremonies. It seems that these took place during the Lent of 1242.

A numerous deputation from Monte Senario assisted at these functions, in which all Christian souls, whatever their state of life, felt bound to take a part. The Fathers of Monte Senario could, perhaps, better than most others, enter into and feel for the sorrows of the Church, and they had long been in the habit of making them a subject of prayer. They were, therefore, among those most eager to answer to the summons of the saintly prelate It was on this occasion that, as with their accustomed modesty and recollection, they formed part of a procession through the City, they were unwillingly made conspicuous in the same singular manner that has been already related Infants, not yet naturally capable of articulate speech, again exclaimed: "Behold the Servants of Mary!" as they passed by. The crowds, present at the ceremony, soon became apprised of this, and crying out that it was a miracle, they looked with reverence on the men whom God was pleased to make the more known, the more they desired to remain hidden, and to be held of no account.

This circumstance added much to the attractive influence which our Seven Founders already possessed. More than ever they were now resorted to by famished souls desiring to be fed of their abundance ; and, since they were no longer apprehensive of erring as to their vocation, they freely lavished on all who came to them instruction, consolation, and encouragement, thus effecting an immense amount of good. Recruits now flocked to them in such numbers that they would soon be able to found several new houses, each containing about a dozen Religious.

They had no intenton, however, of abandoning Monte Senario: "For," says Pietro da Tidi, "so great was their veneration for the ways of God's Providence, whereby, in the beginning, he had prepared for them and made known to them the retreat of Monte Senario, that they were fully convinced it would not be allowable, either for themselves, or for the Brethren who should come after them, ever to abandon it. But, since they saw that the habitation there did not suffice to contain the Brethren whom they had already received, and those whom they proposed to receive, they were obliged to obtain other houses where they could dwell now, and leave for their successors to inhabit hereafter, and where they could devote themselves to the work of souls."

But, although the dawn of peace began to be visible on the political horizon, it was difficult to carry out these plans for the extension of the Order, so long as the sanction of the Sovereign Pontiff was not given to the work begun by the Bishop of Florence and the Seven Founders. The opposition which is ever excited by undertakings inspired by God Himself could only be successfully met by a decree emanating either directly from the Holy Father, or through the medium of an Apostolic Legate. Until the Head of the Church had spoken, everything would be disputed upon one pretext or another. Objections would be taken to the name of the Order, to the habit, to the Rule, to the customs and devotional practices of the Religious, and, in short, to every word and act of theirs. The reasons, too, for these attacks would be all the more plausible, since the General Lateran Council had expressly forbidden the establishment of new Religious Orders · this, in the hands of an adversary, was an unanswerable argument.

Therefore, the Religious of Monte Senario held aloof, and, like timid doves, sometimes remained hidden in their nest, instead of coming forth to spread their wings for distant flights.

The hindrance which proceeded from the most exalted quarter of all was not so great as those which arose close at hand. To their ill-wishers, the Servants of Mary were harmless enough so long as they remained at Monte Senario, which to the world in general appeared an inaccesible wilderness. But, if they left their solitude, and began to preach and teach in the cities, there was no saying to what such steps might lead. We shall find that it was the lot of the Order to endure these trials for more than half a century. This forms the best explanation of the fact that Monte Senario was during several years the only house, and that the advances of the Bishops and some neighbouring cities, who were desirous of having a foundation of the Servants of Mary, were not promptly answered. The household of Monte Senario increased in numbers upon the spot, but was unable to branch out at once in other directions without giving rise to stormy discussions. In those days there were many eager for a fray, and the members of the new Order feared that they might become the cause of painful conflicts if they emerged from their solitude to appear in the busy scenes of city life.

Thus passed a space of about four years, from April, 1240, to the middle of 1243, during which time the Servite Annals present a blank. The swarm of Monte Senario had become a host of working bees ; but they were unwillingly compelled to seek for honey here and there, in their mountain solitude and round about it, noiselessly and in secret. The Religious of Monte Senario dwelt in such impenetrable seclusion that scarcely any sound of their doings reached the outer world. But their time was not wasted. The Seven Founders had set their hands to the work, and were assiduously tending the plants confided to their care by the Blessed Virgin. St. Bonfilius retained the helm of government : St. Amideus was Master of the Novices ; St. Buonagiunta was the Superior's able auxiliary : St. Manettus utilized his learning by imparting it to the others ; St. Alexis was devoted to the material interests of the Community, which in nowise hindered his steady growth in holiness , St. Hugh and St. Sostene vied with each other in zeal, giving a good example in all things, and helping the other Fathers in every possible way , Blessed James di Poggibonzi was, as ever, the tried and faithful counsellor of all. All loved more fervently day by day the things of God, became more versed in meditation, and made greater progress in the virtues which make up the character of the perfect Religious. Therefore, the various hindrances to the visible propagation of the Order were largely compensated for by the even greater harvest of interior graces reaped by the Brethren in their hidden life.

Meanwhile, Our Lady, whose regard for her Servants continually increased, smoothed away all obstacles, and solved difficulties, by unhoped for methods, much sooner than had been expected. In fact, after a few years of expectation, the first foundations were to take place, and the man destined by Providence to open a way for the Order was on the point of making his appearance in Florence.

Thus the work for which our Seven Founders were destined from all eternity, and for which it was necessary that they should become Saints, was now to come forth into the full light of day. At first, indeed, they were to be alone in the desert, far from the tumult of the world, and apparently employed only on the work of their own sanctification ; but now they were commanded to have spiritual children, and to exercise their holy influence for the good of souls. Their field of action was enlarged, and it comprised town and country and distant lands : in whatever corner of the earth

Jesus and Mary were unknown and unloved, there was to be their apostolate And, as in the first and the second period, so in the third, all that they had to do was to be done under Mary's protection and in obedience to her commands ; for she herself appeared to them in dazzling splendour, and revealed to them that she had called them from the beginning in order that, under the glorious title of Servants of Mary, they might be wholly hers ; and it was to be her care that nothing should be wanting to them to enable them to fulfil her designs.

Thus closed the period of the foundation with all its attendant wonders of grace. A new epoch now began, during which the Seven Founders propagated and extended the Order at home and abroad ; endured trials of every kind ; grew daily more exercised in the practice of heroic virtues ; and, lastly, were favoured, each in his turn, with the privilege of a happy and a holy death, in the odour of sanctity.

BOOK III.

EXTENSION—CONSOLIDATION—TRIALS—
TRIUMPH (1243-1310—1717-1888).

CHAPTER I.

First Foundations: Siena, Pistoja, Arezzo—Chapter on Monte Senario—Beginnings of Cafaggio.

(1243—1244).

THE year 1243 had begun, and Monte Senario was still detaining its guests. Some of their number, it is true, went forth occasionally to one place or to another, in order to toil in the Master's Vineyard ; but no regular foundation had as yet been made : the causes already mentioned had hitherto combined to chill the aspirations of St. Bonfilius and his Brethren. But at length a concurrence of favourable circumstances, and especially the earnest entreaties of several Bishops and cities, made the Seven Founders decide upon taking steps towards the foundation of the first Convents of the Order, and it seems that Siena was the first city to possess the Servants of Mary.

Siena was a well-chosen spot wherein to plant an offshoot of Monte Senario. From a geographical point of view, she was the most important city of Lower Tuscany. Situated in the heart of that region, perched on the crest of lofty hills, she completely commanded the surrounding plains. Her origin was lost in the mists of antiquity ; many of her buildings bore traces of Etruscan handiwork, whilst her name was Roman. Seen from a distance, with her encircling walls, her cathedral, and other public buildings, she looked a perfect type of a provincial capital. From a political point of view, she was the seat of a fairly prosperous republic, with an increasing population of between thirty and forty thousand. Although she could not aspire to rule over Florence, she could easily become her rival ; and Florence knew this, and ever feared to be excelled by her. Hence, the city of the Arno looked upon Siena as a foe to whom no quarter should be shown, until she would own herself to be vanquished. A perpetual series of small wars, therefore, ensued, in which Florence was usually the victress. The inhabitants of Siena, as of all Italian cities, were divided into two factions; but that of the Emperor was by far the most powerful, and she was, therefore, counted as a Ghibelline stronghold

By a singular species of self-contradiction, Siena, although favouring the Imperial rather than the Papal party, was yet the most intensely religious city in Italy, and her piety was, moreover, characterized by a devotion to Our Blessed Lady which could nowhere be surpassed. The firm and childlike faith of the Sienese was concentrated on the Mother of God with a fervour which nothing could diminish. This love of the Immaculate Virgin was an heirloom from the far-distant past. A cherished tradition ascribes its propagation to a disciple of the holy Apostles themselves, St. Ansano, who, coming to Siena to preach the glad tidings of the Gospel, had there converted many of the inhabitants. In order to help them to preserve their infant faith, the Saint urged them to look with filial confidence to the Mother of the Redeemer ; and from thenceforth his docile hearers devoted themselves so ardently to the cultus of Our Lady, that it seemed to pervade the entire range of their belief. As years passed, so did their love of Mary increase, till Siena became renowned far and wide by the name of Our Lady's City.

This love of the Blessed Virgin was to the Sienese as a strong shield protecting them against the Manichean heresies of the Cathari, and to this it was due that they were, on the one hand, wholly uninfected by that deadly poison ; and on the other, whilst keeping fast to their traditional policy of fidelity to the Empire, they held aloof from the excommunicated Emperor. It was, then, but natural that Siena should have been eager to welcome the ambassadors of the Queen of Heaven, so soon as the news had reached her of the occurrences which had decided the first Seven Fathers to found an Order bearing the name of Servants of Mary, for nothing could have been more in unison with the feelings of the population towards Our Lady.

The exact date of this foundation is unknown, but it seems to have taken place towards the middle of the year 1243 ; and though the Chronicles are rather obscure as to its origin, we gather from them that it began in the following manner : —

At that time Siena possessed as Bishop an old man, who was beloved and esteemed by all on account of his wisdom and virtue. His name was Bonfilius, like that of the Superior of the Servants of Mary. In former times he had been singularly struck by all the marvellous facts which had concerned our Seven Saints, and from that moment he had never ceased to feel a keen desire to see these Solitaries and to converse with them. The last events which had occurred only increased his desire, and having shortly afterwards occasion to go to Florence, he put his desires into execution and went to Monte Senario. There he was received with all the marks of veneration which were due to his age and his merits ; and he even gladly accepted the invitation of the poor Hermits to dine at their table.

During the repast, St. Bonfilius and his companions related to him the origin of their Order and the kind of life which they had adopted. Further, with the frankness belonging to men of God, they confided to him something of the favours which had been granted them from Heaven The Prelate, fired with holy curiosity, asked them several questions, to which they replied with charming simplicity. During the conversation, the other Religious maintained a profound silence, listening with great modesty. Already the good Bishop felt filled with admiration at all which he heard and saw ; but after he had visited the Hermitage, the Oratory, and the Grottoes, he conceived so great an affection for the Servants of Mary that he quickly formed the project of having some of them in Siena. This he at once named to St. Bonfilius, who, after consulting with his Brethren, believed that it was their duty to acquiesce, and so without further delay he chose St. Alexis and Brother Victor to go upon this mission.

The Prelate took these two away with him to Siena, where he lodged them in his own house. The following day he called together the people of Siena, and briefly related to them the history of the Servants of Mary, their mode of living, their virtues, and their observances, and he concluded by asking them to give a good welcome to their newly-arrived visitors. The Sienese quickly responded to this call upon their sympathy, and they promised to comply liberally with the expectations of their Bishop, and it was then decided that the city should provide for their maintenance, and should also build a Chapel and Convent for them.

When the meeting was over, the Sienese surrounded the two Religious, admiring their habit, which they now saw for the first time, and conversing with them upon everything relating to their Order. St. Alexis and Brother Victor felt quite confused at the attention paid to them, but they replied with modesty and affability to all that their interrogators desired to know. From that time their humility, sweetness, and amiability gained for them the love of the people of Siena, who became more and more attached to the two Servants of Mary.

Soon afterwards Messer Bonfilius proposed to them a piece of ground outside the walls, at the foot of the hill of St. Clement, near to the gate called Castel del Montone. This land belonged to a wealthy proprietor of Siena, who, filled with devotion towards those who wore the habit of the Sorrows of Mary, presented it to the

Bishop for the use of the Servants of the Blessed Virgin. According to the engagement already made, the Oratory and Convent were soon built, and were placed under the protection and name of the Blessed Virgin. When this was accomplished, St. Bonfilius sent six more Religious from Monte Senario to form a Community. From that time the Servants of Mary have ever been a source of edification to the inhabitants of Siena. St. Alexis especially was venerated by all as a Saint, and he captivated the hearts of all those who approached him by his sweet and gentle manners, and his words, which savoured more of heaven than of earth. From the ardour with which he spoke of Jesus and Mary, all saw clearly that his whole soul was absorbed in God. The Sienese were always most liberal benefactors to the Servants of Mary, ever affording them alms when such were solicited.

Then, shortly afterwards, numbers of young men were to be seen hastening, in the springtime of their lives, to dedicate themselves to the service of the Blessed Virgin in this monastery, under the direction of her Servants. Though they were of noble parentage, and were filled with fervour, they were not at once received ; they were well examined, and severely proved, in order to ascertain if their vocation was true, and not the result of momentary enthusiasm. These delays, so far from giving discouragement to the young men, only confirmed them in their design. And the Fathers, seeing their earnestness, admitted them to the clothing. They selected a Feast-day, and sang Mass; and the Postulants, after being fed with the Bread of Angels, stripped off their worldly garments to receive, in the midst of tears from all beholders, the humble livery of the Servants of Mary, trembling with joy at the thought that they had embraced for ever the service of the Queen of Heaven.

These first subjects went through their novitiate with all these good dispositions of piety and fervour, and each of them made great progress in virtue.

Such was the commencement of this Convent of Siena, which was governed at first by St. Alexis, and a few years later by Blessed James of Poggibonzi.

It never ceased to be what we might almost term the spoilt child of the Sienese, both Republic and people All strove to supply its smallest needs, and to heap gifts upon it. Nor did it prosper less spiritually than temporally. The Religious rapidly increased in numbers, and soon this fertile soil, consecrated in an especial manner to be the portion of the Blessed Virgin, brought forth a harvest of great Saints. Here were fostered St. Peregrino Latiosi, Blessed Gioacchino Piccolomini, and Francesco Patrizi, whose holy lives and innocent souls gave glory to the spotless purity of Mary.

Not long after the foundation of Siena another Convent was established.

About five-and-thirty miles from Florence, near the source of the river Ombrone, stands the small city of Pistoja. Her historic record, and the amount of influence which she exercised, seem out of all proportion to her size and population. At the time of which we are speaking, she did not number more than twelve thousand inhabitants, and she could not attempt to compete in arms with Florence. The majority of her citizens sided with the Empire ; and hence they were little friendly to a city so devoted to the Papal party as was Florence. Pistoja, moreover, had been imprudent enough to defy her , and, consequently, had been forced to undergo much suffering at the hands of the irritated Florentines.

In this city dwelt a family, by name Cancellieri, of ancient descent, and possessed of great influence, who were the leaders of the Guelph party. One of the members of this family was a certain Messer Marsilio, of canonical rank, and Rector of a Church situated outside the walls, near the gate which bore the name of his race, the Porta Cancellieri. Whether his age or his health made him unequal to the task, cannot now be known ; but it seems that a certain Brother Luciano, of the Servite Order, was appointed to act as his Chaplain, or Coadjutor. No doubt the good Canon had heard a favourable report of the Order, and was, in consequence, well-disposed towards it, and before long he made up his mind to hand over his Church to the Servite Fathers. After a consultation with the Bishop of Pistoja, Graziadio Berlinghieri, who was himself a Florentine by birth, and who highly approved of the plan, it was decided that the Order should take possession on 16th February, 1244.

The Fathers were desirous that this foundation should be made with all the necessary formalities prescribed by canonical rule. Four Religious were chosen for this first filiation ; but none of the original Seven Fathers were included in the number. Fra Marcellino, one of the first received in the Order, was elected Prior ; his companions were Fra Luciano, Fra Giovanni, Fra Agostino, and Fra Filippo.

Mati, with his quaint simplicity, thus relates the circumstances attendant on the taking possession of the Church :—

"On the sixteenth of February, 1244, we Brothers, Servants of the Virgin Mary, entered upon the possession of the Convent and its out-buildings, all situated close to Pistoja, just outside Porta Cancellieri. The Church, which is called Santa Maria Novellecta, was in charge of Messer Marsilio, the Canon, one of the noble house of Cancellieri. The Chaplain of the said Church was Brother Luciano of our Order, who did duty for Messer Marsilio. We made our entry processionally, singing the *Salve Regina* : we were accompanied by his Lordship the Bishop, by Messer Marsilio, the Rector of the Church, and Messer Marco degli Amadori, both of whom were

Canons and priests, and by many other clergy ; also, by a goodly number of secular persons, both men and women ; among these were Messer Vinciguerra Tinghi, and his son Messer Forte, both of whom, in conjunction with Messer Marsilio, had much to do with our coming to Pistoja. All the inhabitants greatly rejoiced when they saw us installed in their city. The Bishop sang Mass with full solemnities, and then blessed the people, and announced the Indulgence ; and he made known to all that henceforth the Church should be called St. Mary of the Servites, and no longer by its former name.

"Afterwards, my Lord the Bishop, with the venerable Canons Marsilio and Marco, and Messer Vinciguerra and Messer Forte, with many others, remained at the Convent for breakfast. This meal they took, in brotherly love, with the Prior and the Brethren ; and holy poverty was duly observed, although the Bishop and many of the guests had supplied our deficiencies, and abundant gifts had been sent to us by the citizens.

"Grace having been said after the repast, all cordially took leave of the Prior and the Brethren, and then withdrew, full of joy and consolation at the thonght of having among them a Community bearing the name of Servants of the Virgin Mary. For this they gave thanks to God and to his Blessed Mother ; and all the citizens gave thanks likewise ; so that for many days nothing else was talked of but the edification which all found in the company of the Brethren, whose sincerity, simplicity, and kindliness redounded to the glory of God, and the praise of His Mother, Our Lady St. Mary."

St. Bonfilius sent, not very long after the first installation, seven other Religious to Pistoja, in order to have in the Community a number of twelve Religious.

The Convent of Arezzo was founded about the same time as that of Pistoja, either a little before or afterwards. Arezzo, a town of Tuscany, situated on the Arno, was a place of great antiquity, and, having been for a long time mixed up with all the debates in Italy, was considered a place of some importance. She possessed within her walls partizans of both the political factions, which were setting all the cities of the Peninsula at variance.

It appears that a deputation from the inhabitants of Arezzo repaired to Monte Senario in order to solicit that a Community of the newly-formed Religious might be sent to their city. The envoys accompanied their demand by most enticing promises. St. Bonfilius and his Brethren thought it right to give a favourable answer to this request, and shortly afterwards some Religious departed from among them to take possession of this new post. They were gladly welcomed on their arrival at Arezzo, and they were presented with a small Church, called San Salvatore, and a suitable Convent was built for them adjoining the Church. This Convent was to become celebrated fifty years later by the miracle which was wrought there by St. Philip. This was the third Convent which was founded.

After making these foundations, St. Bonfilius thought it expedient to call together all the wisest and most experienced Fathers to confer upon the affairs of the Order at Monte Senario. It was of the utmost importance that all the various observances should be so well fixed that all the new Convents could adopt them, and thus lead a life in perfect accord with their centre, Monte Senario. The formula was therefore rearranged in a manner more precise. Those Statutes formed the first Constitutions of the Order, called the Constitutions of St. Bonfilius. They were, as we have seen, reduced to some essential points; but nevertheless were sufficient at first to characterize the Order, and demonstrate its life and observances. The traditions and the practices of the past, with the initiative of the Superiors and those under him, sufficed to supply the rest.

Moreover, to preserve unity, they added the following resolution:—" In order that the different members of this Institution should be united under one head, it is decided that among the Priors of the different Convents there shall be one Superior to all the others, and to him shall belong the chief direction both of spiritual and temporal affairs, and nothing shall be done without his authority and consent; and it is advisable that in future, as it has been in times past, this superiority shall be vested in the Prior of Monte Senario". This Rule was of the highest importance, because it ought to give to the Order so perfect a combination that it would be a source of benefits without number.

At last they proceeded to the election of the Priors for the different Convents, and especially of the one for Monte Senario. St. Bonfilius was unanimously confirmed by all the Fathers as Superior-General, for each one of them had already had experience of his goodness and his wisdom. They then proceeded to the election of the Priors of Siena, Pistoja, and Arezzo, when the Priors already chosen by the Holy Founders were confirmed in their office.

The property question very likely was also in this chapter brought forward, and it was resolved that the Order should possess nothing, even in common. The Seven Saints had from the beginning advocated absolute poverty; and notwithstanding the many cares which this involved in practice, they perseveringly held to their point. Whilst they were living as Solitaries at Monte Senario, it was easy for them to practise their cherished virtue; but with their present mission involving the expenses of fresh foundations, many difficulties would present themselves. Undaunted by these, they unanimously decided that for the future their vow of poverty was to include the renunciation of all property in right and in fact. They then, with one accord, pronounced this vow which, by wholly removing the burden of worldly cares, left them free to run with greater speed in the race of perfection.

This Conference, which was necessary for the discussion of so many matters affecting the interests of the Order, was likewise a golden opportunity for the renewal of brotherly intercourse between the Religious. Many of them had long been parted from the first Fathers, and now eagerly sought them to pour out all the troubles and anxieties with which the interval of separation had been filled. And the Seven Founders joyfully welcomed their spiritual children, bestowing on them instruction and consolation, with paternal exhortations to sustain the combats which awaited them.

Besides, there was between all those present an intermingling of thoughts, hopes, and fears. They rejoiced to verify the perfect unanimity of feeling subsisting among them. They saw clearly that the numerous obstacles before them were all according to the divine decrees, since suffering would ever be the chief tool wherewith their work was to be wrought. Then, remembering all that Our Lady had hitherto done for them, they said one to another that she would never fail them in their hour of need, and that, therefore, they ought never to give way to discouragement.

When this Conference broke up, the members bade one another farewell, with the hope of frequent meetings of a like nature. They took courage in the thought that they could again hold counsel together, and for a brief space enjoy mutual society in the peace of the Lord, and under the protection of His Blessed Mother. Thus all went forth with glad hearts, ready to encounter future trials, if only they might build up and increase their well-loved Order.

Not long after the Chapter was dissolved, St. Bonfilius went to Bishop Ardingo at Florence in order to place before him the Constitutions and adopted Rules. The good Bishop willingly gave his sanction to all that had been decided upon, and it gave him great joy to see the confidence and affection with which St. Bonfilius was treated, because he also loved him with a very tender affection.

As to Florence, at this time the Order did not possess any Convent in that city. But if our Saints had not yet established themselves in their native place in a regular and canonical manner, it is certain that they had about that period a beginning of installation. The fact is explained as follows:—

St. Bonfilius, seeing the impossibility to provide for the needs of his Brethren at Monte Senario, was alarmed at the risk incurred by their health. For how could they with weakened bodies fulfil all the requirements of their calling? As usual, the good Superior had recourse to prayer ; and after examining into the matter before God, he saw clearly that it could not have entered into the designs of Divine Providence to lead the Servants of Mary into the desert, there to perish with hunger. How, indeed, could they continue to

play the part of Mary at the feet of Our Lord, if the task of Martha
was left undone! Reflecting further, he recognized that the needs
of the poor are designed by Our Heavenly Father to draw forth the
charity of the rich, who thus make friends to themselves of the
mammon of iniquity. He therefore determined to send the Brothers
regularly and systematically in quest of alms, in order that the
Community might be supplied with the necessaries of life. They
were to go forth two and two on appointed days, and, with wallets
on their shoulders and staves in their hands, they were to beg from
door to door through the streets of wealthy Florence. Thus, at one
and the same time an edifying example of humility would be given
to the proud and luxurious city, and a good opportunity would be
offered to the rich of practising those alms-deeds which deliver
from death and purge away sins.

St. Bonfilius rejoiced in having procured some mitigation of the
hardships which his companions had endured; and now he was
desirous of securing an alleviation of the fatigues which the distance
of Florence from Monte Senario, the intense heat during the summer
season, and the inclemency of winter, would entail on those who
were dispatched on those missions. After much thought, he
determined to become possessed of some halting-place near
Florence, where his Brethren could rest for the night before
returning.

Just beyond the walls of Florence, looking in a north-easterly
direction towards Monte Senario, and in one angle of the four cross
ways formed by the intersection of the Via di Balla and the road
leading from the city to Cafaggio, stood a small Oratory, such as
was often built in those days on the highway. This Oratory was
known as Santa Maria di Cafaggio, and the neighbourhood was
retired and almost deserted. All around stretched a meadow,
watered by the rapid stream of the Mugnone, where cattle of a
choice breed grazed. It was there that the Emperor Henry IV.,
after having foresworn himself in 1077, and having been repulsed
before the walls of Rome, encamped in 1081 to besiege Florence;
but having vainly renewed his assaults for the space of three
months, he was forced to withdraw his troops. In thankgiving for
their deliverance, the Florentines had built that Chapel to the
Mother of God. A certain amount of historical interest thus
attached to the spot to which was now allotted a greater destiny:
no longer the camp of an earthly monarch, it was to become one of
the thrones on earth of the Queen of Heaven.

It was this Chapel and a portion of the adjoining ground that
St. Bonfilius had in view for the carrying out of his plan. Thanks
to the munificence of the republic, to which the property belonged,
he was enabled to become the possessor of it. A small cottage was
added to the Chapel: this was all that was needed for the accommo-

dation of the Servants of Mary. There they would be able to seek refuge against fatigue or bad weather.

As soon as the Religious of Monte Senario were free to occupy their temporary lodging at Cafaggio, they again became a centre of attraction. The Florentines besought permission to visit them and bring them alms, and the neighbouring proprietors offered them some adjacent land, expressing their desire that they would have soon a permanent dwelling-place in Florence, for the welfare and happiness of the inhabitants. Among these benefactors are especially named Bonvicino Frenaio, son of Ceci ; Aldobrandino di Drudulo and his son Orlando, of the noble family of Visdomini ; and Bencivenni, son of Guernerio.

The Holy Founders, far from opposing this project, most readily agreed to it, as it fulfilled their most earnest desires. In it they beheld the means of establishing a focus for good in their beloved Florence. They rejoiced also that by diminishing the Religious at Monte Senario, they were able to give to that dear solitude something of its primitive aspect. The Bishop Ardingo, on his side, favoured with all his power a plan which, however, he would not see realized. In every case it was a sweet subject of hope to our Saints ; but it was necessary to wait several years before it became an accomplished fact.

Authors do not agree about the period when that temporary dwelling was commenced. Some place it as far back as 1234, in the beginning of Monte Senario. But it seems more probable that it was only about 1242 that St. Bonfilius took that determination. The admission of subjects on the one side, and the absence of resources on the other, obliged the holy Fathers to seek in regular and frequent rounds the daily bread of an ever-increasing family.

These beginnings were abundant in consolations, but rivalry and opposition were not wanting, and everyone might conjecture that they would increase in violence in the future. Perhaps our Saints would have been disconcerted by this, if the providential care of their Heavenly Mother had not sent to them a man more capable than anyone to communicate that courage which faces all difficulties, and never thinks of retrograding.

CHAPTER II.

St. Peter of Verona at Florence.

(1244—1245.)

AFTER a dreary interregnum of a year and two months, Innocent IV. was at length chosen to succeed Gregory IX. on the pontifical throne, on 25th June, 1243.

The new Pope was a learned man, of great strength of will. He set himself, without loss of time, to seek remedies for the evils then afflicting the Church. He hastened to make pacific proposals to Frederick, but at first unsuccessfully; for the haughty Emperor only met them with the most exacting counter-propositions. Another source of anxiety to the Pontiff was the Catharist heresy, which daily assumed more formidable proportions. He consequently approved of the energetic measures taken by his predecessor to arrest its progress; and as Florence had become one of the chief strongholds of error, he saw how essential it was that the decisive blow should be struck in that city.

It may be said, indeed, that heresy ruled there unchecked. The orders given by Gregory IX. with the view of repressing it had been, from laxity, from prudence, or from inability, imperfectly carried out. The saintly Bishop Ardingo was full of zeal, but he was feebly seconded by circumstances. The search for heretics was not kept up; and even when some were brought before the tribunal, the judge hesitated to pronounce against them. Thus, the Cathari were made aware of their strength, and presumed upon it. The consequences were lamentable, and the evil reached a point at which it became almost past cure. To put a stop to this state of ruin, it became necessary to seek a man of iron will who would be prepared to resort to the strongest measures rather than give way. When the moment of need came, the man was found.

In the north of Italy lived a Religious of the Order of St. Dominic, called Peter of Verona. He was still young, fervent of spirit, and practising virtue even to an heroic degree. For about six years he had been struggling against the Cathari, chiefly at Milan. He knew them thoroughly; and he saw that their tenacity to evil could only be overcome by the light of divine truth, blended with the flame of brotherly charity. Failing these spiritual weapons, there was nothing left but the secular arm in all its rigour. The zealous Dominican was gifted with marvellous eloquence: he was endowed, too, with a most elevated degree of prayer; and his devotion to Our Lady was as loving as that of a child.

Towards this Religious the attention of the Sovereign Pontiff was now directed; or, rather, it may be said that his talents and personal holiness gained for him the favourable opinion of the Holy Father, from whom he received all the necessary powers, together with the order to repair at once to Florence, towards the close of the year 1244.

The intrepid Dominican was speedily installed at Santa Maria Novella, the Convent of his Order, and ready for the campaign which he began at once upon his arrival. The rapid succession of stirring scenes in the tremendous drama which was now enacted culminated in the complete victory of truth over error.

No sooner did the Inquisitor enter Florence than he took a general survey of the state of affairs, and diligently collected all available information. Having made his observations, he resolved to take the initiative, and immediately began a course of sermons, in which he set forth the Catholic doctrine in all its purity, contrasting it with the grave and hateful errors, both of teaching and of practice, adopted by the Manichees. These discourses, uttered by the ringing voice of the eloquent preacher who stood there, regardless of consequences, speaking with that clear-sighted fervour which is the fruit of a saintly life, produced widely different effects upon the hearers. Some of them, touched and enlightened, renounced their errors; others, blinded by pride and passions, remained obstinate; while many, unhappily, swayed by human respect and evil counsel, became more and more hardened. Extreme measures had at length to be resorted to. Those who refused to submit, being brought before the tribunal of the Inquisition and convicted, were condemned to suffer under the stern laws of those days. Justice had her course. Persuasion proving inefficacious, it was necessary to use force, and to cut off the unsound members, in order to preserve the health of the whole body.

This inflexible administration of the law filled the Cathari with rage, and they threatened Peter of Verona and his Brethren at Santa Maria Novella with death. The dauntless Inquisitor, in order to guard against this danger, appealed to those qualified to bear arms to protect the Convent and to defend the inmates. The new troops were clad in white tunics, with a red cross on the breast, and were known as the Captains of Santa Maria. From this time forward they were at the orders of Peter of Verona during his struggle with the heretics, who soon found themselves confronted with the alternative of abjuration or death.

The enraged Cathari, supported by the Podesta, or Chief Magistrate of Florence, and by the family of the Baroni, all of whom were Ghibellines and adherents of their sect, also took up arms. This being made known to the Inquisitors, they cited the leaders of the rebellion before their tribunal. These were at first found guilty, and were made to sign a promise to comply with the requirements of the judges, giving bail, at the same time, to the amount of a thousand pounds. But suddenly the Podesta demanded the revocation of the sentence, which was strenuously upheld by Peter of Verona. The situation soon became critical. The contending parties met face to face, the defenders of the good cause eager to prove their attachment to the faith, and the heretics thirsting for revenge. Peter then summoned the faithful to assemble in the Churches of Santa Reparata and Santa Maria Novella, on St. Bartholomew's Day, 24th August, to hear the condemnation of the Podesta, whose high position only increased the offence of which he had been guilty, in temporizing with heresy. Whilst the people were gathered together in Santa Reparata to hear the sermon, the Cathari and the Ghibellines entered the square, fully armed, and, at a concerted signal, rushed into the Church and drove out the faithful with savage violence, wounding many, and even killing several.

Without loss of time, Peter of Verona, with the approval of the Bishop, collected the people that afternoon in the square of Santa Maria Novella, and in a resolute speech he again pronounced sentence on the Podesta and the house of the Baroni. He then exhorted the defenders of the faith to be ready to shed their blood, if needful, in the cause of God and of His Truth. The Captains of Santa Maria now advanced, headed by Peter of Verona, who bore the white Standard with the red cross. The Cathari were posted near at hand, at a spot called St. Sixtus' Well (Pozzo San Sisto). Soon the troops of Peter of Verona, which were fired with enthusiastic zeal, were attacked; then they fell upon the heretics, who, giving way under the shock of the onset, broke their ranks and fled across the Ponte Vecchio to the district of Oltrarno. The defenders of the faith pursued them, and a general conflict followed, in which most of the Cathari perished.

This stern lesson produced a marked effect on the survivors, many of whom repaired to Santa Maria Novella, and there abjured their errors and were reconciled to the Church.

Thus was Manicheeism stamped out in Florence. The means employed were effectual, but it must be owned that they were extremely severe. Still, it is doubtful whether gentler measures would have sufficed to overcome this obstinate and seductive heresy; and it is certain that a fearful fate must have been in store for the fair city of Florence had this deadly disease been suffered to infect the very springs of life within her.

Be this as it may, Peter of Verona, who seemed only to have come to overthrow the Cathari, had a more peaceful and pleasing mission to fulfil. It was his task to strengthen the hearts of the Servants of Mary, and to speed them on their course. For there was no disguising the fact that, although the internal organization of the devout Community at Monte Senario was complete, and several houses had been already established with the approbation of the Bishops, their external regulations might at any moment be contested. The name, the habit, the Rule—in short, all the prominent and distinctive characteristics of the Order were liable to be called in question so long as the Holy See remained mute. Thus, the work ran the risk of suffering shipwreck; for, if the Order ceased to preserve its own peculiar title, mould, and aim, it thereby lost its claim to exist as a corporate body. The Inquisitor of Milan, who held that office in Florence, could not apply any specific remedy in this case, since he had no authority to do so.

But it was plain that Our Lord and His Blessed Mother had appointed him to be the guide and comforter of the Servants of Mary, to set their feet in the right road, and to cheer them onward in spite of all obstacles.

All Florence came to hear the sermons and conferences of the eloquent Dominican. Nobles, citizens, peasants, churchmen, and laymen, all gathered round him ; and the Seven Founders of Monte Senario distinguished themselves also by their assiduous attendance.

But, whilst Peter of Verona was absorbed in these external labours, a remarkable incident occurred in connection with his interior life. Many times during the night-watches he had fallen into an ecstasy, in which the following vision had been vouchsafed to him : He beheld a mountain enveloped with a profusion of flowers, among which seven lilies, of dazzling whiteness and exhaling a sweet perfume, surpassed in beauty all the rest. Whilst he gazed with delight upon the scene, he beheld Angels gathering these lilies, binding them in a cluster, and offering them to the Blessed Mother of God, who graciously received them with a loving smile. The vision then vanished, and Peter of Verona remained deeply impressed by what he had seen.

For many successive days the Saint vainly sought to interpret this mysterious vision, and prayed fervently to obtain some clue to its meaning, but to no purpose. The vision again and again re-appeared to him ; he saw, but understood it not.

Meanwhile, our Seven Founders continued to attend diligently whenever Peter of Verona preached. By virtue of that instinctive comprehension of divine things which belongs to interior souls, they quickly discerned that the heart of the saintly Inquisitor was on fire with the love of God, and that the zeal of the Holy Spirit inspired his words and actions ; and they felt in his presence an unwonted ardour communicated to their souls. Whether they themselves, or the Inquisitor, took the first steps towards becoming mutually known, certain it is that no long time elapsed before their acquaintance ripened into cordial friendship ; so much so, indeed, that the Seven Fathers chose the holy Dominican to be their spiritual director, and their Master and Councillor in all matters relating to their salvation. They gave him their whole confidence, manifested their hearts to him, and even went to Confession to him.

From the date of their first meeting, Peter of Verona began to surmise that here was the key to the mystery of his visions. But, being a man of much prudence, he did nothing hastily. He made inquiries in all available directions concerning our Seven Fathers, and listened carefully to the various opinions given ; and he found that everyone was agreed as to their great and manifold virtues, but that many took opposite views about their external work ; it was in no way doubtful that the Bishop of Florence favoured it, and that others were opposed to it. He therefore determined to observe the Founders personally, and to draw his own conclusions. This he had many opportunities of doing, as they were now his spiritual children. He led them, accordingly, to relate the history of their several careers before and after their entrance into Community life ; and whilst listening to the communications of souls, so simple and yet so lofty, he was filled with admiring wonder at the marvellous operations of Divine Grace in them. He saw that their holiness was beyond a doubt genuine, free alike from pretence or exaggeration : he therefore felt more and more drawn towards them, and his intimacy with them increased day by day.

The saintly Inquisitor was now persuaded that his visions related to his hearers from Monte Senario ; but still, he did not feel absolutely certain on this point, and he wished for further confirmation. This before long was vouchsafed to him.

The Seven Founders entreated Peter of Verona to visit them at Monte Senario, and he complied with their request. It was in this hallowed spot that he was destined to be at length enlightened in an unmistakable manner, both as to the designs of Our Blessed Lady, and the line of conduct to be observed by himself in regard to them. St. Peter spent several days at Monte Senario, surrounded by the Fathers and the Novices composing the household of the Servants of Mary. Being thus enabled to examine minutely into all the details of their daily life, he was profoundly impressed by the atmosphere of peace and concord which pervaded the consecrated place ; by the holy fear which made the inmates shrink from the slightest occasion of offending God ; by the perfect unity promoted among them by the Holy Spirit reigning in the heart of each ; and by the exact punctuality of their observance. He was especially struck at the aspect of the Seven Founders of this youthful Community. A few years only had passed since their withdrawal from the world ; and yet they could already discourse with profound knowledge on the things of God, and clearly expound the deepest mysteries. Rejoicing in what he now heard and saw, he declared that these men were mines of hidden wisdom ; and he then acknowledged that it was not until he set foot in the solitude of Monte Senario that he fully understood the meaning of the heavenly manifestations which had been vouchsafed to him in Florence.

Peter of Verona was so well satisfied with this first visit to Monte Senario, that he repeated it on several occasions. The Servants of Mary always welcomed him cordially as their father and best friend ; and, on his part, he rejoiced to dwell among them. In these visits he continued daily to discover new secrets of their spiritual life ; for, aided by a special grace, he penetrated to the very depths of these holy souls whose earthly dwelling was in this peaceful Sanctuary of Monte Senario. Besides, he considered that large community of men devoted to the service of the Most Holy Virgin, over whom our Founders presided, and he wondered at such a variety of types remarkable for their sanctity. Thus his admiration went on unceasingly increasing The most advanced in virtue were naturally our Seven Saints, whose spiritual gifts were of a high order ; and their disciples followed in their steps, striving zealously to imitate the virtues of their Fathers. All were united in concord, devoting themselves heart and soul to celebrating the praises of Our Lady, and endeavouring continually to promote her glory, and to render her homage on earth as do the angelic hosts in heaven. Peter of Verona now fully recognized that in these Servants of Our Lord and of His Blessed Mother was realized all that he had seen in his visions ; and from this time forth, in all his sermons, he never failed to utter their praises, and to assert that this new Religious Community advanced daily in wisdom and virtue before God and man.

After many consultations with the Fathers of Monte Senario on the subject of the opposition made to the name, habit, and Rule of the Order, Peter of Verona, in spite of their entreaties, was unwilling to give any decided opinion, not having jurisdiction in these matters. His mission was to oppose heresy, not to pronounce upon the legality of the existence of a new Institute. Nevertheless, he wished to relieve the anxiety of his friends the Servites ; and he therefore had recourse to prayer, addressing himself with especial devotion, and many tears, to Our Blessed Lady. At the same time, the Fathers and their spiritual children at Monte Senario redoubled their fasts and good works, and besieged the Queen of Heaven with supplications that she would be pleased, by some manifest sign, to enlighten the saintly Inquisitor upon all the points in contest.

Our Lady lent a favourable ear to these filial entreaties, and vouchsafed once more to appear to Peter of Verona. Whilst he slept, he saw her before him surrounded by cohorts of Angels, and wearing a mantle beneath the folds of which she sheltered th Fathers of Monte Senario, whom he knew so well. She then gave him to understand, "that these men, and those who should hereafter join them, were called in an especial manner to enlist in her service : that, to this end, they should establish an Order in her honour, and bearing her name ; and that she had obtained for them this favour of her Divine Son". Pointing to the habit which they wore, she added, "that they must keep it as a memorial of the sufferings which she had endured in the most bitter Passion of her Son". Lastly, she told him "that the Rule of St. Augustine must be given to them, whereby to shape their lives". Another chronicler mentions that the Blessed Virgin spoke as follows : "Behold, Peter ! these are the men whom I have withdrawn from the world, and chosen to be my Servants, that so, holding this title, they may never

11

cease to fulfil the duty they owe to me. See, then, that they be careful to bear my name, to wear my habit, and to observe the Rule of St. Augustine."

Rising early, the man of God betook himself to prayer, eager to pour forth his gratitude to Our Lord and to Our Blessed Lady for so great a grace; and in further thanksgiving, he celebrated most devoutly a Mass of the Blessed Virgin; then, without more delay, he, with his socius, proceeded to Cafaggio. There he was joyously welcomed by the Fathers, to whom he announced the good news, telling them "that Mary had appeared, and that she had again made known her will: that they were to keep their habit and their Rule in perpetuity, and that they were to be called the Servants of the Virgin Mary: that this decree was pronounced by herself in the first place, and that, by her authority, he, Peter of Verona, now ratified it from henceforth for ever". Having exhorted the Fathers to thankfulness—which, indeed, it was hardly necessary for him to recommend to them—he took leave of them, desiring them to pray for him. His mission at Florence being ended, St. Peter returned to the north of Italy, where, in 1252, he was put to death by the Manichees. Shortly afterwards, he was canonized by the Church, and is generally known as St. Peter Martyr.

Great was the joy of our Seven Saints at this fresh proof of the divine goodness, and at the encouragement thereby given to their efforts. But, although the assurances given by the holy Inquisitor were of great weight, they did not altogether suffice to decide the question of the Apostolic Authorization. They were, however, a step in that direction, and afforded grounds for the indulgence of hope. The Fathers were, therefore, emboldened to walk on in the path they had entered, since the growth was henceforth to continue in spite of all hindrances both from within and from without.

CHAPTER III.

St. Manettus in France—The First Apostolic Approbation—Chapter at Monte Senario—Cafaggio.

(1245—1251.)

WHILE parting with a good number of its guests, Monte Senario retained the Seven Founders, its greatest treasure. These were ready to quit their cherished solitude, to take leave of their beloved Brethren, and to travel into distant lands if it were needful. But it seemed to them, in their humility, that they would achieve more by remaining on their mountain crest, uplifting their hands in prayer, than by going down armed into the battlefield to share in the combat. Their path was still so beset with obstacles that they had need of retirement and tranquillity to enable them to take counsel together. Their Institute, like a new-born and weakly child, required constant and fostering care. The Lateran decree still hung like the sword of Damocles above their heads. The jealous rivalry which they had excited was another source of danger; and, consequently, they were forced to be ever on the watch to checkmate any hostile move made against them.

The ceaseless solicitude with which they were filled for the well-being of their Order, caused them to turn their eyes towards Lyons, where the Pope had taken refuge, and where a General Council was now being assembled. They thought it not improbable that the Council would discuss the subject of the new Religious Orders; and, having consulted together, they decided that it would be well for one of their number to proceed to Lyons, that so, being on the spot, he might the better protect the interests of their Order. They made an appeal to the zealous devotedness of St. Manettus, whose theological attainments made him a fitting envoy, and to him they entrusted the mission. He set forth, and arrived at his post in an opportune moment. At Lyons he found several prelates, well-wishers to the Servants of Mary, and ready to come to their aid in time of necessity. Among these were Cardinal Goffredo di Castiglione, the Bishops of Florence and Pistoja, and, most probably, the Bishops of Siena and Arezzo also. St. Manettus sought them out at once, and having done this, he awaited, in prayerful tranquillity, the result of the Conciliar deliberations.

The preliminaries occupied about six months. When these were ended, the Pope, on the 28th of June, 1245, opened the Council in person, in the Metropolitan Church of St. John. The Pontiff himself pronounced the opening discourse, and in the course of it he dwelt upon the great troubles which then afflicted the Church, and which he compared to the five wounds of Our Lord. These troubles were: the ravages committed by the Tartars in many parts of Christendom, the Greek schism, the progress of heresies, the desecration of the Holy Land by infidels, and the persecution raised by Frederick II. against Holy Church. On the 5th and 17th of July, two more sittings of the Council took place, during which the necessary measures were concerted for remedying these evils.

Contrary to the expectation of our Saints, the subject of the Religious Orders, with respect to their number and the granting of the Pontifical approbation, was not brought forward at the Council. Consequently, the decree of the fourth Lateran Council of 1215 remained in full force. This decree, of such vital importance to our Fathers, ran as follows :—" Fearing that the too great multiplication of Religious Orders might be the cause of confusion in the Church, we forbid the introduction of any new Order : but such as desire to enter Religion must be enrolled in one of those already approved ". Nothing, therefore, was done ; all remained *in statu quo :* the future of the Servants of Mary appeared neither brighter nor darker than before.   They still entertained the hope that in time, notwithstanding the prohibitory decree of the Lateran Council, they might obtain a formal recognition of their existence, as had been done in the case of the Dominicans, the Franciscans, the Trinitarians, and the Religious of Our Lady of Mercy.   The cultus of Our Lady was daily increasing in the most striking manner within the Church ; and they might, therefore, reasonably believe that the suitableness of recognizing an Order exclusively devoted to her service would be universally acknowledged.   On the other hand, it might be urged that, since they had adopted the Rule of St. Augustine, they were not, strictly speaking, to be classed as a new Order.

But St. Manettus did not occupy himself solely with the debates and decisions of the Council.   As far as circumstances permitted, he strove to propagate the Order in France.   The throne of that country was then filled by Louis IX., the most perfect type of a Christian King.   Some writers assert that St. Manettus was received in audience by St. Louis, to whom he gave the scapular of the Seven Dolours of Our Lady.   If this conjecture be true, his task must have been much lightened by the support of so great a Sovereign.   It is well known that the holy king held all Religious in high esteem : he lived with them on a footing of friendly intimacy, he invited them to his table, he employed them in confidential missions in various parts of his dominions, and he constantly sought enlightenment from their sagacious counsels.

We have no authentic record of the work accomplished by St. Manettus in France.   Some historians attribute to him the foundation of the Convents at Paris and Toulouse, of which others give the credit to St. Philip ; but the establishment of the Convent at Vienne seems to have been indisputably his work.   Be this as it may, St. Manettus made good use of his time.   He caused the Order to become known ; he gave general edification wherever he went ; and he marked out the road for St. Philip, who, twenty-four years afterwards, strengthened and developed the work begun by the holy Founder.

St. Manettus having thus fulfilled his mission, returned to Italy, and went to announce to his Brethren at Monte Senario the results that he had obtained.   Some writers assert that, on his homeward journey, he halted at Bologna, where he had been requested to make a foundation.   This project, however, was not carried out till about the year 1260.

Meanwhile, intestinal divisions reigned in Italy, and especially in Florence; and the great disturbances which ensued did not afford much encouragement to the Fathers of Monte Senario to settle in that city. Everything was in confusion there; and souls thirsting for peace and silence could not long have endured the turmoil and the heated atmosphere of that arena. Besides, the holy Bishop Ardingo their true father and protector, had died towards the end of 1248, after a life marked by meritorious actions and ceaseless anxieties. His See remained vacant for several months, and was then filled, at the beginning of 1250, by Filippo Fontana, who only held it for a year. In this uncertain state of affairs, they could only await a more propitious season to enable them to carry out their plan of establishing themselves definitively in Florence.

However, during the years which elapsed from 1245 to the beginning of 1249, they did not remain idle. Their Novitiate continued to increase. The wretched condition of the country seemed to implant in many minds a distaste for the world. The partizans of Frederick, who were now under the ban of excommunication, were eager to embrace the Religious Life in order to receive absolution. The Servants of Mary had their share of these recruits; and thus, the quiet refuge on Monte Senario gradually became filled with souls seeking shelter from the tempests which raged around.

But, more than ever, the holy Founders were anxious, especially after the death of Bishop Ardingo, of being approved by the Pope. The Catholic Church possesses a centre from whence all its members must derive strength and life. This centre is the Holy See, presided over by the successor of St. Peter. As Christians, to be saved, ought to believe and act in conformity with the decrees of the Vicar of Christ, so the Religious Life, in its forms and obligations, is not less dependent upon the Holy See.

This sanction was the one thing now wanting to the Servants of Mary, though ten years had elapsed since their institution. It is true that they had been cheered by the words and smiles of the Blessed Virgin herself, when she came from heaven, bringing them the commands of her Divine Son; that Ardingo, the holy Bishop of Florence, had thrown his whole heart into their cause, and they had zealously co-operated with him in all things; and that the saintly Inquisitor, Peter of Verona, had recognized and approved their work, and had become one of their staunchest friends. On a former occasion, moreover, a Cardinal, who subsequently filled the Pontifical Throne, had come to visit them, whilst they were living as Solitaries, and had urged them to found a new Religious Institute. But Rome had then, and had ever since, kept silence. The Supreme Head of the Church spoke not, either in person or vicariously through his Legates. Peter of Verona could not be counted among these last; for his task in Florence was to seek out and to repress crime and error, not to give canonical ratification to newly-established Religious

Orders. But now, at length, the hour had come when the Holy See was to bestow the necessary approbation, or, at all events, something of a preliminary kind.

Innocent IV., who at this time filled the Chair of St. Peter, entertained views concerning Religious Orders identical with those to which the Lateran Council of 1215 had given expression. Not only did he oppose the foundation of new Orders, but he was even desirous of diminishing the number of those already in existence, either by suppression or by amalgamation. No sooner was he elected to the office of Supreme Pontiff than, on the 16th of December, 1243, he commanded the various branches of the great Augustinian brotherhood in Tuscany to unite together in one body, so as to form but a single Order. Thus was begun, in a particular province, a fusion which became far more general under the succeeding Pontiff, Alexander IV., in 1255 and 1256. There was, at the time of which we are now writing, much cause to fear that Innocent IV. would propose the absorption of the Servants of Mary in this Order ; and this project seemed to be the more plausible, as the Religious of Monte Senario had adopted the Augustinian Rule. The situation was most critical, and the result justified the apprehensions of the Founders. Theoretically, the prohibition of the institution of new Orders, and, practically, the prevailing tendency to reckon the Servants of Mary as genuine Augustinians, were first for the Seven Fathers, and afterwards for their successors, two sharp nails which were destined for more than sixty years to fasten them to their Cross. But the Providence of God was preparing the first obstacle to an amalgamation with the Augustinians . an obstacle which subsequently proved the chief means of preserving to the Servite Order its name, its mission, its distinctive characteristics, its autonomy ; all, in short, that was peculiar to itself, and, consequently, the groundwork of the sanctification of its members.

In the course of the year 1248, Innocent IV., who was still at Lyons, nominated Cardinal Raniero Capocci his Legate in Tuscany. This Cardinal was the first in Italy who wore the scarlet insignia of his ecclesiastical rank ; these insignia having been conferred on the Sacred College by Innocent IV. at the recent Council, in testimony of the blood shed by members of the hierarchy who had fallen victims to the anger of Frederick. The Legate Capocci was remarkable for his great devotion to the Blessed Mother of God. During a short sojourn at Viterbo he built a sanctuary in honour of the Most Holy Virgin, on which he expended a large portion of his private means.

So soon as the Fathers of Monte Senario heard of his arrival in Tuscany, they resolved to seek an interview with him ; for, since the first beginning of their Institute, they had not seen any direct representative of the Holy Father, and they felt a continually-increasing need of the Pontifical approbation. They determined, therefore, to take this step without delay. This momentous duty devolved upon St. Bonfilius. The Legate was then residing at Fermo, a city of considerable importance, situated in the Marches near the Adriatic seaboard. St. Bonfilius accordingly repaired to this city about the beginning of March, 1249, bearing with him the cordial good wishes of the Bishop of Florence, and the fervent prayers of his fellow-Religious. On being presented to the Legate, he at once informed His Eminence that his Brethren and himself were citizens of Florence, that city ever faithful to the Papal cause, and Servants of Mary—thus putting forward a twofold plea for a favourable hearing. He then gave a detailed account of the chief events leading up to the point at which the Order now stood. He afterwards replied to the questions put to him by the Cardinal, and at the close of a conversation as full and prolonged as the business in hand required, he tranquilly awaited the results of the interview. His expectations were more than realized ; for the Legate presented him with letters completely shielding him and his spiritual family from all the dangers which they had dreaded.

The letters ran as follows :—

" Ramero, by the Divine Mercy Cardinal Deacon of Santa Maria in Cosmedin, representing Our Holy Father the Pope in the Patrimony of St. Peter, in Tuscany, the Duchy of Spoleto, and the March of Ancona, and Legate of the Holy See in Tuscany : to our well-beloved Sons in Christ, the Prior and Brethren of St. Mary of Monte Senario, known as the Servants of Mary, in the diocese of Florence, health and benediction in the Lord :

" The great devotion professed by you, in the sincerity of your souls, for the Holy Roman Church, moves us, not without good cause, to grant you favours as far as is lawful before God. For this reason, taking yourselves and the place known as St. Mary of Monte Senario, where you perform the Divine Office, under the protection of the Apostolic See and under our own : by these presents and in virtue of the authority wherewith we are invested, we confirm the faculty granted to you by Ardingo, Bishop of Florence, permitting you to live under the Rule of St. Augustine, and to establish the said Order of St. Augustine in the aforesaid place, called after the name of the Fathers who dwell there, to whom it is to belong in perpetuity. Nevertheless, I charge you not to suffer any of the Brethren who have made, or who shall hereafter make, their Religious Profession in the said place, to go elsewhere without testimonials from the Prior of the aforesaid place, except it be for the purpose of entering a Religion of stricter observance. And we desire that you should also be at liberty to receive free-born citizens who may desire to withdraw from the world, and to keep them when once they have been received.

" In testimony whereof we have drawn up these letters ; and we have commanded that they should be farther enforced by having our seal appended thereto.

" Given at Fermo, March 13, in the sixth year of the Pontificate of our Holy Father Innocent, Pope, IV." (1249.)

Although this act did not emanate from the Holy Father in person, it was nevertheless a priceless boon, enabling the Order to rank Cardinal Raniero among its greatest benefactors. In a few terse sentences he had exactly defined its status, and conferred on it a more durable tenure of existence, consecrating the joint work of Bishop Ardingo and the Seven Fathers—that work which had cost them so much labour, watching, and anxiety. This act, too, would enable our Founders to obtain other decrees of still greater importance, and to parry any further blows which might be aimed at them. Innocent IV., on his return to Italy, would find the document inserted among the curial letters, and he could not at once disavow the words of his Legate. Thus a great obstacle would be placed in the way of that projected amalgamation so much desired by the Pontiff, and the extinction of the Servants of Mary could be averted.

These letters expressed themselves with clearness and precision upon all essential points of the new Religious body. The name of the Religious Order to which it belonged was clearly said. The title, which included its mission, was set forth unreservedly. Everything necessary to constitute a Religious body was enumerated . the Prior, the Brethren, the Rule, the enclosure, the perpetuity of the Institution, and full permission to receive fresh subjects ; the terms of Order, Religion, or Religious body being expressly employed to designate the foundation. As a mark of especial favour, the whole was placed officially under the protection of the Holy See. In short, the approbation was as explicit as it was possible to make it.

St. Bonfilius, overflowing with gratitude, returned to Monte Senario, where the good news of which he was the bearer filled all hearts with joy. The tidings were at once communicated to the Convents at Siena, Pistoja, and Arezzo. The holy Prior and his Brethren now thought that a favourable opportunity offered itself for a general Conference, in which they could discuss together again all topics concerning the Order, and more especially everything relating to the Constitutions. Accordingly, a Chapter was held ; and, though without any formal preparation, all that had been previously decided upon was thoroughly revised, particularly in regard to the regulations suggested by St. Peter of Verona or adopted since he had stayed in Florence.

St. Bonfilius, in his great humility, thought this a most favourable opportunity to resign his office. By the death of Ardingo the powers which the Saint had received from him expired, and by the Legate's letter the Order began a new life. He therefore put forth

to his Brethren these his considerations, and begged of them to proceed to elect a fresh Superior. But his expectations failed, and for
the third time he was chosen to govern the family of the Servants of
Mary. He was obliged to submit and take up his task once more.
At the same Chapter it was decided that in future there would be a
meeting regularly every year to direct the affairs of the Order, and
that the supreme authority should be vested in the Prior of Monte
Senario, who on this account should be called the Prior Major. In
the peace of the Lord, without any noise, our Saints thus provided for all the needs of the Order, and laboured to consolidate
and extend it.

A new start had now been given by the Legate, and the little
Community of Monte Senario prepared to send forth members in
various directions to found new Convents. The Seven Founders
were about to see their endeavours blessed beyond their hopes. The
impediments which were raised on all sides, instead of checking
their progress, seemed rather to aid it. It had taken ten years to
make the plantations of Siena, Pistoja, and Arezzo take root, but now
hardly a year passed that some offshoots did not spring from the
parent tree.

The Founders' eyes first turned towards Florence, where they
had often desired to be. It is true that they already possessed a
temporary home there; but this could in no sense be looked upon as
a regular foundation. It was intended merely as a shelter for them,
when duty called them to the city; they owed it to charity, and it
was far from being spacious enough to serve the needs of a Community toiling for the good of souls—the Chapel being merely a
small private Oratory. Hitherto no favourable opportunity had
occurred for them to inhabit Cafaggio, and several obstacles had
stood in the way. But at length all was changed. The Pontiff had
spoken by the mouth of his Legate, and the alteration which had
taken place in the Servites' mode of life was sanctioned by his
authority. The political horizon in Florence was beginning to
brighten, especially since Frederick, dragging out the remnant of a
miserable and dishonoured existence, had quitted Tuscany. The
Guelphic city was about to shake off the yoke of the Ghibellines,
who ruled her with a rod of iron. Whilst, to enable the Founders
to carry out their project of a Florentine foundation, some generous
persons promised to defray the first expenses of taking possession,
and gathered together among them a sufficient sum for the purchase
of the house at Cafaggio, and also for the necessary furniture and for
additions to the main building.

The property belonged to several citizens of Florence, who held
it jointly. After some discussion, they agreed to sell it for a sum
which does not sound at all extravagant for these days. The price
was twenty-five pounds sterling, equivalent to about two hundred and

fifty pounds of the present currency. In order to comply with the obligations entailed by the vow of poverty, the sale was made to a representative of the Supreme Pontiff and of the Holy Roman Church, full and entire jurisdiction over the property being vested in the Bishop of Florence, who was to grant the use thereof as an alms to the members of the Order, or, in other words, of the Convent of St. Mary of Monte Senario. The representative who was chosen was a pious citizen of Florence, one Enrico Baldovini, an old and devoted friend of the Fathers. The bill of sale stated expressly that the owners sold the piece of land, of four *staiora* square (a land measurement of the period), and that the sale included both what was underground and what stood upon it, with the house, the surrounding walls, the cloister, and all other buildings upon the property.

This important event took place on July 1, 1250, and was the first step towards the realization of the Founders' golden dream of returning to the city which had been their birthplace and the home of their youth. In order to smooth away the remaining difficulties, it was necessary to seek another interview with the Legate, and to procure from him a written permit which would effectually silence all objections on the part of their opponents It was resolved that St. Bonfilius should take the necessary steps for the purpose of obtaining this sanction. The Pope Innocent IV. was still at Lyons, where he remained till April 19, 1251 ; but his Legate was residing in Italy, and it was therefore the Legate with whom the holy Founder would have to treat. A favourable opportunity was alone wanting, and for this St. Bonfilius waited.

Meanwhile, in Florence, the destruction of the Ghibelline party became more and more imminent. After many reverses, both at home and abroad, a fearful blow fell upon them : Frederick, who had taken up his abode in Apulia, died at Fiorentino during the night of December 12-13, this same year, 1250. By a singular coincidence, his Vicar perished the same night in Florence, crushed by the fall of a stone from the vaulted ceiling of his room. The news of this twofold catastrophe soon spread over Italy. It came like a thunderbolt upon the Ghibellines in Tuscany, whilst it caused great exultation in the Guelphic camp. Once more the Guelphs were masters of the situation, whilst the Ghibellines, withdrawn from public life, passed their days in hatching plots and fostering intrigues of every kind.

The Fathers of Monte Senario, finding that matters looked more promising in Florence than had hitherto been the case, thought that it would be well to defer no longer their plan of settling in that city. The Legate Pietro Capocci was at Ancona, in the Marches. St. Bonfilius went thither, and had an interview with the representative of the Holy Father, in the course of which, though many questions were doubtless discussed, only two received a formal solution.

The first of these questions related to the Florentine foundation. The Fathers had already at their disposal the piece of ground of which mention has been made, with the buildings upon it, including a small Oratory. But they now proposed to build a Church, which would be the centre of a regular Convent. The right of occupancy as private individuals would, therefore, have to be merged in a right of occupancy as a corporate body, which would include the throwing open of the Church to the public. The Legate approved of the proposal, and he wrote letters to the Bishop of Siena (who was Administrator of the diocese of Florence during the vacancy of that See), by virtue of which St. Bonfilius was authorized to rebuild, on a fitting site, the Chapel then standing at Cafaggio, without the walls of Florence, on condition that no existing rights should be infringed. He then begged the Bishop of Siena to give permission for the laying of the first stone.

The second question discussed was concerning those subjects who sought admission to the Order after having belonged, whilst in the world, to the faction of the Emperor, and who had obstinately adhered to the Ghibelline cause after Frederick had been excommunicated and deposed. Being themselves excommunicated, they could not be received among the Religious, for the sentence pronounced upon them deprived them of all part or lot in the spiritual treasures which the Church of God has in her keeping. The Fathers, therefore, desired to have faculties to absolve them. The Legate readily acceded to this request · he granted full faculties to the Prior, and to all the priests of the Order, for this purpose, only stipulating that those who received absolution should make reparation for all wrong done by them to the Church or to individuals ; and that, if they should not be able to discover the persons whom they had wronged, they should then give alms to the poor by way of atonement.

The interview being ended, the Bishop of Siena was at once apprized of the Legate's decision as to the foundation at Cafaggio. The zealous prelate hastened to comply with the directions which were transmitted to him, and in a missive dated March 17, 1251, he gives the Fathers power to take possession of Cafaggio, to build a new Church there, and to lay the first stone with the usual rites. In point of fact, no reasonable objection could be made to the undertaking, nor could any legal right be infringed, since the property in question lay without the walls, in an unfrequented spot.

Everything was now arranged in conformity both with civil law and with religious rule. St. Bonfilius resolved, therefore, to proceed without loss of time, and he himself blessed and laid the first stone, having received authority to do so by reason of the see being then vacant. The saintly Father's heart was filled with gladness as he presided at the ceremony, and poured forth his prayers for a blessing upon the work. Fervently did he implore the divine grace, and earnestly did he beg that both the material building of which the stone then laid was the first-sown seed, and the spiritual edifice which would be the future harvest, might grow and flourish in that spot to the greater glory of God and of Mary, His Most Blessed Mother.

The work, zealously carried on, made rapid progress. The Church was of modest dimensions, and the buildings already on the premises were utilized for the accommodation of the Religious. Those who had become poor for the love of God were bound to house themselves like His poor. The Florentine foundation was characterized throughout by poverty of spirit ; and the smaller and more humble was its beginning, the more was Our Lord pleased to glorify it in after times. The Santissima Annunziata was but a tiny sanctuary at first, which we should vainly seek to trace in the magnificent basilica now existing.

These five years had indeed been years of trial and slow progress ; but two great blessings had been granted to them ; the Papal Legate had sanctioned the work of Monte Senario, and the Convent of Cafaggio had been inaugurated in Florence. The future, indeed, was still clouded ; but these two events shed a hopeful and consoling light upon the onward path, for the Order was for the first time strengthened by the Supreme Authority of the Vicar of Christ, and it had put forth a fair and flourishing branch. And now our Seven Founders, filled with supernatural confidence, were about to obtain from Holy Mother Church an official protector for their Order, and to make further foundations ; nay, they were to receive a token of heavenly favour, proving to them that Mary was, even more than heretofore, on their side, whatsoever might befall them.

CHAPTER IV.

The first Cardinal Protector—Citta di Castello— La Santissima Annunziata—Lucca.

(1251—1253.)

THE great work which the Order and the holy Founders had now in hand was the erection of the Church and the Convent at Cafaggio. The building went on rapidly, the plans being unambitious, and the dwelling-house, which existed there already, forming part of the religious habitation. Under the direction of St. Bonfilius, who often came from Monte Senario to Florence, the indefatigable St. Alexis was everywhere, superintending and giving orders ; and soon all was in readiness to receive a regular Community, which was to undertake in Florence the work which the Order was doing at Monte Senario, in Siena, Pistoja, and Arezzo.

Still, the consoling prospect of possessing a settlement in Florence did not prevent our Saints from continuing to feel apprehensive of the impediments which might be placed in their way by adversaries ; and, therefore, they thought it prudent to take precautions against any misfortune of this kind. They were aware that each of the other Orders had a Cardinal appointed by the Supreme Pontiff to take under his protection the Religious confided to his charge, and to watch over their interests. Our Founders considered that it would be well if they could obtain a similar favour. Whilst they had remained in obscurity at Monte Senario, their seclusion had been their shield, but now that they were to come forth into the light, and were to live and labour in the disturbed atmosphere of Florence, they would need some additional safeguard.

Innocent IV. had resolved, upon the death of his persecutor Frederick, to quit Lyons and to return to Italy. Leaving France on the 19th of April, 1251, he reached Bologna during the month of October. Hither, too, came St. Bonfilius to present his supplication; and here, after bringing forward all the arguments which made for the cause that he had at heart, he obtained his request. On the 23rd of October, letters were handed to him by which he was officially informed that his petition was granted. This document was issued by the Cardinal who was chosen to be the first Protector of the Order, Guglielmo Fieschi, nephew to Innocent IV. It was of the highest importance, since it contained expressions which amounted to an implicit recognition of the Order ; and it also referred to the chief points of the organization of the brotherhood. It ran as follows :—

"Guglielmo, by the Divine Grace Cardinal Deacon of St. Eustachius, to the Religious, his well-beloved in Christ, the Prior and all the Brethren who are styled Servants of St. Mary, health and true charity in Our Lord.

"In order that, by our Ministry, the zeal of your Institute should increase and bring forth yet more fruit for time and eternity, Our Holy Father the Pope has committed to me the supervising care of your Order. Therefore, by the express command of the aforesaid, Our Holy Father the Pope, we take under our headship and benign protection both yourselves and the places wherein you give yourselves to the service of God ; and, by these presents, we enjoin you henceforth to preserve inviolate all the essentials of your Order, placed under the Rule of St. Augustine, in conformity with the settlement and the grant made to you by Ardingo, Bishop of Florence, of happy memory, and the confirmation and concession granted to you by His Lordship Raniero, Cardinal-Deacon of Sta. Maria in Cosmedin, of revered memory.

"In witness whereof we grant you these present letters under our seal.

"Given at Bologna, October xxiii., the ninth year of the Pontificate of His Holiness Pope Innocent IV., the year of Our Lord, 1251."

The new Cardinal Protector had expressed himself as clearly and frankly as could have been desired. He had spoken of the new Order by the name which belonged to it as its very own ; he allowed all that Bishop Ardingo had done, and he approved of what had been done by Cardinal Raniero. In short, it is evident that St. Bonfilius had been able to convince Cardinal Guglielmo, by irrefragable proofs, that the Servants of Mary were lawfully existing.

Our Seven Founders, fearless of the dangers which threatened the Order, and trusting wholly in the goodness of God, and in their heavenly Protectress, continued to carry on their work, and to take advantage of every opportunity of developing it. Whilst the Siennese Republic ceased not to lavish gifts upon the house established in their city, the Convent at Pistoja was in a flourishing state, Arezzo was prosperous, at Cafaggio the building went on apace, and all was getting gradually into order in preparation for hard work ; a new foundation, too, loomed in the near future, that of.Città di Castello, a small Umbrian town on the banks of the Tiber.

In Città di Castello lived a family, by name Mancellari, the members of which, being piously disposed and in easy circumstances, were desirous of setting on foot some good work to be accomplished by the instrumentality of the Servants of Mary. Accordingly, they met together, 24th October, 1251, in presence of the notary public of the town, and made a declaration to the effect that, in what they were about to do, they were moved by the wish of procuring "benefit to their own souls, and to the souls of all their relatives, and of all who were allied to them by ties of consanguinity". Then they conveyed to Brother Christian, the assignee, acting on the part and in the name of the Holy Roman Church, a piece of land, to found a Convent of the Order, situated at Castello, outside the Porta Sant' Andrea, in the place known as the Lime-kilns of Uguli junior. The Bishop of Castello, Pietro, of the family of the Counts D'Agnani, grand-nephew to Innocent III. and Gregory IX., did all in his power to forward the undertaking. The Servants of Mary took possession temporarily of a house in the town until they were able, some years later, to build a Convent and a Church.

Whilst the foundation of Città di Castello was beginning its existence, that of Cafaggio was successfully completed within the limits assigned by prudence. The Church soared gracefully above the small Convent which nestled on its north-western side. To the Fathers of Monte Senario, ardent lovers of holy poverty as they were, these edifices seemed great and splendid ; but, in truth, the new foundation at Cafaggio was of extremely modest proportions, when compared with other monuments in Florence. Our Saints now thought it would be well that they, who had promised a life-long service to Our Lady, should crown their work by bestowing on their Church a visible badge of its consecration to Mary, in the form of a painting representing the great mystery of the Annunciation, at the moment when the Blessed Virgin proclaims herself the Hand-maid of the Lord. Nothing more appropriate could have been devised ; for it was at that supreme moment when, by the Divine Will, she was clad with the unapproachable dignity of Mother of God and Queen of Heaven, that she herself chose that title of Hand-maid or Servant of the Lord, as being sweeter than all others in her ear, and one to be desired before all. And this title, simple as it may seem, implies in the holder the possession of virtues of humility, of strength, of gratitude, and of love. It was in right of this title that Mary uttered her *Fiat*, that all-powerful word which brought about the accomplishment of the most stupendous event of all time. Thus she proved that God alone is great, and the source from which all great things proceed, and that the Creature becomes greater in proportion as he annihilates himself more utterly in the presence of the Creator.

It was, therefore, decided that during the spring of 1252, the Church should be adorned with a fresco, to be painted by the most skilful artist of the day, and which was to represent the Angel Gabriel delivering his message to the Spotless Maiden, whose reply is simply in those words of utter self-surrender : " Behold the Hand-maid of the Lord ".

At that time there existed no Florentine school of art properly so-called. There were painters, indeed, but few ; and these, for the most part, copied indiscriminately the defects of the Byzantine style, which, owing to the persecutions of the Iconoclasts, had long been acclimatized in Florence. It seems, however, that there was one painter of the period, who had, to some extent, emancipated himself from this servile imitation of his predecessors, and who allowed him-self to follow the inspirations of his own genius. His name, we are told, was Bartolomew ; his taste, it is said, was pure and refined, and he was of a deeply religious cast of mind. Whenever this artist undertook any important work, he prepared himself for it by the reception of the Sacraments ; for he well knew that the soul must detach herself from the things of earth, in order to be able fittingly to conceive and shadow forth the image of things divine. When, therefore, the holy Founders requested him to employ his talent on their behalf, he hastened to purify his soul in the fountain of Penance, and then received the Blessed Eucharist, wherein resides the King Who is All-beautiful. Having sketched his design, the artist then set to work, previously asking the prayers of the Religious. The first portion of his task was comparatively easy, and he accomplished it to perfection : the Angel, beautiful in ethereal grace, about to deliver reverently the celestial message ; the Eternal Father, majestically calm, looking down upon the fulfilment of the first act of the great mystery ; and the Holy Spirit, under the form of a dove, descending to complete the wondrous union. These details the painter had represented with no mean skill : and he had traced the outline of the Blessed Virgin's form in her attitude of exquisite modesty and humility ; but he had not yet ventured to limn the face. He knew well what that face should be—how it should shine with heavenly brightness, reflecting the glory that was within ; how faultless should be the features, how pure the expression, with the purity of light itself ; how the intense spirituality of the beauty should swallow up and efface all thought of its material perfection. It was a glorious vision that he beheld with his mind's eye, glorious as the mystery which he was striving to depict. But his hand proved powerless to realize it ; and, after several fruitless attempts, his courage failed, and he laid down his brush, resolving to rest awhile.

The next day, 25th March, 1252, being the feast of the Annunciation, Bartolomew returned to the Church to seek anew inspiration for his task But this time it was not Our Lady's pleasure that mortal skill should portray her celestial loveliness. As the painter drew aside the curtain which veiled his sketch, a cry of awed wonder burst from his trembling lips. It was no earthly pencil that had pictured the Mother Maiden—no human genius, however exalted, could have produced so perfect an embodiment of her whom all generations called Blessed. Bartolomew could not doubt that a miracle had been wrought, and he hastened to proclaim it to the Fathers and the Brethren, all of whom rushed to the spot. From them the news spread throughout the city, and vast crowds soon gathered in the Church, weeping for joy as they gazed on that heavenly countenance, feeling that the Unseen became more real to them as they beheld it. A writer of that time says, that those who looked upon the Virgin of the Annunciation were already drawn in a wondrous manner to the things of God, and were inspired with the utmost aversion from whatever could displease Him.

Our Seven Founders were not less deeply impressed. None, indeed, could feel so intensely grateful as they for this marvellous proof of Our Lady's good-will, which inspired them with fresh courage to continue the work now happily begun. Soon after pilgrims began to flock from distant lands to see the miraculous picture ; for, in those ages of faith, the announcement of a miracle was sufficient to draw throngs to the favoured spot. Hither especially came sufferers, seeking relief from the many ills that flesh is heir to, and of the cures and miracles of various kinds sought at the shrine of Our Lady of Cafaggio many were obtained, so many, indeed, that the new sanctuary was generally known as Our Lady St. Mary, Mother of Grace.

About the same time the Church received the name of *La Santissima Annunziata;* and from then till now pilgrimages have constantly been made to it, not only from every part of Italy, but from all quarters of the globe, to pay homage to the Mother of God, and to ask favours through her intercession. The miraculous picture has been visited by the greatest artists, all of whom have recognized its supernatural character. Michael-Angelo, who had examined it minutely, went so far as to say : "If anyone were to tell me that this picture was painted by man, I should reply (and I speak as one understanding the business) that this was false . for no art of man, however great his powers, could have produced this masterpiece. And I firmly believe that this heavenly face came direct from God, and was the work of no mortal."

The foundation of Cafaggio being completed, the Convent of Our Lady St. Mary, Mother of Grace, became daily more famous and more resorted to. The miraculous picture of the Blessed Virgin was continually surrounded by pious throngs. The Religious who served the Sanctuary were full of fervour. A heavenly fragrance pervaded the hallowed spot, and shed a holy influence over all who approached it, making them taste of that peace passing all understanding, which the world can neither give nor take away.

Such was the work newly organized by St. Bonfilius and the other Founders. It was evident that the blessing of God rested upon it, and all the Brethren redoubled their efforts to correspond generously with the graces bestowed upon them, and to prove themselves not unworthy of the bounties of Divine Providence.

The saintly Prior-General of the Order now became a more frequent resident in Florence, so as to be better able to tend the offshoots of the parent stem, and to plant others. He did not, however, entirely leave the holy mountain or lay aside the title of Prior of Monte Senario : the link between him and the loved cradle of the brotherhood was too dear to be severed so quickly ; and the names of Monte Senario and Bonfilius were inseparable the one from the other.

On the other hand, St. Alexis, who had come to Florence to superintend the works at Cafaggio, never again quitted the city, where his services were almost indispensable. Within the walls of the Convent he gave a perfect example of all the virtues of a good Religious, whilst he humbly fulfilled the various duties of a lay-brother. He was ever ready for the lowest and most fatiguing employments. He was extremely popular in the city, and he had but to speak to obtain whatever alms were needed by the Brethren.

In short, he was one of the pillars of the Order in Florence, and St. Bonfilius was careful to retain him ever at hand.

Meanwhile, St. Amideus remained at Monte Senario, engaged in the responsible office of Master of the Novices. The influence which his birth had given him in the world was as nothing compared with the veneration and implied submission which his consummate virtues now won from all. He seemed on fire, as it were, with the love of God, and he was marvellously enlightened thereby in directing the souls under his charge, all of whom, differing much in character, and also as to their former position in the world, he guided with a wisdom and tact which wrought in them complete transformation, and communicated to them the dispositions which they needed to carry out their vocation.

The other Saints all proved serviceable in their different departments. St. Buonagiunta was employed in making new foundations. St. Manettus, having returned from France, where he had made the Order known, and had paved the way for the future labours of St. Philip Benizi, devoted all his energies to his own country St. Hugh and St. Sostene continued to live in retirement at Monte Senario, where their regularity and fervour made a great impression upon the young Religious. Thus, whether in Florence or at Monte Senario, the Servants of Mary quietly and unostentatiously strove to advance in holiness.

War continued to be waged between Florence and her many rivals ; but these external storms did not hinder the Saints' work — nay, sometimes they even seemed to promote it. The Florentines and the people of Lucca had made common cause together, and had thus been enabled to defeat their foes at Montopoli. Nor was their friendship bounded by political interests, but it extended to ecclesiastical matters ; and Lucca was shortly afterwards endowed with a Convent of the Florentine Order of Servants of the Virgin-Mother of God.

. Lucca was an important city. In the sixth century she had been the capital of Tuscany, and she was long the favourite residence of the Ducal, or Margravine Court. She was as continually at war with her rival, Pisa, as Florence was with Sienna. Having risen in rebellion against the Countess Matilda, Lucca joined the Imperial party, but soon deserted it. From this time forward all her sympathies were with the Guelphic party, and she was on good terms with Florence.

Two brothers, named Simonetti, began this foundation, which appears to have been on a small scale, since two years afterwards St. Buonagiunta was obliged to buy a piece of land for its enlargement.

As we have seen, they neither wasted time nor allowed themselves to be checked by obstacles. The Order grew and spread from year to year, without human support—thus proving that it was sustained invisibly by the hand of Mary. The miracle of the Santissima Annunziata had shown this unmistakably; and, now, another sign was about to be manifested of Our Lady's ever-vigilant maternal care, in the person of one of her most favoured sons, whose steps she was to guide until at length it may be said that she herself presented him to the brotherhood.

CHAPTER V.

Philip Benizi enters the Order—Steps taken by Innocent IV.

(1254.)

At the beginning of the year 1254, a young physician belonging to a family of rank lived in Florence. His name was Philip Benizi. Brought up in a thoroughly Christian household, he had spent his youth in the practice of piety. He had recently returned from Paris and Padua, where he had gone through his medical studies and had taken his degrees. He was only one-and-twenty years of age; and, though actively engaged in the duties of his profession, his life was one of intense spirituality—more resembling that of a cloistered Religious than of a man living in the full tide of worldly affairs. He spent many hours both daily and nightly in prayer; he was bountiful in alms-giving, and was most fervent in devotion to Our Blessed Lady; he gave himself up to every kind of good work, seeking none of the relaxations customary among young men of his age, and he took no part whatever in the political agitations by which, at that time, Florence was disturbed.

The young physician soon felt himself strongly drawn to the Religious Life. On the Thursday in Easter week of this year, 1254, he was praying before a miraculous Crucifix in one of the Churches of Fiesole, when a voice from the lips of the Divine Figure thus addressed him: "Go, Philip, ascend the mountain, and dwell with the Servants of My Mother, and thou shalt be pleasing in the sight of God". Philip instantly promised to obey this command; and, coming down from Fiesole, he paused at the Oratory of Cafaggio, where he engaged in fervent prayer. Whilst he was recommending to Our Lady the resolution which he had taken of promptly obeying the call of her Divine Son, one of the Religious, vested for Mass, entered the Church, and proceeded to offer the Holy Sacrifice.

The Epistle of the day was that which records the meeting of the Deacon Philip with the eunuch of Queen Candace in his chariot, on the road to Gaza, to whom he expounds the prophet Isaias, and whom he subsequently converts and baptizes. The Celebrant was reading the Epistle, and had just come to the following verse : "And the Spirit said to Philip : Go near and join thyself with this chariot" (Acts viii. 29). As these words fell upon the ear of Philip Benizi, a sudden ray of light seemed to flash into his soul, and he felt that the call of the Holy Spirit was addressed to himself. He turned pale and trembled, filled with the religious awe which mortals feel at the approach of the Divinity ; and, becoming lost to all outward things, he beheld the following vision. It seemed to him that he was passing through a desert waste overgrown with thorns and brambles, which wounded him sorely as he forced his way through them. Before him were enormous masses of overhanging rock, ready to crush him in their fall. On each side yawned fearful abysses, into which a single false step might precipitate him. Around him crawled poisonous serpents, whose hissings chilled him with fear. The marshy soil upon which he trod gave way beneath his feet ; and the more he struggled to extricate himself the deeper he sank, till at length he seemed about to be swallowed up and suffocated in the mire.

The stoutest heart must have quailed amidst dangers so great and so various. St. Philip, finding his strength failing him, called on Heaven in his distress : "Save me, O God," he cried ; "for the waters are come in even unto my soul. I stick fast in the mire of the deep, and there is no sure standing" (Ps. lxviii 2, 3). Then, turning himself to the Mother of Mercy, with suppliant looks and heartfelt sighs, he implored her not to forsake him in so great a time of need. Hardly had he ceased speaking, when a voice of heavenly sweetness, addressing him by name, repeated the words of the Epistle of the day : "Go near, and join thyself to this chariot". Looking in the direction whence the voice proceeded, a marvellous sight appeared before his dazzled eyes.

A chariot of pure gold, mounted upon four wheels of exquisite workmanship, and drawn by a lion and a lamb—strange yoke-fellows !—descended from the cloudless sky, and advanced towards him. The fierce aspect of the lion contrasted strongly with the gentleness of the lamb, which was whiter than snow. An ivory throne was placed in the chariot, and on the throne was seated the Blessed Virgin in all her majestic grace, clothed in mourning weeds and wrapped in a long black mantle, whilst sable hangings were thrown over the chariot itself. Nothing which this earth has to show can give an idea, how imperfect soever, of the marvellous beauty of the Mother of God, and the more than royal dignity which clothed her whole person. Above her head, encircled by the starry crown, the Angels bore a silken canopy of azure hue. Other angelic spirits, mingled with countless hosts of Saints, made the air resound with her praises, their voices filling the Church with celestial harmonies unknown to mortal ears. A dove of spotless whiteness hovered around the Queen of Heaven, whilst from its wings darted rays of light brighter than the sun.

St. Philip, beholding this vision, no longer experienced any fear ; a feeling of complete security possessed his soul. Rapt in ecstasy, he contemplated the gorgeous apparition, and could not withdraw his eyes from the mysterious chariot and its heavenly Occupant; whilst the enchanting melody of the angelic songs held him spellbound. Suddenly, the Angels were mute, and the voice which he had before heard spoke sweetly and winningly the self-same words : " Go near and join thyself to this chariot ". At the same time, the Queen of Heaven held out to him a religious habit exactly resembling that worn by the brotherhood of Cafaggio. St. Philip was about to advance in order to receive it, when a hand touched and shook him gently. The spell was broken , he was recalled to earth, and the vision disappeared.

Looking around, he saw that he was in the little Church of Our Lady of Grace, where he had heard Mass that morning. One of the Servite brotherhood stood beside him. It was St. Alexis, on whom the care of the Church devolved, and who, being about to close the doors, had thought it well to rouse Philip Benizi from his absorption. Drawing near to him, he said, softly, " Rise, dear brother, Mass is over ". But, rapt in ecstasy, the young physician heard not a word. St. Alexis, thinking that he had fallen asleep, now spoke in a louder tone : " Rise, holy man," he said, " for Mass is over ; and it is time for you to return home ". Then he laid his hand on the shoulder of Philip, who, opening his eyes, recovered his consciousness, and remembered all that had taken place. Turning with a look of mild reproach towards the holy Founder, he said : " May God forgive you, Brother Alexis, you have brought me back from Paradise ". Without another word he humbly rose, and quitting the Church, returned at once, troubled and thoughtful, to his parents' house.

St. Alexis had, with keen insight, divined what was passing in Philip's soul. He admired and kept silence, fully convinced that Our Lady of Grace was moving the heart of the saintly youth in order to advance him one day to the highest degree of perfection. Meanwhile, the holy Founder, offering his prayers for this intention, proceeded to close the Church, and re-entering the Convent, resumed his customary occupations. Soon he was to see the fulfilment of what his prophetic eye had foreseen, and great and glorious were to be the results therefrom to the Order of the Servants of Mary.

During the remainder of the day, Philip ceased not to muse upon the event of the morning. Every circumstance of the vision, even to the minutest detail, was indelibly graven on his memory. He sought in vain for an interpretation of the mystery ; it remained impenetrable. Night came, but he still pondered and prayed, when, towards midnight, falling again into an ecstasy, he once more beheld the vision which had appeared to him in the Church at Cafaggio. Again he seemed to be a distressed wanderer in the frightful desert, from which he could not make his escape ; again he had recourse to Mary ; and again she smiled gently upon him and he heard her speak. This time she spoke as follows : "Go, Philip, hasten to seek my Servants : their lips will expound to thee the mystic meaning of the chariot which thou hast seen ; do thou whatsoever they shall counsel thee". Having thus spoken, Our Lady returned heavenwards, leaving Philip's heart flooded with sweet joy.

"Go, Philip, seek my Servants" These words rang in the heart of Philip Benizi till daydawn, and he was impatiently eager to obey the summons. He seized the earliest opportunity of leaving the paternal roof, and hastened to Cafaggio. There, prostrating himself before the miraculous picture of Mary, he prayed, followed the Divine Office, and heard Mass. Then he knocked at the door of the Convent and asked to speak with the Father Prior, who was St. Bonfilius. The Founder lost not a moment, but hastened to meet Philip Benizi with words of cordial greeting, which, combined with his gentle kindliness of manner, put the young man completely at his ease, and drew from him the motive of his visit. Philip related circumstantially all particulars of the vision which had twice appeared to him : the first time whilst hearing Mass at the Santissima Annunziata, and the second time during the night in his own home. He concluded by saying that it seemed to him that he was called to enter the Order of the Servants of Mary, and that his greatest happiness would be to live and die in it.

The frank simplicity of the narration delighted St. Bonfilius, who clearly foresaw the great future sanctity of the speaker. Raising his hands and eyes to heaven in fervent thanksgiving, he blessed God from the depths of his soul, and then turning to Philip, congratulated him upon his praiseworthy intention, and gave him all the counsels of which he stood in need.

"The vision," he said, "which has been vouchsafed to you by Our Lady, shows plainly what it is that she expects from you. The gloomy desert, overgrown with thorns which pierced you as you passed along, and where at each step great rocks seemed about to crush you, of course represents the world, which is truly a wilderness, wherein the soul is assailed continually by temptations of one kind or another. Those serpents whose poisoned fangs threatened you with a cruel death, were the evil spirits who go to and fro on the earth, and destroy souls with their deadly venom, by making them the slaves of avarice, ambition, pleasure, dissensions, and other sins. The fearful abyss which yawned beneath your feet, and the mere sight of which froze you with dread, was none other than the bottomless pit.

"You are now, brother, in the midst of all these perils, because you live in the world. But the Most Blessed Virgin, whom you have so often invoked with great confidence, has had pity upon you. Seeing you in danger, she has hastened to rescue you ; she has snatched you from impending death, and has offered you a safe refuge at her feet. This refuge is the Order of her Servants, represented by the mystic chariot wherein she was enthroned in queenly state Mary is, indeed, our rightful Queen, and reigns over our Order with absolute sway.

"This heavenly chariot, you say, was mounted on four wheels. These wheels signify the four cardinal virtues, and also the four Evangelists, by whose precepts and counsels our lives are directed, even as we read in the vision of the prophet Ezechiel. 'The spirit of life was in the wheels' (Ezech. i. 20). And in the Holy Gospel Our Lord says : 'This do, and thou shalt live' (St. Luke x. 28). The chariot was of pure gold, showing the excellence of the Religious Life ; for, as gold is the most precious of all metals, so is the Religious State the most perfect of all states. A fierce lion and a gentle lamb were harnessed together to the chariot, signifying that the true Servant of God and of Our Lady is bound to unite in himself two virtues which at first sight seem incompatible with each other, namely, unalterable meekness and unconquerable energy. The holy Psalmist tells us, that 'The meek shall inherit the land' (Ps. xxxvi.), and Our Lord himself incites us to that virtue saying : 'Learn of Me, because I am meek and humble of heart' (St. Matt. xi. 29). But meekness alone is not enough ; strength and courage must be added in order to enable us to resist temptation . for we also find in Holy Scripture these words : 'Fight the good fight ; lay hold on eternal life' (1 Tim. vi. 12). 'Be strengthened in the Lord and in the might of His power' (Eph. vi. 10). The snow-white dove which you saw hovering over the head of the Blessed Virgin represents that purity of soul which should adorn the Servant of Mary, so that he may be worthy to approach her ; and it is also emblematic of that simplicity, of which Our Lord Jesus Christ spoke when He said to His disciples : 'Be ye therefore . . . simple as doves' (St. Matt. x. 16).

"But you are, doubtless, perplexed as to the reason of the Blessed Virgin being clad in mourning weeds with a long black mantle, instead of the sumptuous robes befitting the Queen of Heaven. It was to remind you, dear brother, of the overwhelming grief and sadness which she endured in witnessing the death of her only Son ; and the black habit which she presented to you is the mourning garb worn by us, her Servants. For you well know that our Order was established on Monte Senario in honour of her Sorrows, which we keep in everlasting remembrance. This habit, at one and the same time, recalls to us the desolation of Our most dear Mistress, and preaches to us the mortification which we are bound to practise. It serves to distinguish us from other Religious ; and, since it was bestowed upon us by the hands of the Blessed Virgin herself, we never lay it aside neither by night nor by day. When Mary spoke to you so lovingly yesterday, saying : 'Go near, and join thyself to this chariot,' she called upon you to be clothed with this habit and to enter this our Order. Do not, then, my son, hesitate to make answer to her summons ; be faithful to grace, and persevere stead-fastly in your holy resolution."

St. Bonfilius, inspired by the Holy Spirit, made many reflections as touching as those we have recorded. Under the influence of grace the words flowed from his lips like torrents of living water. Philip was deeply moved : his heart throbbed, and his eyes filled with tears. When the venerable Founder had ceased to speak, the young man threw himself at his feet, and in a voice tremulous with feeling said : "Dear Father, your words have been most sweet to my ears. I beseech you, by the bowels of the Divine Mercy, not to reject me. I am, in truth, resolved to leave all things ; and I pray you to deign to admit me into your Order among the Servants of Mary. I ask you, as a favour, not to place me among those who are destined to the priesthood, but rather to let me be one of the lay-brothers who wait upon the priests and clerics. For I wish to enter Religion in order to be a Servant of the Servants of Our Lady."

St. Bonfilius, who wished to try Philip's resolution, so as to be assured that it did not spring from a mere passing impulse, answered thus : "My son, to this end you must have a brave heart, firm, un-daunted, and persevering ; for, believe me, it is no light matter that you have taken in hand ".

"By the grace of God, and the help of His Blessed Mother," the young man replied, "I shall be ready to do battle for the glory of Our Lord Christ Jesus, and the salvation of my soul. I shall fight without fear against the world and its vanities, against the devil and his temptations. Therefore, do I, once again, from my heart entreat you to be pleased to give me the habit of the Servants of Mary."

The conversation would have been yet further prolonged, had not the sound of the refectory bell startled them. So wholly had their thoughts been engaged with heavenly things, that they had been unconscious of the flight of time. It was now about three o'clock in the afternoon · for it was Friday, and the Seven Founders had made it a rule that the day sacred to the Passion of Jesus and the Sorrows of Mary should be kept as a strict fast. St. Bonfilius, seeing how ready Philip was to obey Our Lady's summons, resolved to propose him to the Religious as a subject for admission that very day. So as soon as they were all assembled, he led the young man, in their presence, into the enclosed part of the Convent, conducted him to their poor refectory, and invited him to share their frugal repast.

The meal being over, and grace having been said, followed, as was customary, by the *Salve Regina*, St Bonfilius held a spiritual conference with his Religious on the contempt of riches, the vanity of the world, apostolic poverty, religious observance, and the ceremonies and customs peculiar to the Order. His motive in so doing was to enlighten Philip as to the new life which he desired to lead, and that thus, being thoroughly acquainted with it beforehand, he might not, by acting precipitately, expose himself to the danger of regretting the step which he had taken.

The conference was hardly concluded, when Philip, whose resolution was now stronger than ever, knelt down in the middle of the refectory, and extending his arms in the form of a cross, he declared aloud that it was his desire to withdraw from the world, and to give himself to God without reserve. "Dear Father Prior," said he, addressing St. Bonfilius, "I beseech you, by the love you bear to Our Lord and to His Blessed Mother, no longer to defer accepting me as the lowest and least of your servants and novices. My heart is melted within me at the joyful prospect of belonging to the Religious State ; for in this, I am convinced, is the true earthly paradise to be found."

Then he turned to the rest of the Religious, and implored each of them, in turn, to have the charity to receive him among the Servants of Mary. He repeated what he had said to St. Bonfilius, assuring them that his sole earthly desire was to be the Servant of Mary's Servants, to live and to die in that capacity ; and he therefore begged them to admit him at once as a lay-brother. "My dear Fathers," he said, "I pray you, for the good of my soul, to open to me the arms of your clemency, since Our Lord and His Most Holy Mother have been pleased to call me to their service, without any desert of my own."

All present were moved to tears at beholding so perfect a union of fervour and humility in a young man of noble birth, of high-bred bearing, and of distinguished talents. They were touched by the sincerity with which, as he knelt at their feet, he entreated them to admit him among them as the very least of their servants. Philip was naturally graceful in manner, and of a pleasing countenance ; but, at this moment, stirred as he was by high and holy feelings, there was something angelic in his expression.

There was no hesitation as to his being admitted into the Order. The only question was as to whether he should be received, according to his wish, as a lay-brother. St. Bonfilius was reluctant to place a young man of such great attainments in that subordinate position ; but, after consulting the Religious, he concluded that it would be better to consent to the desire of the postulant who was so plainly called to a high degree of perfection, the foundations of which must be deeply laid in humility. When the time was ripe, Almighty

God would have His own ways of bringing His servant forth from this inferior rank, and would enable him to accomplish his high destiny. The holy Founder, accordingly, turned to Philip, raised him from his kneeling posture, and, gently laying his hands upon his shoulders, gave him the kiss of peace, and told him that he was accepted by the Order. At these words the soul of the postulant was filled with unspeakable gladness; the desire of his heart was granted ; and henceforth his life would be spent among the Servants of Our Lady, in that house of God which seemed to him as the gate of heaven itself.

It was the custom, at that period, for postulants, on their admission into the Monastery, to remain for some time before they received the habit. During this interval, the purpose of which was to try their vocation, they were made to practise various acts of obedience, humility, and mortification. St. Bonfilius did not think it well to dispense Philip from this rule in spite of the ardour with which he had sought admission, and of the marvels which had preceded and accompanied his vocation. In so important a matter the prudent Founder would do nothing hastily. He did not spare the new postulant, but laid upon him, as he himself desired, the hardest tasks, and employed him in the lowest and most menial offices, in all of which Philip showed a cheerful readiness which amazed the Religious, accustomed though they were to the daily contemplation of heroic virtues.

The spirit of utter self-abnegation so conspicuous in Philip Benizi, together with the admirable manner in which he bore himself under all the tests by which his vocation was tried, convinced St. Bonfilius that this was no ordinary postulant, and he marvelled as he beheld the high degree of sanctity to which this young man had attained whilst he was yet living in the world. He did not, therefore, hesitate to shorten the usual term of probation ; and, after a briefer period than was customary, he resolved to give the fervent postulant the habit of Our Blessed Lady which he so earnestly craved. The Religious being assembled in Chapter, St. Bonfilius, amidst the solemn chant of psalm and hymn, gave Philip, in exchange for his secular dress, the coarse garb worn by the lay-brothers of the Servants of Mary. The piety, recollection, and humility exhibited by the postulant, as he received from his venerable Superior the rough tunic, the scapular, and the ample cloak of the Order, moved St. Bonfilius and all present to tears, as on the first day of his being presented to them

Although it was usual, at the reception of the habit, to confer a new name upon the postulant, in order to remind him that he was henceforth to lead an entirely new life ; nevertheless, St. Bonfilius deemed this unadvisable in Philip's case. Out of reverence for the heavenly voice which had four times summoned him by his baptismal name, he was allowed to retain it in perpetual remembrance of the maternal goodness of Mary on his behalf.

On the conclusion of the ceremony the saintly Prior formally presented the new Servant of Mary to his Brethren, and then left him to himself in order to give him full freedom to pour out his grateful thanks to his Mother and Mistress.

Philip Benizi's novitiate was marked, from the first day, by extreme fervour. He was a constant source of edification to the Community, both his speech and actions affording them a model of perfection in every particular. His whole bearing preached humility, sweetness, loving-kindness, modesty, patience, and diligence. He kept silence with most scrupulous exactness, and when duty compelled him to speak, his words were so discreet and few, that they seemed not to break the hushed tranquillity of the cloister. His gait was dignified and graceful, free from stiffness or affectation, sedate without slowness, swift, yet not hurried. He observed the strictest poverty as to his habit; yet it was always spotless and neatly arranged. He mortified himself in all things. Like the holy Apostle, he chastised his body and brought it into subjection; he put all his natural inclinations under the yoke of reason and of faith; and he refused himself the most innocent gratifications, and fought continually against self as being the most formidable enemy. He delighted in the hardest toil, and in the most menial offices. He dug in the garden, swept and scrubbed in the Monastery, washed the plates and dishes, and never shrank from any task, how laborious soever it might prove. His love of prayer was not less striking; he was always the first to enter, and the last to leave the Choir; and when the Office, or Meditation, or Conference was ended, he still lingered there, devoting all his free time to prayer and spiritual reading; insomuch that, if he was ever missed, there was no need to search far for him, since he was sure to be found in the Church. Such was Philip Benizi, from the very beginning of his novitiate. It might be said, indeed, that he was a perfect reproduction of the Seven Founders. To St. Bonfilius, however, belonged the merit of having given the first impulse to his holy aspirations, by fostering his longings after heroic sanctity.

The brotherhood of Cafaggio did not long enjoy the privilege of possessing the saintly Novice, for it soon became necessary to withdraw him from the near neighbourhood of his relations and friends, whose frequent visits were undesirable. Philip had found these constant interruptions so disturbing that he had humbly petitioned to be sent to Monte Senario. He had always loved retirement, but it was dearer to him now than ever, since he had been permitted to taste in the silent cloister how sweet is the Lord, and how irresistibly He appeals to the faithful soul. St. Bonfilius readily granted his request, and had, indeed, been on the point of anticipating it. For the enormous throngs of people who frequented the Church of Our Lady of Grace made the neighbourhood most unsuitable for the training of the young Religious, to whom freedom from bustle and excitement is essential. Accordingly, Philip, having obtained permission to remove to Monte Senario, knelt before the miraculous picture of Our Lady, and placed himself under her maternal protection. Then, still kneeling, he received the blessing of the venerable Prior, and joyfully set forth on his way to the holy mountain.

At Monte Senario, Philip was confided to the charge of another of the founders, St. Amideus, whose office it was to train the Novices of the Order. To be brought into immediate contact with this great soul, so devoted to God and to Our Lady, was of itself enough to fan the flame which the younger Saint's craving for perfection had already kindled in his heart ; and under the guidance of St. Amideus, he advanced with rapid strides in the path of holiness. Philip's life at Monte Senario was spent in intimate intercourse with, and under the supervision of, several of the other Founders, whose examples he beheld with reverence, and whom he strove diligently to imitate during the four years which he passed there. Under their influence, he practised continually the austere virtues of which they were such perfect models, and it was not long before he attained to their level.

The long hours of prayer, the incessant penances, the frequent seclusion in the lonely mountain caves, which had trained those heroic souls, became more and more his delight. It was in the same school, too, that he learnt to love Our Lady with that supernatural affection which so greatly distinguished each one of our Seven Saints.

This was a time of great happiness for all the members of the Order. New convents were built in many places : vocations became daily more numerous . all were full of fervour, and eagerly striving after perfection ; and Our Lady's fostering care gave inexpressible sweetness to every detail of their lives. All was going smoothly, when suddenly a bolt from the blue vault fell upon the new centre of the Order, the house of Cafaggio. It was needful that the bitterness of the trial should mingle with the sweetness of success, and that thus the sons of the Queen of Martyrs should fulfil their vocation.

The Convent of Cafaggio, since the occurrence of the miracle to which it owed its fame, was frequented by crowds of pilgrims. The Florentine Republic had also established a weekly market close at hand, to which great numbers resorted ; and the quiet retirement of the brotherhood was continually broken in upon. The Religious of St. Mary, anxious to fulfil all the duties of their state as perfectly as possible, strove to prevent this constant intrusion of the world, but in vain.

Another disadvantage was, that they were much straitened for room in the little Convent of St. Mary ; and the Chapel, also, was far from being sufficiently spacious. It, therefore, became necessary to enlarge the whole edifice. St. Bonfilius, seeing that it was absolutely essential, did not hesitate to adopt measures to remedy the evil. The Government of the Republic, having exhausted all the funds at their disposal in the endless succession of wars in which they had been engaged, were now endeavouring to raise money to meet their expenditure. Among other resources, they proposed to sell the lands belonging to them near the Santissima Annunziata ; and they were ready to part with as much ground as was required for the enlarging of the Convent ; but the difficulty for the Fathers was to find the amount needed for the purchase.

Under these circumstances, St. Bonfilius thought that the best plan would be to have recourse to the Holy Father, who was then at Anagni ; and, accordingly, he proceeded thither and presented to the Pontiff a twofold petition, requesting him to protect the Religious at Cafaggio from the disturbances occasioned by the noisy traffic of the market, and to furnish them with some help towards building a more suitable Convent.

Innocent IV. replied to these two requests by two separate letters. By the first, he approved of the desire expressed by the Brethren of Cafaggio of giving themselves more freely to a life of contemplation ; and to enable them the better to do so, he forbade their hearing the confessions of seculars, and also prohibited the burial of lay persons in their Church, and the admission of women during the celebration of the Divine Office. This letter, dated 17th August, 1254, was the first which the Order had received directly from the Supreme Pontiff.

This letter has given rise to two entirely opposite interpretations. According to the first, our Saints claimed quite another kind of protection, and, far from being a boon, these restrictions were, in reality, a great hindrance to the pastoral work of the brotherhood at Cafaggio. It is difficult to suppose that Innocent IV. did not grasp the full consequences of the decree, by which he responded to the petition of the Fathers We must then believe that he intended either to pave the way for the amalgamation of the Servants of Mary with the Hermits of St. Augustine, or to deprive the former of their privileges, in conformity with a plan which he put into execution, shortly afterwards, 21st November, 1254, with regard to all the Mendicant Orders. In any case, this rescript of 17th August, 1254, threw the Servite Order back by at least fifteen years, and seriously interfered with its fundamental object of uniting the Active to the Contemplative Life. Moreover, the practical results of this prohibition were most disastrous, as the Convent of Cafaggio was thereby deprived of its chief means of doing good to souls, as well as of maintaining itself, and of developing its resources.

According to another opinion, the affair takes a very different aspect. After the miracle of the Santissima Annunziata, our Saints, seeing themselves overflowed by the influx of visitors entreating their ministration, resolved to put a stop to it. Thus, to protect their life of solitude and prayer, and draw as near as possible to their primitive vocation, they themselves spontaneously solicited the prohibitions that Pope Innocent IV. granted them. Thus, this letter, far from contradicting their desires, fulfilled them, and everything was for the best. It must be said that this second interpretation has been only proposed quite recently, and up to this time it was entirely unknown. However, after a lapse of three years, we shall see our Seven Founders begging themselves for the cancelling of the decree of Innocent IV., and obtaining it from his successor.

In any case, whether the first letter was inspired from a motive of benevolence or severity, Innocent IV., on the very next day, 18th August, signed another letter, whereby he granted to the Brothers of St. Mary, in aid of their pressing necessities, two hundred pounds Pisan currency, to be deducted from money lent on mortgage, which could not be restored to the lawful owners. This mode of restitution was much in vogue at that time, when the love of gain induced many traders to lend money at a usurious rate of interest. ˙

St. Bonfilius was thus enabled to acquire some land belonging to the Republic adjoining the Convent and Chapel of Cafaggio, and to carry out the projected enlargement. The Oratory was now beginning to be transformed into a regular church, rectangular in shape, and about one hundred and fifty feet in length by ninety feet in width. The works begun at this period were carried on for a considerable time, and they ultimately produced an edifice of surpassing and unequalled beauty, for the famous Churches, Santa Maria Novella, the Cathedral, and Santa Croce, had not yet been built.

Such were the various events by which the year 1254 was marked. It was drawing towards its close, when, on the 7th of December, Innocent IV. died at Naples. Five days later Cardinal Reginald was elected Pope, and took the name of Alexander IV. The Order, which had been threatened by his predecessor with an amalgamation that amounted practically to its suppression, could not but rejoice at the accession of Alexander IV., whose moderate views and whose amiable disposition were well known. During his reign the Order, like a disabled ship, repaired its damages, and set sail anew towards the port to which the Providence of God had directed it, and which, in spite of all adverse gales, it was destined to reach, under the protection of Our Blessed Lady.

CHAPTER VI.

Borgo San Sepolcro—Perugia—First Monastery of Nuns—Alexander IV.—St. Bonfilius' Retreat.

(1255—1256.)

Our Seven Saints, who had been rather dismayed by the attitude of Innocent IV. towards them, breathed more freely again when they saw the Holy See filled by a Pontiff whose kindliness of nature and sweetness of manner were known to all. Just then, indeed, fortune seemed to smile again upon them. Florence was entering upon a hitherto unknown phase of existence. After having been engaged in perpetual warfare with the neighbouring cities, and after a year of victories, she was now about to inaugurate a time of peace by allying herself with her former foes. Our Founders consequently set to work at once with joyous hearts and renewed courage. All the existing foundations were making satisfactory progress. At Cafaggio the Church was being enlarged under the supervision of St. Bonfilius; at Lucca St. Buonagiunta was purchasing land in order to complete the erection of the Convent; at Siena the Republic was contributing towards the building of the Oratory and the house ; in the other Convents all was going on well. Everything was in their favour, and the Fathers had only to take advantage of it. This they perfectly understood, and they gave themselves up to the direction of Divine Providence.

When the Founders began to enlarge the scope of the Order, they drew lines radiating from their centre, the holy mountain of Senario, and extending to the nearest points in Tuscany, as Siena, Pistoja, Arezzo, Cafaggio, and Lucca ; and here they established themselves, being at the same time willing to occupy more distant posts. Indeed, they had already crossed the frontiers of Tuscany to settle at Città di Castello; and they were about to do so a second time, in order to make a foundation at Borgo San Sepolcro, which then belonged to Umbria. This small city, at about ninety miles distance from Florence, was in those days a fortress town surrounded by towers ; and, picturesque of aspect, it seemed her natural lot to be the birth-place of famous painters. Here, all circumstances combining to favour the project, the Servants of Mary resolved to establish a Convent.

An extraordinary occurrence is connected with this foundation, and we must here pause to relate it, since it redounds to the honour of one of our Founders, St. Sostene, the force of whose holy influence it strikingly displays. In the neighbourhood of Borgo San Sepolcro there was a small property belonging to a certain Count Bonafede della Selva. Anxious to induce the Servants of Mary to settle at

Borgo San Sepolcro, so that he might be within easy reach of them, he had offered to contribute liberally towards the undertaking. A temporary abode was soon found to serve until matters could be placed on a permanent footing St. Sostene was sent with several other Fathers to establish the first Community. Our good Founder and his companions, having arrived at their destination, took possession of the dwelling assigned them, and inaugurated the Convent. Just then Count Bonafede was preparing to celebrate the marriage of his son Donato, with Grazia, the daughter of Andrea, a noble of equal rank ; and he accordingly begged St. Sostene to give the nuptial blessing to the youthful pair. The Saint consented ; and during the ceremony he, as was customary, gave a short discourse on the dignity of the Sacrament which had just united the bridegroom with the bride. But, whilst eulogizing holy Matrimony, the Saint touched on the higher glory of Virginity, and, carried away by his theme, became very eloquent, and gave marvellous utterance to the lofty thoughts which filled his mind. The youth and the maiden who knelt before him were so deeply moved that as soon as the nuptial Mass ended both declared that they were resolved to part for ever at the foot of the Altar. The young man entered the Servite Convent, just founded by his father, and his bride became the Spouse of Christ in a neighbouring cloister. This was truly an unlooked-for sequel to the wedding festivities. St. Sostene's humility made him give all the glory to the most spotless Virgin, who loves to be attended by a numerous company of virgin souls.

The Borgo San Sepolcro Convent was blessed by the grace of God, for it trained its disciples in such wise as to make it a school of holiness ; for it was here that St. Philip, later on, enlisted two of his most distinguished recruits—Blessed Andrea Dotti and Geronimo.

We have little authentic information as to the early days of this foundation from the material point of view. We only know that the site of the Convent was outside the walls, upon the road called the Via Cupa, the Hollow Way. The brotherhood speedily took possession of the ground and began to prepare it for building. On the fifteenth of the following July they requested permission to erect a Church and Convent.

Before these preliminaries, however, towards the close of April, St. Bonfilius had resolved to seek an interview with the new Pope. More than four months had elapsed since the pontifical election, and it was now time to come to an understanding with the Church's Supreme Head, and to endeavour to procure the revocation of the stern decrees of Innocent IV., since the Order, fettered by these, could scarcely be said to live—all its powers of action for the good of souls being utterly paralyzed.

The holy General set forth in hopeful mood, and repaired to Naples, where Alexander IV. was still residing ; and there he was able to confer several times with the Pontiff himself. He found the Holy Father to be, as universal report had described him, benevolence personified. His Holiness would gladly have restored the Servants of Mary all that they had lost under the pontificate of his predecessor ; but he was obliged to proceed with caution. Two questions of the utmost importance had to be considered : in the first place, the existence of the Servants of Mary as a distinct Order, and, next, the conferring of faculties upon the members for the ministry of souls. Too many interests were concerned in these questions, and too many jealousies were aroused by them, to allow of their being disposed of without further examination. Nevertheless, he granted all that it was possible to grant for the moment, by virtue of two decrees which we gladly reproduce.

In the first of these documents, dated 19th May, 1255, addressed to the Religious of Monte Senario, he reminds them of the strict poverty to which they had vowed themselves with the approval of the Holy See, and he gives his sanction to the same in all its rigour. At the same time, in order to furnish the Servants of Mary with the means of carrying out their undertaking at Cafaggio, he permits them to receive alms and bequests given for the purpose of building the new Church and of enlarging the Convent.

This concession only related to an isolated and temporary state of affairs. But, seven days later, on the 26th of May, the Pope issued another decree of a more general and permanent character, the scope of which was far wider. In this he gave the Order formal permission to establish itself wheresoever any of its members existed upon such terms as were essential to the peculiar vocation of the Servants of Mary. This concession, as all-important in itself as it was briefly expressed, was in the following terms :

"Alexander, Bishop, Servant of the Servants of God, to Our well-beloved sons the Prior and Brethren of Blessed Mary of Monte Senario, commonly known as Servants of St. Mary, of the Order of St. Augustine, health and the Apostolic benediction.

"Of Our good-will we comply with your zealous petitions, and by virtue of these presents, without prejudice to the rights of any others whomsoever, we grant permission for you to have, in all places where you may be established, the requisite houses, Oratories, and cemeteries, but solely for your religious exercises.

"Given at Naples, the seventh of the Calends of June (May 26), the first year of our Pontificate (1255)."

During the discussions which ensued upon the granting of these favours, the Pope and the Cardinals, and more especially the Cardinal Protector, did not fail to remind St. Bonfilius of the plan at first conceived by Innocent IV., and afterwards entertained by his successor, of amalgamating all the branches of the Hermits of St. Augustine at that time in existence. The Saint had no difficulty in proving that

13

although the Servants of Mary belonged to the great Augustinian family, they yet could not fairly be included in this scheme. Undoubtedly, they resembled the Hermits in some particulars ; but their name, their spirit, and their mission were wholly unlike. In a certain sense, they might be said to be members of the same Order ; but it would be impossible for them to follow the same Observance, or to be dependent on the same Superiors. It was therefore decided that the Servants of Mary should continue to form a distinct brotherhood, and to be directed by Superiors exclusively their own, whilst belonging by their Rule to the Augustinian Order. Thus ended the debate ; for, shortly afterwards, Alexander IV., on July 15, 1255, formally approved of the Statutes drawn up for all those Congregations of the Hermits of St. Augustine which were to be blended together, but he did not impose them on the Servants of Mary. He convoked the representatives of these Congregations to a General Chapter, but he did not call upon the Brothers of Monte Senario to attend it—there is not, at all events, the faintest trace of his having done so. These are facts full of significance The Servants of Mary had, therefore, neither part nor lot in these transactions ; and the question as to their separate existence remained undecided. It is easy to see why it should have been so. Had the dilemma been settled by a formal act of the pontifical authority, a new Order would have been created ; and to this step the Curia had an insuperable objection. If a negative answer had been returned, the lately established Institute would have been altogether suppressed. A middle course was consequently adopted, namely, that of accepting the *status quo*, as it had existed before the severe edicts of Innocent IV. had been promulgated. It seemed as though the Order, so dear to Mary, was destined, in the mysterious designs of Providence, to pass through an unusually prolonged trial, that thus it might more closely resemble her whom it reverenced as the most sorrowful Mother.

Nevertheless, the journey undertaken by St. Bonfilius may be looked upon as having been partially successful. But now the Fathers had feared that the Order, yet in its infancy, might succumb to the attacks of its enemies. From this time forth there were signs of a victorous issue to the struggle, since they were able, in the face of all opponents, to produce the recent letter of the Pope justifying the existence of their Institute. Our Seven Founders felt like men who have been unexpectedly delivered from the agonies of death and restored to perfect health and unbroken strength. The joyful news was soon communicated to the entire brotherhood, who were filled with joy. The works which had been begun at the various Convents were pressed on with renewed diligence. At Cafaggio additional enlargements were projected at Borgo San Sepolcro and Città di Castello the Prior Pietro Ristoro, who had the superintendence of both foundations, busied himself with the erection of a

Church and Convent in each of those cities. The Bishop of Castello conferred upon him all necessary powers on the 7th of July and the 21st of August, 1255. In these undertakings Father Ristoro enjoyed the co-operation of one, who, notwithstanding his exalted virtues and his superiority in years, was content to be eclipsed by his young comrade. This was St. Hugh himself, whose passionate humility made him ever desire to take the second place, though none were better fitted to hold the foremost rank.

On his return from Naples, bringing with him the pontifical concessions, St. Bonfilius took up his abode for a time at Cafaggio. It had already struck him that the present state of affairs made it desirable to call a Chapter of the Order; and after conferring with the other Fathers upon the subject, he resolved to carry out the idea. In consequence of the many obstacles which had arisen in succession, no Chapter had been held for several years, and all the Brethren now felt the need of meeting together once again to discuss their various plans, and to encourage one another in their labours. It is one of the greatest joys of the Religious Life when the members can meet together, in the interchange of brotherly charity and sympathy, to receive the counsels imparted by the veterans of spirituality. St. Bonfilius had likewise a project which he confided to no one, but which lay very close to his heart. Having now held office as Superior for twenty-two years, he thought that he might claim the right of retirement. Humble-minded as he was, and wholly detached from earthly things, he felt convinced that the post could easily be filled by another as well as, or better, than by himself. He saw, of course, that no change must be thought of during the current year, for the election of a General could not take place without the sanction of the Sovereign Pontiff, failing which, it could hardly be looked upon as valid. It was, therefore, necessary to await a more favourable opportunity, when the clouds which had overshadowed the Order should have entirely dispersed.

In the early days of September, 1255, Florence was enjoying a state of tranquillity, and the time seemed propitious for assembling the Fathers at Cafaggio, which was shortly to become the central point of the Order, and, indeed, might already be considered as such. On the 7th of October following the first session of the Chapter took place. St. Bonfilius presided, and opened the proceedings with a speech in which he gave an outline of the existing situation of affairs, and alluded to the dangers which they had encountered, and the hopes which they were now permitted to entertain. He then spoke of the line of conduct which it would be advisable for them to pursue. Since it was a recognized and incontestable fact that they belonged to the Order of St. Augustine, although they retained the distinctive features and observances of their Institute, he said that it was essential that they should practise the strictest poverty, such

being the marked characteristic of that Order.   It was also necessary
that they should solemnly make profession of this on behalf of the
whole of their Religious family, that so no doubt might remain upon
the point, and that thus they might reap all the benefits accruing
from such profession.   The declaration, if presented to the Holy See,
would undoubtedly predispose the Pontiff favourably towards their
case, and would probably induce him to bestow upon them the
formal approbation which they had so long sought in vain.

All the Brethren replied with one voice that they were ready to
express by word of mouth, and to set forth in writing, the principles
which they avowed from their hearts ; and before the close of the
session they made and signed, in presence of a notary, the proposed
declaration.   In the authenticated record which has been preserved
of the transaction we peruse with vivid interest the names of several
of our Saints.

We here give an epitomized version of this act as it appears in a
Bull of Alexander IV., who, at a subsequent period, gave his approval
to the engagement entered into by the Order with respect to holy
poverty.

"In the Name of God, Amen.   On the nones of October, in the
year 1255, Indict. XIV.

"Be it favourably known by these presents that, the following
being gathered together, namely, Brother Bonfilius, Prior of the
Church of St. Mary of Monte Senario, and the brotherhood belonging to the same place, known as the Servants of St. Mary, and the
other Brethren herein named, dwelling near Florence in their house
which stands in the place called Cafaggio (here follow the nineteen
names, among which are Brother Alexis, Brother Buonagiunta,
Brother James, and Brother Manettus).   Each and all of these, in
honour of Almighty God and of His Son Our Lord Jesus Christ,
in honour likewise of Mary the Holy and Spotless Mother of God, of
all the Saints of God, and as a mark of reverence to the Holy Roman
Church, have promised and bound themselves by vow to Almighty
God and to Blessed Mary never to possess any real property.   And
if it should so chance that anyone were minded to give or make over
to them such real property they shall have no use thereof ; but it
must belong wholly and solely to Our Father the Pope and to the
Most Holy Roman Church.   Let this, however, be done in such wise
as that the Bishop of the diocese may have an entire jurisdiction
over it for the spiritual advantage of the person who has made over
the property, and by way of alms for the Brethren of the aforesaid
Order.   If anyone of them should break any of these engagements,
he will incur the displeasure of Almighty God and of Blessed Mary
ever Virgin.   Moreover, they renounce beforehand their privilege of
appealing to any laws, canonical or otherwise, which might be in
their favour.

" Given in the Church of the foresaid Brothers, situated near Florence, in the place called Cafaggio, in presence of a notary public."

Singularly enough, all the pains taken by the Servites to place themselves in a regular and canonically legal position proved a ground of accusation against them, later on, when they were charged with having endeavoured, in spite of the prohibition issued by the two Councils of Lateran and Lyons respecting the establishment of new Mendicant Orders, to procure the foundation of yet another Order vowed to the strictest poverty. This difficulty was, however, speedily removed. Divine Providence so ordered matters that shortly afterwards the Order was compelled by force of circumstances to hold property. Thus the intentions of the Seven Founders remained fruitless, and a complete refutation was afforded to all attacks upon this point.

In the meanwhile, St. Buonagiunta had already become Prior of the Convent of Cafaggio. In this office all his grand qualities hitherto concealed were brought to light. Full of zeal for the sanctification of others, as well as for his own perfection, he spared no pains to attain both these ends. His charity and sweetness for all around him were inexhaustible ; he was lavish of counsel and exhortation, never relaxing his efforts till grace gained the upper hand ; and thus he saved innumerable souls. The period of his government was rich in the fruits of salvation ; unhappily, the excessive severity of his mortifications caused much apprehension for his health, which was already shattered.

His reputation was great for sanctity and apostolic zeal, and he was also believed to have the gift of working miracles. He had, indeed, given a striking proof of his power in this respect. There dwelt in Florence an aged usurer, named Antonio. St. Buonagiunta knew this man, and was well aware of the iniquitous business carried on by him ; nor did the Saint spare rebuke and warning whenever they met . in particular, he sought to impress upon the moneylender that, besides the avowal of his sins and heartfelt contrition for them, there was but one way of repairing all his wrong-doing, and that was by abundant almsgiving. Antonio, weary of the Saint's exhortations, resolved to put an end to them. He, therefore, affected great sorrow for the past, and an earnest desire to lead a better life for the future ; at the same time, telling the Saint that the fruits of his conversion would soon appear. Shortly afterwards, Antonio's maid-servant arrived at Cafaggio, bringing a large supply of bread, wine, and other provisions as an alms to Father Buonagiunta. The Saint, by revelation from on high, knew instantly that all the gifts were poisoned. Then, addressing himself to the maid-servant, he told her of her master's criminal design, and added that she would find him dead on her return home. Having made the sign of the Cross over the provisions, he was then able to eat of them without injury to his health.   The maid-servant, on reaching Antonio's house, found to her horror that the Saint's prediction was verified : the usurer was dead.

Another Convent was now added to those already possessed by the Order.   In 1251, the brotherhood had taken root at Città di Castello, in the valley of the Tiber, and the Patrimony of St Peter. During the first half of 1255, they made another move in the province of Tuscany, and established themselves at Borgo San Sepolcro: and now they turned their faces again towards Rome, and installed themselves in Perugia, the chief city of Umbria.   Perugia was an influential and fairly populous town, more inclined to the Guelph than to the Ghibelline party, and, therefore, much favoured by the Popes, who frequently made long visits there.   One of the inhabitants, Filippo de Piscina, Count of Cocorano, was strongly attached to the Order : he himself became a member of it, and it was he who built the Convent and Church of St. James in the suburbs of the city.

With the foundation of Perugia there is connected what may be described as the first attempt at enrolling a body of religious women, whose institute was to be modelled on that of the Servants of Mary.

Generally speaking, so far as our Seven Saints are concerned, it is difficult to say what share they took in introducing their rule of life among nuns.   Here, as throughout the greater portion of their career, all is a blank.   Did they themselves take the lead in founding Communities of devout women and virgins living after their Rule ? Or did they only promote the good work by their sympathy and counsels ?   On these points we are left in ignorance.

It may easily be conceived that many pious widows and virgins must have desired to consecrate themselves to Our Blessed Lady in an Order which bore her Name, and which existed chiefly to do her honour.   It is natural that women should rejoice to pay the tribute of their homage to her, the example and glory of all womanhood, to her who is blessed among all the daughters of Eve.   All that was known to the outside world of the origin of the Order must have increased the number of those who shared this desire.   But, on the other hand, the struggle for existence, in which the Order was continually engaged, must have cooled the zeal of many, and, in the majority of cases, have rendered the foundation of Convents of religious women impracticable.

However it may have been, it appears that the earliest trace of such a foundation occurs at Perugia   In that city a lady lived, by name Countess Simona.   Having become a widow, she adopted the garb of the Servants of Mary, and thenceforth lived in strict retirement, wholly given up to the service of God and of the poor.   Then, wishing to copy still more closely the example of our Saints, she sold all that she possessed. and distributed the proceeds in alms. She dwelt in a small house bearing all the outward signs of poverty, and here she was joined by several pious souls who, like herself, wished to consecrate themselves to the Blessed Virgin. Thus was begun a new and genuine Community, popularly known as the Convent of Countess Simona's Poor Ladies, on account of the state of privation in which they lived. As time went on, many members of the most distinguished families of that locality entered the Community, which subsequently bore the name of the Immaculate Conception.

This course of events, which took place in Perugia about the year 1255, was repeated afterwards in many other places. The chroniclers only mention Pistoja, Florence, and Porcheria ; but we have reason to believe that small bodies of religious women were established in other towns The mode of life adopted was not always, it is true, precisely the same. There were, in particular, two distinct classes : the members of one continued to live in the world, and even in the midst of home circles ; whilst those belonging to the other led lives of strict enclosure. It was customary to style the last-named class the Second Order, whilst the former class was termed the Third Order.

Meanwhile an event of considerable importance occurred in the Church, and one especially interesting to the Servite Order. The representatives of the greater number of Congregations of the Hermits of St. Augustine came, by desire of the Pope, to Rome, and assembled in the Church of Santa Maria del Popolo, March 1, 1256. There were gathered the delegates of ten Congregations : those of Valersuta, of Torre dei Palmi, of the Penitenza di Gesu Cristo, of St. Benedict of Montefabalo, the Guglielmites, the Giovanni Boniti, those of Lupocavo, near Lucca, the Britinians, and the Congregations of Sta. Maria di Murceto, and St. Jacobo di Montho. In conformity with the Statutes approved by Alexander IV., Lanfranco Septala was elected sole General of all these Congregations, now amalgamated into a single Order, which Order was divided into four Provinces, those of France, of Germany, of Spain, and of Italy. This arrangement was sanctioned by the Pope on the 13th of April following ; and on May 2, 1256, a solemn Bull of unification was promulgated. In 1257, Alexander IV. put the finishing stroke to this great undertaking, by conferring on this Order of Hermits of St. Augustine the privilege of exemption from the jurisdiction of the Ordinary.

Acquainted with these circumstances, our Saints thought it desirable to profit by them to obtain from Alexander IV a formal approbation. For this object they despatched to Rome Blessed James of Poggibonzi, in whom they had the greatest confidence, as well as other Fathers of note. At the same time they charged the

Convents to pray till they received good news. At once the most fervent supplications went up to the Heavenly Foundress of the Order, that the projected steps might have a complete success.

The deputation from the Order arrived in Rome in the month of March. The Cardinal Guglielmo dei Fieschi, their Protector, being ill, the Fathers presented themselves to Ottobuono dei Fieschi, a relation of Cardinal Guglielmo. He was well acquainted with the Servants of Mary, having visited them in Florence, and he esteemed them highly. He promised the Fathers he would exercise all his power with the Pope in their favour. He well understood that a formal approbation of the Holy See, and a perfect right of self-government, could alone give peace to the Order. The conclusion of the affair was surrounded with serious difficulties, but the good Cardinal took the means of surmounting them all.

At length the day was fixed for the deputation to appear before the Consistory of the Pope and the Cardinals. Being introduced, they prostrated themselves before the Head of the Church and presented their petition. In the most pathetic terms they conjured him for the love of the Blessed Virgin Mary to grant it. Then the Cardinal Ottobuono related the marvels wrought by the Mother of God in the Order of her Servants, the edification they gave the faithful, and all the good they did in the Church, and ended by saying that the Servants of Mary merited having their petition granted. "But," said the Pope, "that would be creating a new Order in the Church, which is acting contrary to the Council of Lateran." "By my soul, Holy Father," answered the Cardinal, "deign to grant these Religious the privilege they ask. All I hear of their virtues makes them worthy to have their petition granted." The other Cardinals rose each in turn and pressed, in the name of the Blessed Virgin, the suit of Messer Ottobuono. Then Alexander IV. cried out : "Messer Ottobuono testifies in so positive a manner to the holiness of these religious men, that I grant their petition for the love of the Virgin Mary, whose Servants they call themselves". And immediately he gave orders that the Bull of Approbation should be prepared ; and while the deputation was still kneeling, according to several authors, he conceded by word of mouth the faculty of calling a General Chapter and of electing their own General.

Then it clearly appeared that the Pontiff, who was filled with anxious care for the branch of the great Augustinian family, did not forsake those children of the great Patriarch who had wholly consecrated themselves to the Mother of God. Notwithstanding the difficulties presented by their canonical position, on the entreaties of the Cardinals he came to a very favourable conclusion on this point. His decisions were precisely similar to those taken in the matter of the Hermits of St. Augustine. These last had met, on

1st March, 1256, to enrol themselves in one and the same Order, by choosing a General to be their sole head. On the 23rd of the same month, in the same year, perhaps on the very day of the interview just named, or a few days later, the Holy Father addressed the following letters to the Servants of Mary :

"Alexander, Bishop, Servant of the Servants of God.

"To our well-beloved sons, the Prior and Brethren of Blessed Mary of Monte Senario, commonly called Servants of St. Mary, of the Order of St. Augustine, health and the Apostolic benediction.

"Your holy Order being both pleasing to God and appreciated by men, we are moved to give a mark of our favour to you who, having resisted the seductions of this world, are desirous of serving Our Lord in perpetuity in your regular observance ; and we are willing to grant your request so far as can be done without departing from what is right. Therefore, sons well-beloved in the Lord, we gladly anticipate your lawful requests, following herein the example of our predecessor Pope Innocent, and we receive under the protection of St Peter and of Ourselves your persons, together with the place wherein you devote yourselves to the Divine Service, together with all the goods of which you are now possessed, or which you may rightfully acquire hereafter with the help of the Lord. For this purpose, Ardingo, Bishop of Florence, of happy memory, had already, as you yourselves affirm, granted to you wise and salutary statutes, published by you in the same place, to be observed in perpetuity under the Rule of St. Augustine. And in consequence thereof, Raniero, of happy memory, Cardinal-Deacon of Sta. Maria in Cosmedin, filling in those parts the office of Legate, confirmed these statutes, as may be seen in the letters drawn up upon this subject. Therefore, ratifying, and being, not without good reason, well pleased with what has been done by yourselves not less than by the Bishop and the Cardinal, we confirm it by our Apostolic Authority, and bestow upon it the privilege of the present rescript.

"Given at the Lateran, on the tenth of the Calends of April (March 23), in the second year of our Pontificate (1256)."

On the 2nd of May, 1256, the Pope gave the Hermits their definitive Bull of Amalgamation. On 16th June of the same year, he granted to the Servants of Mary an Indult drawn up in the following terms :

"Alexander, Bishop, Servant of the Servants of God.

"To our well-beloved sons the Prior and Brethren of Blessed Mary of Cafaggio, near Florence, of the Order of St. Augustine, health and the Apostolic benediction.

"We judge it to be both fitting and in accordance with our duty to be ever most bountiful in all things pertaining to the salvation of souls. Therefore, yielding to your entreaty, and by virtue of these presents, we give permission for all your Brethren who are priests, with the consent of the Ordinaries and of the Rectors of Churches, to hear the Confessions of their parishioners, and to give such penances as may be necessary, unless the sins committed should be such as are reserved to the jurisdiction of the Holy See.

"Let none hereafter presume to violate the terms of this concession, or with rash boldness venture to oppose it. For, should anyone dare to attempt this, he would incur the wrath of Almighty God, and of the Blessed Peter and Paul, His Apostles.

"Given at Anagni, the sixteenth of the Calends of July (June 17), in the second year of Our Pontificate, and the year of Our Lord 1256."

These letters proved conclusively that the Order of the Servants of Mary could in no wise be confused with that of the Hermits of St. Augustine. They also perfectly protected it, and almost reinstated it in the possession of the privileges which had belonged to it before the accession of Innocent IV. The members could now breathe freely : though not definitively approved, they were allowed to exist.

Meanwhile, St. Bonfilius had maturely considered his plan of resigning the post which he had filled for three-and-twenty years. His strength no longer sufficed for the labour which it entailed, and all circumstances seemed to combine at this juncture to make his retirement advisable. The Order had recovered from the effects of the severe trial through which it had passed, owing to the stern edict of Innocent IV., and it had regained almost all the privileges which it had formerly enjoyed. It could carry out its internal organization without hindrance, and it could exercise its external ministry, though with some restraint. And finally, it had been saved from the perils of an amalgamation with other Congregations, which would have deprived it of its essential characteristics. Whilst all the branches of the Hermits of St. Augustine had been united under one General, the Servants of Mary of the Order of St. Augustine remained apart, preserving the twofold title as well as the autonomy of their Institute, with the power of holding their own General Chapters, and of electing their own General. The time was favourable for a change ; and St. Bonfilius, in his abundant humility, took advantage of the opportunity. He therefore summoned a meeting of the Fathers at Cafaggio for the purpose of discussing all matters concerning the Order. The difficulties affecting its regular government appeared to be obviated for the future, by the favours recently granted by Alexander IV. As in other Orders, the yearly General Chapter could now be held, and would be held from this time forward. All that remained to be done was to draw up the regulation for the holding of these important meetings. This Chapter of 1256 was to be the first General Chapter assembled canonically ; and also it was its duty to adopt the Constitution regulating the frequency of the Chapters, their mode of convocation, the members who were to form them, the kind of business which was to be transacted, and the whole order of the proceedings from the beginning to the end.

The Capitular Fathers being gathered together, St. Bonfilius opened the session by an address. He began by expressing the gratitude felt by the whole Order for the goodness of Pope Alexander IV., through whose benignant interposition they had been literally recalled from death to life. He then sketched the task which devolved upon the meeting, and which consisted in drawing up a Constitution to regulate the method of holding the General Chapter. And he concluded by saying that he had a personal matter to submit to the Chapter, in the shape of a resolution which he had taken before God, and which he believed would conduce to the greater welfare of the Order.

Each of the Fathers contributed the fruits of his experience on the important topic of the General Chapter ; and from these deliberations sprang a code of regulations, than which nothing terser or more practical could have been framed.

They ran as follows :

"I. Every year a General Chapter shall be held, at the pleasure of the Superior-General. This Chapter the Prior-General and each of the Priors, accompanied by one or two Professed Fathers, will be expected to attend.

"II. No Prior or Professed Father, who shall be prevented by some good and sufficient reason from attending, can be allowed to appoint another to fill his place.

"III. The Prior-General may resign his office, and the Capitular Fathers may accept his resignation.

"IV. In all Chapters, four of the most discreet Fathers shall be chosen from among the Capitular Fathers, into whose hands the Prior-General and all the Priors shall resign their Office. During the session of the Chapter it will be left to the judgment of these four Fathers to praise what has been praiseworthy, and to blame what has been blameworthy.

"V In holding the Chapter the following prescribed order shall be observed :

"First, on the day appointed by the Father-General, all the Capitular Fathers shall meet together in the place fixed upon by him.

"Next, they shall, all kneeling, salute devoutly the Virgin Mother of God, reciting in a low tone of voice the *Salve Regina* as far as the words *O dulcis Virgo Maria*, with the versicle *Ora pro nobis;* and in like manner shall the Collect *Concede nos famulos tuos* be said.

"After this, the Superior-General, or he to whom the duty is confided, shall give an instruction on any subject which he may think most convenient for the occasion: he will make a panegyric of the Blessed Virgin, or of the Religious Life, or he will speak on other topics of a similar kind.

"This being concluded, the names will be read aloud of such Fathers as have departed from this life to dwell with the Lord, for the repose of whose souls all shall recite together the Psalm *De Profundis* with the Collect *Absolve.*

"Then, each in his turn, in the order of precedence, who may wish to propose fresh Constitutions, for the advancement and good of religion, may do so by permission of the Superior-General; and it shall be declared that such Constitutions shall become law when they have been approved by three Chapters General.

"Also, the General shall place his seal of office in the hands of the four elected Fathers, and he shall then leave the Chapter. And those who may not desire to confirm him in his office shall be free not to re-elect him; and they shall be equally at liberty to re-appoint him to hold the first place in the Order, should they wish it. Having been elected, he shall take the highest place, and all shall do homage to him and kiss his hand.

"Lastly, every Prior shall likewise resign his office into the hands of the General and of the Fathers; and these shall chastise him if he have done amiss; but if, on the contrary, he shall have well acquitted himself of his duties, they shall commend him in the Name of the Lord, and shall show their approval in whatever way may seem to them most fitting.

"All business being now ended, the bell shall be rung, and two chanters shall intone the *Te Deum*, the Choir responding *Te Dominum*, and so on to the conclusion. The Superior-General shall then say *Ora pro nobis* and *Concede nos famulos tuos.* He shall then bless the Fathers in the Name of the Lord, and shall let them depart in peace to their several destinations."

This Constitution of the Chapter General combined all the requisite qualities. It was short: so much could hardly, indeed, have been said in fewer words. It was clear; the whole mode of procedure being formulated in terms which made mistakes impossible. And lastly, it was extremely practical: from the opening to the close all seemed to move on by some noiseless machinery, without hitch or friction of any kind.

We find, too, in this Constitution unquestionable evidence as to the principles on which authority is conferred, and by which it is exercised, in the Order. To begin with, we see that it is a self-governing body, as forming a distinct Institute provided by Holy Church with all that is necessary to enable it to be carried on in a regular manner. Moreover, its government is to some extent democratic with respect to the source from which both the supreme and the inferior powers are derived, and to the manner in which they are controlled. In point of fact, all the members have a voice, either directly or indirectly, in the election of the General, since each house deputes, besides the Prior, who is an elector *ex-officio*, and himself elected by the General Chapter, one or two other electors chosen themselves to take part in the election. Moreover, the General, in the exercise of his authority, is so completely amenable to the Order at large that its representatives, the Chapter General and, more particularly, the four Definitors chosen by the Chapter, may examine him yearly as to the manner in which he has discharged the duties of his post, may praise him or censure him, may confirm him in his office, may depose him, as circumstances may render advisable. The Priors of the different Convents are elected in the same way, and are subjected to the same ordeal. The essentials of these fundamental principles have been faithfully preserved by the Order, although, as time has gone on, important modifications have been introduced in some particulars.

We must, however, add that, although the authority takes its rise from and is controlled according to democratic principles, it is practically an absolute monarchy. Once elected, the General is king, a king clothed with power which has been conferred upon him by the general voice, and which none therefore seek to contest. The same holds good, within a more restricted area, in the case of the Priors of each separate house. Thus, besides the bond imposed by the vow of obedience, all the subjects place themselves in the hands of their Superiors to fulfil all their behests unrestrictedly and unreservedly ; and authority being enforced by those in power, and submission willingly tendered by those under them, perfect unity reigns throughout the Order.

The democratic aspect of the Order was satisfactory to the subjects who were thus governed by Superiors of their own choice, and, at the same time, it acted as a warning to these Superiors, should they ever be tempted to misuse their authority. The monarchical side of the Constitutions strengthened the hands of those in office, and kept in check any symptoms of insubordination among the subjects. One side thus balanced the other, and the reciprocal action of each formed an admirable corrective to excesses on either hand, and maintained a spirit of general harmony to the great benefit of the Order at large.

But the drawing up of these regulations had not been the only important business calling for the attention of the Fathers. St. Bonfilius had spoken of another matter affecting himself, namely, his resignation, which for some time past had been much in his thoughts. He, therefore, addressed the Chapter, telling them of his intention, with which they were already acquainted. He urged it upon them, recalling briefly the early days of the Order, the difficulties which it had encountered, and the many years during which he had been called upon to guide it through its perplexities. He then said that he thought the time had now come for him to give place to another, and to withdraw into solitude, there to give himself up to the work of his sanctification.

Then, without farther preamble, the good Father, shedding tears, threw himself upon his knees before his Brethren, and begged them to dismiss him, declaring that he, for his part, resigned his office. He at the same time placed the seals, the insignia of his dignity, in the hands of the Definitors. The Fathers, deeply touched, could not without sorrow see so admirable a Superior laying down his authority. But, knowing how much Father Bonfilius longed to be released from his charge, they did not venture to make any opposition to his wishes, and they proceeded to elect his successor.

The common choice fell upon St. Buonagiunta, the youngest of the Seven Founders, who was then forty-nine years of age. He had already shown what he was during his Priorate at the Convent of Cafaggio. He had a strong sense of duty, and was devoted to the Rule ; he was a man of much strength of character, clear-sighted and inflexible ; at the same time, his heart was as tender as his courage was undaunted, and he was thoroughly apostolic in his zeal, never sparing himself, and continually working to the full extent of his strength, and even beyond it. Being duly elected, he was forced to take the helm in hand, and he did so, confiding himself wholly to God and to His Blessed Mother.

The work of the Chapter was completed by the election of the first Procurator-General of the Order at the Papal Court. Many of the Orders already possessed such a representative. At that period, as at the present time, the government of an Order involved the transactions of so much important business with the Supreme Authority, that it was essential to depute a learned and zealous man of ripe experience to confer with the Head of the Church upon questions affecting the interests of his Brethren in Religion. The Chapter General chose Blessed James of Poggibonzi, who was admirably fitted for the post.

After having provided for the needs of all the Convents, the Chapter was closed, according to the regulation just adopted, by the chanting of the *Te Deum*, in which all joined with feelings of intense thankfulness. The members then dispersed, each returning to his appointed place. St. Bonfilius repaired to his beloved solitude at Monte Senario ; whilst the new General, St. Buonagiunta, applied himself to the duties of his important office. The government of the Order was now transferred from the hands of one Saint to those of another, and the results could not, therefore, fail to be fruitful and blessed to all the members ; and such, indeed, proved to be the case during the too brief Generalate of St. Buonagiunta.

CHAPTER VII.

St. Buonagiunta's Generalate—His Death.

(1256—1257.)

THERE being now every reason to expect a continued development of the Order, Cafaggio was better fitted to be the residence of the first Superior than Monte Senario. There he would be more easy of access to those from outside, and in a better position for keeping up communication with the surrounding districts. Florence had become so important a centre of intercourse that the Order naturally chose that city for its headquarters. Henceforth, Cafaggio was to be the capital of the Servites, as Monte Senario had been their cradle. But few hours of leisure were allotted to the recently chosen General: every moment not devoted to the visitation of the different Convents of the Order was absorbed by anxious cares which exhausted his strength. His tenure of this high office was of the briefest. he had barely time to assume the reins of government, to visit his several Communities, and to transact some weighty business, when he was snatched away by death.

Almost immediately after his election, St. Buonagiunta was apprised of the death of the first Protector of the Order, Cardinal Guglielmo Fieschi. On receiving the tidings, he set out at once for Anagni; and, in spite of his great bodily weakness, caused by incessant toil and rigorous penance, he insisted upon making the journey on foot. Arriving at his destination, he sought an audience of the Sovereign Pontiff, who, addressing him in gracious words, exhorted him to courage in the fulfilment of the duties of his office. St. Buonagiunta then spoke of the chief object of his visit, and, doubtless, of other matters also. As regards the choice of a new Protector, the Holy Father made not the slightest difficulty, but at once ordered the vacancy to be filled by another nephew of Innocent IV., Cardinal Ottobuono Fieschi. By one of those remarkable dispensations of Providence which may be frequently observed in human affairs, the nearest relatives of Innocent IV. appeared to receive a special mission to smooth away all traces of the suffering caused by that Pontiff's decrees. St. Buonagiunta was able to speak freely of all matters concerning his Order with the new Protector. The result of these interviews was that a fresh reparation was made to the Servants of Mary for the injuries which had formerly been inflicted upon them.

It may be remembered that, two years previously, the Brethren of Cafaggio were suddenly confronted by the suspension of the faculties necessary for the prosecution of the most fruitful work of the priesthood—the direction of souls. Alexander IV., continuing to act under the influence of his kindliness of heart, hastened to efface these painful recollections ; and by his Apostolic brief of 17th June, 1256, the suspended faculties were restored, thus giving the Servants of Mary fresh cause to bless the Pontiff for his constant efforts to console them under their trials. The memory of Alexander IV. has been ever cherished in the Order as that of a true father and benefactor ; and a visible proof of the strength of this feeling was subsequently given by the erection of a memorial statue in his honour at Cafaggio.

Duty was the guiding star of St. Buonagiunta : hence, notwith-standing the intense heat of the summer, and his consequent bodily exhaustion, he had no sooner quitted Anagni than he began the visitation of his Convents, a task which involved much minute inspection and considerable fatigue. This, together with the severity of his rule of life, which he would never relax in the slightest degree, contributed to hasten his end, which was still farther accelerated by the many engrossing affairs he transacted at the same time. He was especially desirous of presenting to the next General Chapter a more complete summary of the Constitutions. Although no great length of time was needed to draw up this code, yet much deep and serious thought had to be given to the subject. But, at this period, the Saint, constant in his love of the hidden life, fulfilled his duties in such wise that the outer world heard no word of him. It is, therefore, almost impossible to find any record of this portion of his history.

Month after month rolled away, and the time had once more come round for the holding of the General Chapter. St. Buonagiunta gathered together at Monte Senario the Fathers who were to take part in it. Doubtless, he had himself gone thither some time pre-viously in order to see to the preparing of the new edition of the Constitutions which he proposed to lay before the Chapter. In this cherished spot there was something so full of hallowed recollections, and the fervour of the early days of the Order was so religiously preserved, that it seemed to inspire ideas tending to the greater good of all, and to make it easier to carry them out. Then, too, St. Bonfilius and the majority of the other Founders were there, ready to aid him with their enlightened counsel. In fine, the holy Superior felt his physical weakness increasing day by day, and, knowing that his life hung on a thread, he liked to await the final summons on the beloved heights of Senario.

The new Constitutions were proposed, discussed, approved, and finally adopted. Simple, indeed, they were, yet full of wisdom, and showing a marked progress in that organization which had been ceaselessly advancing in the way of perfection, as the years went by. These Constitutions, taken as a whole, display a striking character-istic of the Order in its first beginnings, namely, that everything was done quietly, and without effort. The regulations were few and brief, because any breach of them was almost unknown, and was never habitual. Postulants placed themselves, like docile children, under the guidance of their spiritual Fathers, who had no need to command : the wish of a Superior superseded all orders. The plan of life being settled, the minor details were carried out with that spirit of simplicity and self-surrender which distinguishes those souls wherein divine grace rules supreme. Mary ruled with queenly sovereignty over all. Inspired by her, each moment of her children's existence drew them more closely to her Divine Son. Like a bright star, she shone with never-failing lustre, fixed high and immovably in the horizon of her Servants' hearts

We here give the text of these Constitutions :

" I The Brethren shall wear woollen garments The outer tunic, the scapular, and the cloak shall be of transalpine or German cloth, black in colour : the under tunic is to be white. The black tunic is not to be made so long as to hang below the instep : the cloak is to be sewn at the breast for about a hand's length, and must be clear of the ground by the same length the girdles are to be of black leather, with plain buckles.

" II. No one shall lay aside the scapular and tunic on going to bed, unless suffering from grievous sickness.

" III. All the Brethren shall keep silence in Choir, in the Refectory, and in the Dormitory, and none shall speak in these places but by permission of the Superior, who can grant such leave when he thinks fit.

" IV. All the Brethren shall fast every Friday, from the Feast of All Saints till the Nativity of Our Lord, and from Quinquagesima Sunday till Easter. No Superior, save only the Superior-General, can dispense from these fasts and no dispensation whatsoever can be given for the eves of the Feasts of Our Lord, of Our Blessed Lady, and of other Saints, to which the Church has specially appointed a Vigil. The same fast is to be observed on the Vigils of the Holy Apostles, of St. John Baptist, of all Saints, of the Feasts of the Blessed Virgin, on Ember Days, and on all Vigils appointed by the Church. On these days the same kinds of food may be taken as during Lent.

" V. On all fast days, as soon as High Mass is ended, the bell shall ring for None ; and after Vespers, when the bell sounds for Compline, the Brethren shall enter the Refectory, and the Chanter shall say, *Jube domne ;* and the blessing shall be given . *Fratres noctem quietam ,* and *Benedicite* and *Largitor* having been said, those who wish to do so may drink ; then, at the given signal, *Tu autem* shall be said, and so, returning to the Church, Compline shall be recited.

" VI. Those who are on a journey, although not fasting at such

14

times, shall, nevertheless, abstain from flesh-meat and from milk : they shall take the ordinary Lenten fare ; but, when not in their own houses, they may eat what is set before them, provided that it be nothing that is forbidden by the Church, or that it be not the eve of a feast of Our Lord.

"VII. No one shall rashly presume to fast, except at the prescribed seasons, without the consent of his Prelate.

"VIII. None shall eat meat in the Refectory ; the Superior may, nevertheless, occasionally dispense from this rule.

"IX. Before the Brethren sit down at table, the blessing shall be given ; and when they rise from table, the thanksgiving shall be said, together with the Psalm *Miserere mei.*

"X. In all places where we have Chapels, none shall be permitted to eat elsewhere than in the Convent, except it be with the Bishop, or in other religious houses, or with discreet seculars. But, permission for this shall be seldom granted.

"XI. If anyone shall see him who sits next him at table in want of anything, let him speak to the servers.

"XII. If anyone should cause any disturbance in a public part of the Monastery, as in the Choir or Refectory, let him forthwith rise and ask pardon of all present, returning to his place only when the Superior signs him to do so.

"XIII. All strangers seeking hospitality shall have their needs supplied with charity proportioned to the length of their journey and to their bodily fatigue.

"XIV. Let an Infirmary be prepared in each of our houses, wherein the infirm and sick shall sleep, and let them be treated with the utmost care. If any of the number be lepers, let them be separated from the rest ; nevertheless, they are to be nursed within the enclosure of the Monastery ; if, for some reasonable cause, this cannot be done, they may be transferred to some other house of the Order, upon the General, or the Superior, giving orders to that effect.

"XV. All shall sleep upon straw beds ; they may have woollen sheets to lie on ; linen sheets are to be supplied only to the sick and to guests.

"XVI. The tonsure is to be made twice a month.

"XVII. None shall be received into the Order before the age of fifteen, nor after forty. If any desiring to enter shall have passed the latter age, he may be admitted by special permission of the General. If the postulant shall have left his Order, or if he have been professed in another Order, the consent of the whole General Chapter will be necessary for his reception. All who present themselves for admission shall be examined, and if any impediment appear, they must be rejected."

All these regulations, it will be observed, relate to external matters. The springs of the interior life must be sought in the Rule of St. Augustine, and in the history of the origin of the Order. The Rule of St. Augustine simply formulates the counsels of the Gospel, that is to say, the practice of Christian perfection in the highest degree. The title-deeds, if we may so style them, of the Order contained but one name, that of Our Lady, to whose service all the actions of each one of the members, and the whole of their lives, were consecrated. The dearest and most distinctive devotions of the Servants of the Most Blessed Virgin were treasured in their traditions, and were hidden with jealous care in the inmost recesses of their hearts.

All the Capitular Fathers joyfully welcomed the promulgation of this rule of life, as did the Communities of the Order dispersed in various places. The Servites now possessed, in addition to the Constitution of the General Chapter, what in those days were called the Observances. This important department of the Religious Life was thus placed beyond the influence of individual caprice, or instability. In the Middle Ages the Religious Life had its own special characteristics. Many simple and childlike souls found all their spiritual instincts satisfied by the constant mortification of all natural inclinations with respect to clothing, food, and sleep; by the life of retirement, whence they saw the world only through loopholes and by snatches; by placing their freedom in the hands of their Superiors with infantine docility. Every interval of time between their daily occupations was filled by prayer, meditation, and various devotional practices. And thus their days sped swiftly and sweetly by, filling them with a tranquil happiness, which left them nothing to desire here, till the hour came which summoned them to the unspeakable bliss of Paradise.

In those days, although disorders were frequent, an intensely religious spirit prevailed among the mass of the people, and the need for Apostolic labourers was not so pressing as nowadays. The members of the new Orders, though ready for action, not seldom therefore remained secluded in their cloisters, like the Religious of the older Orders. In this mode of life holiness, fostered by exterior observances, often attained to an extraordinary height. Such was the case at this time with the Order of the Servants of Mary: there were many of its members whose aspirations did not soar beyond that of a blameless life, spent in the practice of virtue, under the eye of God, and the protection of His Blessed Mother.

Meanwhile, St. Buonagiunta felt that his days were numbered, and that few more months remained for him to spend on earth. In spite of the disease which was slowly wasting him away, he was resolved to toil on whilst life remained. He spared himself in nothing, and insisted on resuming his visitations notwithstanding the overpowering heat of the weather. He had even intended to return to

Rome on business concerning the Order, but was prevented by the critical state of his health. He struggled on, still on foot, till he reached Monte Senario, hoping to resume his journey after a short rest; but God had willed otherwise, and his career on earth was now about to close

The Saint recognized his danger and spoke openly of it to his Brethren. The fever which was consuming him became more and more intense. The grief of all around was great, and prayers for his recovery were offered without ceasing; but he remained absorbed in God, wholly occupied in preparing himself to appear before His Maker. He lost no time in summoning the Capitular Fathers to Monte Senario in order to consult with them as to the well-being of the Order; then, in a prophetic spirit, he named the day of his departure. All this time he continued to say Mass daily.

At length the day dawned which he had himself foretold would be his last—Friday, August 31, 1257. He rose as usual, though scarcely able to stand, and having vested, he prepared, in perfect peace of soul, and with an utter abandonment of himself into the hands of God, to celebrate his last Mass in the same spot where he had said his first, in all the early fervour of his priesthood. He was obliged to be supported at the Altar. Almost all the Fathers and Brothers then living at Monte Senario were gathered round him. With ardent devotion he offered the Divine Victim, heedless of his own sufferings. Tears flowed abundantly from his eyes, and his emotion frequently impeded his speech. All saw that he was wholly absorbed in God, and that to the Offering of the Lamb without spot he united the sacrifice of his own life When the Mass was ended, he turned, still vested, towards those present, and, in words burning with divine love, addressed them at considerable length, in an earnest voice, though husky from weakness, exhorting them to holiness of life, as their one great duty, and to brotherly love, as the first of all virtues. He besought them to be careful to preserve and increase that cherished tradition of the Order—devotion to the Passion of Our Lord and to the Sorrows of His Blessed Mother, adding : "Herein consists the spirit peculiar to the true Servants of Mary . she herself told us so, in this holy spot which was sanctified by her august presence ". He predicted the development of the Order in spite of the furious tempest by which it was to be almost overwhelmed. Then he desired that the Passion of Our Lord should be read to him. He listened to it with the utmost attention, and when the reader came to the Crucifixion, the holy old man shed floods of tears, sighing deeply as he thought of the many sins of mankind. When the words, "Into Thy Hands I commend My Spirit," were read, he repeated them, and then, leaning against the Altar, he stretched out his arms in the form of a Cross, and calmly expired. "Immediately," says the worthy Mati, "his face shone like that of an Angel, and it seemed as though the saintly and venerable man yet smiled upon us."

During this touching scene, all the Religious present wept abundantly, feeling at the same time penetrated by divine grace. Great as was the sorrow with which their hearts were filled, for the loss of a Father of such heroic virtue, it was yet surpassed by the joy which they felt in thinking of his holy death and of his eternal happiness. .

His death left a great blank in the Order, for it removed the member who seemed above all others to be the most endowed with the gifts necessary for extending it. St. Buonagiunta was the youngest of the Seven Founders, hence so many hopes were centred in him ; and it was for this reason that—when St. Bonfilius retired— he had been unanimously chosen to succeed him as General During his short tenure of office, he had fully justified the expectations formed of him. He had displayed all the qualities of a master mind—keen intelligence, quickness of perception, great energy in the practice of all the virtues of a good Religious, and in the fulfil- ment of his duties as Superior. He was himself a living embodiment of the Rule, the smallest infraction of which was never tolerated by him. All who approached him found in him a fatherly heart united to an Apostolic soul. He never wearied in seeking to win souls to God, by every ingenuity that both zeal and charity could suggest. But, when all gentle means failed, he knew well how to rouse those who were sunk in the lethargy of avarice, sensuality, and unbelief, by bringing before them the chastisements of Infinite Justice. When he spoke of Our Blessed Lady, the fulness of his heart over- flowed from his lips ; and wherever he went he displayed all the power of his eloquence in setting forth her greatness, the mysteries of her life, and, above all, her Sorrows On this last theme he never wearied of holding forth. His soul was filled with the sweetest and most loving spirit of devotion. To him it would have been the greatest of all privations to omit the holy Sacrifice of the Mass, which he celebrated daily, and whilst so doing his whole bearing vividly expressed the intensity of his faith. The reward of his great devotion to the holy Mass was granted by his death at the very Altar where he had just celebrated, and whilst listening to the Gospel narrative of the Supreme Sacrifice on Calvary. He felt deeply all marks of favour shown to the Order, and he could never do enough to show his gratitude to those who assisted it in its temporal needs. In going to, and returning from, the Refectory he always recalled to mind these benefactors, and often prayed for them with tears. It is recorded of him that he always recollected himself at the beginning and end of every meal, in order to offer to God this tribute of grateful remembrance.

This loss was a heavy blow to the six remaining Founders. It broke asunder a bond knitted by thirty years of tried friendship and perfect confidence. Nothing but submission to the Divine Will could heal the wound made in the heart of each one of the number.

The body of the Saint was laid to rest in the little Chapel of Monte Senario under the High Altar. All took part in the ceremony with mingled feelings of sorrow and gladness, keenly sensible of their own loss, but realizing the fulness of joy of which their Father, Buonagiunta, was now partaking in heaven, where he was rejoicing in the presence of God and Our Blessed Lady, and from whence he would continue to protect his beloved Order.

His death took place at a period when all hopes were raised high. The Holy See was favourably disposed, the Order was steadily advancing, its Convents were daily growing in number, and subjects were hastening from all quarters to take refuge under the mantle of the Queen of Heaven. Among these many chosen souls were to be found. It was already plain to be seen that the holiness of the Founders would not die out ; above all, the marks of sanctity shone out in the youthful Father, Philip Benizi, with a concentrated brightness which could not long remain hidden. By all these favours Mary granted to her sons a brief interval of consolation to prepare them for the coming trials which St. Buonagiunta, with prophetic inspiration, had predicted at the moment of his death.

CHAPTER VIII.

Blessed James of Poggibonzi chosen General — Favours granted by Alexander IV.—St. Philip's Ordination—Orvieto—Sant' Angelo in Vado-Bologna—Provinces of Tuscany and Umbria—Death of St. Bonfilius.

(1257—1262.)

THE majority of the Capitular Fathers had repaired to Monte Senario on learning the critical state of St. Buonagiunta's health. They were present at his death, and they assisted in paying the last duties to his venerated remains. They then without delay assembled at Cafaggio, under the presidency of St. Bonfilius, in order to elect a General. They would gladly have nominated him who had been the first head of the Order, and who had held the office for so long a period, but the reluctance of the Saint to be reappointed could not be overcome. The good Father pleaded his advanced age, his infirmities, and the necessity of superintending the works then being carried on at Sta. Maria delle Grazie, in order to evade a burden which his humility made him more than ever dread. The Capitular votes were then given to one of the worthiest and most deserving of those assembled, namely, to Blessed James of Poggibonzi. No better choice seemed possible for the Fathers to make; and the Holy Founders themselves were only too glad to withdraw into the background, and to give place to one whom they had so long loved and so highly venerated.

James of Poggibonzi was, in truth, one of the pillars of the Servite Order. He had been actively concerned in all the wonderful manifestations which had occurred in the early days of its foundation, and his attachment to it was the ruling principle of his life. He was ready to undertake any labours, and to submit to any sacrifices, in order to secure its welfare or to extend its influence. He was also thoroughly imbued with its spirit, and Our Lady had no Servant more faithful or more devoted. The various posts which he had filled had made him singularly skilful in conducting public business. In particular, his residence at the Papal Court as Procurator of the Order had given him a perfect insight into the many difficulties of the position and the delicate handling which they required. Moreover, his upright character and sound learning made him especially useful to the Order, as being one likely to insure its safety and well-being.

He was forced to accept a responsibility the extent of which none knew better than himself · he was well aware how thorny his path was likely to prove; but his strong sense of duty and his love for the Order gained the victory over his longing for retirement and obscurity, and he generously accepted the burden.

The one black cloud in their sky was the stern decree of Innocent IV., which completely frustrated all attempts on the part of the Religious to work for souls outside the bounds of their cloister. The worst effects of this decree had been much mitigated, beyond a doubt, by the favourable concessions obtained from Alexander IV.; still, the document itself formed part of the written law of the Church, and until it was formally repealed it could always be used as an effective weapon by the enemies of the Order. It was, therefore, essential to procure its speedy abrogation; and this was now the task which Blessed James of Poggibonzi set himself to accomplish.

Two days after his election he laid before the Fathers assembled at Cafaggio a plan for obtaining the withdrawal of this decree. He proposed to despatch two procurators to the Papal Court, who would act as representatives of the Order, and who, it was hoped, would be the means of bringing about a favourable solution of this momentous question. The great importance attached to this mission was shown by the terms in which the act was drawn, conferring powers on these delegates. The Fathers, twenty-one in number, amongst whom all the surviving Founders were included, commissioned Father Octavian and Father Juncta, although absent from the meeting, to solicit the reversal of the decree of Innocent IV., so as to empower the Order to hear Confessions, to permit the interment of seculars in their cemeteries, and to admit all persons freely to their Churches. But, notwithstanding these efforts, the Order was not at this time irrevocably to win the right to exist, and the dreaded sword of suppression was still to hang for many years over its head.

Whilst Blessed James was thus engaged in fulfilling the duties of his office, and in watching over these important matters, the Holy Founders continued to toil obscurely in the shade. So humble and so hidden were their lives, that scarcely a trace of them remains As far as can now be known, St. Bonfilius appears to have been settled at Cafaggio, engaged in the Church's work ; St. Alexis, who could never be induced to quit the Santissima Annunziata, led there a life of complete self-abnegation, fulfilled with unobtrusive duties ; and the other Saints undertook different employments from time to time, according to circumstances. St Manettus' aptitude for weighty business increased year by year St Amideus gave himself wholly to the training of the younger members of the Order, in which he was particularly successful, owing to his special gift of gentleness, in drawing all hearts to himself St. Hugh and St. Sostene pursued with unwearied delight their solitary and penitential life at Monte Senario, which they were, nevertheless, always ready to relinquish at the slightest call of obedience.

Thus life flowed on calmly in the bosom of the Order, filled with work, prayer, study, and such external labours of the ministry as they were permitted to undertake. Year after year passed, until a quarter of a century had elapsed from the day when the little seed of La Camarzia and Monte Senario had been cast into the earth ; and now that seed had sprung up and become a tree, the roots of which had not, however, as yet taken a firm hold of the ground A storm of more than usual violence might easily overthrow it, were it not shielded by the divine protection Many sympathized with the Order , but, on the other hand, it was often attacked. It seems that the Hermits of St Augustine had not given up all hope of uniting the Servites to their Order. The situation of affairs was extremely critical, and a combination of prudence, energy, and tenacity of purpose was essential in those by whom they were directed These qualities were all united in Blessed James of Poggibonzi, who, during the seven years in which he held the reins of government, was able to consolidate and spread the Order in spite of all the dangers by which it was threatened.

The year 1258 proved to be an uneventful one. It was a time of perfect tranquillity for the Order, which continued its course of labour, and made constant progress, with no outward hindrance Blessed James of Poggibonzi ceased not to urge the definitive repeal of the decree of Innocent IV. , and in order to hasten this measure he continually roused the zeal of the procurators who had been sent as delegates to the Papal Court Matters proceeded, however, slowly and languidly Father James, having exhausted all human means, resorted to prayer. The whole Order, by his desire, earnestly implored Our Lady to touch the heart of Alexander IV. The Mother of God heard the prayer of her Servants, and did more than touch the Pontiff's heart indirectly, for she appeared to him in person, entreating him no longer to delay the bestowal of those favours which he intended to grant to her children. It is to be regretted that no details can be given of this miraculous vision, as contemporary authors only briefly mention the fact. The Father-General himself had repaired to the Court of the Pontiff, to make a final effort to obtain the desired concessions Then, after two years, they were at length granted.

The first of these concessions granted by Alexander IV. related to the privilege, so much coveted by the laity, of being interred in monastic cemeteries Mother earth seemed to rest more lightly on the departed in those hallowed spots, where the prayers of holy Religious continually echoed over their graves. Alexander IV, under the date of April 1, 1259, addressing himself to the whole Order, to the General, Priors, and Brethren of the Servants of Mary, declared that he was willing to grant their petition, being moved thereto by beholding the holiness of their lives ; and that he, therefore, gave them leave to grant the right of sepulture in their cemeteries to whomsoever should desire it This permission encouraged the Order to ask for farther favours. Here we must reluctantly own that the state of uncertainty in which the Order continued at this period was not favourable to the exercise of authority. The steps taken by Innocent IV., the reserved attitude of the reigning Pontiff, and the pretensions of the Augustinians had fostered a spirit of rebellion in certain of the members. Hitherto there had been no means of checking this, since no formal document had been issued by the Holy See to legalize the authority exercised by the first Superior of the Order. Alexander IV. was pleased to dispose of this difficulty once and for ever, by writing specially to the General of the Order as follows ·

" Alexander, Bishop, Servant of the Servants of God, to Our well-beloved sons, and particularly to the Prior-General of the Servants of Mary, of the Order of St. Augustine :

" Health and the Apostolic Benediction.

" Being desirous of returning a favourable answer to the prayers prompted by your pious zeal, We, by these presents, grant to you and to your successors full power both for yourself and for the said successors freely to correct, according to the rules of your Order, the other Priors and all the Brethren under your obedience, and likewise to fulfil towards them all the other duties of your office; and to confer this power, as often as you shall think well to do so, upon others of your Brethren who are fitted for the discharge thereof.

"Let none presume to oppose this Our will, &c.

"Given at Anagni, the third day of the Ides of May (May 13, 1259), in the fifth year of Our Pontificate."

Nothing could be clearer or more explicit than this letter, which in few words conferred indisputable authority upon the Father-General, and at the same time clearly defined the constitution of the Order. Hence, it now became evident that the strictest uniformity was to characterize the Institute, and that under no pretext whatever could any individual or any party in the Order be independent of the head. The Order of the Servants of Mary was a closely united body under a single Superior, and with a perfect autonomy and a distinct character of its own; that is to say, the supreme authority of the General, conferred upon him by the members of the Order, was exercised by him with their control according to the Constitutions.

This was the sixth favour granted by Alexander IV. to the Servants of Mary. Hence, unquestionably, this Pontiff deserved to be inscribed by them among the chief benefactors of their Order. No one had done more for it than he. He it was who had saved it from inevitable shipwreck: he had supplied the oars and the sails which enabled it, under St. Philip's guidance, to reach the haven in safety, notwithstanding the fury of the storms by which it was assailed. The holy Father had the greater right to the gratitude of the Servites, since he had to encounter a strong opposition before pronouncing a favourable decision; but resolutely closing his ears to the objections suggested by their enemies, he fearlessly decreed that the Order should continue to live to give glory to Mary; and it yet lives to revere his memory, and to promote the honour of the Queen of Heaven.

Great as were the favours thus granted by Alexander IV., something was yet wanting, namely, an official recognition of the right to hold the General Chapter and to elect the Prior-General. This right was admitted implicitly by various letters of that Pontiff; but the strictness of Canon law required more than this. With regard to these two essential points, the Order could only allege tacit permission of verbal approval. To no man is it given to bring a work to completeness; and it was reserved to Alexander's immediate successor, Urban IV., to make this concession which finally and for ever insured the perfect unity and characteristic of the Order.

The last boon of Alexander IV. was received by the whole Order with an outburst of joy and gratitude. A touching instance of this is recorded. The messenger who brought the good news to

Monte Senario was hastening to reach the Convent. It was on a Saturday, and the Community was gathered before the Statue of the Blessed Virgin reciting the prayers appointed for the needs of the Order. Just as the line in the *Ave Maris Stella: Monstra te esse Matrem* (Show thyself a Mother), was being sung, the bearer of the glad tidings crossed the threshold of the Church. In order to perpetuate the remembrance of this striking coincidence, it was at once resolved that in future this line should always be repeated by both sides of the Choir.

Another pious practice still in use in the Order dates from the granting of this favour. In testimony of gratitude it was decided that a special prayer called *Vigile*, or *Benedicta tu*, should be recited daily in Choir before Vespers. This *Vigile* was composed of the three psalms and three antiphons of the first Nocturn of the Office of the Blessed Virgin, with three Lessons followed by responses; all expressive of the most tender devotion to Mary. The twofold title given to this devotion was full of beautiful and mystic meaning. The *Vigile*, recited standing, expressed the ardent desire which should be felt by the whole Order to be ever found watching before Our Lady's throne, whilst the *Benedicta tu* marked the resolve of the Servites to profess unceasingly with their lips the praises of their Queen and Mother, blessed above all creatures

It was now considered advisable to convoke the General Chapter. This Blessed James proceeded to do immediately upon his return to Florence; and the Capitular Fathers assembled at Monte Senario on the 1st of June.

The General opened the Chapter by formally announcing the favours which had been conferred, and of which all present were well aware. He enlarged upon the great debt of gratitude due to Mary for her visible protection; and he exhorted all the Fathers to enter more and more deeply into the spirit of their vocation, which was to honour Our Lady and to cause others also to honour her.

The Chapter then addressed itself to the work before it. The Fathers, ever seeking to promote the well-being of the Order, created a new office. When the General was obliged to leave his usual residence to discharge the various duties incumbent upon him, no one remained to fill his place at the headquarters of the Order. It was now thought advisable to give the General a *Socius*, or colleague, who could replace him in any case of urgent necessity.

The choice of the Chapter fell upon St. Bonfilius. The former Superior and General would gladly have declined office: but he was forced to conquer his humility and his love of silence. He begged to have, himself, a coadjutor on account of his age and infirmities, a request which was readily granted. St. Philip was appointed to this post. It was a great consolation to the spiritual parent and child to be thus united in the same work.

St. Philip, who had given constant edification by the proofs of eminent virtue which he displayed, and who had but recently revealed the treasures of heavenly wisdom which he possessed, had been constrained by obedience to receive Holy Orders. He had spent about five years at Monte Senario and at Siena, in the fulfilment of the humble duties of a lay-brother, when Blessed James of Poggibonzi suddenly resolved to confer upon him the dignity of the priesthood, in order that the great graces which God had so plentifully imparted to him might be more widely utilized for His glory. Accordingly, Philip was ordained on the 12th of April, 1259, and after a preparatory retreat of fifty days at Monte Senario, the celebration of his first Mass took place on the occasion of the holding of the General Chapter, and on the glorious Feast of Pentecost. A great miracle made the day for ever memorable in the annals of the Order; and as it was witnessed by nearly all the holy Founders, the narration cannot be omitted here

When the moment came for him to offer up for the first time the tremendous Sacrifice, the young Father, radiant with the grace of ordination and overflowing with seraphic love, vested himself as soon as Tierce had been sung, and proceeded towards the Altar with an aspect of blended modesty and dignity. The Fathers all knelt around in silent devotion; the holy Founders were wholly absorbed in God, and filled with the memories recalled by that hallowed spot where the Blessed Virgin herself had appeared to convey to them the heavenly summons.

The holy Sacrifice was begun. The devout Celebrant was only thinking of the great mystery which was about to take place through his ministration; he was deeply moved; and all present followed him with earnest devotion. The time for the elevation was at hand, and Philip, with all present, bowed in adoration. The newly-made priest raised in his trembling hands the pledge of our salvation, when suddenly, amidst the dead silence, the sound of singing was heard No order had been given for the singing on this occasion of any portion of the Liturgy, yet voices were distinctly heard to sing in exquisite harmony the words. *Sanctus, Sanctus, Sanctus, Dominus Deus.* Never had Monte Senario re-echoed such sweet and melodious sounds: they had no earthly origin; such tones proceeded from no mortal lips.

A miracle, like that which took place amidst the mountains of Judæa on the night of the Nativity, was now accomplished on Monte Senario. The Angels sang when the Divine Child lay for the first time in His Mother's arms, illuminating the darkness of the stable at Bethlehem, and they now sang again when the same God became incarnate, mystically and in very truth, in the anointed hands of Philip Benizi.

All present, and especially the saintly Founders, shed tears as they heard this unquestionable proof of the holiness of Philip ; for as such all understood and rejoiced in it. "But he," says the Chronicle of Poccianti, "though he was thus exalted, did but humble himself more and more before the God and Lord of all "

At the same time that the General Chapter conferred the office of Colleague of the General upon St. Bonfilius, it nominated two other Founders to important posts, St. Amideus being placed at the head of the establishment at Cafaggio, and St. Hugh at that of Monte Senario. Both submitted themselves to the call of obedience. St. Amideus was forced to quit his cherished solitude, so loved by him, and where he was beloved by all, and to reappear amidst the feverish turmoil of Florence, where political passions surged as restlessly as did the waves of the sea. When he returned to his native city, he no longer found any of his kindred ; all had been exiled by the dominant faction, and their palaces and fortresses had been razed to the ground.

St. Hugh, on the contrary, remained in the tranquil solitude of Monte Senario, where scarcely a distant echo of these tumults could reach him. His task henceforth, like that of St. Amideus, to whose office he succeeded, was to train the postulants who came to swell the ranks of the Order.

As regards the other Founders, we only know that St. Alexis never left the Santissima Annunziata, and that apparently St. Manettus and St. Sostene filled various employments, the first in one of the more important Convents, and St. Sostene in the Umbrian Province, which was shortly inaugurated.

About this time, too, the Order was preparing to acquire several of the Convents which were soon to be founded. In consequence of their march towards the south of Italy, favoured by circumstances, the Fathers established also themselves in Orvieto, in the Patrimony of St. Peter. Orvieto is a small but beautifully-situated town surrounded by massive ramparts. She was always intensely Guelph in her political tendencies, and hence she was often a place of refuge for the Popes in those troubled times, when they were not seldom forced to quit Rome. No less than thirty-two of the Pontiffs have, on different occasions, sojourned within her walls.. Some of the Fathers were sent hither to take possession, and on 27th September, in the following year, Father Ristoro, whose mission it seemed to be continually making fresh foundations, received from the hands of the Bishop Giacomo the Church of St. Pietro-in-Vetera, which was close to the city.

The Convent of St. Angelo in Vado was likewise founded about this time. St. Angelo in Vado was a small town of the Apennines, situated at equal distances from Borgo San Sepolcro and Urbino. The beginnings of this new offshoot are obscure, and bear the seal of great poverty. The Fathers were obliged to appeal to the charity of the inhabitants in order to establish themselves. Happily the good Arch-priest of Mercatello did all in his power to stimulate the charity of the inhabitants of the country in favour of the Servants of Mary, and, according to the custom of the time, he even granted indulgences to reward their zeal. This Convent had the happiness of giving three beatified members to the Order — the Blessed Gieronimo of Borgo San Sepolcro, the Blessed Thomas of St. Angelo in Vado, and the Blessed Gieronimo Ranuzzi.

In the same year negotiations were entered into which decided the foundation of the Convent at Bologna. Bologna held the same rank among the cities of the Æmilia that Florence held among those of Tuscany. Picturesquely seated at the foot of the Apennines, inhabited by a large industrious and religiously disposed population of Guelphic sympathies, she was in all respects a desirable home for the Order, which settled there about this time—for the exact date cannot be accurately fixed. Some authors are of opinion that St. Manettus, on returning from France after his journey thither, had already paved the way for this foundation. It was made at the collective request of the Council of the Republic and of the people, with the consent of the Bishop Ottavian of the Ubaldini. The little Church of St. Petronio was given to the Order. The Servants of Mary were so prosperous in this city, which boasts of possessing the celebrated Madonna of St. Luke, that they simultaneously possessed there three Convents.

Continual extension on all sides made it necessary for the Order to follow the course adopted by the Mendicant Orders, namely, of dividing itself into provinces, so as to facilitate matters for the Superiors, and make their Rule the more efficacious. The Chapter held in May, 1260, at Cafaggio, was chiefly concerned with this important matter. The question was put to the assembled Fathers, and after due consideration it was decided in the affirmative. The simplest method, and that which was already sanctioned by the practice of other Religious, was to conform to the civil boundaries : this was accordingly done, and two provinces were constituted, to one of which belonged all the Convents in Tuscany, to the other all those of Umbria. The area of these provinces was thus already clearly defined without farther trouble. The next question concerned the choice of Superiors for these provinces, who were to govern them independently and to be coadjutors of the General in ruling the Servite Republic. "Because of the goodness of their lives, and the greatness of their learning," as one of the Chroniclers expresses himself, St. Manettus and St. Sostene were chosen to be the first Provincials. St. Manettus was appointed to the Tuscan Province, and St. Sostene to the Umbrian. Each held his office for three years.

After the holding of this Chapter, nothing occurred for some time to break the routine of tranquil activity which characterizes monastic life. Like busy bees within and without their hives, the Servants of Mary, headed by their holy Founders, were ever occupied, how different soever might be their employments and their capacities, in striving to promote the glory of God and of His Holy Mother, and to co-operate with the graces bestowed in their vocation. Therefore, there is nothing to record except the foundation of the Convents of Saint Angelo in Vado, Orvieto, and Bologna, which opened new ground to the Order.

Politics appear to have engaged the thoughts of all during the year 1260. The events which led up to and followed upon the disastrous defeat of the Florentines by the Sienese at Montaperti, on 4th September, 1260, were especially exciting, and the Annals of the Order, meanwhile, remain a blank. Time, however, brought round the usual period for the holding of the Chapter General, which was opened 15th May, 1261, at Borgo San Sepolcio.* This place was chosen because Count Bonafede di Selva di Casentino, whose son had bid farewell to the world and to the prospective happiness of a marriage already contracted, that he might enter the Order, had generously offered to defray all the expenses of the Fathers attending this Chapter. At this meeting the Fathers were still occupied with legislating for the Order : they added several Constitutions upon the rights and duties of the General and of the Provincials.

A few days after the closing of this Chapter, the sad news was received of the death of Alexander IV., on 25th May. The Order mourned deeply the loss of one of its greatest benefactors. The deceased Pontiff was succeeded by Urban IV., a Frenchman by birth, who was at that time Patriarch of Jerusalem. He was at Viterbo on business, when the Cardinals, now reduced to the number of nine, eight of whom were present, and unable to come to any other decision, cast their eyes upon him and he was elected.

Meanwhile, St. Bonfilius, who was now sixty-four years old, and bowed down more by his labours and penances than by age, had returned to Monte Senario towards the close of 1261. The many journeys which his office as Colleague of the General obliged him to take had completely exhausted his strength. He had been, indeed, frequently called upon to supply the General's place in the visitations of the Convents. He quietly realized the fact that his days were numbered. Far from dreading the approach of death, he hailed it as the hour of his release. His sole desire was to be united for ever to Jesus and His Blessed Mother after all the trials of this vale of tears. Each day saw him therefore preparing for the all-important passage from time to eternity : he was more than ever given up to prayer, and he neglected none of the exercises appointed by the Rule.

On the night of the 1st January, 1262, in spite of his infirmities and of the wintry cold, he assisted in Choir at the Office of Matins.

According to the custom, after the life of the Saint of the day had been read, the Fathers held a Conference on spiritual matters, and especially on the great mystery of the Feast. Suddenly a voice of heavenly sweetness uttered these words, which were heard by all: "Come, thou, Good Son (Bonfilius), for as much as thou hast hearkened to the call of My Son, when He bade thee leave all things for His Name's sake, father, mother, brothers, sisters, and home ; and since then hast with inviolable fidelity kept all His commandments, thou shalt receive an hundredfold, and shalt possess life everlasting".

It was Mary who spoke these words ; and hardly had she ceased to speak when the holy old man sank down, and, without a moment's struggle, passed away. The startled Religious crowded round him, but he had ceased to breathe. As they were about to give vent to their sorrow, the same sweet voice again spoke, saying : "Come, ye Saints of God ; hasten, ye Angels of the Lord, take this soul which has served me so well on earth, and bear it to the kingdom of the Blessed. And you, my well-beloved Servants, lay his body to rest in the grave." The Religious remarked that the countenance of their Father "shone," as Niccolo Mati records, "like a star, whilst from his body exhaled a fragrance like that of Paradise". Filled with gladness, they sang no Mass of Requiem for him, but laid his venerated remains beside those of St. Buonagiunta, beneath the Altar of their Oratory.

He who had been the father, and the first originator of the brotherhood of Monte Senario, who had been ever careful to act, to counsel and to guide in accordance with the Spirit of God, was now no more. His prudence had been manifested by the gentleness and impartiality of his rule, and by his discretion in relinquishing his superiorship in order to accustom them to the guidance of another, and to prepare them for his approaching end. After having been so long the head and soul of everything, he was quite content to be but a humble subordinate : having spent the greater part of his life in a post of authority, he was well pleased to crown its close by practising the virtue of dependence—a proof of the genuineness of his humility.

Gentle, sweet-tempered, and warm-hearted, he ruled more by an imperceptible influence than by the exercise of authority ; he loved all the Brethren as though they had been truly his children, and he gained their affection by the strength of his own for them. Thus he trained them to the fulfilment of their duties without the slightest difficulty.

His love for Our Blessed Lady was as the axis on which his whole being revolved. For her he sacrificed his most cherished possessions , the entire strength of his loving nature was drawn towards those mysteries of her life which to the ordinary Christian are the least attractive—the sufferings and sorrows of her sword-pierced heart. These were his constant study ; and having completely interpenetrated his thoughts with the sweet bitterness of her Transfixion, he strove to lead all souls, especially those of his spiritual children, to the understanding of this devotion which is the choicest fruit of Divine Love.

The large share which he took in the planning, the foundation, and the propagation of the Order of the Servants of Mary gives him the right to a foremost place amongst the Seven Founders. In the eyes of posterity he will ever remain the chief star of that pleiad of holy souls, linking them one to another, and consecrating them to the Mother of God. He it was who knit together in indissoluble bonds those seven hearts whose earthly friendship was supernaturalized by grace into brotherly charity. He it was who took the lead and drew them after him to the path whither the Will of God and the voice of Mary directed them. St. Bonfilius Monaldi is, beyond a doubt, the foremost among the first Seven Servants of Mary, and he is likewise the chief Founder of the Order after her who first called it into being, and provided the means for the realization of her plan.

After St. Bonfilius had passed away at Monte Senario, the Order continued to enjoy a state of comparative tranquillity, which, unhappily, proved to be but a truce of brief duration. The foundations already made were taking firm root; others were being planned —the internal organization of the Institute was being gradually perfected. Many chosen souls, amongst whom St. Philip shone with conspicuous lustre, had already given themselves to the work, or were about to do so. The five surviving Founders spread around them that fragrance of virtue which increases with years. And all this time, as subsequent events made known, Mary beheld with complacency her children, who strove with constant loving homage to repay her fostering care.

CHAPTER IX.

Montepulciano—Cesena—Asti—The Province of Romagna—St. Manettus chosen General—Gubbio—Death of St. Amideus—Generalate of St. Philip.

(1262—1267.)

St. Bonfilius, having rejoined St. Buonagiunta in their true home, there to enjoy eternal peace in the Court of the Queen of Angels, the surviving Founders, in spite of their natural sorrow, pursued their task with fresh courage. Each at his separate post did all in his power to aid the General, Blessed James of Poggibonzi. Thus the progress of the Order continued unchecked, whilst it became more firmly rooted, and better able to resist any storms which might assail it in the future.

On the 3rd of April, 1262, the Servites, with the consent of the Bishop of Arezzo, took possession of the Church of St. Andrew at Montepulciano. Montepulciano was a Tuscan fortress-town of some importance, lying beyond Siena, and near the frontier. It had always looked to Florence for protection against Siena, the little town being politically Guelph. Placed as it was, like an apple of discord between the rival republics, it was in a perpetual state of turmoil. Thus the Servants of Mary came there opportunely to fulfil their mission as peacemakers.

About this time, later on, new foundations were made at Cesena, a little town in Æmilia, and at Asti, the most northerly point which the Order had yet reached in Italy. Asti was destined to be the nucleus of a new Province, which was subsequently constituted under the title of Cisalpine Gaul.

Siena was now about to be chosen for the first time as the place of meeting for the General Chapter. This city had attained to a large measure of independence since the battle of Montaperti. Her citizens had always shown a marked preference for the Servite Order, on which they continued to bestow liberal benefactions; and they used every endeavour to persuade the Religious to reside once more within the city walls, and to take possession of the Church of St. Clement. In this Church the Chapter of 1262 was held, in the month of May. During this Chapter the Definitors were elected. these were the Fathers Ristoro of Florence, Francesco of Siena, Peregrino of Città di Castello, and Philip Benizi of Florence. All of these had already done good service to the Order. St. Philip, in particular, had been Master of Novices at Siena since the beginning of the year; and, in spite of his youth—for he was only twenty-nine years of age—he had in all respects fulfilled the expectations which he had excited. The venerable Founders, during this meeting, kept humbly in the background, full of holy pride and joy at beholding their sons and disciples chosen to fill the highest offices. Several of their number had to give an account to the Definitors, like all the other Superiors, of the posts which they themselves occupied. St. Manettus, in particular, had to submit to their judgment the manner in which he had discharged his duties in the Umbrian Province.

A fresh Chapter was held at Cafaggio in the following year, 1263. These meetings, appointed by the Constitutions, had become most important constituents of the existence of the Order, and from this time forth they were held with the utmost regularity. Not only did the government of the Order benefit thereby, but the outer world saw herein a visible proof that the Servants of Mary were a distinct Religious body, the members of which were bound together in perfect unity. However, the right of the Order to hold these General Chapters was not established without a struggle, for its enemies were numerous ; and when repulsed on one side, they at once renewed the attack upon another.

The meeting was, accordingly, held at Cafaggio. The rapid growth of the Order, in defiance of all obstacles, made it necessary for the Chapter to take into consideration the erection of a third Province, to be styled the Province of Romagna. This Province was to include all the Convents in Italy north of the Apennines ; and Bologna was to be its central point. Nothing could have been better planned. The geographical features of the district made the arrangement necessary, for it would have been almost impossible for the Provincial of Tuscany to take under his charge so many distant places which were by no means easy of access. In those days the Religious usually travelled on foot ; the Provincial had to make frequent journeys ; and it was, therefore, desirable that this duty should be lightened by shortening the length of each journey. Two of the Definitors, chosen by the General Chapter of the preceding year, now became Provincials. Father Ristoro of Florence was appointed to the new Province of Romagna, and Father Francesco of Siena to the Tuscan Province. The Umbrian Province was confided to the charge of Father Stefano of Borgo San Sepolcro. St. Philip, in spite of his reluctance, was, at the same time, nominated *Socius* or Assistant to the Father-General. St. Amideus was relieved from the government at Cafaggio, and was allowed to retire to Monte Senario : his place being filled by St. Manettus, who ceased to hold the Tuscan Provincialate. Thus, the five surviving Founders relinquished the chief posts in favour of younger men. They were only too ready to withdraw into solitude, and to be forgotten . the sense of their own nothingness possessed them so completely, that it gave them no concern to be set aside. But, though removed from active service, they continued to promote the general good of their beloved Order by the fervour of their prayers, and by the strong and holy influence of their unceasing self-abnegation.

In the course of this last meeting, the subject of the General Chapter was again discussed, and it was agreed that every effort must be made to establish this right beyond all dispute. In consequence of this decision, the General, Blessed James of Poggibonzi, and his *Socius*, St. Philip, set off without delay for Orvieto, where Urban IV., who had succeeded Alexander IV., then resided. To him they desired to prove their need of protection against their inveterate enemies. Through the friendly intervention of Cardinal Ottobono, the Protector of the Order, who smoothed all difficulties for them, the Pontiff yielded to their entreaty. He would gladly, from prudential motives, have deferred doing so ; but, upon being fully acquainted with the state of affairs, he at once, in clear and unmistakable terms. granted the indispensable right of summoning the General Chapter. In order to obviate all possible objections, he conferred this power as though it had not been previously bestowed either in writing or by word of mouth.

The favour was granted in the following terms :

" Urban, Bishop, Servant of the Servants of God, to all the Priors and Brethren of the Servants of St. Mary, of the Order of St. Augustine, health and the Apostolic Benediction.

" The good works shown forth by your Order in the discharge of the duties of the Sacred Ministry dispose Us to grant, with the utmost good-will and affection, whatsoever we think may conduce to the welfare of the said Order. For which reason, yielding to your earnest supplication, We give you permission, by the authority of these presents, to hold the General Chapter of your Order, and to elect thereat a Prior-General. If this Chapter be held at a distance of more than five days' journey from the place where the Papal Court resides, the Prior-General shall have his election confirmed by the Ordinary of the diocese , and if it be held less than five days' journey, the election shall be confirmed by Us and Our successors And pending this Confirmation, it shall be permitted to him to have one or more Vicars Councillors.

" Let none, then, presume to violate this concession, or rashly to oppose it. Should anyone presumptuously do so, be it known to him that he will incur the anger of Almighty God, and of His Blessed Apostles, Peter and Paul.

" Given at Orvieto, on the eighth of the Calends of August, the second year of Our Pontificate " (25th July, 1263).

These letters were such as to leave no doubt whatsoever as to the right of the Order to meet in General Chapter. Yet, even now, the opposition from which the Servants of Mary had suffered so cruelly was not completely overcome. They continued, however, to hold their yearly meetings, and the Chapter had now become an institution, as had also the office of the *Discreets*, or Councillors, chosen from among the Fathers. Each Province assembled in Chapter annually, and each Convent held its weekly Chapter. All were held upon the same plan. The authority, lodged in the hands of one, was controlled and strengthened by the counsels of those whose prudence and wisdom had caused them to be chosen for that purpose. No system could be better adapted to check any excesses on the part of the rulers, and to meet the requirements of their subordinates. Upon the whole, the Order had now good cause for exultation : it had gained a substantial victory, over which the venerated Founders rejoiced even more than did their Brethren.

It would seem that St. Manettus was at that time Prior of Lucca, whilst the other Founders were either at Cafaggio or at Monte Senario, each unbrokenly pursuing a life of silence and of good works, in the practice of all the virtues of his position.

Wheresoever they were, the chief desire entertained by them was to see the completion of the Church of Our Lady of Grace at Cafaggio ; but their resources were exhausted. The second plan of the building, and that which had been finally chosen, was one of considerable magnificence : it had been begun, and it was essential that it should be well carried out. St. Alexis, who was especially interested in the undertaking, took advantage of an opportunity which now offered itself for the completion of the work. His brother, Chiarissimo, was a wholesale dealer in cloths of foreign manufacture, and had amassed a large fortune in the business, not always, it may be feared, by lawful means. Both in buying and in selling he had from time to time broken the rules of strict probity ; but, being a good Christian at heart, he felt the prickings of conscience. He wished to make reparation for all wrong-doing ; but it was not easy to remember and to trace out every instance, for he had been engaged in trade for many years. He consulted St. Alexis, who solved the difficulty by applying to the Holy See, whence a decree was issued on 5th June, 1264, ordaining that Chiarissimo Falconeri should cause his desire of making restitution to be publicly announced in every Church in Florence ; and this precaution having been taken, whatever sum remained unclaimed by those to whom he owed reparation, he was at liberty to hand over to the Servants of Mary for the completion of their Church.

During the progress of these events, Pope Urban IV, attacked in his retreat at Orvieto by Manfred and the Ghibellines, took refuge in Perugia, where he died 2nd October, 1264. On the 5th of February, in the following year, he was succeeded by another Frenchman, Guy Fulcodi, who took the name of Clement IV. The new Pontiff had long been one of the most valued Councillors of St. Louis, and he was remarkable for his fairmindedness, and for his tact in State affairs. St. Manettus, who had visited the French Court during the Council of Lyons, had there become acquainted with him, and the acquaintance had ripened into intimacy, there being much affinity between their characters. The Pope gave a proof of his friendship by granting, on 20th May, 1265, at the request of St. Manettus, then Prior of Cafaggio, an indulgence of twenty days for all who helped in the building of the superb Church. These were the first indulgences which the Order had ever received from the Holy See. The Pontiff had already, on 17th April of the same year, interposed to procure from the Premonstratensians of Orvieto permission for the Servants of Mary to build an Oratory, of which they were in need in that city.

Soon afterwards the Chapter General was again summoned to Siena, where it met on Whit Sunday, 24th May, 1265, in the Church of St. Clement. Blessed James of Poggibonzi had resolved to take advantage of this opportunity of retiring from office. He had now held the Generalate for eight years ; he was old and spent with labours, and he longed for retirement in order to prepare himself for death. These and other reasons made him anxious to withdraw from the turmoil of active life. He also thought that St. Manettus' intimacy with the new Pope might be turned to account for the good of the Order. He explained his views to the Capitular Fathers, who consented, although regretfully, to relieve him of his office, and to confer it on St. Manettus, whom he had himself indicated as the fittest person to succeed him. St. Manettus accepted the Generalate, with the stipulation that he should be allowed to retire after holding it for a short term. His diffidence sprang from his humility, for he was gifted with all the qualities essential for the office—holiness, learning, great and varied experience—so that his Brethren found their choice fully justified by subsequent events.

Before the Chapter broke up, he obtained the consent of the Fathers to the erection of a new Province, to be called the Province of Lombardy, or of Hither Gaul, Father Rota of Florence being appointed Provincial. The Order now extended from the centre of Italy to the north, and only the southern parts of the country remained open to this pacific conquest. Father Ristoro was at the same time appointed Prior of Cafaggio, and the holy General, accompanied by St. Philip, who had been confirmed, notwithstanding his reluctance, in the office of *Socius*, set out at once for Perugia, where the Pontifical Court then resided.

Clement IV received his old friend with much cordiality, and the business upon which he had come to confer with the Holy Father was quickly settled. The election of St. Manettus was confirmed by Cardinal Rodolph in the name of the Pope, on 29th May, and on the 8th of June following Clement IV. himself renewed the Bull of his predecessor, Urban IV , relative to the meeting of the General Chapter and the election of the Prior-General. St. Manettus returned to Cafaggio at the beginning of October, 1265, and it was at this time that an episode occurred in which the holy General took a leading part.

There dwelt in Florence a worthy man, by name Enrico Baldovini. He was married, and was possessed of considerable means, but he sought rather for those treasures which are laid up in heaven for faithful souls. The Servants of Mary were dear to him as his own brethren, and he had contributed generously towards the foundation and enlargement of the Convent of Cafaggio. His highest ambition was to be received among them, but he was a husband, and he could not break those bonds which Almighty God has Himself pronounced to be indissoluble. Since his wishes could not be fulfilled in the manner desired by him, he begged to be admitted as a *Divoto*, or Oblate. These titles were given to persons who, having a special devotion to some particular Church or to a Religious Community, consecrated thereto their personal service, and either the whole or a portion of their property. Such persons usually lived either in the Convent itself or in some of the out-buildings ; they promised obedience to the Superiors, and occasionally they bound themselves by vow to observe poverty and chastity. This pious custom possessed great attractions for the fervid devotion of the Middle Ages. St Manettus gladly complied with the request of the generous benefactor of the Order, and on the 6th of October, 1265, he received the oblation of Enrico Baldovini, who thenceforth was a true member, though in a subordinate position, of the Community of the Servants of Mary.

Notwithstanding his many labours and his advanced age, the saintly General continued to watch vigilantly over the interests of the Order. He was always well received by Clement IV., who gave a fresh stimulus to the works now proceeding uninterruptedly at the Church of Cafaggio, by granting forty days' indulgence to all who contributed in any way to the undertaking. The lofty soul of St. Manettus was at this time filled with an eager desire to carry the tidings of salvation to the multitudes sitting in the shadow of death in heathen lands, and especially in the remoter countries of the East. Most joyfully, therefore, did he respond to the appeal of the Holy Father by making choice of a band of apostles who, armed with the blessing of the Head of the Church, and that of their own General, were to embark for distant shores to impart the knowledge and love of Christ Jesus our Saviour, and of His Blessed Mother. These missionaries set forth for the scene of their labours, and toiled there faithfully and courageously, some among them being so happy as to shed their blood for the glory of their Master and of their Queen.

Thus the holy General was favoured by great consolations ; but, at the same time, he was tried by many severe sorrows. Of these, one of the most painful was caused by the faithlessness of some of his subjects. The establishment of the Mendicant Orders had been hailed as a hopeful prognostic ; their virtues and their active charity had won for them almost universal sympathy. A few dissentients had raised their voices against them : of these the loudest and most bitter was Guillaume de St. Amour, a doctor of the University of Paris. By various specious arguments he scrupled not to depict the friars as hypocrites, seducers of the people, and false apostles. Although this propagator of slanders was condemned by Innocent IV. and by Alexander IV., and refuted in the most masterly manner by St. Thomas Aquinas and St. Bonaventure, yet his falsehoods had taken root and borne fruit in the minds of certain Religious who were weary of the yoke of discipline, and who were now strongly tempted to break loose from engagements into which they had entered of their own free will. It stands to reason that duty to God and to the dictates of conscience must be carried out in opposition to all the suggestions of our evil nature ; and reluctant as St. Manettus was to take strong measures, he felt that the only remedy was to pluck up the tares by the root, the Pope having granted him full powers, authorizing him, as was then customary, to pronounce the major excommunication against them, and to have recourse to the secular arm if necessary, in order to reduce them to submission. At the present time, when similar cases occur (which but rarely happens), the only course to be pursued would be to allow these rebellious members to quit the Order, leaving to them the sole responsibility of their disloyal conduct.

About this time the Order was busied in making a new foundation in Umbria. Close to the frontiers of that Province, at the foot of the Apennines, looking westward, was the small, quiet, unpretending town of Gubbio, now destined to be edified and sanctified by the Servants of the Mother of God, who established a Convent there.

Whilst the Order was thus peacefully and unostentatiously spreading itself in various directions, the Saintly Founders were one by one passing away to their reward. It was now the turn of St. Amideus, who had reached his sixty-eighth year. For more than a year he had dwelt in retirement at Monte Senario, when at length he felt that his end was rapidly approaching. His bodily strength was exhausted, yet the holy Founder had relinquished none of his bodily austerities. His heart was so inflamed with the fire of divine love that he could hardly sustain the vehemence of its ardour, which often caused him to swoon away. Yet still he did not think himself sufficiently prepared for death. Often did he withdraw to his grotto, passing there whole days absorbed in God, and refusing to accept any of the little comforts which were procured for him, it being his desire to give himself uninterruptedly to the raptures of divine charity which urged him heavenwards. This grotto became to him, amidst the fervours of his almost unceasing prayer, an abode of unspeakable bliss. Here it was that death came to him whilst rapt in an ecstasy, on the 18th of April, 1265, the third Sunday after Easter.

A remarkable phenomenon, which may, indeed, be styled miraculous, was witnessed on this occasion. At the moment when the soul of the Saint was freed from its earthly prison, a brilliant light was seen without the Convent, illuminating the whole of Monte Senario, and it was visible from a great distance ; doubtless this light marked the passage of that ardent soul to heaven, and was typical of the fervour of his charity. At the same time, the Convent was filled with a delicious fragrance, in token of the purity which in that soul had been inseparably blended with the love of God.

Many tears were shed by the Brethren over the bier of the Saint, but their sorrow was tempered by supernatural gladness. The venerated remains were laid to rest beneath the altar of the original chapel, in the shrine which contained the bodies of St. Bonfilius and St. Buonagiunta, thus reuniting in death those who in life had been so closely bound together in the bonds of the love of God and of His Blessed Mother. The dust of the three was now mingled in the grave, as their souls were absorbed in the unity of the Beatific Vision.

The memory of the holy Founder who had just been taken from the midst of his loving children was henceforth held in benediction among them. His whole life had been full of edification, and in every respect he was a model of religious perfection.

His life in religion was spent in the practice of heroic virtues. It was his delight to be counted as nothing, and to remain in utter obscurity : penance and mortification were to him joy unspeakable. He was continually rapt in prayer, and almost always in a state of ecstatic contemplation. Indeed, so completely was he united with God, that he was unable to conceal his raptures. Whatever might be his occupation, whether in public or in private, he would suddenly fall into an ecstasy and remain perfectly motionless At other times, when saying office he united himself to the Angelic Choirs, praying with such fervour that his face became illuminated, whilst his heart was so on fire with divine love that he was forced to loosen his habit to enable himself to breathe, and once he was seen to rush to a spring of water to assuage the heavenly ardour which consumed him. His Brethren manifesting some wonder at this, he said to them . "If you only knew, dear children, what a fire is kindled in my heart !" He said Mass with profound recollection and with intense feeling . so absorbed was he that it might have been thought that he beheld Our Lord face to face : and after the Elevation and Communion the expression of his countenance showed how overflowing a source of sweetness the most holy Mysteries ever proved to him.

Nor did the charity of St. Amideus restrict itself to God alone, but rather did it extend itself from him over all mankind with endearing tenderness. Bodily infirmities and mental sufferings were equally alleviated by it. The holy Founder never spared himself, if by any means he could procure the sanctification of souls : prayer, exhortation, argument, all were employed in turn until he gained his end. He took great delight in visiting the sick poor, whom he consoled and encouraged by his unfailing sympathy. Those in distress found in him their best friend ; he gladly became a beggar to obtain the means of relieving them; and he well deserved the honoured title of "Father of the poor".

Having been for many years engaged in the direction of others, he was a model Superior, ruling with a combination of gentleness and strength, of humility and dignity, of discretion and charity, which made obedience easy and submission attractive to all. Under his headship discipline was perfect, each one striving his utmost to fulfil those duties which became a labour of love as soon as he gave the word. He never spared himself, being always foremost in all the religious exercises. When suffering from painful maladies he never lost patience; he joyfully endured all the privations imposed by evangelical poverty, and he was ever calm and cheerful in the midst of harassing anxieties. All his counsels were full of heavenly wisdom. he could speak sternly when circumstances made it necessary that he should do so; he preserved an unalterable sweetness of temper with all, but he was never to be turned from his purpose. It only needed to look upon him to behold the personification of a true Religious. He was always the first to obey the summons of the bell, especially in going to Choir, and he influenced others to imitate this exactness by the force of example rather than by words. He continually counselled perfect detachment and holy indifference. When he was obliged to administer a reprimand, the most sensitive culprit perceived by his gentle manner of censuring that it was dictated by fatherly love rather than by the authority of a Superior, and the fault, whatever it might be, was forthwith amended.

Several of his counsels have been preserved, which illustrate his admirable method of directing those who were subject to him. Speaking of the importance of choir duty, he said. " Recollect, my Brethren, that your psalms are accompanied by the melodies of the Angelic Spirits, who, in union with you, praise the Lord in this His Sanctuary. Be, therefore, devoutly attentive; for it is not enough to praise God with our lips only; our hearts must take their share by meditating on the meaning of the hymns and psalms which with our tongues we say; for the offering with which God is best pleased is that of our inmost affections."

On one occasion he felt it necessary to refuse a request made by one of his Religious, who withdrew, downcast and sorrowful. Then, St. Amideus, calling him back, said, with a gentle smile: " My son, why are you grieved? Why do you look so ill at ease? You are doubtless displeased with me for having refused your request; but know, my dear child, that asking for dispensations and exemptions in the hope of obtaining such, without actual necessity, deprives a Religious of the merit and of the graces which he would acquire by the strict observance of all the orders and regulations of his Superior. A Religious who is possessed of the true spirit of obedience should, when he asks for a dispensation, remain in a state of holy indifference, ready to accept whatever it may please his Superior to appoint, because in his will he recognizes the will of God. Moreover, he should be fully persuaded that, when his own will conflicts with that of his Superior, the sooner he obeys the more perfectly does he accomplish the Divine Will, the greater is his merit, and the more abundant will be his reward. For, in so doing, he tramples self-will under foot to do homage to God's most holy Will, and this is the most acceptable sacrifice which can be made, and the most conducive to the glory of God." The Religious, hearing these words, left St. Amideus' presence much edified and consoled.

Another time, a Religious, who was envious of the greater virtues of one of his Brethren, presumed to sit in judgment on him, detracting from his merits by attributing to him unworthy motives. St. Amideus, perceiving this, said to the Religious gently and with a smiling countenance : " My son, the Religious Life is a school where all, under pain of punishment if they fail, must learn two lessons : one is the lesson of self-mortification, the other that of self-conquest. The first teaches us to acquire by practice the virtues which we see displayed in our Brethren ; and through the second, he who fights most courageously and resists most strenuously attains the highest perfection. Hence, the great advantages of Community life : we can never thank God enough for setting before us so many beautiful patterns of religious excellence. If we do not imitate them, ours will be the shame ; but never let us allow ourselves to utter one word of detraction concerning them." This gentle reproof produced its effect, and the offending Brother hastened to correct the fault of which he had been guilty.

With his exalted virtues, his lofty standard of religious life, and his wonderful tact in dealing with souls, St. Amideus could not fail to train many eminent subjects for the Order Several Saints passed through his hands, among others St. Philip, who spent some time at Monte Senario, when St. Amideus was Master of Novices there. The holy Founder was thus the source of incalculable benefit to the Order, by the spirit which he infused into the many whose spiritual education was entrusted to him.

St. Amideus had a great reputation even during his lifetime as a worker of miracles. His heroic charity made him ever prompt to succour others, and it continually happened that sick persons and cripples were brought to him to ask his prayers. Then were many marvellous cures wrought by him : evil spirits were cast out, the sick were restored to health, the lame recovered the use of their limbs, the dying were snatched from the brink of the grave, and even the dead were restored to life. An instance of the latter is on record, in the case of a youth who was drowned in a deep pond at the foot of Monte Senario.

This youth was diverting himself on the banks of the pond, and by some mishap he fell in. His parents, who were near at hand, endeavoured to save him, but in vain, and in their distress they uttered loud cries. St. Amideus was, providentially, passing by, and, touched by the grief of the poor parents, he strove to console them. Meanwhile some peasants had drawn the lifeless body of the youth from the water, and laid it at the feet of the Saint, whilst the weeping father and mother implored him to take pity upon them. St. Amideus, in his charity, raised his heart to God, strong in faith, and, kneeling down, he took the youth's hands into his own, commanding him, in the name of the Lord Jesus Christ, to rise up. At the touch of St. Amideus' hand, and at the sound of his voice, the youth opened his eyes, rose up, and, full of joy, embraced his father and mother, exclaiming, "I am alive, I live again!" All present burst forth into expressions of gratitude to God and praise of St. Amideus, who, all abashed, hastily withdrew to the Convent.

No wonder, then, that the people called him a Saint, and that he was so beloved by them. As he passed along, he was surrounded by crowds, all sounding his praises, striving to kiss his hands and his habit, and to get his blessing. His humility shrank from these demonstrations, but he took advantage of them to influence for good the hearts of those who sought to do him honour, by turning their thoughts to God and to His Most Blessed Mother.

Such was St. Amideus, and great, indeed, was the blank which his death left in the Order. But, whilst one star sank below the horizon, another of no less brightness was rising to its zenith We allude to St. Philip Benizi, the beloved disciple of the Seven Founders, and the pupil of St. Amideus himself, who, since 1263, had filled the post of Assistant to the Father-General, and who, at the age of thirty-four, was himself destined to succeed to the Generalate. Here we shall quote a few pages from the work of St. Philip's modern biographer.

"The Servant of Mary was ready, and the time had now come when his mission was to be confided to him. On Whit Sunday, the 5th of June, 1267, the Fathers, assembled at the Convent of Cafaggio in order to hold the General Chapter, visited in procession the picture of Our Blessed Lady. Kneeling humbly at the shrine of their Queen and Mistress, they recited together the *Salve Regina*, the proper versicle and response, and the prayer following, *Concede nos.*

"It was thus that the Servants of Mary were accustomed to open their General Chapter, and the ceremonial remains in use unaltered to this day. The Fathers then proceeded to elect the four Vicars Capitular, or Definitors. St. Manettus next came forward to resign the Generalship into their hands. As the Definitors were empowered either to confirm the General in his office or to accept his resignation, as might seem to them best in the sight of God, St. Manettus, knowing their intentions, entreated them not to lay anew so heavy a burden upon him, his advanced age and many infirmities making him unequal to the complicated duties of the post. At the same time he suggested to them the advisability of electing in his stead his Colleague, Father Philip Benizi, who in past years had given abundant proofs of his capacity for the office. Not only were the suffrages of the Definitors at once given for St Philip, but all the Fathers voted for him with one accord, and his election was unanimous.

"The humble Religious was completely overwhelmed. It was in spite of himself, and only after a strenuous resistance, that he had accepted the office of Colleague, which had been forced upon him four years previously. But now, to take the first place, to be responsible for the well-being of the whole Order, and to command the obedience of so many holy men who had grown old in the service of God, whilst he, still young, had only been admitted to the priesthood eight years before—this was more than he could resolve to undertake. Moreover, he knew that it is safer and more meritorious to be ruled than to rule. Very modestly, therefore, he declined the proffered dignity; and kneeling in the midst of the Chapter, he implored the Fathers, with tears, to choose another, since he knew himself to be an instrument unworthy of so great a work, and also wholly wanting in the qualities which should mark a true Superior. The Fathers, however, knew both his humility and his merits; and, refusing to listen to his plea, they, with what Rucellai calls 'courteous persistence,' forced him to take the yoke upon his shoulders. It was not without considerable trouble that his objections were overcome. Indeed, it was only after a contest carried on with perfect charity between the Fathers and himself, and when a direct communication from heaven intervened to close the discussion, that he finally yielded. Whilst the Fathers were vainly endeavouring to persuade him, a voice was heard in the air, which, in a gently authoritative tone, spoke thus · ' Philip, do not resist the Holy Spirit, for I have called thee out of the world, that thou mayest rule my chosen people'.

"These words of their Queen filled the Religious with joy, and St. Philip at once bowed to the Divine Will of which she was the messenger. He humbly took his place as General, and all the Religious in turn knelt before him and kissed his hands in token of respect and obedience. He then rose and addressed his sons in words burning with divine inspiration, taking for the subject-matter of his discourse the thirty-second Psalm, which opens with these words: 'Rejoice in the Lord, O ye just : praise becometh the upright,' and he commented and developed the text of holy David in a manner which, from its freshness and its fervour, at once arrested the attention of his hearers. He showed that they were in a special manner bound to praise the Lord, Who had called them into the Order of the Most Blessed Virgin, Who had gathered them together like 'the waters of the sea in a vessel,' Who had collected into 'storehouses,' that is, their first Fathers, 'depths' and treasures of learning and holiness, and Who had made them 'blessed' by placing them under the protection of the Mother of their Redeemer, and by choosing them 'for His inheritance,' for the habitation which He had prepared from all eternity.

"He added that 'the Lord would bring to naught the counsels' of the wicked who desired to destroy their Order; and that He would protect the Servants of His Mother against all the devices of their enemies. Thus he continued, drawing beautiful meanings from each word of Holy Writ; and, like the householder of whom Our Lord spake, bringing forth 'out of his treasure new things and old'. The Religious listened in hushed attention, almost fearing to breathe lest they should lose a single word which fell from the lips of one in whom the Spirit of God so evidently dwelt. They could not sufficiently admire his profound knowledge of the Sacred Writings: and when he ceased to speak, they only regretted that his discourse was so quickly ended.

"After the address of the newly-elected General, the Chapter proceeded, in accordance with the prescribed Rule, to the election of the other dignitaries of the Order, beginning with the Colleague, or *Socius*, of the General. It frequently happened that the General directed the choice of the Fathers in a matter of such personal importance to himself, and it was not otherwise on this occasion. He whom St. Philip designated to fill this post was a Religious of great discretion and prudence, well known both for his learning and for his holiness, Blessed Lottaringo della Stufa. He belonged to the noble and worthy house of Lottaringhi. He had passed through his studies with considerable distinction, and he was an excellent classical scholar. A brilliant career, to all appearance, awaited him in the world, but at five-and-twenty years of age he renounced everything—ambition, wealth, and literary success—that he might hide himself in the poor and obscure Order of the Servants of Mary. St. Philip himself had some share in bringing about his choice.

"Blessed Lottaringo had been in fact a friend of the General's from his childhood upwards, and their bond of affection, knit together by their common piety, only grew stronger as time advanced. When Philip withdrew from the world, his example made a deep impression on Lottaringo, who shortly afterwards was induced by his friend's exhortations to do likewise, and to dedicate himself to the service of Our Blessed Lady. Like his friend also in this, he became so humble and obedient that his self-will appeared to be completely uprooted and cast out. In order to crush his pride of birth, he delighted to be employed in the lowest offices in the Convent. He was, in short, well worthy of being St. Philip's Colleague, and their long-standing friendship ensured his being more than commonly zealous in the discharge of the duties of that post. So helpful did he subsequently prove to the General, and so perfectly did he justify the confidence which his Superior reposed in him, that he was maintained in office throughout St. Philip's lifetime, and on his death succeeded him in the Generalship.

"After the election of Blessed Lottaringo, the Chapter nominated the Superiors of the four Provinces which belonged to the Order—namely, those of Tuscany, of Umbria, of Æmilia or Romagna, and of Cisalpine Gaul or Lombardy. St. Philip, in conferring office on the new Provincials, exhorted them to procure without delay the names of those Religious in their respective Provinces who were versed in the Greek and Hebrew languages and in the Syrian and Arabic tongues, and to see that the same were taught to all those among the Brethren who showed any aptitude for such studies. The zealous General was eager to follow the grand example of St. Manettus, and to send anew missionaries to the East. He knew that the work of converting the heathen was especially dear to the Sovereign Pontiff, and that His Holiness was desirous of finding apostles willing to spend themselves in evangelizing the Tartars and other Asiatic tribes. The story of the heroic labours of the Friars Minor and Friars Preachers was familiar to him, and he longed to see his own Brethren hasten, like them, to the rescue of those poor souls who were enslaved by error. The Provincials, fired by his enthusiasm, promised to exert themselves unremittingly to find labourers for the spiritual harvest. We shall shortly see them, faithful to their pledge, bringing him several subjects, whom he himself took and presented to the Pontiff.

"The Provincials having been elected, the Chapter proceeded with its business in the usual course. The other Superiors, in order of precedence, resigned their offices into the hands of the Definitors, who reappointed some and replaced others, as they in the interests of the Order judged to be best. Then, the work of the meeting being over, two of the Religious intoned the *Te Deum* in thanksgiving, in which hymn all the Fathers joined antiphonally. The new General then recited the versicle *Ora pro nobis, Sancta Dei Genitrix* and the prayer following, after which he blessed them all in the name of the Lord, and dismissed each one in peace to the duty assigned to him.

"Shortly afterwards, in conformity with the decree of Urban IV., he presented himself before the Bishop of Florence, by name Giovanni Mangiadoro, to announce to him his election to the Generalship, and to request the episcopal ratification of his appointment. The Bishop received him graciously, inquired how all had passed at the Chapter, and declared the election valid.

"As some of the early biographers express themselves, those who raised St. Philip to the chief dignity of the Order were truly inspired by the Holy Spirit. No one else could so well have replaced the Blessed Founders, who were then, one after another, fast passing away ; and no one else was equally capable of carrying on and consolidating their work. Surely he was a ruler and a father trained by Our Lady herself to preside over her well-loved Servants. During his eighteen years of headship, the Servite Order derived from him a strength and lustre hitherto unknown—qualities which prepared it for the great things which, in after years, it was destined to accomplish." (Fr. Soulier, *Life of St. Philip Benizi*, pp. 112-118.)

CHAPTER X.

Ⱬ𝔥𝔢 Conⴼ𝔱i𝔱u𝔱ion𝔰 of 𝔱𝔥𝔢 𝔒r𝔡𝔢r of 𝔱𝔥𝔢 Ⴝ𝔢r𝔳an𝔱𝔰 of Ⴘ𝔞r𝔶.

(1267—1268.)

At the very earliest beginnings of the Order, the Seven Holy Founders had endowed it with Constitutions, the first of which were composed by St. Bonfilius, when the Religious body of which he was chosen Superior came into being at Monte Senario. These primitive Constitutions were the germ of those subsequently sanctioned by St Buonagiunta in the General Chapter of the year 1257, which, although somewhat amplified, were still exceedingly laconic. Additions were made at each succeeding Chapter, and, finally, they were completed and codified by St. Philip, the new General whom God had appointed to carry out this work, to strengthen and extend the Order at the head of which he was placed, and to preserve it, humanly speaking, from extinction.

St. Philip possessed all the talents necessary to enable him to revise these Constitutions, to put the finishing touch to them, and bring them into perfect working order. He had thoroughly grasped the fundamental ideas of the Seven Founders, whose favoured disciple he was, whose chief hopes were placed in him, and whose relations with him had always been most cordial and brotherly. St. Bonfilius had received him into the Order after expounding to him his vision at the Santissima Annunziata, and had subsequently taken him as his companion in the journeys which it was his duty to make for two years as *Socius* of the General ; and his last sigh was breathed, as was that of St. Buonagiunta, in St. Philip's arms. St. Amideus had trained him for four years at the Novitiate of Monte Senario, and had instilled into him all the virtues specially appertaining to the Order. St. Manettus had retained him for two years as his Colleague in the Generalate. Thus it cannot be doubted that the saintly Founders had on numberless occasions admitted their youthful Brother to their innermost counsels, and had imparted to him their most cherished projects; and the course of events proved him to be the rightful inheritor of their life-work. He was thoroughly imbued with their spirit and their ideas; and he was, therefore, peculiarly fitted to embody these in the rules which were intended to shape and direct the lives of the Servants of Mary.

Moreover, St. Philip was endowed with a brilliant intellect, which he had cultivated by assiduous study. Although still young, he had acquired an extensive and varied experience of men and things in the different offices which he had filled. Above all, he was a man of saintly life, practising virtue in the heroic degree, and united to God in the highest kind of prayer. And since he had been chosen to govern the Order, he thereby received in addition a special grace to enable him to discharge the duties of his post, and particularly that of drawing up wise and holy rules.

Accordingly he set to work, and by the help of prayer, united to assiduous labour, he managed, in spite of all the difficulties of the task and the many interruptions occasioned by the duties devolving upon him as General, to complete the drawing up of the Constitutions in less than a year. Step by step he followed the track marked out by St. Bonfilius and St. Buonagiunta, and by the various Chapters which had decreed additional Constitutions; and thus at length he completed a document which settled once and for all every essential point St. Philip, whilst carrying on and completing what had been sketched out by his predecessors, availed himself of all the assistance which he found ready to hand, profiting both by previous experience and by the Constitutions of other Orders—particularly that of St. Dominic, which had originally borrowed a good deal from the Premonstratensians.

We cannot transcribe the whole of his work, but we shall here give an outline which will give a general idea of it to our readers, and which will enable them to enter more fully into the spirit of the Order which Our Lady herself desired the Seven Founders to establish in her honour. These Constitutions, originally consisting of twenty-one or twenty-two chapters, relate chiefly to the five following subjects:—I. Religious Duties and Devotional Exercises; II. Religious Discipline; III Admission and Training of Subjects; IV. Religious Perfection; V. The Government and Administration of the Order.

I. *Religious Duties and Devotional Exercises.*—The principal aim of the Order is set before us in the head of the Constitutions, for the first chapter is wholly taken up with the homage to be rendered to Our Lady, the various modes of which are enumerated with loving

16

iteration. The chosen devotions are in keeping with the spirit of the age, the object of the Order being chiefly carried out by liturgical means, but to these public tributes of veneration were to be added the private practices of devotion which each Religious was at liberty to choose for himself. If the Sorrows of Mary are not expressly named, it must be because this devotion was so deeply imprinted in the hearts of the Brethren that it was needless to mention it in the Rules Besides, the devotion itself long retained an esoteric character, being faithfully handed down by a pious tradition from one generation of the Order to another.

CHAPTER I.

Of the Marks of Veneration due to the Most Blessed Virgin.

Every week, on Wednesday and Saturday, there shall be said in the houses of the Order the Mass *de Beata*, to which shall be added, on Saturday, the *Gloria* and *Credo*.

Every evening the Office of the Vigil of the Blessed Virgin shall be said, and after the third Lesson the *Salve Regina* shall be recited.

At the beginning of each Hour the Officiant for the week, after having said in a low voice the *Pater Noster*, shall intone the versicle *Ave Maria, gratia plena, Dominus tuum ;* and the Brethren shall respond : *Benedicta tu in mulieribus, et benedictus fructus ventris tui.*

The *Salve Regina* shall be recited at the close of each Hour, and after meals, all through the year, with the exception of the three last days of Holy Week. Every evening this Antiphon shall be sung with great devotion after the Lesson of the Office of the Vigil of the Blessed Virgin, when that Office is said : when it is not said, this Antiphon is to be sung immediately after Compline.

All the Churches belonging to our Order, and the High Altar of each Church, shall be raised and consecrated in honour of Our Lady, at least where this can, without inconvenience, be done.

Whenever, according to the rubrics of the Roman Liturgy, the Hours of the Blessed Virgin are to be omitted on great Solemnities, the Brethren, gathered together by twos or threes, as may be most convenient, shall devoutly recite them.

The second chapter concerns the Divine Office and the Sacraments. The Divine Office is to be recited in common, in the Church, and with moderate speed. This manner of saying Office, besides being most conformable to the directions of Our Blessed Lord, clearly indicates that the Order is an active one, which is not devoted to prayer alone, but which is bound to labour for the salvation of souls.

With regard to the Sacraments, the rule adopted is that of frequent Confession and of Communion at long intervals, such being then the practice.

CHAPTER II.

OF THE DIVINE OFFICE.

The Mass and the other Divine Offices are to be celebrated after the usage of the Roman Church, all the manifestations of veneration for the Most Holy Virgin being added thereto.

The Hours and other Divine Offices are to be recited with moderate speed, lest too great slowness should diminish the devotion of the Brethren and of those who assist thereat. the points and stops must be observed without prolonging the sound of the voice, which must cease at once.

The Brethren must go to Confession twice at least in each week.

They shall go to Communion on the First Sunday of Advent, at Christmas, on the Feast of the Epiphany ; on Ash-Wednesday, Maunday Thursday, Easter Sunday, Ascension Day, and Whit Sunday , on the four Feasts of Our Lady, namely, her Purification, her Annunciation, her Assumption, and her Nativity ; on the Feast of the holy Apostles, SS. Peter and Paul, in the month of June ; and on the Feast of All Saints.

The third and fourth chapters are occupied with the external signs of religion which must be observed in the Church and in the Choir during the Divine Offices : these form the special Liturgy of the Order.

Each Order is in itself truly a family, the members of which are united by bonds which not even death can sever : the departed are, therefore, the objects of continual and anxious care. On this point the Order of the Servants of Mary yields to no other. Many special prayers are offered after the death of each member, as prescribed in the fifth chapter.

CHAPTER V.

OF SUFFRAGES FOR THE DEPARTED.

Upon the death of one of our Brethren, the Conventual Mass shall be offered for him, and those who are Priests shall each say three Masses for him.

The Anniversary of the fathers and mothers of the Brethren shall be kept on the day after the Octave of the Epiphany.

II. *Religious Discipline.*—Nothing is so strengthening to the soul as privation, or use being restricted to that which is of absolute necessity, especially in those things which are most likely to enervate the body. Thus the danger is avoided of becoming attached to a multiplicity of things which absorb the attention and weigh down the soul, even sometimes wholly enslaving it. Religious discipline breaks all these bonds asunder, increases tenfold the powers of the soul, and restores to it full freedom.

Silence—that most powerful lever of religious discipline—is exacted in the three places where it is most needed—in the cells, to promote the mental occupations of the Religious ; in Choir and in Church, to increase the fervour of prayer ; and in the Refectory, to give sobriety to the animal function which is there performed, and to diminish the dangers attendant upon it. Silence is kept with especial strictness during the night time, so as to enable the Religious to enjoy that unruffled tranquillity which is the inheritance of all Orders, and which is so great a promoter of the union of the soul with God, as well as a powerful aid in preparation for the sacred ministry of the Altar.

CHAPTER VI.

CONCERNING SILENCE.

Silence is to be observed by our Brethren in the dormitory, in the cells, and in Choir, from Compline until Prime of the morrow : in the Refectory during meals, both at the high table and at all others within the house and without. Nevertheless, should anything be wanting at table, it is permitted to ask for it once, speaking quickly, and in a low voice, to the Server, so as to be barely heard by those on either hand.

He who presides at the table may, when he thinks well, give dispensations on this point to the other Brethren.

Fasting, that most potent queller of our bodily nature, is held in honour in the Order. It is observed during Advent and Lent, on all Fridays throughout the year, at Ember-tides, and on certain Vigils

CHAPTER VII.

CONCERNING FASTING.

Fasting is to be strictly observed from the Feast of All Saints until Christmas, and from Quinquagesima until the Feast of the Resurrection of Our Lord : to these are to be added every Friday, from Easter until the following Quinquagesima, the Vigil of Pentecost, and all Ember Days.

For the rest of the time, and in order not to be too heavy a burden upon those with whom we may be staying, it is permitted for the Brethren to partake of that which is provided for them, to quote the text of the Gospel, and doing all in the name of Christ, " Eat such things as are set before you ".

It is not permitted for anyone to add to the number of these prescribed fasts, excepting with the permission of the Superior, who can increase the number.

All things concerning food, and the manner in which it is to be taken, are spoken of in the ensuing chapter. Perpetual abstinence is to be observed, as in those days meat was looked upon as a luxury totally unsuitable for Religious. The Priors had, however, the right of giving dispensations from this rule. When St. Philip drew up the Constitutions, the Order no longer observed the vow of poverty with pristine strictness, it having been considered more prudent to yield this point in order not to be included under the decree of the Council of Lyons forbidding the establishment of any new Mendicant Order : the Order consequently became possessed of permanent revenues. These conditions enabled it to conform to the traditional custom, forbidding the use of meat as an article of diet in Religious houses.

The ninth chapter prescribes the manner of taking collation, which in those days was performed very expeditiously.

CHAPTER VIII.

On Food.

At the proper time, before dinner and supper, the bell shall ring for the washing of hands, after which all shall proceed in silence to the place appointed outside the Refectory. And when the bell is again sounded, the Brethren shall enter the Refectory.

No Brother who has been present at the first table shall remain in the Refectory without permission, saving only the Servers and the Superiors.

All others who have not been able to take their meal with the Community shall eat at the second table.

No meat shall at any time be eaten in the houses of the Order, but it is allowable to use cream with the food as a condiment. As to this matter, however, the Priors may occasionally grant dispensations to their Brethren, but this must be done with due circumspection.

In places where our Communities exist, none of the Brethren, whether Priors or ordinary Religious, shall eat out of the Monastery, except in a Bishop's house, or in the house of another Religious Order, or in the company of ecclesiastics or laymen of known virtue ; and even then it must be but seldom, and only by permission of the Prior.

No one shall keep any description of food in his cell.

CHAPTER IX.

Concerning Collation.

On fast-days, after the first bell for Compline, when the Server gives the signal, the Brethren shall go to the Refectory for Collation.

The sick are nowhere tended with such watchful and devoted care as in Religious Orders : everything is done for them that can relieve bodily suffering and cheer the spirit, for in times of sickness sadness often clouds the soul. But whilst lavishing on the sufferers every attention which their health demands, all over-indulgence should be avoided, since such often leads to the relaxation of discipline.

CHAPTER X.

CONCERNING THE SICK.

Let the Superior be careful that the sick shall not be neglected, but that they shall have such relief as may quickly restore them to health, as our Father, St. Augustine, prescribes.

To insure a perfect disengagement on the part of the Religious from the countless trammels created by indolence, vanity, and the spirit of independence, everything respecting bedding, clothes, the care of the hair, travelling, and correspondence is minutely provided for. In each detail, often small in itself, but important as a means of spiritual advancement, the will of the Religious is ruled and guided by the authority of the Constitutions.

CHAPTER XI.

CONCERNING BEDS AND BEDDING.

Our Brethren shall not sleep upon mattresses, but they shall lie on straw beds , they may have pillows under their heads and sheets of wool or of serge.

Without the Convent they shall take whatever kind of bed is offered to them, so as not to be troublesome to those who show them hospitality.

When they go to bed they shall take off their shoes and mantle, keeping on their tunic and scapular, except in cases of grievous sickness.

CHAPTER XII.

CONCERNING APPAREL.

The apparel of our Brethren shall be of wool : the tunic, the scapular, and the cloak, or cappa, shall be made of transalpine or German cloth, the colour being black : the white tunic may be made of either foreign or of native cloth. They shall wear no linen except upon the legs · the girdles are to be of black leather, with black bone or iron clasps Each year the Brethren shall receive two golden florins apiece, which they are bound to spend wholly in buying their clothes.

CHAPTER XIII.

CONCERNING THE TONSURE.

The tonsure shall be of suitable dimensions, as is fitting for Religious, so that the circle of hair left on the head shall not be above three fingers in breadth.

CHAPTER XVII.

CONCERNING JOURNEYS.

When the Brethren are sent upon a journey, he who sends them is to choose one to act as Superior. If he does not make known his choice, the elder of the two is the Superior.

Those who are under obedience to go from one place to another are to kneel down before the Superior, and, bowing to him, beg his blessing.

Before they go forth they shall pray, kneeling before the Altar, or before some picture which is held in veneration : they shall do likewise on their return, and the same practice shall be observed whenever they go out or come in.

They shall go to no other place but that to which they are sent.

The Brethren, when travelling, must always carry with them letters commendatory, and they are to deliver these upon their arrival to the Prior of the Convent, or to his Vicar.

III. *On the Admission and Training of Subjects.*—The reception of recruits for an Order, and the preliminary training which they receive, contribute largely to the harvest of virtue and sanctification produced therein, to the tranquillity and content which it secures to its members and to its own expansion ; briefly, everything depends upon the seed-time. Thus, we see that the Constitutions deal with all essential points in a manner proportioned to their gravity.

In the three succeeding Chapters the Constitutions deal with the Postulate, the Novitiate, and the Profession, entering into all the precautions to be taken in order to secure the admission of none but good and worthy subjects, such as may readily be trained to the perfection required by the religious state, and thus be prepared to undertake a solemn and life-long engagement. All necessary guarantees of discreet behaviour and a true vocation are secured before admission. The subject cannot enter the house until he has been examined by two experienced Religious, the Prior being one of them. A fresh examination is required if the subject is intended for the priesthood. Admission to the Novitiate only takes place after three favourable reports from the Community, and by permission of the Provincial or of the General.

Chapter the fifteenth contains a complete educational code for the Novices, the rules or principles of which are chiefly taken from the Dominican Constitutions, which were themselves derived from those of the older Orders.

CHAPTER XIV.

CONCERNING POSTULANTS.

None shall be admitted under fifteen, or above sixty years of age, except by the authority of the Prior-General.

Postulants shall only be received in the Convent of the district to which they belong.

When a subject desires to be clothed with our habit, the Prior, together with at least one other discreet Religious, shall, before he be admitted to our Order, examine whether there be any obstacle to his reception.

No Postulant shall be admitted as a candidate for the priesthood who is not well versed in plain chant and grammar. The Prior of the Convent may in such case accept him, by the advice and with the consent of the Brethren of the Community assembled three times in Chapter, and after having given notice to the General or to the Provincial, and having obtained their permission.

CHAPTER XV.

CONCERNING NOVICES.

The Prior shall set over the Novices a careful Master, who shall instruct them in all things relating to the Order, and who shall diligently reprove them by word or by sign when they show themselves negligent either in Church or elsewhere.

He must procure for them all things needful, as far as may be in his power. When one of them has been guilty of any public fault, he must ask pardon therefor; and the Master shall give him a penance, or else may reprimand him in the private Chapter of the Novices.

Let the Master instruct them how to practise both interior and exterior humility, according to those words of Our Lord : " Learn of Me, for I am meek and humble of heart ".

Let him teach them to confess their sins frequently, discreetly, and straightforwardly.

Let him train them so to live as possessing nothing of their own, to wholly give up their own will, and to place that of their Superior above their own in all things.

He shall instruct them how to bear themselves in different places, and under divers circumstances , and how they are bound to remain wheresoever they may be placed.

Let him teach them to bow themselves whether anything is given to them or taken from them, whether they are spoken to gently or harshly ;

And how they should comport themselves in the Community rooms ; that they should not raise their eyes ;

How they should pray, what prayers they should say, and that these should be said silently, so as not to disturb the others;

Likewise, how they should ask pardon in Chapter when they are reproved.

If one of them shall scandalize his brother in any way whatsoever, let him remain prostrate at his feet until this one shall be appeased, and shall raise him up.

Let them also be trained never to dispute with anyone.

Let them obey their Master in all things. In Processions let each give heed to his companion. Let them not speak at times or in places where it is forbidden to do so.

Let them strictly refrain from judging anyone, but if they see anything done which appears to them wrong, let them interpret it for the best, or, at all events, as having been done with a good intention, for human judgments are often fallible.

Let them not speak of the absent, except it be in their favour.

Let them often take the discipline.

When they drink they must hold the cup with both hands, being seated.

Let them be very careful of the books, of the clothing. and of all other things belonging to the Convent.

If one of them shall ask for anything, let not another make the same request without giving his reasons for so doing.

Let the Confessions of the Novices be heard before their Profession, and let them be instructed as to the manner of making their Confession, and all other things needful

Before their Profession let the Novices discharge all their debts ; and whatever may remain over and above, let them lay it at the feet of the Prior, so as to be wholly detached from all things.

Let the Novices, during the time of their probation, diligently study psalmody and the Divine Office.

During the year of their Novitiate let them not be sent to a distance, except in case of necessity ; and let them not be employed in any office.

Let not their clothes be taken from them before their Profession without their consent.

Let them not be ordained before their Profession.

When the time comes for them to make their Profession, let them be sent to the Prior-General or to the Provincial, with letters giving their names and the name of their Convent , and, at all events, let them not be professed without the special consent of the Prior-General or of their Provincial.

If one of them, when the given time has passed, should not be willing to be professed, let him be excluded from the Order

Let them keep silence amongst themselves and when with externs , but, having permission from the Prior or from their Master, they may speak with those with whom they would otherwise be forbidden to do so.

CHAPTER XVI.

CONCERNING THE PROFESSION.

The formula of the Profession is as follows :

" Ego, N., facio professionem et promitto Deo omnipotenti, beatæ Mariæ Virgini et universæ Curiæ cœlesti, et tibi Fratri N. priori generali Fratrum Servorum Sanctæ Mariæ, Ordinis Sancti Augustini, et omnibus tuis successoribus obedientiam, vivere sine proprio, et castitatem et vivere secundum regulam beati Augustini toto tempore vitæ meæ, in hac religione ".—" I, N., make profession and promise to Almighty God, to the Blessed Virgin Mary, to the whole court of heaven, to you,

Brother N., Prior-General of the Brothers, Servants of Mary, of the Order of St. Augustine, and to all your successors, to observe obedience, poverty, and chastity, and to live all my life long in this Religion, after the Rule of St Augustine."

The habits of the Novices, at their Profession, are to be blessed as follows .

"V. Ostende nobis, Domine, misericordiam tuam.

"R　Et salutare tuum da nobis.

"V　Dominus vobiscum.

"R. Et cum spiritu tuo."

Oremus.

"Domine Jesu Christe, qui tegimen nostræ mortalitatis induere dignatus es, obsecramus immensæ largitatis tuæ abundantiam, ut hoc genus vestimentorum, quod Sancti Patres, ad innocentiæ et humilitatis indicium, ferre sanxerunt, ita bene ✠ dicere digneris, ut qui hoc usus fuerit te induere mereatur.　Qui vivis et regnas. . . .

"R. Amen."

And then they shall be sprinkled with holy water.

IV. *Concerning Religious Perfection.*—The twentieth, twenty-first, and twenty-second chapters, which were added afterwards in St. Philip's time, are entitled—Concerning Serious Faults ; Concerning More Serious Faults ; Concerning Most Serious Faults.　They comprise all omissions opposed to the essence and to the perfection of Religious Life.　Therefore, in the exact reverse of these transgressions, we find a correct portrait of a perfect Religious whose life is in perfect harmony with the vocation he has embraced, and who, by shunning all these faults, practises the virtues belonging to his state in their most heroic completeness.

V. *On Government and the Management of Business.*—The Constitutions solve the important problem of Government by turning to account the experience of older Orders.　They are more especially modelled upon the Dominican and Premonstratensian Constitutions.

As, however, the Order, whilst forming a perfectly united whole, is nevertheless divided into separate Provinces, and as a certain number of Convents are contained in each Province, the Constitutions relegate the governing power to three different ranks of Superiors : first, the General, whose authority extends over the entire Order, without reserve or exception ; secondly, the Provincial, who exercises supreme authority within the limits of his Province ; and, lastly, the Prior, whose authority is restricted to the Community residing in his Convent.

The government of the Superiors includes the power of giving orders, dispensations, reprimands, fraternal correction, and making loans, alienations, purchases, &c , all of which are carried on within certain limits which are the more strictly defined when the Superior is lower in dignity and the business in hand is more important in its nature.

In each Convent the management of affairs is divided between the Prior and several officials, namely, the Procurator, who receives and disburses the finances; the sub-Prior, who sees to all the requirements of the Brethren, in health or in sickness; the Sacristan, who has charge of everything belonging to the Church; the *Œconomus*, who has the care of the stores of provisions, which he gives out as they are needed; and the Porter, who receives visitors. The duties of all these offices are carried out under the superintendence of the Prior and in subjection to his will. For this reason, no Father is allowed to interfere in the business of any office to which he has not been appointed.

The Superiors and the other Officials are appointed by election, and they are bound to give an account of their administration at the General Chapter. The election of the General, of the Provincial, and of the Prior takes places at the yearly meeting of the General Chapter: that of the subordinate Officials is carried out by the majority of votes of the Religious in each house.

For the election of Officials and for the settlement of accounts, the General Chapter possesses a complete code of procedure, in which the four Definitors, invested with exceptional powers, play the chief part.

Thus, by this mode of government the Order lives in peace, without jarring discord, protected from any excess or abuse to which human imperfection is but too liable, avoiding both the harshness and unsympathetic nature of an autocracy, and the fickleness and the excitability of democratic rule.

CHAPTER XVIII.

CONCERNING THE AUTHORITY OF SUPERIORS.

The General shall exercise supreme authority in all matters, both spiritual and temporal.

He shall have full power to give dispensations upon any point of the Constitutions whatsoever, after consulting thereon with several discreet Religious and taking their opinions.

He shall visit, either personally or by his deputies, all the Cisalpine Communities at least once a year, and the Transalpine Communities once every three years. The Provincial shall not be empowered to borrow any money until he shall have consulted all the Priors of his Province.

He shall have full authority from the General for the government of his Province, unless the General shall desire to reserve certain cases for himself. He shall be bound to visit every Monastery in his Province thrice in a year at the least, and oftener if it be necessary.

The Prior-General shall send visitors when he may think it expedient to do so.

The Prior of a Convent shall not cause any of his Brethren to be ordained without the consent of the General or the Provincial. he shall not build nor pull down any building without the advice of his Counsellors: he shall not settle any account nor receive any legacy without consulting them: he shall have full power to correct any of his Brethren in the Convent, according to our Constitutions, after having consulted his ordinary Counsellors in serious cases He shall hold a Chapter every Friday at the least. This Chapter is to be held immediately after Matins, and the Prior shall therein hear the Brethren tell their faults. When he is obliged to absent himself he must appoint a deputy, charged to rule carefully and vigilantly · he shall cause the Constitutions to be read before the assembled Brethren at least six times a year.

In each Convent there shall be a Procurator, chosen by a majority of the votes of the Community duly met in Chapter: to him shall be handed over all sums received as alms in the Convent or laid upon the Altar, and all such as come into the hands of the Brethren in any way whatsoever. These sums he may use and lay out by permission of the Prior he must write down all that he receives and expends, and he must hand in his accounts monthly to the Prior and his Counsellors.

In each Convent there shall be, likewise, a Sub-Prior, chosen by the most able and prudent members of the Community: he shall see to the outlay and to all things needful for the maintenance of the Brethren: he shall be careful that the sick, the Religious in good health, and all visitors, have food, shoes, furniture, and all other requisites: it is solely by his permission, or by that of the Prior, that any furniture for the Brethren can be made elsewhere than in the Convent.

A discreet and zealous Sacristan shall be chosen, who will carefully and conscientiously fulfil the duties of his office: he shall neither exchange, nor give away, nor alienate any articles under his charge, to any brother or stranger, except by permission of the Prior.

The Œconomus must be provident and discreet: he must keep watchful care over the bread, the wine, and all the other provisions: every day he shall give out to the Servers at the appointed time the bread, the wine, and the other things necessary. When the Brethren at the second table have finished their meal, their Server shall give everything back again to the keeping of the Œconomus.

Let the Porter be a prudent and upright Religious, in whom all confidence may be placed · he shall diligently discharge the duties of his office as they have been marked out for him by the Prior.

CHAPTER XIX.

Concerning Prohibitions.

Let no one keep money in his own possession.

Let no one sell any book or other article belonging to the Order for more than cost price.

Let no priest of our Order hear the confessions of our Brethren, of seculars, or of women, unless he have received authority for so doing from the Prior-General or from the Provincial.

Let the Conventual Priors examine, once a month, the cupboard, drawers, and wallet of each Brother during his absence.

None shall send letters addressed to a Brother or to a stranger without first showing them to the Prior. And if one of the Brethren shall receive a letter from without, he likewise must give it first to the Prior.

No one can be elected to the office of Prior-General, of Vicar-General, or of Visitor until he shall have passed a period of four years in the Order.

No one shall sell or buy, give or receive, anything without permission from the Prior.

Let no one, without permission from his Superior, intermeddle in the administration and management of any property, whether real or personal, if belonging to strangers, or even if it belong to Novices.

CHAPTER XXIV.

Concerning the Chapter General.

We desire that the Chapter General be held yearly at the Calends of May. For this Chapter there shall be summoned . the Prior-General, his Colleagues or Vicars, all the Provincials, and the Priors of every Convent, numbering, at least, thirteen Choir Brethren.

Each of these shall be accompanied by two Religious chosen by the most able and prudent members of the Community.

The Prior of a Convent containing fewer than thirteen Religious shall only take with him one companion.

If one, or several, of those convened to the Chapter should be unable to attend, they cannot give their votes by proxy.

At the opening, Mary, Our Advocate, is to be invoked, kneeling, with great reverence, the Antiphon *Salve Regina* being recited instead of sung, followed by the versicle *Ora pro nobis* and the prayer *Concede nos.*

Then, if anyone desires to speak, or if he is commanded to speak by the Prior-General, the sermon, which must be short and concise, shall be preached. Those who desire edification can remain for the sermon

The sermon being ended, as it is well to be speedy in helping those who suffer, all shall join in reciting the Office of the Dead for those Brethren who have died during the past twelve months a general absolution shall be given for them, and the Psalm *De Profundis* shall be said , followed by *Kyrie Eleison, Pater Noster,* with the versicle *A porta inferi,* and the prayer *Absolve.* .

These prayers being said, the Brethren who do not take part in the Chapter withdraw.

Then the Brethren present elect four Definitors, thus : each elector writes his name, then the name of the Definitor chosen by him : after which the names of the elected, with those of the electors, are read aloud. Let the Brethren Electors follow in all the inspiration of God

Then shall the Provincials and the other Priors forthwith place their seals and warrants of office in the hands of the Definitors.

Then the said Definitors shall *rectify* the Prior-General, his Colleagues and Vicars, and all who have filled those offices. And then the Prior-General, in conjunction with the four Definitors, rectifies the wrongs of the Provincial and Conventual Priors and others. Then the Brethren present in Chapter elect two Brothers, priests, who, in conjunction with the General, shall rectify any abuses committed by the Definitors previous to the meeting of the Chapter.

Then any new Constitutions which may have been brought forward shall be discussed: those which are approved by the majority shall be recorded in a separate register, not in the same book with the old Constitutions, unless they shall have received the approbation of three successive Chapters.

No Constitution sent up by a Convent shall be examined by the Chapter General, except it be authenticated by the seal of the Prior of that Convent.

Then, the Prior-General and the four Definitors shall elect the Provincial and Conventual Priors, and appoint the Religious to be sent to the different Convents of the Order: after which prayers shall be asked for the benefactors of the Order, and, all things necessary having been settled, the names of the Priors of each Province and of each Convent shall be given out. This being done, the *Te Deum* is intoned at the sound of the bell, and when it has been sung, the versicle *Ora pro nobis Sancta Dei Genitrix* is added, together with the prayer *Concede quæsumus*, &c.

Afterwards the *Confiteor* is said, and the Absolution and Blessing given to all And this is the customary manner for holding the Chapter General.

The Brethren who have been present at the Chapter General cannot alter or modify anything which has been decreed in the same Chapter, except it be done by unanimous consent. And, similarly, a general statute, or a custom of long standing which has always been approved, cannot be modified in any particular whatsoever, either by a General or a Provincial, unless these should have obtained the approval of three successive Chapters.

A sentence pronounced by the Definitors shall be strictly carried out, so as that no person shall be able to appeal against their judgment. Any such appeal, if made, is to be considered as void and of no effect: for we forbid any appeal to be made in our Order, seeing that we do not enter into it to dispute, but rather to correct and cure our faults.

The Prior-General and the Definitors shall always decide upon the time and place of meeting for the succeeding Chapter.

Such are the first complete Constitutions of the Order of the Servants of Mary. Their structure is extremely simple, their rules are full of wisdom: all is marked by that spirit of moderation and gentleness so characteristic of Our Blessed Lady. Truly, they are a masterpiece; and we cannot, therefore, wonder that they have been, and still are substantially, preserved with religious faithfulness. Undoubtedly St. Philip drew them up with his own hand, and impressed upon them his own individuality; but, nevertheless, in giving expression to his own ideas, he never ceased to be the mouthpiece of our Seven Saints : it was their views which he consigned to writing : it was their decisions of which he made a code of laws. The disciple transmitted to after generations the words of his Masters, by whom he was inspired, by whose intellects he was enlightened, and whose souls guided his soul. It may, therefore, be truly said that these Constitutions were the joint work of the Seven Holy Founders—by whom their outlines, at all events, were conceived—and of St. Philip, who completed those outlines and put them into shape. The glory of the work belongs equally, therefore, to the Fathers and to their son, all having an equal right to be styled the Lawgivers of the Order of the Servants of the Most Blessed Virgin Mary.

CHAPTER XI

St. Philip's Headship—The Works and Deaths of St. Manettus, St. Hugh, and St. Sostene.

(1267—1285.)

AFTER the election of St. Philip to the Generalate, the surviving Founders retired more and more into the background. From this time forth they became passive but vigilant spectators of all the doings of the Order ; and, whilst following with the deepest interest the proceedings of the great Saint who had been appointed to govern it, their own lives remained hidden, silent, and almost forgotten.

St. Manettus withdrew into seclusion to prepare for his approaching death. St. Hugh and St. Sostene had still fifteen years of life before them, during which time they would, on two or three occasions, reappear for a brief space, returning quickly to their retreat. St. Alexis, still at his post at the Convent of Cafaggio, was to continue for forty-three years to lead, without outward change, his humble, hidden, saintly, and edifying life.

But, although no longer engaged in the active Religious Life, the holy Founders did not relax their labours in the enclosed vineyard where perfection is cultivated. There they toiled with all their old fervour, and there they set forth holiness in its most winning aspect to those who were privileged to behold them, and offered to the younger generations of the Order, who strove to follow in their track, perfect models of every virtue.

Above all things, they devoted themselves to prayer, lifting up their souls to God and to His Blessed Mother with ardent and sweet devotion. Whilst the rest of the Brethren, led by their General, were engaged in battle on the plain, they, on the mountain-top, held up their hands like Moses in supplication to heaven; and the prayers which uprose from those pure hearts winged their way unerringly to the Hearts of Our Lord and of His Mother, and brought down a plenteous dew of grace upon the whole Order.

Thus the holy Founders, in their calm and peaceful retreat, continued to be the moving spirits and the protectors of their Institute; and under this restful aspect did they appear to their spiritual sons whilst St. Philip was engaged in those active toils by which his vital powers were to be exhausted in less than twenty years.

One of the first cares of the new General was to determine the wording of the Constitutions. This task being completed, he presented it, on the 27th of May, 1268, to the representatives assembled at Pistoja, by whom it was unanimously approved. Among those present were the surviving Founders, who were not chary of their admiration for St Philip's work, which they pronounced to be a faithful version of the purest traditions of the Order, as transmitted from their first Superior, St. Bonfilius.

Shortly afterwards, as the holy General was journeying from Arezzo to Perugia, he learnt by a messenger that St. Manettus was seriously ill at Monte Senario. It was in the month of August; but, notwithstanding the intense heat, St. Philip hastened at once to Florence, on his way to the cradle of the Order.

Thither St Manettus had retired more than a year previously His age was not very advanced, he being then only sixty-five; but his strength had been sapped by toil and mortifications, whilst it had been completely exhausted by the anxieties inseparable from the government of the Order. His bodily frame was wasted by several painful diseases; but the soul of the holy old man remained youthful and vigorous, though pent in a frail, earthly tabernacle. He continued to be absorbed in prayer, wherein he found perpetual delight, and he could still drag himself to his beloved grotto, where he passed hour after hour in contemplation. Nor did he relax the severity of his penances. If any personal exertion was necessary for the good of others, it was made instantly, especially with regard to poor sick persons, who were frequently brought to him; and not long before his death he wrought upon one of these a miraculous cure, the details of which have been preserved.

In that part of the country dwelt a family, one of the members of which was powerless in all his limbs, and, moreover, both deaf and dumb. Many physicians had been consulted in vain, and at length it was resolved to have recourse to the venerable Saint. The poor cripple was accordingly carried to him, and attended the Father's Mass, who, after the Communion, went down to him, and, taking him by the hand, caused him for the first time in his life to walk and kneel, and then gave him Holy Communion. From that moment the cure was complete; and the man hitherto so fearfully afflicted was enabled to use both his tongue to give thanks to God for His great mercy, and his limbs to return unaided to his own home.

Meanwhile the good Father grew daily weaker, and, courageous though he was, he was at length compelled to keep his bed. The other Fathers saw plainly that there was no hope of his recovery, and they, therefore, sent for the General without delay. The meeting between St. Philip and St. Manettus was most touching: those two holy souls pouring out their hearts to each other, and each giving comfort and edification to the other by words glowing with the inspiration of divine love. The young General strove in every way to soothe and brighten the last moments of one who had so long been his father and master in the spiritual life, whilst the aged Founder rejoiced to show his full sympathy with the young General, and his entire confidence in him. Between them there was, as it were, a contest as to who should show the greatest generosity and affection towards the other.

The whole Community watched anxiously by the bedside of St. Manettus, but neither their watchful care, nor the joy caused by St. Philip's visit, could check the rapidity of the saintly old man's decline. The hour of his departure was at hand. The Religious gathered around him, and, with a voice faint but audible, he gave his last exhortation, urging them to lead the lives of Saints, to be tenderly devout to Our Lady, and never to forget the obligations imposed upon them as bearers of the title of her Servants. Then, embracing each one severally as a much-loved son, he gave him the counsels most needful for him, together with a few words of fatherly encouragement; and, finally, he took leave of them all with an allusion to their reunion in a better world in presence of the Queen of Heaven.

Then, with his mind and his heart wholly detached from the things of this world, and filled with a child-like love of Mary, he made his preparation for death with the assistance of St. Philip, who remained with him to the end. He received the last Sacraments with the utmost fervour, resigning himself wholly to the Divine Will. As he was suffering intensely from the complication of his maladies, St Philip supported him in his arms; and during the long final agony, the dying Saint listened with rapture to the inspired words of the pupil who had now become his master; whilst with his failing breath he sang with Philip in alternate strophes the hymns in praise of Our Lady which had been so often chanted by them both. Thus, on the 22nd of August, within the Octave of the Assumption of the Most Blessed Virgin, he breathed his last sigh,

17

leaning upon the breast of a Saint—surely the best pillow on which a dying head can rest ; and after his soul had fled, his lips still smiled, as though he were yet singing the glories of Mary.

The Brethren of Monte Senario prepared to pay the last duties to St. Manettus. They clothed his body in the religious habit, and laid it on a bier with the face uncovered, in the Chapel where the Order had received its charter from on high, and where the simple and touching funeral rites were carried out. Whilst thus engaged, they felt far more moved to beg the intercession of the departed than to pray for him. They laid his mortal remains near those of the three holy Founders who had gone before him, beneath the altar of that sanctuary so dear to him. He rested with them in that peaceful sepulchre for many years, until the translation of their venerated bodies took place.

The life of St. Manettus ended as it had begun. From first to last it formed one beautiful and consistent whole It closed in an ecstasy of love of Mary, leaving behind it the fragrance of consummate virtue, and bearing all the tokens of divine election. There was one holy soul the less on earth, and one Saint the more in heaven.

St. Manettus was the fourth of the Seven Founders who had finished his earthly pilgrimage and taken his place in the Court of the Queen of Angels. Thus, of the original number, the majority, and these the most able of the band, were no longer of this world ; the three who had been Generals—St. Bonfilius, St. Manettus, and St. Buonagiunta—with St. Amideus, the great trainer of the youthful Novices, had all departed. But, amidst these afflicting losses, the wonderful dealings of Divine Providence are more than ever clearly marked. Whilst the chief props of the Order were being one by one withdrawn, a new upholder was given in the person of St. Philip, who was competent to fill the place of all. The three surviving Founders, perfect in obedience, and rejoicing in their humility to be held as nothing, were only too happy to be passed over in favour of St. Philip. Henceforth, so hidden were their lives, that scarcely the faintest record of them can be found ; they came and went at the command of their saintly General, having no will but his. They were all growing old : at the time of St. Manetto's death, St Hugh was sixty-four years of age, St. Sostene was sixty-three, and St. Alexis was sixty-eight.

About two years after the death of St. Manettus, St. Philip resolved to carry out his plan of journeying beyond the Alps, taking with him St. Hugh and St. Sostene, than whom he knew he could have no better coadjutors The two Founders, in spite of the infirmities of age, accordingly set out with their General. They went first to France, where together they made a visitation to the foundations, which were the fruits of St. Manettus' labours there. Then St. Philip, having finished the business which had brought him to that country, left St. Sostene there as Vicar-General, delegating to him very extended powers.

St. Philip proceeded thence with St. Hugh to Germany, where, after travelling into various parts of that vast country, he handed over to his saintly companion the government of all the houses of that Province ; he then returned to Italy, passing on his way through France, where, as on a previous occasion, he found a General Council assembled. This was in the course of the year 1274

The two Vicars-General remained at their respective posts as long as obedience required ; they continued to practise, in Germany and in France, all those virtues of which they had in Italy given such bright examples ; and their presence at the head of these two important Provinces became the source of abundant graces which caused them to be esteemed as Saints even more than heretofore they had been.

St. Hugh founded several Convents in Saxony, Thuringia, Brandenburg, and other parts of Germany

Meanwhile, St. Sostene assiduously cultivated the seed sown by St. Manettus and St Philip. Residing in Paris, he became intimate with the son of St. Louis, Philip the Hardy, who held him in great esteem. One day, indeed, the King, in presence of his whole Court, spoke of him in terms of the highest praise, saying : " In the Vicar of the Order of the Servants of Mary in this country we have before us the example of a spotless life ; he is in truth a Saint ". And when St. Philip came to salute him, he repeated this eulogium almost word for word : " Your Vicar," said the King, " leads a most exemplary life, and by the eminence of his saintliness the whole kingdom is edified ".

In the year 1276, St Hugh and St. Sostene were recalled to Italy by their General : they set out immediately, leaving behind them honoured memories and flourishing good works, and gladly did they return to their beloved solitude at Monte Senario, where they could once more refresh their souls athirst for silence, for prayer, and for penance.

St. Philip, who himself had but recently returned from a journey into Germany, now received a sudden summons to the Pontifical Court. The new Pope, Innocent V., who had succeeded Gregory X., desired to suppress the Order, thinking this to be a duty imposed upon him by the Council of Lyons. In his view, the extremely precise wording of the conciliar decree left no room for doubt upon this point ; and although he was grieved to the heart at being obliged to put in force this destructive measure, his conscience, he considered, would allow of no alternative. This news overwhelmed the holy General with sorrow. He offered up special devotions to obtain the intercession of Our Lady, and then, full of anxiety, proceeded to Rome ; but before he arrived there, he was informed of the death of

Innocent V. The Cardinal Protector of the Servites was chosen to fill the Chair of Peter in succession to the deceased Pontiff; but five weeks only after his election he too was called from this world. The Servants of Mary now had recourse to his successor John XXI., who, after a favourable consultation, held by the Consistorial pleaders, decided that the Order should continue to exist under the same conditions as heretofore. Soon afterwards, however, John XXI. died, and after an interval of six months Cardinal Orsini, who was well disposed towards the Order, became Pope. He at once nominated the Cardinal, Latino Frangipani, Protector of the Order, in the spring of 1278. The Order was now safe, and could at length breathe freely, after this sharp trial which had continued for two whole years, during which time a most fierce tempest had raged against the work of the Seven holy Founders What pangs had not the three surviving Saints endured during this space! Yet, were they not overcome by their trial, for they were supported by a firm confidence in the promises made by their Most Blessed Mother.

St. Hugh, St Sostene, and St. Alexis again took up their accustomed life of prayer and good works: the two first-named at Monte Senario, and the third at Florence where he usually dwelt. St. Philip, too, resumed all his habitual occupations, which did not afford him one moment of leisure. Over and above these, he had now the laborious task of restoring peace within the bosom of the Order, which had been much disturbed by the threats of suppression proceeding from the Holy See, and by the attacks from without to which these had given rise. This storm was not, alas! to be the final one.

Four years later St. Philip again returned to Germany to answer the summons of the Emperor Rodolph, and to visit the houses of the Order; but before a twelvemonth had elapsed he was recalled to Italy. Martin IV., who had been elected Pope on the 22nd of February, 1281, was contemplating the inclusion of the Order in the decree of suppression issued by the Council of Lyons.

There was no time to be lost. It was the period at which the General Chapter was usually held. St. Philip summoned it to meet at Perugia, desiring most especially the presence of St Hugh and St. Sostene, whose far-seeing wisdom was indispensable under these critical circumstances. The two holy old men, in spite of their three score and ten years, left their solitude in obedience to the call of their Superior. The Chapter being opened, St. Philip gave a brief outline of the state of affairs, the alarming features of which he pointed out, concluding by desiring counsel from all present.

At this appeal St. Hugh, breaking the bonds of his habitual humility and silence, rose up to speak. He saw those around him cast down, and he felt it his duty to strive to inspire them with hope. With that simple and apostolic eloquence which is the prerogative of those who are closely united with God, he made a touching address, reminding his hearers that it was no new thing to see works highly pleasing in the sight of God, profitable for His glory, and fruitful for souls, decried and thwarted. They should not, therefore, fear and be troubled, but should look upon this trial as a proof of God's love, and a pledge of His divine protection. Our Lord has, indeed, promised to be with those who are in trouble ; and all good works come out of the furnace of persecution, intended for their destruction, far stronger and purer than before. This was seen when the Divine Master founded His Church upon earth. Neither could the lowly Servite Order escape from the operation of this law, that so it might be seen of all that the foundation and preservation of the Institute was no human work, but that it proceeded wholly from the intercession of the all-powerful Mother of God : and she who had protected it so wondrously in the past, would certainly not forsake it in this present peril. In conclusion, he advised that the Father-General should straightway betake himself to the Papal Court, in company of two of the most discreet Religious, and there strive to disperse the clouds which had gathered around the Order. The holy old man succeeded in his aim ; the hopes of his hearers were rekindled ; and seeing this, he spoke words of encouragement to St. Philip, whilst St. Sostene declared himself of the same opinion as his venerable brother.

In conformity with their advice, St. Philip accordingly hastened, in company with Blessed Lottaringo and Buonaventura, to Orvieto, where the Pontifical Court was then residing.

The two saintly Founders, soon after their return to Monte Senario, learned that St. Philip had so convincingly pleaded the cause of the Order, that Martin IV. had wholly relinquished all idea of suppressing it. This joyful news filled up the measure of their desires, and they continued uninterruptedly to pursue their life of retirement, prayer, and mortification, until they were once more summoned to the Chapter General, which was on this occasion to be held at Viterbo, before the 1st of May, 1282.

The Jubilee of the Order was now at hand ; soon it would enter on the fiftieth year of its existence. All were filled with joy at the approaching anniversary, in spite of the uncertainty in which the future was involved. This joy found expression at the meetings of the Chapter, and the two venerable Founders, Hugh and Sostene, were received with enthusiasm by all, from the Father-General to the youngest of the Brethren.

After their joyous welcome at Viterbo, St. Hugh and St. Sostene at the close of the Chapter hastened back to Monte Senario . the journey was long and occupied several days. They were accompanied by several other Fathers who were returning to their respective Convents. On the way the two saintly old men held converse

together : like the disciples at Emmaus they reminded each other of
all that had passed from the birth of the Order to this its year of
Jubilee. They recalled especially the most striking events which
had marked its history—the happy day when the Most Blessed
Virgin had inspired them with the design of quitting their life in
the world , the title of Servants of Mary bestowed upon them by
infant lips ; the miraculous picture, that heavenly masterpiece, at
the Santissima Annunziata ; and the extension of the Order into
several other countries. They spoke with admiration of the virtues
and holiness of their Father, St Philip ; of his great merits, which
obtained for him the grace of such marvellous works ; of his wisdom
and learning, which enabled him to draw so many souls to God ; of
all his gifts which, exerted to the fullest extent, made all the seed
which he had laboriously sown and watered spring up and bear good
fruit in the enclosure of the Order. Then they spoke of their holy
companions who had already departed, and of their deaths, precious
in the sight of God, by which they had passed to the life of unfading
blessedness. And, so speaking, they could not refrain from sighs
and tears, asking God most earnestly to reunite them speedily to
those beloved companions in the peace which knows no end.
"Alas !" they said, "why are our souls so long in exile, dwelling
with the inhabitants of Cedar ? Here we continually offend God
and our Brethren : we have never done one good thing. When
shall we depart ? When shall we say as our companions have done :
' Our soul hath escaped like a sparrow from the net of the fowler :
the snare is broken and we are delivered !' Alas ! this world is like
a deep sea, filled with venomous creatures. Everywhere is there
mourning, lamentation, and woe. O thrice-blessed souls who have
crossed the stormy ocean of this mortal life, and who are now safe in
the port of eternal salvation, we entreat you of your charity, now
that all your perils are over, to think of us who are still surrounded
by dangers. You are in the enjoyment of unfading glory, have pity
then on our wretchedness. O beloved Brethren, we beseech you, in
the Name of Him Who chose you and made you what you are, Who
gives you to drink of the torrent of His delights, and Who has made
you sharers of His immortality, forget not us your comrades in our
sorrow, bestow on us some consolation ; pray that we may not long
be separated from you. Intercede for us without ceasing, that it
may please Our Lord to deliver us poor sinners from this vale of
tears."

Whilst thus speaking, they halted from time to time, and knelt
down to pray. They had almost reached the crest of the mountain,
continuing unceasingly to lift up their hearts to Heaven, when
suddenly they heard a voice afar off, which thus addressed them :
"Men of God, weep no more ; rejoice, for soon will your prayer be
granted". Amazed, they lifted up their eyes and looked around

them, but could see no one. The mysterious voice filled them with
awe, and they dared not speak, but went on in silence till they
reached the monastery. They went at once to the Chapel to return
thanks to God for the glad tidings they had just heard ; and from
that time forward they joyfully awaited the longed-for day of their
departure, for which they prepared themselves by prayer and
penance They had not long to wait ; for both were shortly seized
with an illness, apparently slight at first, but which soon became
serious ; and they then received the last Sacraments amidst trans-
ports of holy joy at the prospect of their approaching deliverance.

These worthy Servants of Mary died as they had lived—with the
praises of their Queen upon their lips. Lying side by side upon
their poor beds of straw, they were reciting together the Crown of
Our Lady, when two Angels, approaching St. Sostene, spoke to him
in tones of heavenly sweetness "Come, O Sostene," they said,
"it is now time for that pure soul of thine to return to its Creator !"
And, bearing this precious pearl with them, they winged their way
upwards to the throne of Mary. St. Hugh, seeing this, cried out :
"O Sostene, my beloved brother, wait, I beg of thee, wait for me !"
And, as he was thus speaking, his soul, too, took flight, and, being
received by one of the Angels, was presented, together with that of
St. Sostene, to the Most Blessed Virgin, amidst the joyful acclamations of the whole Court of Heaven.

That very night, after the two holy Founders had breathed their
last sigh, St. Philip, whilst at prayer, fell into an ecstasy He beheld
two Angels who, plucking two beautiful lilies on the holy mountain,
offered them to Our Lady, and she, receiving them with a radiant
smile, presented them to her Son, and He then placed them together
in a precious vase for all the heavenly hosts to contemplate their
beauty, and to admire in them a perfect model of brotherly love.
By this mystical vision, St. Philip knew that the two Saints had
departed to the life eternal.

When morning came, calling together his Brethren, he said to
them : " Rejoice, my brothers, the two lilies which flourished in our
field, amidst the warfare of this world, have been transplanted to the
garden of the heavenly Jerusalem, where now they bloom in the
presence of the Lord The venerable Fathers, Hugh and Sostene,
who, with their five companions, founded this our Order, who with
us have laboured to spread the Gospel, have fallen asleep this night,
and now flourish like two olive-trees. and stand like burning lamps in
the Divine Presence. Their tongues are now as keys to open to us
the gates of heaven. Let us, therefore, beseech them to intercede for
us, that we may one day with them partake of the life eternal."

It is thus that Poccianti records these two deaths. Nicolo Mati
gives us the same narrative in his quaintly simple style, as follows :
" In 1282 the Blessed Hugh and Sostene, two of our first Founders,

departed to God. It was they who, when asking for alms in the streets of Florence, were for the first time greeted by the name of Servants of Mary by the lips of infants at the breast, who spoke by heavenly inspiration. Together they went to Germany to spread the Order, and to glorify God by their labours and good example among the heretics, showing themselves always most humble, devout, patient, and mortified, more like Angels than mortal men. And so many marvels did they work that the Florentines spared not openly to call them Saints. When they were worn out by age, the saintly Father, Philip Benizi, permitted them, for their consolation, to withdraw to the holy mountain. As they journeyed thither, kindling their hearts by speaking of death and the glory to come, they heard a voice from heaven, and all things fell out as they had foreseen ; for soon afterwards they both fell sick and died, as they had lived, like Saints, reciting together the Crown of Our Lady, on the third of May This was revealed to our Father, St. Philip, in a vision, wherein he beheld two Angels plucking two lilies upon the holy mountain and presenting them to Our Lady. ' My children,' he said, now I know that our two holy Founders are dwelling in paradise.'"

Thus gently passed away these two Saints, whose chief characteristics were simplicity of soul, gentleness of heart, and a great love for retirement and silence. United by the bonds of holy friendship to their five companions, they were yet more closely linked to each other by an attachment no less holy, springing direct from the source of all love, whereby brotherly affection is expanded and purified from all earthly dross. During the course of their long lives they often dwelt together : we are told, indeed, that they shared the same grotto, and that it was there that they expired almost at the same moment. It would seem that their friendship must have been pleasing in the sight of God, since during their lifetime He stamped on their countenances an expression of great holiness, and since He favoured them by permitting them to depart together in perfect peace. The hearts of Saints are full of tenderness, since they possess in abundance that which Almighty God possesses in infinite fulness : they are overflowing with charity. Of this, the first-fruits are poured out upon God, and upon Mary, the purest of His creatures ; but they have still a heaped-up measure left to bestow, without stint, upon their Brethren, of which they reserve a choice portion for those whose dispositions and tone of thought are most in accordance with their own. Among these ranked St Hugh and St. Sostene, and thus they have left us an example, by no means uncommon in religion, of faithful friendship grafted on charity, and bringing forth fruits of holiness.

Six of the Founders had now left this vale of tears, and only St. Alexis remained. From this time forth he was the only witness left of the original number, to give testimony of the life and works of

St Philip, and of the progress and the many vicissitudes of the Order. He remained at Florence, fulfilling the same lowly duties as before, edifying all by his life, and inclining all hearts to virtue. He continued to make his rounds in quest of alms ; and these were always to him so many opportunities of doing good work for souls He never relaxed in his zealous efforts to procure for the younger members of the Order sufficient funds to enable them to complete their studies at the University of Paris. His influence over his own relatives was great, and productive of the happiest results: he constantly impressed upon them all the vanity of earthly possessions ; but his special work among them was to train for God his young niece Juliana, who had been born to his brother Chiarissimo in his old age. Many in the city came to consult him , even the magistrates of Florence often sought his counsel.

In the silent obscure life which he led, his thoughts turned much to St. Philip, who to him represented in some sort the whole Order. He kept up constant communications with his beloved General, whose headquarters were at Florence. All the concerns of St. Philip were at once known to the venerable Founder who rejoiced in his joys and mourned over his trials Thus passed three years, during which St. Philip completed his allotted task, and made a final, though fruitless, effort to place the Order in a position of perfect security. Then came the hour of his departure.

On the 20th of May, 1285, he presided over the Chapter General at Florence ; and shortly afterwards he received an intimation from on high that the day of his death was not far off. Being thus warned, he hastened to put all things in order, gave his final instructions to St. Juliana, whom he had received into the Third Order during the preceding year , passed several days in strict retreat at Monte Senario ; and gathering the Capitular Fathers together at Florence, on the 14th of July, he bade them a last farewell, often repeating these words, "Love one another, my children, love one another". Lastly, having nominated Blessed Lottaringo his Vicar-General, he set forth accompanied by him Before leaving, St. Philip saw St. Alexis for the last time . each gave expression to the devoted affection which had ever subsisted between them, and they parted with the promise to meet again in heaven, before the throne of their Mother Mary

By short stages St. Philip reached Tivoli, beyond Rome, whither the Pope had retired. There he obtained an audience from Honorius IV., who received him with the utmost kindness, but did not touch upon the still disputed point of the approbation of the Order. The Saint left the charge of this matter to Blessed Lottaringo, and proceeded to Todi, where the Order possessed an extremely poor Convent, and where for this reason St. Philip, in his humility, desired to die and to be buried.

At the gates of Todi he moved to repentance two poor abandoned women, named Flora and Helena, who afterwards became noted for the holiness of their lives. he then entered the town, where he met with an enthusiastic reception. The following day, the 10th of August, St Philip preached : on the Feast of the Assumption he once more spoke of Mary, in tones which seemed not to belong to this world. That afternoon, about three o'clock, he was seized with a violent fever. He told the Community that he should die on the following Wednesday, being the Octave of the Feast, and from that moment he ceased not to edify, instruct, and console his spiritual children, who surrounded his humble bed. On the 21st of August, he prepared himself with the most vivid faith, the deepest humility, and the most ardent charity to receive the last Sacraments. He insisted upon kneeling to make his confession , and on the 22nd of the month, after praying for a long time prostrate upon the ground, he received the Body of Our Lord with an expression of countenance more seraphic than human. He then seated himself upon his bed, and prayed at considerable length, reciting the Penitential Psalms and the Litany of the Saints. Hardly had he ended, when he became unconscious, and for three hours he remained apparently lifeless. At this moment Blessed Ubaldo Adimari, one of his spiritual sons, who had come in haste from Monte Senario, entered the cell and called loudly upon the Father, who, as though awaking from a deep sleep, recognized Ubaldo, and leaned lovingly upon his shoulder. Then, making a great effort, he spoke briefly of the fearful assaults which he had suffered from the Evil Spirit, and from which his soul had been delivered by the merciful interposition of Jesus and Mary. When he ceased speaking Extreme Unction was administered at his desire Thus inwardly strengthened by the reception of the holy rite, the end was gradually drawing nearer, when he suddenly became agitated, and appeared to be seeking something, in the meantime calling eagerly for "his book". Those about him knew not what book he meant, and accordingly they offered him several, but he put them from him. At length one of the Religious gave him a Crucifix, and this he seized, joyfully exclaiming, "Yes, this is my book ! From it I have learnt everything : it has taught me how to follow in the footsteps of my Master, and has shown me the way to heaven." Then, having recited the thirtieth Psalm, "In Thee, O Lord, have I hoped," he saw in a vision Mary and her Divine Child smiling upon him, and into their hands he gave up his blessed soul, and thus ended his earthly pilgrimage.

The news of his death speedily reached Florence. All the Religious of the Order were overwhelmed with grief, but the sad tidings flooded the soul of St. Alexis with an even deeper sorrow. For he who had justly been styled the Eighth Founder of the Order was now no more ; and henceforward, of those eight souls chosen by the

Mother of God herself, there remained but the humble recluse of Cafaggio. To him, in the mysterious designs of Providence were to be allotted twenty-eight years more upon earth, to enable him to witness the progress and the definitive recognition of the Order, and that in him might be seen a representative of the Servites who had beheld the birth of the Institute, its growth amidst grievous trials, and finally its establishment on an unshakable foundation by the supreme decision of the Holy See.

CHAPTER XII.

𝖣efinitive 𝔄pprobation of t𝔥e 𝖮rder—𝔖t. 𝔄lexis— 𝔥is 𝖣eat𝔥.

(1285—1310.)

MORE than fifty years had passed away since our Seven Saints had heard the call of Mary in the Confraternity of the *Laudesi*, and six of them had left this world for heaven before being permitted to see their work safe from all danger. As in turn they bade farewell to earth, their beloved Order was still like a fragile bark driven hither and thither by the winds and the waves. Doubtless, amidst the bliss which was now theirs beside the throne of the Queen of Heaven, it was given them to know that the tempest would cease; that, although it might yet rage for awhile, it would not endure for ever. Yet, in their mortal lives they had suffered, as it were, a martyrdom by slow fire from not knowing how or when the trial would end.

St. Philip, their beloved disciple, in whom they had all seemed to be born again, who had been the soul of their souls and the mirror of their virtues, was now, himself, no more. He too had departed with the same thorn of anxiety piercing his heart. Perhaps he felt it more acutely than any of them, having more accurately gauged the danger, from knowing how deadly was the hatred with which the foes of the Order were filled But, from these haunting apprehensions he was now set free, for he had passed to the clear vision of the One and Only Good; and Mary, his beloved Mother, was the channel whereby the secrets of futurity were gradually revealed to him, and he was shown the frail bark safe in port, after having battled with the storm for the allotted term of years Thus, for those who had quitted the earth, all sorrow was ended; and sorrow was succeeded by peace and joy and unalloyed happiness.

One alone of the Founders still survived, St. Alexis Falconieri. It was necessary, in the designs of God's Providence, that a witness should remain who had seen the birth of the Order; who, himself a

Founder, preserved intact the spirit of his colleagues; who knew what had been their designs; and that this witness should be reserved to see the triumph of the Order after its many and prolonged struggles. It was the humblest of the Seven who was chosen for this lot. He it was who was to be the representative of his departed Brethren during the final revolutions through which the Order had to pass, and therefore his life was prolonged far beyond the usual term.

St. Alexis had become the dearer to his Brethren, since on him was concentrated all the veneration and love which would have been shared by the other holy Founders and St. Philip had they been still living But the saintly old man would not hear of any special indulgence or privilege being accorded to him. He continued to practise all the austerities of his Rule as he had done for fifty years. Father Niccolo Mati, the Chronicler of Pistoja, has left us in his simple narrative so touching a picture of our Saint that it would be a pity to omit a word. "How many obligations (he says) are we not under to that holy old man! Our Lady called him from the Confraternity of the *Laudesi* with our other Blessed Fathers, when he was thirty-three years old, and he never lost his baptismal innocence. He was learned, too, for he had studied with much diligence, leaving to his brother the care of their house and of their business. Never would he consent to be ordained, for he had so lowly an opinion of himself that he seemed to be as nothing in his own eyes; he was the servant of all, he undertook all the begging rounds, all the most wearying and most lowly tasks; he was ever cheerful, and he prayed continually Being full of zeal for our holy Order, he made it a great point that the young Religious should study diligently and be holy; and to obtain means for sending Brother Clement and Brother Christopher, and many others, to Paris, he became a beggar, asking money from those who were friendly to us.

"So great was the esteem in which he was held by the Florentine Republic, that for him to ask a favour was to obtain it. It was he who built at Cafaggio the courtyard, and the dormitory, and the whole of the Church besides. All that we know of the first beginning of our Order is from what he related to Brother Pietro di Todi; we should otherwise be ignorant on this point. A holy old man he was, in truth, for he never lost his baptismal innocence. Owing to the severity of his mortifications, he was nothing but skin and bone he always slept in his habit: he wore a hair shirt under his tunic, next to his skin; his bed was usually but a few planks laid on the bare ground. How many, owing to his example, led holy lives, both in the Order and elsewhere! He disciplined himself nightly; and for many years he fasted continually on bread and water, scarcely ever taking wine"

Another chronicler—the above-named Pietro da Todi—has preserved for us, from his own personal knowledge, some remarkable characteristics of the life led by the holy old man, when bent by the weight of more than a hundred years. After a few introductory words, the chronicler devotes himself especially to putting before his readers the marvellously mortified spirit shown by the Saint, and the perfection of his humility and of his charity.

"Of my own consciousness I know," he says, "and with mine own eyes have I seen, that the life of Father Alexis was such as to draw all who beheld his virtues to follow him . for his life was in itself a convincing proof of his own perfection and that of his companions, as well as of the excellence of the Order to which he belonged.

"Notwithstanding his great age, the weakness of his body, and the length of time during which he had borne the burden and heat of the day, he never sought any of those things which others reasonably look for—neither rest, nor food suited to his failing health, nor warmer clothing, nor a softer bed for his wearied limbs On the contrary, far from desiring more delicate food, he always took thankfully his share of what was served to all in the common Refectory. Even when he was too ill to go to the Refectory with the Community, he would allow nothing to be set before him different from what his Brethren had. At the most, he sought in the garden for a few strengthening herbs. In what concerned clothing, he had a great horror of anything of finer texture than ordinary ; but he was extremely discreet in this matter, always wearing garments of medium quality—neither too squalid nor too fine. He would never suffer a bed to be provided for him, even when his infirmities seemed to make one needful ; but, as all who dwelt in the Convent have affirmed, even in his most advanced years his preparations for sleep were of the roughest kind. So far from shunning hard work, as at his great age would have been only natural, he sought for it eagerly, in spite of the frequent remonstrances of the Brethren, giving his whole strength to it, and often undertaking more than he could actually get through.

"Both in his words and in his actions, he practised humility and charity to an unequalled degree. The holiness of his life was plainly to be seen of all. The Brethren all held him in veneration, as being one of the First Seven Founders by means of whom Our Lady had been pleased to establish her Order ; yet did he never pass by any opportunity of humbling himself. However hard or disagreeable any employment might be, he took it in turn with the youngest Brothers, working at it till his strength gave way. As long as he could do so, he went upon the begging rounds, taking upon himself this wearisome task with as much alacrity as though he had been the sturdiest and lowest member of the Community ; and though the Brothers did all they could to circumvent him, he never would allow his turn to be passed over. And it was just the same with all other conventual duties, such as the world consider slowly and degrading: he made a point of fulfilling them like the rest of the Brethren. Thus did he exercise charity towards them, whilst the humility of his heart was made manifest to all ; and thus he gave to those who aimed at perfection an example meet to inspire them with courage for that undertaking"

These traits, so simply recorded by our two chroniclers, give us a more complete idea of Alexis than we could gather from a lengthy biography or from an elaborate panegyric. As we read of the unshakable resolve with which he persevered in his utterly obscure life, in the most absolute poverty ; we recognize in him one of those types, rare even in the annals of sanctity, which put us to the blush, as we contrast their strength with our own feebleness. And the humble Brother of Cafaggio gained additional merit owing to his abnormal longevity ; for it is given to few to sustain heroic virtue, and to practise unceasingly the duties of the Religious life, during so long a span of years.

His mortified life. together with his many other virtues, gave great weight to his words ; and he never lost an opportunity of instilling into his hearers the true spirit of the Order. One of his instructions on this matter has been preserved. It is exceedingly touching, and may be looked upon as his spiritual bequest to his Brethren.

"My little children," he said, "the spirit of our Order is far loftier and more noteworthy than that of the sons of St. Francis and of St. Dominic ; for our aim is to attain sanctity ourselves and to make others holy by meditating and causing others to meditate with true compunction of heart upon the Sorrows of the most afflicted Mother of God and the Passion of her Beloved Son. Whatsoever trials and persecutions you may have to undergo, believe me, you can never be overcome so long as you diligently do the will of Our Blessed Lady ; but woe to you if you are disobedient ! My dear children, I am telling you what I heard from the lips of our heavenly Patroness herself, whose Servants we are : therefore, believe these words and trust in them. Blessed will you be if you obey them ! "

Michael Poccianti, the famous chronicler of the sixteenth century, has gathered together in a charming sketch all the most salient features of this life so enlightened by holiness. "Blessed Father Alexis," he writes, " was, both in the world and in Religion, God's servant in the fullest meaning of the word. In the world he was, from his earliest youth, so devoted to his duties, to study, and to the practice of virtue, that he was looked upon by all as a model of excellence. Those who followed in his footsteps, though far behind, yet felt assured that they were on the right path. This pious youth, as did another Alexis in Rome, scorned the advantages of birth and of wealth, and, with his companions, he forsook a condition of prosperity in his native place. He took up his abode on the crest of a rugged mountain, and there he spent his days in fastings, temptations, prayer, and mortifications of every kind. From his lips no words fell but such as were modest and edifying, and his hands were continually engaged in virtuous and holy works. He held rank and honours to be vain and fleeting vanities, since the truest glory is to be humble and of no account in the household of God. Several times was he chosen Provincial, and even General, but he would never take office. He was ever firm in the practice of the faith, whereby he overcame the world, and his meekness of spirit enabled him to bear all the rough and sharp trials of life. When he was in the company of others, his countenance was always calm and cheerful, so as not to depress them ; yet he was never known to laugh loudly. He lived to a great age, although his constitution was undermined by several diseases, and although he was troubled by many infirmities ; but his soul remained youthful and did not bend under the burden of the weak body. He undertook all kinds of work allotted to the younger Brethren, continuing meanwhile to fast, to keep vigil, and to pray, so that all wondered at him and feared for him. He only drank wine when forced to do so under obedience ; even then, he mingled it with so large a quantity of water that hardly any flavour of wine remained. He was scarcely ever absent from the Night Office, and was never known to miss the Sacred Office by day. He was always the first in Choir and the last to leave it. When he assisted at the great and tremendous Sacrifice, he often shed tears. In the Refectory, he ate of the same food that was served to all ; and if any special dish was prepared for him, he either refused it, or he took it so reluctantly that the Brethren were distressed to see him. His great delight was to relate the first beginnings of the Order, to tell of the heroic lives of his companions, and to recall to his spiritual children all that God had permitted to take place in former years, that thus the memory of these things might never be effaced from their minds. His hearers took such delight in listening to him that they seemed ravished with his discourse. It was not wonderful that such should be the case, for he was all on fire with charity, eager for all good works, most humble-hearted, and exceedingly gentle in speech. And therefore did he find favour with men, and not less with God, before Whose Throne he now intercedes for us."

From his beloved retreat at the Santissima Annunziata, in Florence, St. Alexis watched the gradual succession of events until the close of his long life. He followed them attentively both with heart and intellect, for the Order was all in all to him. If the thoughts and feelings to which the vicissitudes of more than thirty years gave rise in his mind could have been recorded for us, we should now be in possession of the life history of one of the most beautiful of souls.

At length, after the many anxieties and trials which marked the fifteen years' Generalate of Blessed Lottaringo, St. Philip's successor, St. Alexis beheld the dawn of a new epoch for the Servants of Mary. It had taken nearly twenty years to bring about this change in the prospects of the Order; but now the final approval of the Holy See was about to be granted. Father Andrea Balducci, who was elected General after the death of Blessed Lottaringo, was the instrument through whom it pleased God to bestow this favour; and it was by the voice of the Pope Benedict XI., a member of the Dominican Order, of happy memory, that the long-contested right of the Servants of Mary to a corporate existence was finally proclaimed. Barely four months after the accession of Benedict XI., the question was thoroughly gone into and decided in the most favourable terms: the Apostolic letters, approving unreservedly of the Order of the Servants of Mary, were signed by the Sovereign Pontiff, acting in the fulness of his authority. We give the letters in full ·

"Benedict, Bishop, Servant of the Servants of God:

"To Our well-beloved Sons, the General, and all the Priors and Brethren of the Servants of St. Mary, Order of St. Augustine, health and the Apostolic benediction:

"When We cast Our eyes around, contemplating on all sides (as it is Our duty to do, being Shepherd of the fold) the flock which the Lord, notwithstanding Our unworthiness, has committed to Our care, in accordance with the designs of His Wisdom, We anxiously watch, to the best of the capacity which has been given to Us, over those who toil in the vineyard of the Lord God of Hosts, that they should apply themselves to the work of saving souls so zealously as to extend more and more the branches of the Vine, and to cause it to bring forth more abundant fruits of holiness   Doubtless, Our Apostolic solicitude extends over all who labour in the vineyard, more especially those who belong to ecclesiastical bodies; but it is fitting that Our chief care should be for those Religious who, having crushed under foot all worldly temptations, are unceasingly striving to lead a life of holiness in the contemplation of heavenly things: it is fitting that these should possess a more abundant share of Our goodwill, since they are more especially devoted to the defence of the Holy See. Undoubtedly, you, who belong to the Order of St. Augustine approved by the Apostolic See, you have, on the one hand, moved by devotion to the Blessed and Glorious Virgin Mary, taken from her your title, humbly styling yourselves her Servants; and, on the other hand, you have nevertheless up to the present time continued to observe (and therefore do We commend you) the Rule of the said Order of St. Augustine, and do still observe it, as your own Rule piously and laudably prescribes. Moreover, the Holy See has granted you, by special privilege, the faculties for summoning a General Chapter and for electing thereat a General who shall have authority to correct the Brethren of the Order, and freely to fulfil all the duties of his Office ; and you have also been granted permission to inter within your precincts those who desire burial in your houses. Considering all these things, it is evident to whosoever examines into the matter that your Rule has been already in great measure tacitly confirmed by the Apostolic See. Now We, who are desirous of testifying to Our Blessed Lady as much devotion as is in Our power, would on no account suffer the possibility of any attack being made either upon yourselves individually or upon your Rule, as though the said Rule had not received the fulness of the Apostolic Sanction : and in order to dismiss from the minds of all the faintest doubt upon this point, and in answer to your petitions, We, in virtue of Our Apostolic Authority and in the most explicit manner, confirm, nay more, We approve, with all the additional weight of this decree, your Rule and all the provisions thereof : We grant you this Rule, and we desire that it may ever be inviolably observed by you. Henceforth, it is absolutely forbidden to any person whomsoever to criticise or to oppose this paper containing Our confirmation, approbation, concession, and decree. If anyone shall venture upon so great a presumption, let him know that he will thereby incur the wrath of Almighty God and of His Blessed Apostles Peter and Paul.

"Given at the Lateran, on the third of the Ides of February (11th), in the first year of Our Pontificate (1304).

" BENEDICT XI., Pope."

By this formal and explicit approbation, Benedict XI. finally closed a dispute of sixty years' standing. He destroyed at one stroke all the arguments of the opponents of the Order, and he placed, as it were, in the hands of the Servants of Mary a two-edged sword, wherewith to smite both those who refused to allow the new Religious to belong to the recognised Order of St. Augustine, and those who denied them the privilege of constituting an independent Order, that of the Servants of Mary. From this day forth, the Order enjoyed the fruits of its labours in peace ; the cloud which had cast so gloomy a shadow over the past had now vanished, and the toils and anxieties of the Seven Holy Founders at length received a well-earned reward.

Benedict XI. had evaded with great skill the technical difficulties caused by the decrees of the Councils of Lateran and of Lyons. In the widest interpretation of the terms, no new Order had been founded ; it was simply an offshoot which had sprung from an Order already existing. Consequently, the decision of the Lateran

Council was in no wise departed from. On the other hand, this new branch could not be said to belong to the ranks of the mendicants, since, in point of fact, it possessed, or even if this were the case, it benefited by the authorisations granted to the Augustinians. In no way whatsoever, therefore, could it be said to violate the decrees of the Council of Lyons.

Moreover, the Pope had, by the wording of his Bull, sanctioned the special object of the Order, which was to devote itself chiefly to the service of the Blessed Virgin. He showed that the characteristic devotions of the Servants of Mary was an essential feature of the Order, and, in fact, the cause and origin of its existence.

In pursuance of his design, which was to place the entire organization of the Institute beyond the reach of any further attacks, he verified the authenticity of the Constitutions and of the privileges granted by the Sovereign Pontiffs, his predecessors ; thus showing that he considered all the internal legislation of the Order as being already confirmed by the Holy See. But, in order that no shadow of doubt might remain, the Pontiff was pleased to give, both to the Institute and to its regulations, his entire and explicit approbation

At the news of this great boon granted by the holy Pontiff, Benedict XI., the whole Order was filled with gladness, which found vent in various ways. Among other tokens of joy they sang all those verses of Holy Scripture in which the Latin signification of the Pope's name, Benedictus (blessed), was to be found, as "Blessed be the Lord God of Israel, because He hath visited and wrought the redemption of" the Servants of the Blessed Virgin Mary. "Blessed is he that cometh in the Name of the Lord."

Unquestionably, this approbation was a priceless boon to the Order, for Benedict XI.'s reign only lasted eight months and seventeen days ; and his successor, Clement V., who was French by birth, after four years spent in moving from one part of France to another, took up his abode finally, in 1309, at Avignon, which made the transaction of business extremely difficult for all who dwelt in Italy.

Among all the Servite Religious, overflowing with happiness as they were, one seemed to have a special right to rejoice and be thankful. This was the humble lay brother of Cafaggio, St Alexis, the only Founder of the Seven who survived to witness the triumph of his Order. Since St. Philip had slept the sleep of the just, now almost twenty years ago, St. Alexis had watched over the many vicissitudes through which his beloved flock had passed, his heart meanwhile fluctuating between hope and fear, but sustained by an inward conviction that Mary, the Queen of Heaven, would never forsake her Servants. This confidence was at last rewarded by the fulfilment of his ardent desires, and he could not sufficiently express his gratitude.

St. Alexis had made no change in his way of life since the burden of years had begun to weigh him down Although he had reached the great age of a hundred and four, he was not surpassed by the youngest brother in the rigorous observance of discipline, in the severity of his mortifications, or in the punctuality of his attendance at the Divine Office both by night and by day. He was a standing model of holiness to all the Community , and his peaceful, smiling countenance seemed to impart cheerfulness and tranquillity to all who beheld him. He was ever ready to answer any questions about the early days of the Order, and to satisfy the natural curiosity of the Brethren upon this subject. But, towards the close of his life, these recollections of the past moved him so deeply as often to cause him to shed tears ; and it therefore became necessary to be sparing of allusions to the topic, since any emotion was now hurtful to his weakened frame. Pietro da Todi, however, gathered from him sundry particulars which he has recorded in his chronicle.

As the days went on, the holy old man grew weaker and weaker ; but nothing could persuade him to relax the severity of discipline, which he unflinchingly observed as in former years. At length it became necessary to put him under obedience, in order to overcome his predilection for penance. Fathers Giovanni di Pesei and Adimario degli Adimari, who were successively Priors of Cafaggio towards the close of St. Alexis' life, were obliged to exert the whole weight of their authority to induce him to sleep on straw instead of on the bare ground, and to eat a small quantity of meat. He did not long indulge in these mitigations of his Rule, for he shortly announced that his death was at hand, and he even named the exact day of his departure ; and he at once set about his preparations for the reception of the Last Sacraments.

All the Brethren gathered round the lowly bed on which St. Alexis was stretched ; and whilst they grieved to see the holy old man, whom they loved as the kindest of Fathers, about to breathe his last, they beheld with joy the heavenly expression which dwelt upon his wasted features. The dying Saint, having returned fervent thanks to Almighty God for having vouchsafed to visit and strengthen him for the great journey, spoke touchingly to those around him, exhorting them to observe his two cherished virtues—humility and purity. He then began to recite, as was his daily practice, one hundred *Aves ,* and whilst his lips uttered the praises of the spotless Virgin, his eyes were raised with a smiling expression towards heaven, where he appeared to contemplate some glorious vision seen by him alone. Suddenly he paused in his prayer, exclaiming, "My Brothers, do you not see the holy Angels round me under the form of doves ? Kneel down, my brothers—kneel down and adore the Infant Jesus, who is crowning me See you now, we shall all have a share in this crown if we practise purity and religious humility, and if we endeavour to imitate the most pure and humble Mother of God, our heavenly Patroness." He then finished repeating his hundred *Aves,* and, as he concluded them, his pure soul took its flight to the throne of God

Father Lapo Benizi, one of the Religious of the Order, and a holy and upright man, was present with the other Fathers of Cafaggio at this deathbed ; and he afterwards declared upon oath that he had himself seen birds of snowy whiteness fluttering round the Saint, and in the midst of them the Infant Jesus, holding a crown of flowers, which He placed on the head of the dying patriarch, whose soul, a few moments later, He carried back with Him to heaven.

Father Niccolo Mati has left a description of this scene, written with all the charming simplicity which marks his style ; and truly it may be said that it was a scene more calculated to console than to sadden those who witnessed it. " Happy old Saint that he was ! " Mati writes. "Jesus called him to His Paradise after seventy-seven years of faithful service ; for he was one hundred and ten years old when he died.

"All our Brethren hastened to surround his deathbed ; and truly it was a joy to all to see how he welcomed death. He saw doves flying about him : these must have been Angels under that form, for certainly no birds could have got in by any natural means. And all of a sudden he called out joyously : ' Kneel down, all of you ; do you not see Jesus ? Happy are those who serve Him faithfully, with great humility and purity, for a glorious crown awaits them ! ' And then he repeated, as was his custom, one hundred *Ave Marias,* and when he had said the last of these, he died. All the people were deeply grieved, for they held Alexis to be a Saint And for many days they were allowed to come from all parts to venerate the holy remains ; after which Father Amideus, the Prior, caused the body to be carried to the holy mountain to rest with those of our other saintly Fathers."

Such was the death of the last of our Seven Founders. It is impossible to imagine one more peaceful or more beautiful ; and it fitly crowned a life so fragrant with the sweet odour of sanctity. Even whilst yet on earth, the humble lay brother who had spent so many years in obscurity and lowliness was honoured more than any monarch ; for Jesus, the King of kings, with the Angels, who are His ministers, had visited him, making themselves visible even to his mortal senses. How triumphant, then, must have been his entry into heaven, bearing with him the record of his hundred and ten years of innocence, during which he had preserved his baptismal robe free from stain ! By his own choice he had remained the last and least of his companions. By the Divine Will he was the last of them to reach the abode of the blessed. May we not believe, also, that in him, as the reward of his heroic humility and his long years of toil, were verified the words of the Master, "The last shall be first"?

Certainly no more beautiful or fitting scene could have been pictured wherewith to close the story of these seven men of God and Servants of Our Blessed Lady. The last moments of him who so long survived the others are in keeping with the lives of all. Here we can trace the plan of the great Designer by Whom these seven souls were so closely knit together as to form but one: the object which He has had in view throughout becomes more and yet more clearly visible; and we may without hesitation declare that Mary, in the Divine Intelligence, was the primary cause of this design, as in its execution she was the final end and aim.

Our task would now be ended were it not necessary to its completion that we should give a brief outline of the virtues of which our Saints left such bright examples to the world, a hasty sketch of the generation of Saints who were their spiritual children; a list of the numerous foundations in existence at the death of the last survivor of their number; and lastly, the history of their Canonization. Under each of these heads the lives of the Seven Founders of the Servants of Mary may be said to be prolonged beyond their actual term, and therefore to make these additional chapters a biographical necessity.

CHAPTER XIII.

Heroic Virtues of the Founders—A Holy Generation —Numerous Descendants.

THE Seven Founders of the Order of the Servants of Mary were Saints, for they practised all virtues in the heroic degree, and it is in this that true saintliness consists These heroic virtues are the most precious portion of the inheritance which, when leaving this world, they bequeathed to their spiritual children; and, since the records thereof which remain to us are scattered here and there in the pages of their lives, it may be well to gather these together, as it were, in a trophy, so that their grandeur and beauty may be seen of all men And it is the more needful that this should be done, since the heroic humility of the Seven Saints caused them carefully to conceal any facts which were likely to redound to their honour.

First and foremost, we find that the whole of their supernatural life was built and founded upon the theological virtue of Faith. Faith, which soars at once to God as the Only and Sovereign Good, was to them the very principle of existence. By Faith they dwelt continually amid those things unseen which they alone loved and sought. In their eyes, thus enlightened by the divine glory, all earthly splendour seemed faded and worthless : wealth, honours, pleasure, were but as smoke which a breath disperses. All that is of faith they believed beyond the possibility of a doubt. All that we are taught by faith concerning the existence of God, the Most Holy Trinity, the Divinity of Our Lord Jesus Christ, Our Blessed Lady, the Church, and the life everlasting—all these topics were to them the only subjects of real importance ; and in accordance with this belief was their conduct—no human considerations ever entering into their thoughts or their scheme of action. The penetrating light of this faith colours the whole of their lives in a remarkable manner. It was this faith which preserved them in their youth from all the attractions which pleasure offers to its votaries, by pointing out to them, as their supreme object, the First and Only Fair. It enabled them to fulfil their vocation when Mary called them to her, by inspiring them with courage to break the bonds which might otherwise have held them back It made them carry out their great work—the foundation of the Servite Order—in defiance of all obstacles, by showing them that such was the will of God, and that, therefore, they must ultimately triumph over whatsoever opposition they might encounter. It was this faith, in short, which gave them strength to persevere in following their rule of life under the eye of the Great Master, ever ready to obey the least indication of His will, and devoutly serving Our Lady, thus sanctifying their own souls and labouring for the salvation of others And it was this which won for them the grace of dying happily, filled with sweet thoughts of Jesus and Mary, and of a blessed eternity.

From this lively faith which distinguished the Seven Saints sprang that great dread of offending God, which inspired them throughout their lives with an intense horror of sin, causing them to be perpetually on the watch to guard themselves from unlooked-for assaults ; and since their humility made them always distrustful of themselves, they put on the strong armour of penance and mortification, whereby they obtained the graces of a quiet conscience, of a soul possessing itself in peace, and of a cheerful spirit. We may thus judge how perfect was their faith, since we see how abundant were the graces which it procured for them.

The virtue of Hope was also practised by them in great perfection. In every phase of their lives, whether they were busied about their own sanctification or that of others, this strong hope in Almighty God, in Our Blessed Lord and His Most Holy Mother, never faltered for one moment. They confided themselves with child-like trustfulness to Our Lord, Who is infinite power, consummate goodness, and unfathomable love, and to His Mother Mary, who, of all creatures, approaches most nearly to His perfections. And, therefore, when, humanly speaking, their cause looked desperate, they were still buoyed up by hope ; and of them it may be truly said, in the words which St. Paul uses in speaking of the Patriarch Abraham, "against hope" they "believed in hope". Not all the many crosses and trials by which their work was assailed during so many years could depress them or shake their confidence. Their lives, under all circumstances, were sweetened by the thought that they belonged to Jesus and to Mary ; and their deaths were gladdened by the conviction that they were now about to "behold what they but dreamed before". Throughout their course they spared neither toil, nor prayers, nor tears, to obtain this blessed consummation, and their hope was not confounded.

All the virtues in which our Seven Saints abounded were built on the strong foundation of that peerless virtue—humility. Nothing is more marked in their lives than that absolute conviction of their own nothingness which possessed them. When they were members of the Confraternity of the *Laudesi*, they loved to be wholly undistinguished and hidden among their fellow-devotees. How gladly they withdrew from the world to live in obscurity at La Camarzia ! How did they rejoice to retire to the wild solitudes of Monte Senario ! How reluctant they were to turn their peaceful hermitage into a busy Novitiate ! When they were charged with the duty of founding an Order, how earnestly did they impress upon everyone that Our Lady was the sole Foundress, and that to her all the praise was due ! When they were placed at the head of their Order, how consistently did they conceal their gifts, keeping silence, and shunning every opportunity of being brought into notice. And, as the close of their lives approached, with what perfect absence of self-consciousness did each in turn retire to breathe his last unnoticed at Monte Senario ! What a marvel of humility was the prolonged life of St. Alexis ! It may, indeed, be said of all the Founders, that the stamp of humility was so deeply impressed on them, that it was undoubtedly their characteristic virtue.

Not less remarkable than their humility was their spirit of mortification, which remained unabated to the close of their lives From their earliest years they had waged war on their bodies, sometimes carrying their penitential rigour to the verge of imprudence ; but, ever obedient to the voices of those in authority over them, they avoided excess whilst maintaining unrelaxed severity. No mode of exterior penance was unfamiliar to them ; but, at the same time, they remembered that the most efficacious of all mortifications is that which chastens the heart and the will, making them ever submissive to the good pleasure of Almighty God. From the dawn to the close of their religious career they were ardent disciples of this virtue of mortification, which, in their truly enlightened eyes, seemed full of charms.

As they possessed the virtue of mortification, which seeks suffering for the body and inflicts it unshrinkingly, so were they also

accomplished in patience, which awaits suffering and accepts it un-
murmuringly. They had much to endure whilst living in the great
world of Florence which they abhorred. They had also much to
bear in consequence of their peculiar vocation, and of the work
which they were appointed to carry out. They were spared in
nothing—neither in bodily fatigues, nor in mental anguish, nor
in spiritual combats, nor in opposition from their Superiors in
religion, and even from their friends To all these trials they bowed
patiently, humbly, and in silence, rendering good for evil, and
calmly awaiting the passing of the storm, knowing that God gives
strength in proportion to the needs of each moment. And though
they were called to suffer poignantly and for many succeeding years,
their patience never failed ; and as it was supernatural, so did it
receive a supernatural reward when the final hour of triumph
sounded.

The Seven Founders also practised in the heroic degree those
three great virtues which are the triple cord of the Religious Life.
Their poverty was absolute. Despising all worldly possessions, they
renounced for ever everything in their power ; and having done this,
they passed the remainder of their days in the same condition of
utter poverty, having recourse as mendicants to public charity for the
supply of their daily needs. Whilst they observed exterior poverty,
they were wholly detached interiorly ; and having nothing whatever
which they could call their own, they died leaving their virtues to
be the sole inheritance of their spiritual children.

The joys of chastity were also theirs Having broken all those
ties which bound them to their homes and families, they looked
back no more, but remained henceforth severed from all that makes
so large a share of earthly happiness All their affections were concentrated on Jesus and Mary : nothing else appeared to them worthy
of a moment's thought. He, in Whom all beauty, all goodness, all
love are centred, was the object of their passionate attachment ; and
next to Him came Mary, so closely resembling her Divine Son.
Thus were their loving hearts so filled to overflowing that no
room was left for any earthly idol.

They also renounced the privileges mostly prized by men—those
of personal freedom and independence, by placing themselves under
strict obedience. In order to carry out this essential point of religious
discipline, they, for a considerable period, religiously obeyed one of
their number, their equal ; and subsequently they were frequently
under the orders of those who had been their disciples, and who
were their juniors. They did not enter into considerations with
respect to the age, the ability, or the qualifications of their Superior,
but obeyed him implicitly, seeing in him the visible delegate of the
Master, in Whom is all authority, and Who can confer it upon
whomsoever He pleases.

By the unceasing practice of these virtues they gave proof of possessing the queen of all of them, namely, Charity. The Seven Saints loved God with their whole heart, with their whole soul, and with their whole strength, and their love manifested all the tokens of true love. It was an active love which bore fruit in heroic actions throughout their lives. It was the fountain which fertilized all their other virtues, and which caused these to attain such heroic proportions. Their love was undivided; they sought none other; and they longed ardently for the moment when it would be theirs for ever, beyond all fear of change or loss. On this love they poured out the full power of their wills, keeping their hearts and their minds immutably fixed thereon. Their lives were an eager race, in which their love continually spurred them on, for the possession of the Sovereign Good. St. Amideus, in particular, often felt his heart so burning with this divine love, that he was forced to bathe his breast with cold water to temper that heavenly fire.

To this love of God the Founders joined a love of Our Lady, not of that feeble, lukewarm kind which many pious Christians entertain for her, but a love almost unequalled for loftiness, strength, and constancy. She was the mainspring of their lives, their consolation in all difficulties. She was first in their thoughts when they began any work, from her they drew inspiration during its progress; from her they looked for approval at its completion. They acknowledged that to her they owed everything; they gloried in being her Servants and in belonging wholly to her. They invoked her help in all difficulties, and in all tribulations they took refuge beneath her mantle. Their greatest joy was in serving her themselves, and in teaching others to know and to love her. For this purpose they crossed valleys and mountains, speaking to all of her greatness, of her sorrows, of her goodness. In their familiar intercourse, her praises were their constant theme, and they were ever ready for any undertaking calculated to increase the love and reverence wherewith she was regarded by the nations. Thus did they live and thus did they die, after having more than once enjoyed the privilege of beholding Mary herself descend from heaven to bestow on them a smile of maternal love.

Though their love was centred in God and Our Lady, yet it overflowed abundantly on the souls of men. They were most zealous in fulfilling all the duties of that charity which recognizes in every fellow-creature another self. They looked on all mankind with the eyes of faith, seeing in each one a soul loved from all eternity by God, Who had sent His Only begotten Son to become Incarnate and to die for its redemption. They made no distinction of persons, but rather preferred those most loved by Our Lord—the humble and the poor. They bore all the defects of others with gentleness, doing all in their power to edify them and lead them to virtue, performing penances for them, and refusing no labours, however painful, which might tend to set their feet on the path of salvation.

Great, too, was their love for Holy Church. In her life they lived, in her joys they rejoiced, in her sorrows they sorrowed. Whatever pain her decisions might cause them, they were wholly submissive to her decrees, which they obeyed unreservedly. They judged everything from her standpoint; they threw themselves heart and soul into all her interests ; and they gave all their powers to the carrying out of her mission, which is the salvation of the souls of all men.

This brief sketch will show our readers that the holiness of the Seven Founders of the Servite Order shone forth under the most various aspects Vainly did they strive to remain concealed by the enshrouding veil of humility. Their biographer can but represent them in their own colours, as true heroes of sanctity. Undoubted evidence of this was given by the miracles which in after years corroborated the witness of history insomuch that the Church no longer withholds from them the honour of being placed on her altars, but, by an irrevocable decree, has raised them thither in one bright constellation, thus recognizing in them followers of Our Lord, Who have imitated Him even to an heroic degree.

This accumulation of heroic virtues was the first legacy left by the Seven Founders to their spiritual posterity. As with veins of precious ore buried in the earth, we cannot tell how great may be the amount of the treasure ; but we know enough to be sure that, if it was brought to the surface, it would surpass our expectations. There was also another bequest made by our Seven Saints to their Order and to the Church, in the form of a whole generation of Saints springing up as if by magic to follow in their steps on earth, and to be the brightest jewels of their crown in heaven. It is but due to the memory of the Founders to make known in some degree this marvellous growth of sanctity which was fostered by their benign influence in the garden of divine grace.

At the head of all stands St. Philip Benizi, of whom we have already spoken, the most eminent among the disciples of the Seven Founders, both as regards his labours, the amount of good accomplished by him, and, above all, his holiness. So great was the splendour of his virtues as almost to cast into the shade those of the masters who had trained him in Religion, and whose chief glory he yet remains. No one ever more fully imbibed their spirit, or entered more thoroughly into their ideas, or more perfectly carried out their plans. He seemed to combine in himself all the finest qualities of each of them. He was—if we may use so modern an illustration— the telephone by which their words were transmitted to the outer world. He was their favourite son, their best beloved disciple. Had they done nothing else, to have given St Philip to the Church would have been enough to entitle them to the gratitude of succeeding generations.

But, when they trained St. Philip, they did more than give a great Saint to the Church. they gave to the world a leader of Saints. For Philip, who at the feet of Saints had himself learned to be a Saint, became in his turn the spiritual father of other Saints and Blessed, a whole cohort of whom surround him in heaven. At least twelve of this number, as stars of the first magnitude, encircle his head with a diadem of glory. It was he who first met them, as Our Lord met His disciples, and who, speaking to them of the things of God, touched their hearts, decided their vocations, enrolled them in the squadron of Our Lady's Servants, and sped them on the path of self-sacrifice, making them soldiers of Christ, lovers of the Cross, and children overflowing with filial tenderness for the Mother of Jesus.

Undoubtedly the largest share of merit belongs to him who first instilled the rudiments of sanctity into these chosen souls ; but some portion of the glory reverts to the Seven Saints from whom St. Philip had in great measure received what he so generously communicated to others. It is but just that some rays of the brightness of the third generation should be reflected back upon the first. The great Saint can lose no particle of his blessedness by this giving of honour where honour is due. Indeed, the twelve Saints and Blessed who were trained by St Philip belonged to the Order during the lifetime of the three last surviving Founders, with whom some of the number were privileged to hold personal intercourse ; and we may be sure that, like their own spiritual progenitor, they felt the love of virtue largely increased in their hearts as they contemplated three such admirable models of holiness

This garland of Saints comprises many and various types. We find in it the simplest wild flowers, as well as the most carefully cultivated blossoms. We need but give their names without comment ; they were : Blessed John of Frankfort, Blessed Joachim of Siena, Blessed Bonaventure Buonaccorsi, Blessed Andrew Dotti and Jerome, Blessed Ubaldo Adimari, Blessed Thomas of Germany, St. Peregrine Laziosi, St Juliana Falconieri, Blessed Francis Patrizi, and Blessed Helena and Flora.

St. Philip, escorted by his troop of Saints and Blessed, is a splendid jewel in the diadem of the Seven Fathers · so splendid, indeed, that he may well be judged unsurpassable. Yet we could add to this long list of names those of many others who died in the repute of sanctity, and whose lives were more closely linked to those of the Seven Founders. But here we find the same contrast as that which existed between the career of these venerable Fathers and that of their beloved son St. Philip. A brilliant light illumines the actions of those trained for God by the disciple, whilst deep obscurity enfolds every incident connected with those whom the Fathers taught to aspire to perfection. To begin with, all are not known to us, even by name ; and of those whose names have been preserved, only fragmentary notices remain. We only know that these followers of the saintly Founders were to be found in every branch of the Order : some among them were priests, others were lay brothers, others were simply members of the Third Order. Several of these heroic souls belonged to the weaker sex, and included both some who had vowed themselves to Our Lord as His spouses in the cloister, and others who, as Tertiaries, remained in the world, living with their families. We subjoin the names of a few of these disciples of the Seven Saints : Blessed Victor, Blessed Lottaringo della Stufa, Blessed Antony of Viterbo, Blessed Bartolo, Blessed Pangino Benincasa, Blessed Illuminata, Albaverde, Margaret of Montepulciano, and Giovanna Benizi.

We may, then, with truth aver that the Seven Founders were the fathers of a generation of Saints. In the spiritual firmament it is only stars of the first magnitude that are surrounded by satellites. Those Saints who stand forth conspicuously among the hosts of the blessed prove their pre-eminence by their spiritual fertility. And in this class we may, therefore, claim a place for the Seven Founders.

In addition to the splendid legacies of heroic virtues and of a whole generation of Saints and Blessed bequeathed to the Order, the Seven Founders left a third legacy, in the shape of a numerous progeny of spiritual descendants. This might, indeed, be termed a deed of gift made whilst they were yet living ; for, at the time of St. Alexis' death, in 1310, their children were already established in several parts of Europe, and numbered not less than ten thousand souls. This was a surprisingly rapid growth, especially when we take into consideration the many obstacles calculated to check the development of the Order, their limited resources, and the popularity of other Orders—more particularly those of St Francis and of St. Dominic. But the grace of God and the protection of Our Lady, with which favours the holy and heroic Founders fully co-operated, explain the enigma which would otherwise perplex us.

The Order was at this time divided into six Provinces, comprising about one hundred Convents. We subjoin the names of the different Provinces and of the principal Convents in each of them.

The first in rank, as in date, was the Province of Tuscany, containing the cradle of the Order, Monte Senario, and the residence of the General, Our Lady of Grace of Cafaggio, besides the Convents of Arezzo, Lucca, Montepulciano, Caminata, Pistoja, Prato, Siena, Città di Castello, and Selva di Casentino.

The second, inaugurated by St. Sostene, was the Province of Umbria and the Patrimony of St. Peter, and it was as rich in Convents as the Mother Province. It contained those of Celladi,

Barnicola, Borgo San Sepolcro, Biviliano, Città della Pieve, Cortona, Gubbio, Foligno, Montamiata, Spoleto, Todi, Orvieto, and the hermitage of Montevicchio.

The third Province was that of the Æmilia or Romagna, the principal Convent of which was at Bologna, with others at St. Angelo in Vado, Broilo, Cesena, Forli, Parma, and the hermitage of Sant' Ansano.

The fourth Province, that of Lombardy or Cisalpine Gaul, was founded later than the others; it contained the Convents of Alessandria, Asti, Gorgonzola, Mandello, and Tortona.

The whole of Germany, divided into two chief districts, Thuringia and Saxony, constituted a kind of Province under the administration of a Vicar-General. In this vicariate there were a great many Convents. We give the names of those of which some records have been preserved: In Saxony, there were houses at Halberstadt, Himmelsgarten, Erfurt, Halle, Radeberg, Gutterboitz, and Storbera, at Hayn, in Cassel: at Bernberg, in Anhalt; at Vach, Spires, Neuberg, Altham, and Assnetet in Bavaria; at Germesheim in Rhenish Bavaria, at Scornsheim in Bohemia; at Schonthal in Wurtemberg; at Sbigt, Linz, and Vienna, in Austria; at Marienthal in Thuringia; at Cracow, in Poland; at Embden in East Frisia; Patére in Rhenish Prussia; Bamberg in Franconia; Weisskirchen in Moravia; Hale in Westphalia; Passau in Hungary; and at Frankfort. We must add those at Brussels, Antwerp, Louvain, and Ghent in Belgium, which also belonged to this Vicariate. All these Convents were founded in the thirteenth century or at the beginning of the fourteenth, in very few cases can we give more than an approximate date.

France, like Germany, formed another Vicariate, in which we can only give the names of the Convents of Paris, Toulouse, Vienne, Avignon, and Montpellier. There were others, but no documents exist to enable us to give any precise information as to their respective localities.

Besides these formally established Provinces and Vicariates, the Order had undertaken distant Missions in Crete and India; but the scanty records of this Apostolate make it impossible to give any details upon this interesting subject.

Such was the aspect of the Order when St Alexis passed away at Cafaggio. It had not spread over the whole world, but it had taken root in the heart of Europe in three great nations, Italy, Germany, and France; and it had begun to carry on its labours in those lands which had not yet received the light of the Gospel, or which had lost it after having formerly possessed it.

Scanty and imperfect as this list may be, we cannot peruse it without wonder, when we reflect that the Order which gave such signs of vigorous life had pined for years under what threatened to be a sentence of death. Like those trees which bear more abundant fruit the more closely they are pruned, the Order of the Servants of Mary stretched forth its branches and multiplied its offshoots whilst it was being harassed on all sides, whilst its very right to exist was contested, and every engine was set at work to crush it. Without doubt, the blessing of Our Lady was upon her Servants, and was as balm to their wounds. The Queen of Heaven did not abandon her beloved children in the strife, but abided with them more closely than ever. And the Seven Founders, by their prompt co-operation with the designs of their Mother and Patroness, contributed in no small measure to this rapid increase of their cherished Order. It is but just, then, to give them the praise so richly deserved. These numerous descendants were truly their own, and when they passed to their reward, this widespread posterity was an additional proof that they were indeed men of God and chosen Servants of Mary.

Thus, then, was their sanctity made manifest in many ways; and it only remained for this general testimony to receive an authoritative confirmation from the seat of Infallibility, which would be received with joyful submission on earth, whilst it was fully ratified in heaven. It belonged to the Church alone to confer this unquestionable authenticity upon the testimonials of the saintliness of the Seven Founders, by impressing on them her sign-manual; and when the appointed time for so doing was come, then would she speak with the voice of one to whom power had been given, and would perform the sacred duty delegated to her from on high.

CHAPTER XIV.

Ｔｈｅ long hidden Glory of the Founders is at last made manifest.

(1717—1888)

THE Seven Founders of the Orders of the Servants of Mary had possessed in an eminent degree those virtues which impress an indelible mark of sanctity on the lives of holy men. Their deaths had been a foretaste of the joys awaiting them. Their souls had flown with arrow-like swiftness to their heavenly centre, and they had received a reward great in proportion to their merits. From henceforth they rested from their labours in the bosom of God, and shared in those unspeakable and inconceivable joys which are the portion of His chosen souls: they saw, face to face, the Three Persons of the Most Blessed Trinity, the Sacred Humanity of Christ, and the Virgin Mother from whom He took His earthly form. They had left for ever this vale of tears; and now, for all eternity, their dwelling was in the City of which the Glory of God is the Light, and whereof the Lamb is Himself the Lamp.

Meanwhile, all that was mortal rested in a common grave, on the mountain where they had lived, and which they had loved so much. As one after the other had succumbed to the stroke of death, their spiritual children had tenderly and reverently laid them to rest in the same shrine, beneath the very altar at which they had so often knelt. No spot was better fitted for their sepulture; for to none had they, in life, been more attached. There, with trembling awe, they had offered the Adorable Sacrifice; there had their famishing souls been nourished by the Bread of Life; there, in contemplation of the divine mysteries, their hearts had melted within them; there, in colloquies with Mary, the Sorrowful Mother, they had poured out their most treasured feelings; there the Queen of Heaven had revealed herself to them, and had spoken to them words full of sweetness; there had they sung, by night and by day, the praises of God; there had taken place all the most memorable and decisive events of their lives; and there it was that they slept the sleep of the just, watched over by their pious descendants. They had every right to rest there, for the holy mountain belonged to them: it was given to them by the good Bishop Ardingo; and Cardinal Raniero, as legate of Pope Gregory IX, had assured them that it was to remain their property in perpetuity.

The goodness of Divine Providence had ordained that, as they had been always united in life, so they should not be divided in death. From the day when, in the Confraternity of the *Laudesi*, they had been of one heart and one mind, they had continued to live in the closest intimacy, each of them finding true happiness in the companionship of the others. From time to time the calls of duty obliged them to make the sacrifice of this happiness, but no separation, no distance, could break or weaken the bonds of religious friendship, which remained firm as ever to the last moment of their earthly existence. So truly supernatural was their brotherly affection, that, in contemplating their lives, it strikes us as being one of the most marked characteristics of their holiness. Even death could not wholly sever the links which united them, rather did it seem to rivet them, and as a crowning testimony to the strength of their love, the remains of the Seven Holy Founders were laid together, beneath the same altar, and in the same shrine, side by side, so that their very dust became commingled. And, as an outward symbol of this unbroken union, the altar above their grave was raised on seven marble columns, typical of the whole Order being sustained by the Seven Saints as by seven immovable pillars.

Our Seven Founders, having thus heroically fallen at their posts, soon reaped the fruit of their labours here below in the form of earthly glory. It is an universal law that when embodied holiness passes away from earth it leaves so bright a ray of glory in its track that it is recognized, venerated, and invoked by the faithful. But we owe it to the truth to acknowledge that, in the case of the Seven Founders, the first ray of this glory was so faint and flickering as to be barely perceptible. Devout persons undoubtedly visited their shrine to venerate and invoke the whole group, without distinguishing one from another. Many graces and favours were obtained through their intercession, but the impulse to flock to the consecrated mountain where the holy remains were deposited was only experienced in a moderate degree, and did not extend to the great masses of the population. At first sight this circumstance appears inexplicable, yet the solution is not far to seek.

Although their entrance into Religion had made some sensation, yet, at the time of their deaths, after the lapse of twenty, thirty, forty, and even of seventy years, the Seven Founders had long withdrawn into the shade and were all but forgotten. They had taken the utmost pains to conceal themselves in the interior of their convents, and in the cells where their days ebbed tranquilly away. When they were forced to leave their enclosure their only anxiety was to be unobserved as they passed along Entirely absorbed in their religious duties, they dwelt in an atmosphere far above this world, and their virtues shed fragrance on all around them wheresoever they went. But then humility made them feel so absolutely nothing in their own eyes, that they shrank from everything which seemed calculated to bring them into notice. Thus, when the hour of their departure came, they had long since, of their own free choice, so arranged all things as to be able to quit this world unnoticed and almost alone.

Another circumstance which prevented any great concourse of pilgrims to the shrine of the Seven Holy Founders was that Monte Senario was situated in a wild and solitary spot, at some distance from any high road, and difficult of access. From nine to ten miles lay between it and Florence. Fervent and devoted souls who loved the memory of the Founders might think little of the distance, but those among the faithful whose piety was less ardent would consider the length of the road a sufficient reason for stopping at home. Besides, long after the deaths of the first six Founders, the very existence of the Order was precarious; more than once had its death-warrant been signed amidst the rejoicings of its enemies, for the Holy See had construed the decrees of two General Councils to imply the suppression of the Order of the Servants of Mary. Who then could have foreseen that the halo of sanctity would one day encircle the heads of those who had originated an undertaking which seemed destined to extinction? Saints may fail like others, but a failure on so extensive a scale casts over the most heroic virtue a cloud which ordinary eyes cannot pierce.

At a later period, when all the Founders had passed away, and when all the storms which had assailed the Servants of Mary had been lulled for ever, the supreme authority of Rome ratified the existence of the Order. And now another hindrance debarred the Seven Saints from receiving the honours to which they were entitled. St. Philip, after his death, continued to eclipse, as he had done during his life, his seven predecessors ; the disciple was glorified before his masters. The chief instrumental cause of this remarkable circumstance was a member of the Order, who at that time was its ruler—Pietro da Todi, elected to the generalate in 1314, and, as his name implies, a native of the city where St. Philip died and where his bones were laid. '

The young General Philip Benizi left behind him a name greater and more widely known than did any of the Seven Founders. He was not less humble than they were, but the circumstances in which he was placed during his life brought him more conspicuously forward. Then, too, no sooner had he breathed his last, than many striking miracles took place through his intercession, and these were continued for a long time, and, indeed, have never altogether ceased.

Pietro da Todi, who was barely forty years old, and whose energy was untiring, took in hand the interests of his beloved St. Philip, and exerted himself to the utmost to promote his cause at Rome. With this view he arranged at Todi the translation of the Saint's relics. This ceremony created a great sensation, and largely increased the popular devotion to the departed General. He also published a *Chronicle*, in which, keeping the same purpose in view, he related the first beginnings of the Order, giving the lives of the Seven Founders and of St. Philip ; his predilections leading him throughout to exalt the disciple above his masters. He fully recognized the great holiness of the Founders ; but he added that "he could not, as in the case of St. Philip, bring forward any proved miracles in their honour · it was not that they had worked none, but that no authentic details could be given on this point". He then proceeded to demonstrate that this uncertainty in no wise detracted from their sanctity, as follows .

"The most undoubted sign of the perfection to which they attained in Religion is, that it pleased Our Lady, when they had already entered into that state of life, to make use of them to found the Order of her Servants. If they had not, then, been most pleasing to her, as well as to her Divine Son ; if they had not already reached a high degree of holiness, she certainly would not have chosen them, in preference to all others, to consecrate souls to her in her Order, and to bestow on that Order her own name.

"And what has here been said concerning their great sanctity is nowise contravened by the circumstance of no miracle being here recorded as having been wrought by them either whilst they were

19

living, or at the time of their deaths, or afterwards. For it is quite possible that all of them, or some of them, may have worked miracles at sundry times; but, owing to the lapse of years and the deaths of the older members of the Order, it is not to be wondered at that nothing deserving of record has been transmitted to us.

"Another reason is, that to work miracles is not in itself alone a proof of sanctity. The true mark of a perfect soul is to love God above all things, to practise charity, and to preserve interior humility. Our Lord did not say, 'Learn of Me to raise the dead, to give sight to the blind,' &c., but, 'Learn of Me, for I am meek and humble of heart,' and 'A new commandment I give you, that you love one another, as I have loved you'. And He likewise tells us that many at the last day will plead their miraculous powers in proof of their holiness, saying, 'Lord, have we not cast out devils in Thy Name, and done many miracles?' and that His reply will be, 'I never knew you; depart from Me,' thus clearly showing that miracles are not necessarily a sign of sanctity.

"And, again, it may well be that Our Lady did not desire that any of the holy men who first instituted her Order should work miracles, in order that it might be recognized by all that she was herself the sole Foundress, and that she alone had a right to give her name to this Order so exclusively her own."

The result of all these efforts on the part of the General was, that the cultus of St. Philip spread and flourished more and more each day, whilst that of the Seven Founders remained stationary. From the day of St. Philip's death to that of his beatification in 1516, and thence onward to his canonization in 1671, all the members of the Order, from Blessed Lottaringo downwards, vied with each other in their endeavours to get the holy General placed on the altars. During all these years absolute silence was observed regarding the Seven Founders, as though an order to that effect had been given and strictly observed, that so, even in their graves, their humility should remain untroubled by human praise.

Yet, still their shrine was visited by some pious souls; they were still held in veneration as Saints, and they were invoked with great confidence; but their cultus remained, it might be said, almost of a domestic character, hardly known except to the members of the Order and to a few privileged persons who were allowed to share in their devotions. But it did not utterly wither away; rather did it surely though slowly wax strong, like those trees the roots of which are taking deep hold in the earth whilst the stem hardly shows above ground. It gained in solidity, though its outward growth was imperceptible.

Nevertheless, the glory of the Seven Founders, carefully concealed though it was for many years, was destined to shine forth one day visibly to all men. Before this could come to pass a long chain of events had to be unrolled. That it should be so seemed a fitting sequel to the countless difficulties which they had themselves encountered in founding the Order. All the ways of God with His creatures are in perfect harmony ; He stamps upon all and each of them the image and superscription which befit them ; and those which He impressed on the Order of the Servants of Mary were the same as those borne by their heavenly Patroness and Model— Humility and Sorrow.

It was immediately after the beatification of St. Philip Benizi that the first steps were taken to procure the same recognition of the virtues of the Seven Founders. In the year 1516, all the necessary preliminaries to the canonization of the Saint took place, and the Apostolic Process began in 1619 amidst all the disturbances caused by the Thirty Years' War. At this time an incident occurred which produced a reaction in favour of the Seven Founders. In 1630 Francesco Falconieri died. He was a scion of the same family as St. Alexis—a race eminent for piety and good works no less than for nobility of birth. Francesco Falconieri was extremely desirous of seeing those among his ancestors raised to the altars who had been conspicuous by their holiness. He counted more than one among the members of his house ; two, indeed, had flourished in the Order of the Servants of Mary—St. Alexis and his niece St. Juliana. For this purpose Francesco left in his will twenty thousand gold crowns, equivalent to rather more than sixteen thousand pounds of our currency—a large sum, especially in those days He desired that this sum should be put out at compound interest, and to accumulate until the cause could be introduced. At length, after more than three centuries of lethargy, the moment of awakening seemed to have come, and a new era was begun, though even now thirty-six more years passed away before the first step was taken.

Here we must observe that, at the period of which we write, it was sufficient, in order to obtain the beatification of any holy person, to prove that he had previously been the object of a cultus in the Church. This cultus was recognized as being authentic, chiefly in the following instances : If there was a general consensus on the part of the Church ; if no opposition had been made to it within the memory of man ; if any mention was made of it in the writings of the Fathers ; if it had been tacitly permitted by the Holy See, or by the Ordinary, for a considerable time and with a full knowledge of all the circumstances.

At length, in 1666, the cause of Alexis Falconieri was introduced ; Cardinal Azzolino was appointed his Postulator ; the Congregation of Rites gave a favourable opinion ; and the reigning Pope, Innocent IX., signed the commission for the introduction of the Apostolic Process on the 4th of October, 1667. Twenty-five years later, on the 20th of December, 1692, the remissorial and compulsory letters were despatched to Cardinal Morigia, the Archbishop of Florence, enjoining him by Apostolic authority to furnish full information as to the cultus actually rendered to Alexis Falconieri This prelate being absent from his see, the Nuncio of Florence was deputed to act for him, with the approval of the Pope, on the 11th of July, 1699. But, from divers causes, the Process was not yet begun; and, consequently, repeated applications were made by the Falconieri family, and especially by Monsignor Alessandro Falconieri, to the Congregation; upon which fresh letters were despatched on the 31st of July, 1700, followed by a Papal Rescript dated 19th August of the same year.

After these prolonged delays the Apostolic Process, on which the solemn declaration of beatification depended, at last began.

Meanwhile, in 1707, whilst information in furtherance of the Process was still being collected in Florence, an incident happened at Monte Senario in connection with all the Founders. A knight and senator of Florence, Donato dell' Antella by name, of the family of one of the Seven Saints, had lately died, leaving a large sum of money to the Order for the purpose of thoroughly restoring the Convent Church of Monte Senario, and of building a separate Chapel in honour of his collateral ancestor, St. Manettus dell' Antella. In the course of the restoration, the shrine containing the remains of the Seven Founders, which had always remained undisturbed under the same altar, was moved. Upon opening it, the celebrated medical Professor Zamboni examined the bones, and stated that they had unquestionably belonged to seven different skeletons. Thus was confirmed the constant unvarying tradition handed down from one generation to another, both at Florence and at Monte Senario, that the seven bodies lying in that tomb were those of the Seven Holy Founders. These proceedings took place by the advice and under the superintendence of Father Luigi Garbi, the Continuator of the Annals of the Order.

The Apostolic Process concerning St. Alexis, being now carried on uninterruptedly, was happily completed on the 12th of November, 1712. It was drawn up at full length, and proved by unbroken tradition that from time immemorial a genuine cultus had been paid to Alexis Falconieri. Great, then, was the joy in the ranks of the Servite Order, and among the Florentines, especially the members and connections of the Falconieri family. After many years they found themselves at last on the point of obtaining what they had so long hoped for.

The Florentine Process now passed into the hands of the Congregation of Rites, which spent five years in examining the case. At length, on the 20th of November, 1717, Cardinal Fabroni being the Postulator of the cause, the Cardinals assembled in general congregation pronounced unanimously in favour of the beatification of Alexis Falconieri. At the same time, they approved and confirmed by rescript the cultus hitherto rendered to him; they recognized this cultus as being in all respects equal to that which had been rendered to other Blessed beatified by the Holy See; and they declared that it constituted a beatification equivalent to that which the Church proclaims in accordance with the rules established for that purpose.

All that was essential was now completed, as far as regarded Blessed Alexis; and the Congregation of Rites was pleased to supplement its work by granting various favours during the following years.

The whole course of these events had taken everyone by surprise, and proved afresh that Almighty God in His infinite wisdom over-rules all circumstances at His pleasure, and brings about the desired end by the most unlikely means. Among the Seven Founders, he who had always desired to be held the lowest and the least, he who had been the last to pass from earth to heaven, was now the earliest promoted to the highest place; he was the first of his companions to be raised to the altars; he was the first to receive publicly, and with the Church's sanction, the honours which are paid to those who have attained to the highest pitch of heroic virtue.

This beatification caused great joy among the Servites of Mary, and encouraged them to hope for a similar result in the case of the other six Founders. Together they had received their first call to the Religious Life, together had their lives been spent, together did they rest in death, together were they enjoying their reward in heaven; why, then, should they not be glorified together on earth? That strong and superhuman bond which had made them all of one heart and one mind could not be severed by the decree which enthroned them as Saints, and hallowed all their past lives. On the contrary, it seemed the more essential to consecrate for ever this unbroken union. The Order, therefore, prepared to enter boldly upon the path opened by the beatification of Alexis Falconieri, and to endeavour to secure the joint canonization of all the Seven Founders. Great difficulties remained to be overcome, but the energy of the Order was equal to the occasion. And its efforts were so successful that after about eight years, on July 7, 1725, the cultus of the Seven Founders was approved by the unanimous vote of the Congregation of Rites, and immediately confirmed by Benedict XIII., who thus completed the undertaking which had been brought to a happy conclusion in the short space of five years.

The earthly triumph which crowned the Seven Founders in their solemn beatification was followed by a time of pain and suspense— as during their lives trials followed quickly on every success. When at length the great victory was gained in their canonization, it seemed, on looking back, as though the struggles and reverses of six centuries before had been carried on to our own day. Some traces of the Sorrows of their heavenly Patroness were to be deeply impressed upon the closing act of their glorification here below. But, as in life they had reached their goal, in spite of every obstacle, so, after a weary waiting for a hundred and sixty years, they were finally to triumph and to be proclaimed Saints.

There were three successive stages in the progress towards the great act of their canonization.

The first stage lasted seventeen years, and bore a character of special importance owing to the discussions carried on between the *Promotor fidei*, whose duty it was to oppose the canonization, and the Postulators, who were charged to promote it.

Whilst the liturgical regulations following on a beatification were being carried out, Benedict XIII., on December 7, 1728, issued a dispensation from the examination into the virtues of the Founders, and ordered that the examination of their miracles should be proceeded with at once. On July 11, 1729, the Holy See took two important steps. In the first place, the Pope united the cause of Blessed Alexis to that of the six other Founders, so that in future the two causes should make but one. Moreover, he dispensed with the examination as to the virtues of Blessed Alexis in the same manner as with the other six Founders, for the Pontiff desired that they should be canonized collectively, since the miracles had been granted to the joint invocation of the Seven Holy Founders. Now was the perfect union of the Seven, which had been momentarily severed, once more re-established, and that for ever. In the second place, Apostolic letters were despatched to order the drawing-up of the inquiry as to the miracles.

All seemed to be going on favourably. There was abundant evidence as to miracles, and there would be no difficulty in bringing forward the number exacted by the ecclesiastical laws. The canonization itself appeared to be at hand. The Pope was personally watching over the proceedings, in order that there might be no needless delay, when his death took place on February 22, 1730. This was the first mischance.

Clement XII. was shortly after elected as successor to Benedict XIII. The new Pope hastened to assemble a special Congregation to examine the different rescripts concerning the Rites. Those relating to the cause of the Seven Blessed, and that in particular dispensing from the examination into the virtues in their case, were also discussed. On September 7, 1730, this Congregation came to the conclusion that it was necessary to make, if not a strict examination, at all events a judicial statement, respecting the virtues of each of the Seven Founders. This was a new departure, of which the vexatious consequences were, however, soon checked. The Postulators, without further loss of time, referred this decree to the Pope, who, on the 18th of the same month, confirmed the decision of his predecessor, gave a fresh dispensation from the examination of the virtues, and ordered that the discussion concerning the miracles should begin at once. Of these five were brought forward.

The Processes relating to the miracles being now ready, they were despatched to Rome, where they were opened and examined and discussed. On August 23, 1732, the *Promotor fidei* was ordered to bring forward his objections, and the cause was adjourned to January 17, 1733. On that day the validity of four of the miracles was admitted, the difficulties raised as to the fifth were removed, and on March 21, 1733, this last miracle was accepted together with the others.

Nothing now seemed likely to oppose the crowning object which the Order had so long and so ardently desired. All the debates concerning these five miracles had to be analysed and despatched, according to custom, to the *Promotor fidei.* This was speedily done, and he then formulated his objections in a brief document. But now, when the harbour appeared actually within sight, the anxious Servites found themselves once more driven out to sea. Greater difficulties than any which had yet arisen now sprang up in opposition to the canonization. They proved fatal to the cause, and occasioned its being postponed for many weary years; indeed as it proved, for more than a century and a half.

The objections brought forward were the following : On the one hand, the miracles obtained by the collective invocation of the Seven Founders were considered to be inadmissible, because, in such cases, it was not known whether these were attributable or not to the power of each individual Founder ; and on the other hand, it was a thing unheard of to canonize Seven Confessors together. Consequently, it was held that the invocation, the miracles, and the canonization must be separate and distinct for each Founder. The Servants of Mary were much surprised : the cause had been introduced and accepted on precisely the opposite grounds : it had been clearly understood that the invocation and miracles and canonization should be considered collectively. Pope Benedict XIII. had himself so decided. The spirit of opposition in the two kinds of proceedings was patent to all.

However, the Postulators of the cause were not put out of countenance. With great deference to their opponents, they admitted that the aspect of affairs was much changed, and that the case demanded the closest attention ; then, taking their adversaries' arguments one by one, they refuted them in a work, the extent and depth of which may well cause modern readers to recoil with alarm.

So promptly was this rejoinder made that, on the 28th of September, in the same year, 1733, was held a meeting of what is called the Ante-preparatory Congregation, because it serves as an introduction to another Congregation which still further advances the cause. This meeting was somewhat stormy. Fresh difficulties were raised on the subject of the general and collective invocation, and it was argued that two miracles obtained by this invocation, and recognized as valid, would suffice for canonization.

Just at this time Pope Clement XII. died, and was succeeded by Benedict XIV. The Order was now most anxious to learn whether the new Pope would be as favourable to the cause as he had been when Postulator. The suspense on this subject was not destined to be of long continuance.

Soon after his accession, Benedict XIV. summoned to his presence a Congregation to examine into the question of the general invocation, and to decide whether or not the joint cause of several Confessors was admissible. The Congregation met for this purpose on 13th January, 1742, and, having postponed the examination of the proposed topics, it decreed that a judicial statement as to the virtues of each of the Seven Founders should be made before the Congregation of Rites, and that then the question as to the general invocation might be reopened. This decision was received with respectful submission. Far from making any complaint, the Servites rejoiced in a result so distinctly advantageous to the cause : the required statement could only convince the world at large of the many marvels which had marked the foundation of the Order, as well as of the sanctity and wonderful works of the Seven Holy Founders themselves.

The required judicial statement was accordingly drawn up, the answers to the objections raised by the *Promotor fidei* were appended, and these documents were placed in the hands of the Congregation which met on 31st August, 1743, under the presidentship of Cardinal Accaremboni, the successor of Cardinal Pico. This time nothing was done, because a doubt attached to the legality and identity of several documents quoted in the summary of the virtues. The Congregation therefore ordered the Postulators to produce all the said documents, especially the manuscript of Pietro da Todi, which was preserved in the archives of the Santissima Annunziata at Florence. The documents were immediately forwarded to the Cardinal Postulator and to the *Promotor fidei*. Then another Congregation was held on 1st February, 1744, at which the following rescript was agreed upon . "The present case, as regards the matter in question, can be proceeded with, if His Holiness so pleases". The Pope approved this rescript on 5th February.

The critical moment was now at hand: the all-important questions were about to be brought forward once more. What would be the fate of the cause ? None could solve the enigma ; it was the secret of the Most High. The suspense lasted for six months, for it was not till 1st August, 1744, that a new Congregation assembled This time it was a full gathering of the Congregation of Rites which met, together with the *Promotor fidei* and the Postulators, to give their decision as to the starting-point of the cause of the Seven Founders. The Pope himself presided. The Congregation examined, discussed, pronounced, and, on 8th August, the Pope decreed as follows : " With respect to the canonization of the Seven Founders. We desire proofs of miracles obtained by the separate invocation of each one of them ; and with respect to miracles obtained through their collective invocation, their evidence shall be admitted as super-abundant." The Sovereign Pontiff therefore required proofs of two miracles worked by each of the Seven Founders individually. This testimony the Order could not produce ; for the close union which had ever existed between the Founders was so established a fact in the minds of the faithful that, as Divine Providence had willed, they had been usually, if not invariably, invoked together, as being inseparable. None would divide those whom God had thus united. The cause was consequently cast aside ; and it remained unheard of and forgotten for the space of a hundred and thirty-four years.

A second attempt was then made ; but it was not sustained, and made only a momentary impression, although the initiative was taken by one whose heart and soul were absorbed by all noble aims, Father Giovanni Angelo Mondani, General of the Servites from 1868 to 1882. He was passionately attached to the Order, which he had entered in early youth, and in which, after having filled every office in succession, he was raised to the highest of all. He was perfect in manner and bearing ; tender and kind and loving as a true father with his spiritual children ; clear and keen in intellect, well versed in every branch of theological science, for which he had a remarkable aptitude ; full of generous enthusiasm for every undertaking calculated to promote the glory of God and of his Order. It was his cherished dream to gain the crown of saintship for the Seven Founders, who were his countrymen, for he was himself a native of Tuscany. He had long and carefully examined into the matter ; and in spite of the length of time during which the affair had been laid aside, and the many obstacles which presented themselves, he resolved to attempt to bring forward once more the cause which was so dear to him.

Pius IX., of happy memory, was then seated in the Chair of Peter. He naturally took an interest in the cause of the canoniza-tion of the Founders, for his birthplace was in the immediate neighbourhood of a Convent of the Order founded by his family, and he had himself been cured of a dangerous illness through the prayers offered by his pious mother for the intercession of Blessed Joachim Piccolomini. Father Mondani applied to the Pontiff, who received him with the utmost kindness. Pius IX was pleased to. appoint a special Commission of Cardinals, who were to examine whether the cause could be reintroduced by accepting miracles obtained by collective invocation. The Cardinals met and debated the possibility of reversing the decree of 8th August, 1744. On 14th December, 1878, they decided in the negative. The chief reason given was, that nothing appeared to have occurred to alter the state of affairs sufficiently to justify a departure from the rules established by ecclesiastical law. Pius IX. had died whilst the Commission was sitting, and Leo XIII. had succeeded him on 20th February, 1878.

Here we ought to say that the Order could have obtained the canonization of those among the Founders in whose favour miracles obtained by their individual invocation could be proved. This, indeed, was the case with several of their number. But the Servites had too profound a veneration for the bond of union which linked the Founders indissolubly together to venture on any such step. The cause, in consequence, was again suspended. The disappointment of the Order at this failure was keener than ever; and the eagerness with which the day of the wished-for glorification was awaited only increased in ardour.

The day was, after all, not far off. Father Mondani gave up his soul to God on the 21st of July, 1882, after an anxious and laborious generalate of fourteen years. He was succeeded by the Very Reverend Father, Pietro Francesco Testa. The new General was a Religious of lofty intellect and of a noble heart, a consummate theologian and canonist, always acting with supernatural prudence and self-command, and never allowing himself to be discouraged by any obstacle when once he was fairly engaged in an undertaking. He was thus the very man fitted to be the instrument of Divine Providence in the work of the canonization of the Seven Founders. It was allotted to him to make the third attempt, and bring it to a happy conclusion. Others had sown with much toil, and had only gleaned the merit of their fruitless labours: he was to sow, indeed, in sorrow, but to reap in joy.

Leo XIII. was now ruling the Church with that power and wisdom which in these trying times are a most striking manifestation of the all-guiding Providence of God. He had speedily acquired throughout the world an influence so great that heretics, free-thinkers, powerful monarchs, all alike vied in showing him the utmost respect and deference, for all agreed in recognizing the fact that in him resided the greatest moral power known upon this earth. Among the members of the Order a strong feeling of discouragement had sprung up since the adverse decision given by the Congregation of Cardinals on December 14, 1878, and all hopes of the canonization of the Seven Founders were apparently at an end, when suddenly the aspect of affairs entirely changed.

At Viareggio, a small town on the Mediterranean shore, where one of the parish churches is served by the Fathers of the Order, a miracle of a striking character was obtained in February, 1881, by the collective invocation of the Seven Blessed Founders. The Archbishop of Lucca, being informed of this, questioned several trustworthy eye-witnesses, who testified to its truth. His Grace, however, still desired further proofs, and particularly the attestation in writing of the physician who had attended the sick person now miraculously cured. The physician unhesitatingly declared in the paper which he sent in, on December 23, 1882, that the person in question had suffered from a dangerous illness, which had reached such a crisis that, without the intervention of a miracle, death would have been inevitable He concluded by expressing in the strongest terms his conviction that the cure was an undoubted manifestation of supernatural power.

The Archbishop of Lucca then determined himself to take steps in the matter, and he accordingly despatched a letter to the Sovereign Pontiff, in which, after speaking of the devotion of his diocese to the Seven Blessed Founders, and of the miracle recently obtained through their joint intercession at Viareggio, he entreated the Holy Father to take up once more the cause of their canonization. Leo XIII , yielding to this petition, began by ordering a fresh examination being made as to the well-known point on which all the previous discussions had turned By his command the Congregation of Rites met on June 26, 1884, to inquire "whether the miracles worked by Almighty God, in answer to the collective invocation of the Seven Blessed Founders, could be brought forward in proof of their claims to canonization ?" Thanks to a decisive opinion given by Cardinal Zigliara, of the Order of St. Dominic, this question was decided in the affirmative. The examination as to the miracles, four of which were necessary, could now be proceeded with.

More than two years were spent in preparing this examination, and the ante-preparatory Congregation for the purpose was not held till September 28, 1886. The miracles were brought forward by the Postulator of the cause, Father Corrado, himself a member of the Order. Of the four miracles admitted, three were of ancient date, and had been already laid before the Congregation at the time of the first attempt to obtain the canonization They had subsequently undergone the criticism of the *Promotor fidei*, and had been successfully defended, and, as we have already seen, allowed to be authentic. They were now to be examined anew as though no previous inquiry had been made. The fourth miracle was that of Viareggio, which was of recent date, and had not hitherto been debated at all

The first miracle was one of considerable importance, being that of the restoration to sight of a blind person, eighty years of age. The second was the cure of a fever, complicated by several other diseases, which had continued for fifteen years. The third was a case of complete recovery from a fearful nervous attack of the most alarming character. And the fourth was the cure of a patient suffering from puerperal fever, which had reached the acute stage. We subjoin an account of these four miracles, as they stand recorded in the reports of the sittings of the Congregation.

First Miracle.—In the town of Rimini lived a widow named Giovanna Lugli Silvestri, born at Castello di Misano. She was nearly eighty years of age, and her strength was failing her much, when, during the month of December, 1728, she suddenly felt an intense pain in her head, caused by a severe cold which impeded her breathing, and which after a time injured the optic nerves to such an extent that she became blind. As she could no longer distinguish one object from another, it was necessary to lead her to the neighbouring Church of St. Augustine on days of obligation in order that she might hear Mass. She was attended by Dr. Mattiolo, who pronounced the catarrh from which she was suffering to be one of exceptional severity, and even likely to prove fatal. He prescribed remedies, but advised the administration of the Last Sacraments if there were no signs of improvement in her health. The patient grew no better.

Meanwhile, one of her daughters, a nun in the Monastery of St. Clare of Rimini, whose name in Religion was Sister Clare, being much distressed at her poor mother's sufferings, was desirous of obtaining some relief to them. This Sister had a special devotion to the Seven Holy Founders of the Order of the Servants of Mary ; and one day she sent her mother, by the portress of the Convent, a small print of the Seven Founders, begging her at the same time to ask their prayers, when she would certainly obtain the help of which she stood in need. The Mother, on receiving her daughter's message, began to experience a feeling of confidence in the Seven Founders , and accordingly invoking their assistance, she devoutly applied the little picture to her forehead. She was instantaneously relieved from the acute pain in the head, which she had felt without intermission from the beginning of her illness.

This improvement in her health increased her confidence in the intercession of the Founders , and she sent continually to tell her daughter that she would soon go to the Convent to have the sign of the Cross made on her eyes with the venerated picture by Sister Clare's own hands. On the eve of the Conversion of St. Paul, accordingly, she was led to the Monastery, and then begged her daughter to do her this favour, from which she expected a complete cure. Deeply moved by her mother's request, Sister Clare brought her into the parlour, recited with her a *Pater*, an *Ave*, and three *Glorias*, in honour of the Seven Saints, and then, with full confidence in their powerful intercession, she made the sign of the Cross with the picture on the brow and eyes of her blind parent. Instantly the aged woman felt as though a bandage had fallen from her eyes : her sight was perfectly restored . she could clearly distinguish the features of her daughter, and she recognized the other persons who were present; and lastly, at the request of Sister Clare, she enumerated and described the figures represented in the picture with which she had been blessed In short, her sight was now restored, nor did she again lose it.

Second Miracle.—Sister Mary Pulcheria Thun, born Countess d'Arco, in the Tyrol, was seized in August, 1715, with a continuous fever, accompanied by severe pains in the head and stomach, nausea, and other serious symptoms. In this state she remained for fifteen years, during the last three of which she also suffered from a most painful sciatic affection, which confined her to her bed for many months at a time, attacking her more especially in the autumn and winter, at which seasons she was completely crippled and unable to move. In summer her health improved slightly, but she did not gain strength, and she had great difficulty in going up or down stairs. The doctor attended her regularly and prescribed various remedies, but without effect . a temporary relief was sometimes obtained, but the disease appeared incurable. In 1728 she was so far discouraged as to resolve to dispense with the doctor's services She now became worse than before her strength diminished daily; swelling of the legs set in; and the pains in the head, and the torture from sciatica, became almost unbearable; and the digestion was so impaired that she could no longer retain the slightest nourishment On the eve of the Epiphany, 1729, she was reduced to the last extremity : her sufferings were intense ; her face and eyes were swelled , and she could no longer raise herself in bed, being lifted up and laid down like a child—and, as she was extremely restless, this had to be done continually On the Feast of the Epiphany there was no change, except that to the bodily pains was now added a great increase of the mental distress from which the patient had suffered to some extent from the first beginnings of her illness. All the Sisters thought that the end was at hand ; and they prayed that it might please God to hasten the moment of the poor sufferer's release

On this same day the Confessor of the Community came to the Convent to bless another nun who was ill, with some relics of the Seven Blessed Founders. Sister Mary Pulcheria Thun, hearing this, expressed a wish to receive the same blessing. Permission being obtained, the patient received Holy Communion in the morning, and after Vespers she was taken with difficulty to the place where the blessing was to be given. The Confessor came, and the sufferer most fervently recommended herself to the prayers of the Seven Blessed Fathers, beseeching them by their intercession to obtain her deliverance from her physical and mental afflictions.

No sooner had she received the blessing than she at once found herself a new creature, both in body and mind, and she was completely cured of all the diseases to which she had so long been a prey. Overwhelmed with joy, she hastened to the choir to return

thanks for so great a miracle to God, to the Blessed Virgin, and to
the Seven Holy Founders. From this time forth she was able to
partake of the food usually served at the Community table, which
she had not been able to do during her illness, she having been dispensed from the obligation of fasting on Friday and Saturday ; and
she continued to enjoy perfect health.

Third Miracle.—Teresa Romagnoli, of Bologna, was a single
woman, of a sanguineo-bilious temperament and a delicate constitution. When still young she was seized with an hysterical attack,
accompanied by fearful convulsions, constant fainting-fits, nausea,
distaste for food, continual thirst, and other alarming symptoms,
the worst of which was nervous fever. In this state she took
scarcely any nourishment, and on many days none at all. Her
strength, in consequence, gradually diminished, and her emaciation,
particularly during the latter years of her illness, was extreme.
Her sufferings increased in proportion to her weakness, and more
than once the poor patient appeared to be dying, and the Last
Sacraments were administered to her. At length she could no
longer leave the house, or even rise from her bed. On one occasion,
however, being Christmas Day, 1728, she tried to go to Mass ; but
she became so ill that she was forced to return to bed, where she
remained till July 13 of the following year, 1729.

She was frequently visited by physicians, who prescribed for her ;
but she only grew worse and worse. At length they gave up the
case as being hopeless. More than once the patient, or her friends
on her behalf, sought the intercession of the Saints, but without
effect.

In these sad circumstances the Confessor of the sick woman, and
several Tertiaries of the Servite Order, entreated the Fathers of that
Order to carry to her the relics of the Seven Holy Founders. Two
of the Fathers accordingly brought the relics to her house on 13th
July, 1722, and spoke to her and to her sisters of the blessing which
they were about to give her. At that moment she became unconscious. The Fathers then thought it better to wait till she revived.
In about a quarter of an hour she came to herself. The Fathers
then exhorted her to confidence in the Seven Holy Founders, assuring
her that Almighty God would cure her through their intercession.
The patient and her sisters then invoked the Founders, and the
benediction with their relics was given to her. She immediately
felt that she was cured. No sooner had the Religious left the house
than she asked for her clothes, dressed herself, and rose briskly from
her bed, without being assisted by anyone. She then attended to
her household affairs, moved actively about the house, and sat down
to her sewing as usual, all without the slightest assistance. Her
relish for food returned, and she was able to eat eggs, meat, bread,
and, in short, whatever was set before her, with good appetite, none

of which things had she been able previously to touch. She slept well, rose refreshed, and on the 16th of the same month of July she went to hear Mass in a Chapel dedicated to Our Lady of Mount Carmel, and there she returned thanks to the Seven Holy Founders for the great miracle which they had obtained for her by their intercession. From that time forward she enjoyed good health, and never experienced any return of her former sufferings

Fourth Miracle.—Maria Anna Barsotelli, wife of Marco Bellotti, was of a weakly constitution. On 2nd February, 1881, she gave birth to her fifth child   Eight days afterwards symptoms of puerperal fever appeared, and she was soon in great danger   She grew worse and worse for about a month, suffering acute pain ; besides which the whole of her body was fearfully swollen.

The doctor attended her assiduously, but in vain. At length, seeing the patient reduced to the last extremity of weakness, suffering intensely, and frequently delirious, he told the priest that it would be advisable to give her the Last Sacraments, since there was no longer any hope of her recovery. The priest accordingly anointed her, gave her the Apostolic benediction *in articulo mortis*, and read the prayers for the dying. All the relatives surrounding the bed thought she was on the point of breathing her last. As her mind remained perfectly clear, the priest exhorted her to a generous detachment from all the goods and vanities of this short life, after the example of the Seven Blessed Founders, who, long before their deaths, renounced all things in order to be more pleasing to God and to Our Blessed Lady. He gave her a brief account of their lives, adding : "You know that there is an altar of the Seven Holy Founders in our parish church ; beg of them from your heart to become your intercessors, and say to them ; 'If it is for the good of my soul and for the welfare of my five little children, obtain for me the recovery of my health ; but if otherwise, pray that I may be wholly detached from all things, and that in the strong bonds of charity I may rest in the peace of God for all eternity'."

The priest then left the room   In about a quarter of an hour he returned to encourage the sick woman afresh. As he entered, she exclaimed : "The Seven Blessed Founders have obtained the boon I asked ; I am cured.   I no longer suffer any pain, and I feel perfectly well."   "You must be mistaken," said the priest, "this is but the effect of your imagination, you are not really cured."   "It is not the effect of my imagination," she replied, "the Seven Holy Founders have obtained my cure."   "Well," answered the priest, "if it be true that they have obtained your recovery, sit up in bed at once."

Instantly, without the slightest help, she sat up in bed. Some nourishment was brought : she took the basin of soup in her right hand and the glass of wine in her left hand, and began to eat and drink. Two or three days later she was able to rise from her bed without assistance After about twenty-five days her strength was completely restored, and she went to church to return thanks to the Seven Blessed Founders for the favour which they had obtained for her. She herself carried back to the sacristy the book and stole which had been used by the priest on this occasion. She had been, in short, perfectly restored from a mortal sickness

These miracles having been brought forward, they were debated in the Congregation of Rites. The *Promotor fidei* attacked not only the last-named miracle, which was now under discussion for the first time, but the other three as well. He was not shaken by all the objections raised and refuted during the first Process. He made a great point of the marvellous progress of medical science, and he endeavoured to show, by arguments which were not wanting in force, that the authenticity of the miracles was doubtful. But, in spite of these attacks, the Postulator of the cause proved that the four miracles were alike genuine and unquestionable.

All these discussions took place in the meetings of the Congregation, which were held on the following dates : the first, or ante-preparatory, on September 28, 1886 ; the second, or preparatory, on March 1, 1887 ; and the third and final one, in presence of the Holy Father, on May 31 of the same year. Nothing which passes at these meetings is allowed to transpire publicly, all the members being bound to strict secrecy. The favourable issue of any one meeting is only known by the fact of the next being held. At the conclusion of the final one, the Sovereign Pontiff pronounces his decision, after taking as much time as he considers desirable to form his opinion. He then publishes a decree, in which he announces his acceptance of the miracles proposed for the canonization. This brings the cause to a favourable conclusion. With the decree which practically formulates the canonization is issued a subsequent decree announcing that it is perfectly permissible to proceed with the said canonization, accompanied by the *placets* of the Cardinals. These, with the three prescribed Consistories, complete the preliminaries. Nothing more remains but the solemnity itself, when the Sovereign Pontiff, by virtue of the fulness of his powers, declares those to be Saints who have been shown to be worthy of that honour.

At length, on November 1, 1887, the Pope declared that there was no longer any doubt remaining as to the validity of the four miracles presented for the canonization. On the 27th of the same month of November he announced that this canonization might be proceeded with Shortly afterwards, the Cardinals responded with a unanimous *placet* to the question of the Sovereign Pontiff as to whether they thought it well to proclaim solemnly that the Seven Founders were worthy of the crown of sanctity. The three Consistories—secret, public, and semi-public—were then held.

No longer could doubt remain. It was now absolutely certain that the Seven Founders of the Order of the Servants of Mary were to be proclaimed Saints, by the infallible verdict of the Pope. This crowning honour was awarded to them six hundred and thirty years after the death of St. Buonagiunta, the first of the Seven to pass from this world, and five hundred and seventy-seven years after the departure of St. Alexis, the last survivor of the group. The Order was filled to overflowing with gladness, which was shared by the whole of the Catholic world. Nothing more remained but to fix the day for the canonization, and the Holy Father appointed January 15, 1888.

But, whilst the preliminary ceremonies of the canonization were being proceeded with, a tide of enthusiastic loyalty was bringing the faithful from all parts of the globe to the centre of Catholicity—to the feet of the Sovereign Pontiff, Leo XIII. The cause of this outburst of filial devotedness was not far to seek. On December 31, 1887, exactly fifty years had elapsed since a young priest received the holy unction of the priesthood, on December 31, 1837 ; and he who on that day offered for the first time the Adorable Sacrifice was Joachim Vincent Pecci, who, forty-one years afterwards, was enthroned as successor to Pius IX, by the name of Leo XIII, and who, consequently, was now about to celebrate his Golden Jubilee.

Such was the reason of this universal enthusiasm : all true Catholics loved their Father, and were eager to give proof of their affection. From remote shores, from centres of civilization, and from wild and barbarous tribes, came gifts, messages, bands of pilgrims, all testifying to the devotion of the faithful to the successor of St. Peter. Emperors, Kings, Queens, Presidents of Republics, and Princes, even those without the Church, came forward to express their veneration for the Pontiff. All voices were united in a general tribute of homage not alone to the personal character, the talents, and the virtues of Leo XIII., but to his supreme dignity as Head of the Catholic Church.

The Holy Father, deeply moved by the enthusiasm displayed towards himself, resolved to celebrate his Jubilee with the utmost solemnity, and to respond adequately to the filial devotion of the faithful by bestowing additional consolations on devout souls, and thus giving greater glory to God. With this intent, he resolved to proceed to the canonization and beatification of a certain number of holy persons who had died in the odour of sanctity, and whose causes had been favourably viewed by the Congregation of Rites. Of this number were the Seven Founders of the Order of the Servants of Mary. The other heroes of virtue whose triumph was to be celebrated at the same time were. Peter Claver, priest ; John Berchmans, Scholastic ; and Alphonsus Rodriguez, temporal Coadjutor, all three members of the Society of Jesus, who were to be proclaimed Saints; and Felix of Nicosia, a Capuchin lay-brother; John Baptist de la Salle, Founder of the Congregation of Brothers of the Christian Schools; and several others, who were to be beatified. It would be impossible to imagine a more glorious solemnity, or one more fitting the occasion. Thus may we truly say, that God had so ordered all things as that the Seven Founders should be immeasurably exalted after their deaths, since during their lives they had set no bounds to their practice of humility.

After having carried their self-abnegation to the point of heroism during the whole of their earthly career, after having hidden their sanctity so carefully that even death, the great revealer, did not entirely withdraw the veil, they were to appear, in the midst of the pontifical rejoicings, crowned with celestial glory, the objects of universal devotion. Now, all could recognize and venerate in them that love of Our Lord which made them renounce all things to follow Him; that devotion to Mary, the spotless Queen of Sorrows, who chose them to be her faithful servants, her valiant champions; those heroic virtues, of which the brightest and most precious gem of all was humility. Now, too, all marvelled that they should have remained unknown for so many centuries; and they seemed to be the more honoured for having been so long concealed, and so tardily made known.

Being now, as it were, given afresh to the world, they will still by the simple beauty of their example carry on the good which they did during their earthly career; the fragrance of their virtues will lead many to love more and more her who was the centre of their lives, Mary, the Mother of Our Lord, and the great Victress of souls. And this their work will be perpetuated from age to age, and will add, if it be possible, to the felicity which is now theirs in heaven.

O Holy Founders of the Order of the Servants of Mary, your son has now concluded a grateful task which has been to him an unspeakable consolation. Gladly did he undertake it, whilst deeply realizing the inadequacy of his power to depict the supernatural beauty of your souls, and the attractiveness of your chosen mission. But he trusts that you will look less to the execution of the work than to the filial love which induced him to undertake it, and which has encouraged and sustained him throughout; and that, in return for the little which he has done for your honour, you will obtain for him some small portion of that burning love of Mary which was kindled in your hearts.

And since your advocacy is so powerful with the glorious Queen of Heaven, ask of her for the writer of these pages those graces which are most necessary for him. Ask for him that patience which bears joyfully alike the keenest sorrows and the most bitter contradictions; courage to work unceasingly, wheresoever, and in whatsoevei manner, may be appointed, to spread the kingdom of God and to save souls ; and fidelity to his vocation, so that death itself may not avail to extinguish in his heait the love of Mary.

And, lastly, beg of this most sweet Mother, by her gentle and most potent mediation, to place him in the Heart of her beloved Son, Jesus, that so he may remain there during this mortal life, bieathe there his last sigh, and there continue for ever in the enjoyment of that unfading happiness which is summed up in knowing, and adoring, and loving that God Who is Himself all Truth, all Beauty, and all Goodness.

THE END.

CPSIA information can be obtained
at www.ICGtesting.com
Printed in the USA
BVHW042137130620
581472BV00007B/671

9 781376 122022